Western Lands and Waters Series
XVIII

This map of Big Horn County as it existed before the formation of Park, Hot Springs and Washakie counties, was distributed about 1906 to customers of the Stock Growers National Bank in Cheyenne. Many of the postoffices on the map have long since disappeared. *Author's collection.*

WYOMING'S BIG HORN BASIN TO 1901

A Late Frontier

by
Lawrence M. Woods

UNIVERSITY OF OKLAHOMA
NORMAN

Library of Congress Cataloging-in-Publication Data

Woods, L. Milton (Lawrence Milton), 1932—
    Wyoming's Big Horn Basin to 1901: a late frontier / by Lawrence M. Woods.
        p. 288 cm. —(Western lands and waters series; XVIII)
        Includes bibliographical references (p.) and index.
        ISBN 978-0-8061-6576-9
        1. Bighorn Basin (Mont. And Wyo.)—History. 2. Frontier and pioneer life—Bighorn Basin (Mont. And Wyo.) I. Title. II. Series
F767.B4W66   1997
978.7'3—dc20   96-43310
                                                                 CIP

The paper in this book meets the guidelines for permanence and durability of the Committee on Production Guidelines for Book Longevity and the Council on Library Resources. ∞

Originally published in hardcover by the Arthur H. Clark Company, copyright © 1997 by Lawrence M. Woods. Paperback edition published 2020 by the University of Oklahoma Press, Norman, Publishing Division of the University. Manufactured in the U.S.A.

All rights reserved. No part of this publication may be reproduced, stored in a retrieval system, or transmitted, in any form or by any means, electronic, mechanical, photocopying, recording, or otherwise—except as permitted under Section 107 or 108 of the United States Copyright Act—without the prior written permission of the University of Oklahoma Press.

Contents

Introduction		9
CHAPTER		
I	The First Inhabitants	13
II	Explorers and Trappers	25
III	Troopers and Teamster	35
IV	The Big Horn Expedition of 1870	49
V	Goldseekers in the Basin	61
VI	The Cattle Come	71
VII	Fleurs-de-lis Along the Stinking Water	85
VIII	The Union Jack on Canyon Creek	101
IX	The End of the Range Cattle Era	117
X	The Frontier Spirit	133
XI	The Old Counties in the Basin	147
XII	Water and a Governer from the Basin	157
XIII	Before Big Horn County	169
XIV	Counties Inside the Basin	183
XV	More Than a Wild West Show	197
XVI	Saints in the Basin	209
XVII	Towns and Farms in the Southern Basin	219
XVIII	The Railroad	225
XIX	A Man Named Boysen	237
XX	Through the Wind River Canyon at Last	247
Appendix A		261
Appendix B		262
Bibliography		267
Index		273

Illustrations

Map of the Big Horn Country	*frontispiece*
Chief Washakie	12
Judge William L. Kuykendall	48
The Little Cannon	67
William Clay Lovell	77
John Dwight Woodruff	81
Shield Ranch Headquarters	84
Count Jean de Hedouville	91
Gilbert Henry Chandos Leigh	113
Albert "Slick" Nard	141
William Alford Richards	161
Hyatt's Store in Hyattvile	168
Joseph DeBarthe	175
Colonel William Douglas Pickett	182
William Frederick Cody	196
The First Boysen Dam	251

Introduction

Those who travel by automobile in the Big Horn Basin and see the majestic mountains rising about them on three sides may not fully comprehend how formidable a barrier they represented in the days before highways or railroads made possible the easy access we now have to this area.

Shortly after the census takers finished compiling the results of the 1890 census, an obscure pamphlet was published which contained some comments on the subject of the frontier. "Up to and including 1890, the country had a frontier of settlement, but at present the unsettled area has been so broken into by isolated bodies of settlement that there can hardly be said to be a frontier line."[1]

We all have an idea of what the frontier was, but precise definitions are hard to come by. The first use of the word merely understood the frontier as being the place where one was facing the enemy; later, it came to signify the territorial jurisdiction as well. In the case of the western frontier, the meaning is closer to the former than the latter definition, since the region was at least inhospitable, if not actually hostile.[2]

Still, it is interesting to speculate where the separate pieces of the frontier line may have finally disappeared in the lower forty-eight states; there is good evidence that one of the last to go may have been in the Big Horn Basin of Wyoming, that enclosed area north of the Wind River Mountains, which is drained by the Big Horn River and its tributaries.[3]

---

[1]When Professor Frederick Jackson Turner read the quoted statement, he was stimulated to write his famous paper which connected the existence of the frontier with the development of the distinctive institutions of the United States. According to Turner, it was on the frontier that new traits and new institutions were born. *Extra Census Bulletin No. 2. Distribution of Population According to Density: 1890* (Washington, D. C.); and Frederick Jackson Turner, "The Significance of the Frontier in American History," *The Frontier in American History* (New York, 1920), 1-38.

[2]Peter Sahlins, *Boundaries: The Making of France and Spain in the Pyrenees* (Los Angeles, 1989), 6.

[3]The Big Horn River is a geographical oddity in that it has two names, being the Wind River before it enters the Wind River Canyon, and the Big Horn River as it passes through the Basin and

When the transcontinental railroad was finished, it effectively linked the settled areas in the east with the areas already settled on the West coast. From that day in 1869 it was only a question of time until all of the frontier regions would be filled with settlements. But in Wyoming, there were reasons for the long delay in settling the northwest quadrant of the territory that became a state in 1890.

The extreme northwest corner was very rugged, and its thermal wonders were discovered as early as John Colter's journey to the region in 1807-08; following the Washburn-Doane expedition of 1870, Congress set aside the entire area to be the first national park (March 1, 1872). Cornelius Hedges, who was with that expedition, suggested that the region should be attached to Montana Territory, because it was impracticable to reach it from Wyoming across the "impassable and eternally snow-clad" Wind River mountains, but this suggestion never bore fruit.[4]

The central part of Big Horn Basin itself is the driest part of the state of Wyoming, with six inches or less in annual precipitation, although, ironically, the area escaped being included as part of the Great American Desert when Major Stephen H. Long fixed that label on a large region of the American West. When Captain William Albert Jones visited the Basin in 1874, he gave the area the description Major Long had overlooked, saying it was generally barren, rugged and parched. The dry climate of the Basin includes huge temperature variations, and while it is generally not the coldest place in Wyoming in the winter, it is often the warmest in the summer.[5]

Transportation by rail and highway soon weakened the characteristics of the frontier, and we end this narrative with the events that assured such

---

on to the Yellowstone to the north. In the summer of 1908 there arose a dispute as to the precise point where the name should change, with the United States Surveyor General opting for the arbitrary point where the stream crossed the middle line of Township 5 North about three miles south of the old Boysen Dam, and just above the head of the canyon. The State Engineer unsuccessfully argued for the point where the Popo Agie River joined the Wind River. *Thermopolis Record*, July 25, 1908. In December 1963, the U. S. Board on Geographic Names issued a formal decision requiring that federal agencies use the spelling "Bighorn" to refer to the region; this usage has not had wide acceptance in other circles. We have followed the more common usage, referring to the Big Horn Basin and the Big Horn River, and reserving "Bighorn" for federal designations, such as the Bighorn Forest.

[4]Aubrey L. Haines, *The Yellowstone Story: History of Our First National Park*, I (Boulder, Colorado, 1977), 135.

[5]The central Big Horn Basin shares with the Great Divide Basin of southern Wyoming the distinction as the driest part of Wyoming, both regions having six or less inches of precipitation. Robert Harold Brown, *Wyoming Occupance Atlas* (Cheyenne, 1970), 16. Major Long's Great American Desert

access to the Basin, from both north and south. Accordingly, the bulk of the commentary ends with 1901, when the first railroad came to Cody, in the north Basin, except for some few comments where events in a later period serve to complete the account. Because access from the south was exceptionally difficult, it was not accomplished until later, and the last two chapters reach further into the twentieth century to tell that story.

---

did not reach as far north as the Basin; it extended westward from the 96th meridian to the 106th meridian and north from the 35th parallel of latitude to the 42nd parallel, which runs across the southern part of Wyoming. Richard H. Dillon, "Stephen Long and the Great American Desert," *Montana*, XVIII, No. 3 (July, 1968), 68. Also, *Report of the Reconnaissance of Northwestern Wyoming Made in the Summer of 1873* by William A. Jones, Captain of Engineers (Washington, D. C., 1874), 52.

Chief Washakie, for many years the leader of the Shoshoni tribe, who had a special fondness for the Basin, both as a hunting ground and as the site of the prized hot springs at the new town of Thermopolis.
Courtesy Wyoming State Museum.

CHAPTER I

The First Inhabitants

Even though the Big Horn Basin was not easy to reach, and its physical environment may not have been as attractive as some of the regions on both sides of the high plains, there were those who passed through the Basin, and spent some part of the year in it. The of earliest of those people appear to have come from Asia, and they reached the Americas from the north.

Geological evidence supports the assumption that these people crossed over from Asia at the time that the two continents had a dry land connection where the Bering Strait is now. We do know that during the last glaciation, the sea level dropped by 460 feet, or so, which would have produced a broad plain, perhaps a thousand miles wide, connecting the two continents. This plain would have been dry perhaps 15,000 years ago, so that the Asian natives must have crossed over during the 3,000 years before the sea again arose, perhaps 12,000 years ago. During the time when the Asian land bridge existed, there were ice sheets over much of Canada and the northern United States, but the valleys of the Yukon and Mackenzie rivers were open grasslands.[1]

Archaeological evidence also points to a northern source for the early people; specimens taken from sites on the north shore of the Great Salt Lake include items that are characteristic of the frigid north. Linguistic analysis suggests that there were only three major migrations, each accounting for a separate language group, each of which can be related to Asiatic languages. The Asiatic tribes apparently migrated southward from

---

[1]Clark Wissler, *Indians of the United States* (New York, 1966), 22-23, 24. Also, Christy G. Turner II, "New World Origins: New Research from the Americas and the Soviet Union," in Dennis J. Stanford and Jane S. Day, eds., *Ice Age Hunters of the Rockies* (Niwot, Colorado, 1992), 8, 41.

the region west of Canada's Mackenzie River and spread out across that portion of North America now within the United States.[2]

Certainly, in the Big Horn Basin, there are archaeological sites that can be dated back 10,000 years, when a resident population of mammoths were hunted by human beings. But who were these people in the Basin? The mammoth hunters had been on this continent for a couple of thousand years, and their tribal affiliations may well have changed in that period, but we cannot say what these changes may have been. It is a long leap in time from the dating of the archaeological sites from 10,000 years ago to the period when we can identify artifacts with individual tribes.

Because of their distinctive pottery, it is possible to argue that the Crows may actually have been in northern Wyoming several times over a period of several hundred years; there is a site with Crow ceramics 400-500 years old at the base of the Big Horns west of Sheridan, and another half that old on Medicine Lodge Creek.

There is evidence that some of the American tribes lived fairly settled lives for long periods of time, growing crops, such as maize, but there is no consensus as to what caused them to give up such a lifestyle. In the East, the Iroquois League, which may have been formed more than 200 years before the Europeans began writing treaties with them, was apparently a stabilizing factor in tribal relationships, for a fairly long period of time. Whether the Iroquois were really at peace is a matter of dispute among the experts, with some respectable opinion claiming that they were at war with all about them.[3]

If we do not always know why they moved from place to place, it is in any case certain that, at least from the time of contact with the white explorers, a number of the major tribes moved a great deal. Food shortages and intertribal warfare may well have been major factors in many of these moves, and some argue that contact with Europeans was the cause of some tribal warfare, among people who had formerly lived at peace.

---

[2]Linguistic origins of American Indians are discussed in Joseph H. Greenberg and Merritt Ruhlen, "Linguistic Origins of Native Americans," *Scientific American* (November, 1992), 94-99. The specimens from the Promontory Point area in Utah include four-piece moccasins, fur mittens, sinew-backed bows and beaver-tooth dice. George E. Hyde, *Indians of the High Plains: From the Prehistoric Period to the Coming of Europeans* (Norman, Oklahoma, 1959), 5. Also George C. Frison, "The Foothills-Mountains and the Open Plains: the Dichotony in Paleoindian Subsistence Strategies Between Two Ecosystems," in Dennis J. Stanford and Jane S. Day, *Ice Age Hunters, op. cit.*, 323ff and George C. Frison, *Prehistoric Hunters of the High Plains* (New York, 1978), 23, 110.

[3]Francis Jennings, *The Ambiguous Iroquois Empire* (New York, 1984), 40.

The Europeans upset the balance of power and created tensions by acquiring land from the tribes by methods fair and foul.[4]

Those tribes who were strong enough to maintain a fairly stable area of occupation or settlement seem to have developed a sense of property regarding the area where they lived. When the British took possession of West Florida in 1763, they found the strong tribes living in towns, and some of them definitely reluctant to discuss land cessions. But that did not necessarily mean the tribes were thinking in terms of a static boundary. Their concept of boundaries was not the modern idea of metes and bounds; instead, they identified their land as the area over which they exercised control, a conception akin to that which existed in Europe before the sixteenth century. According to this concept, when the zone of control changed, so did the claim to land. Under that primitive definition of boundary, the frontier of a nation was literally the point at which one faced the enemy, rather than some notional line drawn on a map.[5]

It is clear that the competitive position of the various tribes was dramatically altered by the introduction of the horse and the firearm, both introduced by Europeans. The firearm was introduced by the French and English from the north, while horses first came to the southern tribes, who secured them from the Spanish. Spanish regulations prohibited trade of firearms to the natives, a factor which seriously upset the balance of power among the tribes, for those tribes dependent on Spanish trade lacked the means to defend themselves during the critical period when their enemies began to acquire firearms from the English and French.

By the same token, the tribes without horses were also vulnerable to mounted foes, and the sight of even a single horse in the distance was enough to alarm an entire Indian camp. In this transitional period, those tribes who did not have both horses and firearms were at a serious disadvantage in warfare.[6]

By 1650, the French had reached the west end of Lake Superior, and

---

[4]R. Brian Ferguson, "Tribal Warfare," *Scientific American*, CCLXVI, No. 1 (January, 1992), 108-09 and Dorothy V. Jones, *License for Empire: Colonialism by Treaty in Early America* (Chicago, 1982), 23.

[5]Cecil Johnson, *British West Florida, 1763-1783* (Chapel Hill, N. C., 1971), 42. Also, Peter Sahlins, *op. cit.*, 6.

[6]Although there is now evidence that man was riding the horse in the Ukraine as early as 6,000 years ago, those who came across the Bering land bridge to the New World apparently did not bring that asset with them. Daniel Anthony, Dimitri Y. Telegin and Dorcas Brown, "The Origin of Horseback Riding," *Scientific American* (December, 1991), 94. This may suggest that the settlers in the New World had lost contact with Asia before horseback riding became general.

the English had a factory on Hudson's Bay in 1668. The Crees and Assiniboins received firearms from the English and French, and by 1690 they were pushing west in a movement that drove the Blackfeet and Arapahoes from their older homes, which were perhaps in the region of the Red River of the north. When Pierre Gaultier de Varennes, the Sieur de la Verendrye reached the Mandans in 1738, he did not mention horses among them, but they were already being visited (presumably from the southwest) by people who did have horses.[7]

The Shoshonis, who are lumped into the designation "Snakes" in this period, were a part of the large Uto-Aztecan family that had been in the Great Basin before coming to the northern plains late in the seventeenth or early in the eighteenth century. It appears that at this time the Snakes and their allies, the Flatheads and the Kutenais, had the Montana and Wyoming hunting grounds, including the Big Horn Basin, much to themselves. According to the Crees, the Snakes began receiving horses between 1735 and 1740, and for a time, they were the terror of the northern plains, so that the Assiniboins and the fierce Blackfeet, so feared by Indian and trapper alike in later years, were afraid to cross the Shoshoni hunting ground to trade at York factory, on Hudson's Bay.[8]

The favorable competitive position of the Shoshonis changed when the Blackfeet received guns, and in the 1770's the Shoshonis were forced west of the Rockies; by 1785-90, the Blackfeet were raiding them and carrying off female captives, and in the closing years of the eighteenth century, the Shoshonis withdrew southwesterly from their former hunting grounds in Montana and Wyoming.[9]

Some argue that the migration of strong tribes, rather than the appearance of the white man, may have been decisive in causing tribal warfare and the shifting of customary locations. For the Indians of the northern high plains, it would have been the Sioux whose migrations destabilized conditions, according to this argument.

The Sioux had at one time been located in what is now the southeastern part of the United States; indeed, the presence of some remnants of this family on the Atlantic coast suggest that their community had been split at

---

[7]Lawrence J. Burpee, ed., *Journals and Letters of Pierre Gaultier Varennes de la Verendrye and His Sons* (Toronto, 1927), 337.

[8]Anthony McGinnis, *Counting Coup and Cutting Horses: Intertribal Warfare on the Northern Plains, 1738-1889* (Evergreen, Colorado, 1990), 6.

[9]Virginia Cole Trenholm and Maurine Carley, *The Shoshonis: Sentinels of the Rockies* (Norman, Oklahoma, 1964) 3, and George E. Hyde, op. cit., 137, 153.

some date before the voyages of Columbus, with a major group moving west. During the sixteenth century, the Sioux moved westward to the headwaters of the Mississippi. The Teton and Yanktonai Sioux were the first to reach the edges of the Great Plains, around the middle of the seventeenth century, and their near relatives, the Santee Sioux, were further east, in the woodlands. Although we cannot be certain of the reason for their movements, this timing would accord with the assumption that the Sioux were then under attack by the Crees and their allies, who were already armed with guns.[10]

Whatever their reasons for coming west to Minnesota, by the time the Teton Sioux moved out on the prairies of Minnesota, they were already well armed, having acquired their guns from the French, and as early as 1707, they also had horses. In the two centuries after 1685, the Sioux were no longer retiring before superior enemies—if, indeed, they ever were—but they had seized the initiative and were pressing relentlessly westward, dispossessing and subjugating numerous other tribes, until their influence was felt as far as the headwaters of the Yellowstone River.

When Lieutenant Zebulon Montgomery Pike encountered the Sioux, they were scattered along the upper Mississippi River, and at that time there were no Sioux villages east of that river, although the tribes still claimed the right to hunt the lower valleys of the Chippewa and St. Croix rivers. The Lewis and Clark expedition reported that the Sioux claimed west as far as the Missouri and further to the lower reaches of the Cheyenne, White and Teton rivers. Nevertheless, these claims continued to be fluid, as we shall shortly see. The availability of game often played a key part in these movements, as when the Brule Sioux moved from the White River region to the North Platte after 1832, because the buffalo had disappeared from the former location.[11]

As the Sioux continued to press westward, they participated in the fur trade to obtain guns and trade goods, and they pursued the numerous buffalo for food. For a time, the populous Mandan and Hidatsa villages

---

[10]George E. Hyde, *Red Cloud's Folk: A History of the Oglala Sioux Indians* (Norman, Oklahoma, 1937), 3-4. Also, Clark Wissler, *op. cit.*, 165, and Richard White, "The Winning of the West: The Expansion of the Western Sioux in the Eighteenth and Nineteenth Centuries," *The Journal of American History*, LXV, No. 2 (September, 1978), 321.

[11]Leroy F. Jackson, "Sioux Land Treaties," *Collections of the State Historical Society of North Dakota*, III (Bismarck, 1910), 498-500. Jackson states flatly that it is "impossible" to set boundaries for the Dakotas before 1825. Also, George E. Hyde, *Spotted Tail's Folk: History of the Brule Sioux* (Norman, Oklahoma, 1961), 28.

were able to resist the advance of the Sioux, but after the buffalo herds east of the Missouri were depleted, the Sioux were faced with the need for more hunting grounds, if they were not to imitate the settled tribes and grow food crops. Indeed, for a time, the Sioux settled with Arikaras and tried the latter culture, but when smallpox struck the tribes at the end of the eighteenth century, the settled tribes clearly suffered more from the disease than the nomadic tribes did, and it is perhaps for this reason that the settled life lost all of its appeal for the Sioux. Moreover, the other settled tribes decimated by smallpox were no longer strong enough to stand in the way of the Sioux advance.[12]

Thus it was that by the time the United States government was trying to open the Bozeman Trail along the eastern flank of the Big Horn Mountains, the Sioux and their allies, the Cheyennes, were claiming this region as their own, although they had taken it from the Crows only in the recent past. Margaret I. Carrington reported a conversation with some Cheyennes in 1866, when the question was raised about the legitimacy of their claim in opposition to that of the Crows. She records this matter-of-fact response: "We stole the hunting-grounds of the Crows because they were the best."[13]

Before 1676, the Cheyenne lived on the river bearing their name, and apparently had come from Minnesota before that. They then moved westward to the Missouri and lived on its banks for a time. The Cheyenne, Arapahoes and Crows had apparently been growing crops and making pottery before they gave up this lifestyle to become roving hunters of buffalo; it seems the Crows and Cheyenne were making pottery as late as 1760.[14]

Later, the Crows and their relatives, the Hidatsa, may have been living west of the Mandans and near the Little Missouri River. From there, the Crows moved westward to the lower Yellowstone, near the present location of Glendive, Montana. In 1742, they were on the Little Missouri north of the Black Hills, and twenty-five years later they had apparently been driven west by the Arapahoes and Cheyenne, to the Yellowstone, a land formerly hunted by the Snakes.[15]

By 1795, the Crows were on the Big Horn, and it was at this time that the Mountain Crows separated from the River Crows. The River Crows

---

[12]White, op. cit., 324-25.

[13]George E. Hyde, Red Cloud's Folk, op. cit., 3. Mrs. Carrington was a partisan of the Crows. Margaret I. Carrington, Absaraka: (Ab-sa-ra-ka), Home of the Crows (Chicago, 1950), 7.

[14]George Bird Grinnell, The Fighting Cheyennes (Norman, Oklahoma, 1915), 3, and George E. Hyde, op. cit., 47.   [15]George C. Frison, Prehistoric Hunters, op. cit., 67, 70.

held the Yellowstone valley and the Big Horn Basin, while the Mountain Crows had the region east of the Big Horn Mountains, and after 1815, the Wind River country as well. The two tribes met annually in the late summer on the Yellowstone above the mouth of the Big Horn River.[16]

Although the tribes moved across the Big Horn Basin in response to various pressures, they left little evidence of their tenure here. Nevertheless, there is one structure in the Big Horn Basin which remains to testify to some previous presence; unfortunately, it cannot be identified with a particular native group. The Medicine Wheel, or Great Medicine Wheel, is located in the Big Horn Mountains, on the western slope of Medicine Mountain, overlooking the Big Horn Basin.

The wheel is a nearly circular pattern of rock, about 75 feet in diameter. In the center is a stone-walled cairn about two feet in height, with an outside diameter of 12 feet and 7 feet on the inside, and from this center 28 "spokes" radiate to the periphery. Around the periphery are six other cairns, each of about the same height as the central one, but of varying size; all but one of these cairns touches the outer circle.

There is no agreement as to why the wheel was built, or by whom. Although the opinion has been expressed that the structure was built about 1770, one would expect that a date this late could be independently corroborated from some tribal tradition; unfortunately, such traditions as there are differ widely.[17]

Although the major Indian tribes now have well defined reservations, many of those lands do not represent the location of the several tribes for any long historical period. For the tribes on the high plains in the nineteenth century, the concept of a settled, immovable land boundary was introduced to them by the United States government in the course of the several treaty negotiations.[18]

---

[16]George E. Hyde, *op. cit.*, 149-50, 177, 178, 181.

[17]Taft Alfred Larson gives the 1770 date, which was derived from an investigation of the site by the Wyoming Archaeological Society in 1958. Tart Alfred Larson, *History of Wyoming* (Lincoln, Nebraska, 1978), 8 and "Wyoming Archaeological Notes, A Report of the Medicine Wheel Investigation," *Annals of Wyoming*, XXXI, No. 1 (April, 1959), 94-100. The northern Shoshonis knew nothing about the structure, while the Crows said it was given by the gods to show them how to build tipis. A report of an interview with a Sheep Eater woman says that the "spokes" of the wheel represent the divisions of the tribe. Virginia Cole Trenholm and Maurine Carley, *op. cit.*, 24-25.

[18]Clark Wissler, *op. cit.*, 184-85 and George Carr Frison, *Archaeological Evidence of the Crow Indians in Northern Wyoming: A Study of a Late Prehistoric Period Buffalo Economy* (dissertation, University of Michigan, 1967), 233. Robert A. Williams, Jr., *The American Indian in Western Legal Thought: The Discourses of Conquest* (New York, 1990), 211.

While a fluid concept of boundary made sense to the tribes, as they ranged over trackless land to pursue the game they needed, it was important for the United States government to have each tribe claim a specific area, and also to have each tribe give up any claim to other areas. Only in this fashion could the government obtain good title to the land it subsequently purchased from the tribes. As a consequence, the earliest treaties signed by the United States followed the precedent of the British colonial governments, and recited fixed boundaries for the Indian lands.

In the early part of the nineteenth century, the federal government had the unpleasant task of removing the Indians from Georgia to new reservations west of the Mississippi. This policy was in part the result of the intransigence of Georgia, which insisted on removal as a condition for its cession of claims to western lands. At first the western reservations were created piecemeal for each tribe, but in 1834, all of the remaining territory west of the Mississippi was set aside as Indian Territory, where white people could not trade without a license from the government. It was an ironic coincidence that the predecessor of old Fort Laramie was built in this new Indian Territory that same summer of 1834 in order to serve the fur trade, and soon it became apparent that this huge insulated territory could not last for long.[19]

In 1851, at the Fort Laramie treaty conference, the United States government asked the tribes on the high plains to agree to specific boundaries for their land, and in the Wyoming country the result was a map of tribal claims that covered the entire area, each claim neatly dovetailed into the next, with no empty spaces or overlap at all.

The 1851 treaty conference was the creation of Thomas Fitzpatrick, who was the first agent appointed to the Indian tribes of the high plains. Fitzpatrick recognized that the massive emigration over the Oregon trail was the source of great tension with the tribes, and he recommended that a treaty council be held to show liberality to the Indians. Congress appropriated $100,000 early in 1851, and the conference was set to convene on September 1, at Fort Laramie. The Commissioner of Indian Affairs, Luke Lea, instructed David D. Mitchell, as treaty commissioner to set bound-

---

[19]Maryland, which had no claims to western lands, had steadfastly refused to ratify the Articles of Confederation until those states with western claims relinquished them to the central government. Georgia was the last state to do so, in an agreement on April 24, 1802, ratified by the Georgia legislature on June 16, 1802; the fourth condition of the agreement contained the promise to remove the Indians. Thomas Donaldson, *The Public Domain: Its History with Statistics* (New York, 1971), 80-81. The Indian Intercourse Act was effective June 30, 1834. 4 *Statutes at Large*, 729, 733. Fort Laramie was originally called Fort John, then Fort William.

aries within which the tribes would reside; "... [E]ach should agree not to intrude within the limits assigned to another tribe without its consent." This was a sensible objective, but not one the tribes were used to.[20]

Mitchell dispatched expresses up the Missouri, Arkansas and Platte rivers in the spring of 1851, calling for a treaty conference at Fort Laramie, to convene on September 1. He left St. Louis on July 24, and arrived at the fort on August 31, to find the tribes camped in uneasy groups scattered on both sides of the river; Mitchell's first success of the conference was to convince the tribes to adopt a common camping ground.[21]

The conference convened on September 1, and lasted for eighteen days. The government had drawn up the treaties it wanted the tribes to sign, and on the 12th the maps which conveyed the substance of the agreement were discussed with the tribes, using the assistance of Father Pierre-Jean de Smet and James Bridger to explain the geography intended. Bridger, whose name would be associated with much of the history of the West, was then 47 years old, fluent in English, Spanish and French, as well as perhaps a dozen Indian tongues. Father de Smet was three years older than Bridger, and had begun his mission to the Indians in 1838.[22]

By the end of the day on the 12th, all except the Sioux had accepted the boundaries the government was proposing; the Sioux insisted that they should be able to hunt below the North Platte, in the region assigned to the Cheyenne and the Arapaho. When this conflict could not be resolved, the commissioner gave all the tribes freedom to hunt outside their assigned regions, although this hunting privilege did not change the boundaries claimed by the tribes.

Most of the territory that later became Wyoming was covered by tribal claims set forth in this treaty. To the tribes, there must have been a certain

---

[20]The Kansas Nebraska Act of 1854 reduced Indian Territory to an area where Oklahoma is now located, and opened the remaining land. Fitzpatrick was born in Ireland in 1799. Leroy R. Hafen, *Broken Hand: The Life of Thomas Fitzpatrick, Mountain Man, Guide and Indian Agent* (Lincoln, Nebraska, 1981), 7. Also, Leroy R. Hafen and Francis Marion Young, *Fort Laramie and the Pageant of the West, 1834-1890* (Glendale, California, 1938), 178.

[21]David D. Mitchell to Luke Lea, November 11, 1851, National Archives.

[22]Luke Lea to David D. Mitchell, May 26, 1851, National Archives. Also, Remi Nadeau, *Fort Laramie and the Sioux Indians* (Englewood Cliffs, N.J., 1967), 79. James Bridger was born at Richmond, Virginia, March 17, 1804, and first came to the Rocky Mountain region with Ashley's party in 1822. He died on his farm in Missouri, July 17, 1881. Colonel William O. Collins said that Bridger was "totally uneducated," but that he could speak Snake, Bannack, Crow, Flathead, Nez Perce, Pend' Oreille and Ute. Father Pierre Jean de Smet was born in Termonde, then under French rule, but later in Belgium, on January 30, 1801 and came to the United States in 1821. He died in St. Louis, May 23, 1873. Father de Smet made it clear that the treaty had been prepared "beforehand. " Hiram Martin Chittenden and Alfred Talbot Richardson, *Life, Letters and Travels of Father Pierre-Jean De Smet, S. J. 1801-1873*, II (New York, 1905), 676.

lack of substance in the tribal designations, for although the treaty recited fixed boundaries, the Sioux insisted on retaining hunting rights elsewhere, and the text was amended to give each signatory tribe the right to hunt on all of the land parceled out by the treaty; obviously, hunting was the chief activity for which the plains tribes needed and claimed lands.[23]

Another concept forced on the tribes in this treaty conference was the designation of a chief who would be the contact with the government, and here again the government objectives could not be realized in full. The Sioux, who were the largest tribal group in the conference, were split into separate bands, and were unwilling to recognize a single paramount chief. When Mitchell insisted they do so, and finally suggested Brave Bear, a Brule chief for the position, that chief at first declined, and the designation was made only after more jawboning from Mitchell; the tribes nevertheless regarded Brave Bear only as a "paper chief." The business of the council was now completed. By some standards, it was a success; certainly Father de Smet thought so, for he had baptized nearly 900 Indians.[24]

At Horse Creek, the Crows were assigned the entire Big Horn Basin of Wyoming (along with other lands), a region that had only a few years before been the hunting ground of the Shoshonis. Washakie, who led the Shoshoni group at the conference, did not agree with the assignment of the Big Horn Basin to the Crows, but his objections counted for nothing. Although the Shoshonis were present at Horse Creek, they were not permitted to sign the treaty; a separate treaty with the Shoshonis in 1863 assigned to that tribe an area in southwestern Wyoming bounded by the Wind River Mountains on the north and the North Platte River on the east.[25]

The 1851 and 1863 tribal allocations were changed dramatically in what came to be called the treaty summer of 1868. In a series of treaties, the entire southern part of Wyoming was cleared of Indian claims so that the railroad could be built without interference from the tribes, and the

---

[23]The commissioners even set aside territory for the Blackfeet, who did not bother to attend the conference. The Blackfeet finally entered into a treaty at a council on the Judith River, on October 17, 1855. 11 *Statutes at Large* 657.

[24]Father de Smet reported that he had baptized 305 "little ones," 253 Cheyennes, 280 Brule and Osage Sioux and 56 from the camp of Painted Bear. Chittenden and Richardson, *op. cit.*, 679. Also, Remi Nadeau, *op. cit.*, 79-80.

[25]Virginia Cole Trenholm and Maurine Carley, *op. cit.*, 123. The treaty of 1851 was not proclaimed by the President, as required by law, and in 1928, the Interior Department tried to have this act performed to clear up the technicality, but concluded it could not be done because Congress had in the interim forbade further treaties with the Indians. 16 *Statutes at Large* 566, March 3, 1871. One of the several memoranda on the subject is dated May 15, 1928.

THE FIRST INHABITANTS

Big Horn Basin itself was also vacated, although it was still nearly surrounded by Indian lands.[26]

South of the Basin, in the center of the newly-created Wyoming Territory, a permanent reservation was set aside for the so-called eastern band of Shoshonis by the Fort Bridger treaty of July 3, 1868; in 1878 the government forced the Shoshonis to accept a part of the Northern Arapaho tribe as joint occupants of this reservation.

Access to the Basin from the east was barred by another of the 1868 treaties. When the Sioux agreed to accept reservations in Dakota Territory (in the Fort Laramie treaty of April 29, 1868), the entire area in Wyoming east of the Big Horn mountains and north of the North Platte River was also set aside for them as a hunting ground. They were not to live on the hunting ground permanently, but for some years they had not lived permanently *anywhere*, so this sort of distinction must have been lost on the Sioux; the Sioux hunting ground was effectively an eastern barrier to the Basin.

To the north, the Crow reservation lay like a great cap across the top of Wyoming, taking in all of Montana lying south of the Yellowstone River and west of the 107th meridian. Since the Shoshoni reservation lay to the south of the Basin, and to the west was the Yellowstone cordillera, the Basin itself was effectively surrounded by natural and Indian barriers.[27]

Although their new reservation was entirely south of the Big Horn Basin, the Shoshonis continued to conduct an annual buffalo hunt in the Basin. We have an account of the 1874 hunt, giving us a late glimpse of a lifestyle that was fast coming to an end.

The reason we have this account arises from the efforts of a government teacher on the reservation to augment his income. It seems that the commissioner of Indian affairs had declared that the teacher should receive no salary during the period when the tribe was absent from the reservation, apparently on the reasonable assumption that there was no teaching work to be done. Accordingly, when the tribe made ready for its hunt in the fall of 1874, the teacher, James I. Patten, devised the clever plan of conducting a sort of "roaming" school, which would meet in a 60-foot tent erected wherever the tribe might halt. The commissioner approved of this plan, and Patten therefore made ready to accompany the Indians to the Basin.

---

[26]The Horse Creek treaty was signed downstream from Fort Laramie on September 17, 1851 and the treaty with the Eastern Shoshonis was signed at Fort Bridger on July 2, 1863. 11 *Statutes at Large* 749 and 18 *Statutes at Large* 685.

[27]The Crow treaty was signed at Fort Laramie on May 25, 1868 and ratified July 25, 1868. 15 *Statutes at Large* 649. The Shoshoni treaty was ratified February 26, 1869. 15 *Statutes at Large* 673.

The departure date was October 16, and the group was large: 1,800 men, women and children, as well as some Bannocks from Idaho. By the 19th they were at the Owl Creek Mountains, where there was a brief scare over the discovery of a wide trail made by hostile Indians; Chief Washakie then altered the route to Red Canyon to avoid the hostiles. On the night of the 20th, there was a terrific snow storm, and soon food became scarce and the children began to suffer from the cold. Finally, the tribe struggled to the summit, where for the first time Patten beheld the Basin stretching out to the north, "a vast ocean of milky whiteness."[28]

Once across the summit, the tribe camped on Owl Creek, and several deer stampeded through the camp, which occasioned some indiscriminate and totally inaccurate gunfire by the Indians, who were as surprised as the deer must have been. Runners sent out to find the buffalo returned with the news that there were large herds on Gooseberry Creek, some forty miles above its mouth. The tribe hastened to this area, and when Washakie signaled the charge, made a great rush which resulted in a fine kill of 125 buffalo. The meat was shared throughout the tribe, but each hide was the property of the one killing the animal. While the hunt was a success, Patten's teaching objectives could not be realized, for the constant movement of the tribe in search of game prevented him from conducting the school he had contemplated.[29]

Before the Europeans arrived, the Basin was used by natives whenever it supported game in sufficient numbers to justify the chase. The Europeans came with their conception of boundaries, and justified taking the land from the inhabitants by making "treaties" and later "agreements" that generally confirmed what had already been decided by the superior party to the arrangement. When this taking was completed, the Basin passed into several new stages of occupation.[30]

---

[28]Patten said there were a few Mexicans, one Portugese and one Penobscot Indian with the camp.

[29]James I. Patten, "Buffalo Hunting with the Shoshone Indians, in 1874, in the Big Horn Basin, Wyoming," *Annals of Wyoming*, IV, No. 2 (October, 1926), 296. The account was written in April, 1917 for Grace Raymond Hebard. Grace Raymond Hebard, *Washakie: An Account of Indian Resistance of the Covered Wagon and Union Pacific Railroad Invasions of Their Territory* (Cleveland, 1930), 159n.

[30]The appropriation act of March 3, 1871 ended the practice of treaty-making with the Indians, so that all subsequent arrangements of this sort be concluded as agreements between the government and the tribes. The practical consequence of this change was that the House of Representatives, which had the sole right to originate taxation measures, would have a vote on the agreement itself, rather than being forced to fund a *fait accompli*.

CHAPTER II

Explorers and Trappers

As schoolchildren, we learned that Columbus discovered the Americas in 1492, but "discovery" could only have meaning to Europeans who did not know where the New World was, for the people living in the Western Hemisphere did not need to be discovered: they knew full well where they were. Indeed, the Europeans themselves acknowledged that the Western Hemisphere was not an empty region, but already had inhabitants, so that we need to understand what discovery meant to those who were using the word.

Soon after Columbus returned to Spain, the Spanish Pope Alexander VI issued a papal bull to recognize the priority of the Spanish claims in the New World. This bull, dated May 3, 1493, recognized that there were inhabitants in the territories the Spanish had discovered, but the Pope made it clear that the claims of the Spanish monarchs were superior to that of anyone else among the *Christian* world who had not already established themselves in the region. This is a rather vague way to indicate primacy, but the Spanish needed the Pope's confirmation of their position, since the King of Portugal had received a similar bull in 1481, confirming him in the territories he had discovered.[1]

The papal bull left unanswered the question whether the Spanish had the right to displace non-Christian rulers who had claims in the New World, and when that displacement occurred it was variously justified on the grounds the Indians were barbarians. A long dissertation opposing this view was written by Bartolome de Las Casas, bishop of Chiapas. Las Casas' efforts caused Cardinal Cisneros to send a commission to the New World to investigate conditions there, and some of Las Casas' recommen-

---

[1] L. Milton Woods, *The Wyoming Country Before Statehood: Four Hundred Years Under Six Flags* (Worland, Wyoming, 1971), 6.

dations were incorporated in the Laws of the Indies in 1542, although there were no significant changes in the treatment of the natives.²

To make matter more certain between them, Spain and Portugal agreed on a line of demarcation between their two discovery regions, and this treaty of Tordesillas was confirmed by the Pope on January 24, 1506. According to this treaty, the Big Horn Basin fell within the claims of the Spanish, although nobody in Rome, or in Spain or Portugal had the foggiest notion that the Basin existed, or where it was. Nevertheless, as between Spain and Portugal, the matter was settled, at least for a time. The claims of the native inhabitants still existed, but naturally were often in conflict with these legalistic pronouncements, made thousands of miles from the locations they affected. Moreover, the other European nations regarded the declarations of the Pope with skepticism, and Francis I of France is said to have remarked that he would like to see the clause of Adam's will which excluded France from the New World; England similarly opposed the intent of the papal bulls.³

We are justified in ignoring those Spanish claims to the Big Horn Basin that were based on the papal bulls, but soon there was a more serious Spanish claim, which followed the more customary procedure. If a European explorer came upon a stream draining a large area, he would commonly take possession of all the land drained by the stream, and in this fashion, nearly all of the North American continent soon fell within territorial claims of the European powers. The action of this sort affecting the Big Horn Basin was the discovery of the Mississippi River by the Spanish explorer, Hernando De Soto. Although he died while his expedition was returning down the river in 1541, he clearly established a Spanish claim to all of the land drained by the Mississippi.⁴

The French were also active in exploration, and Louis Joliet first reached the Mississippi River in 1673, although his powers were somewhat limited, and it fell to Rene Robert Cavelier, Sieur de la Salle to take possession of the Mississippi drainage for Louis XIV, on April 9, 1682. The French claims were clearly inferior in time to those of the Spanish, and we must recognize that even the accepted method of "discovery" was

---

²Carlos Fuentes, *The Buried Mirror: Reflections on Spain and the New World* (New York, 1992), 131. Las Casas, who was born in 1474, wrote *The Defense of the Most Reverend Lord, Don Fray Bartolome de Las Casas, of the Order of Preachers, Late Bishop of Chiapas, Against the Persecutors and Slanderers of the Peoples of the New World Discovered Across the Seas*, c. 1548-50.
³*Ibid.*, 8.
⁴*Ibid.*, 10.

only effective if the nation doing so was able to follow up the discovery promptly and with sufficient strength. In the case of the French, the important difference was the establishment of French settlements on the Mississippi in 1699, which brought a permanent French presence within the region they claimed.[5]

The French called their new possession Louisiana, in honor of Louis XIV, the Sun King, and soon French traders were moving westward. In 1730, an expedition was authorized, charged with the task of finding the legendary river of the west, which supposedly flowed to the Pacific Ocean, under the leadership of the two sons of Pierre Gaultier de Varennes, the Sieur de la Verendrye. The expedition did not get underway until 1738, as the French government required that it be financed from the fur trade. A second journey in 1742 came at least as far west as the plains of South Dakota, and on New Years Day, 1743, they saw mountains on the horizon, which may have been the Big Horn Mountains, although opinions differ on this. If they came that far west, they would have been the first white men to do so.

Larger considerations caused the French to give up their claims to the Big Horn Basin, when they transfered the province of Louisiana to Spain on April 21, 1764, as a part of the settlement of the Seven Years' War. The change of sovereignty had no immediate effect in the Basin. In 1793, *La Compagnie de Comerce pour la Decouverte des nations du haut du Missouri*, generally called the Missouri Company, was organized in St. Louis, apparently in the hope that this company would divert the fur trade with the Indians away from the British. Unfortunately, the first expedition the following year was stopped by the Sioux, and it was 1796 before the Missouri Company reached as far up the Missouri as the Mandan villages. By the last decade of the eighteenth century, the French trappers from Canada had reached the Wyoming country.

When Napoleon came to power in France, he negotiated a treaty with Spain, which transferred Louisiana back to France; this Treaty of San Ildefonso was signed October 1, 1800. It was from France that the United States purchased Louisiana, for $11,250,000, on April 11, 1803, and the Big Horn Basin fell under the control of the United States.

Formidable canyons on the north and south of it made the Basin difficult to explore by water; consequently, when Lewis and Clark made their great journey of exploration across Louisiana to the Pacific coast and back in 1804-06, making use of the major rivers, they passed north of the

---
[5]*Ibid.*, 15-16.

Basin, although John Colter, a member of the expedition, left the main party for a journey to the Yellowstone Park region that brought back to the States the first eyewitness account of the wonders there. Later, the great migrations to the west coast chose the easier terrain offered by the South Pass, skirting the Basin on the South.

Soon the search for beaver pelts brought trappers into the Basin. In 1807 George Drouillard came south into the Basin from Manuel Lisa's Fort Raymond, at the mouth of the Big Horn, and met a village of Crows on the Stinking Water, near the present site of Cody. In 1823, Andrew Henry established a new fort at the mouth of the Big Horn River and Jedediah Strong Smith, about 24, was captain in charge of one of the companies sent south from the fort to the Big Horn region. After trapping the eastern slope of the Big Horns in the fall of that year, Smith crossed into the Big Horn Basin from the Powder River Basin by descending Shell Creek; he was fresh from an encounter with a grizzly bear, which mauled him by taking nearly his entire head in its mouth. Smith survived, but lost an eyebrow and bore a scarred ear to the end of his life.[6]

On the way west, Smith encountered a Missouri Fur Company party under Charles Keemle and William Gordon, and the two companies proceeded to the Big Horn River. It was November, and they now headed southward over barren country, as most of the game had been frightened away by a Crow village moving through the same area. The trappers hurried to overtake the Crows and later spent the winter with those Indians in the Wind River valley; apparently the yield of peltry was disappointing, for Henry abandoned the fort on the Yellowstone in 1824.[7]

In 1825, the Basin was visited by a large number of trappers headed by General William H. Ashley, then about 43 years old. The general had earlier been involved with an educational institution in Missouri Territory and became interested in developing a territorial militia, in which he advanced to the general's rank he carried for the rest of his life. A foray into politics landed him the office of lieutenant governor of the new state of Missouri, but when he ran for governor he was defeated. His business ventures fare little better, and by 1822 he was perhaps $100,000 in debt.

In 1822, Ashley secured a license to enter the Indian country and advertised for "one hundred young men" to ascend the Missouri to its

---

[6]Leroy R. Hafen, *Broken Hand, op. cit.*, 29. Smith was born in Jericho, New York, January 6, 1799; he was killed by Indians on the Cimarron River, May 27, 1831.

[7]Dale L. Morgan, *Jedediah Smith and the Opening of the West* (Lincoln, Nebraska, 1953), 84-86.

source. He pioneered the rendezvous system, where trappers could trade peltry for supplies, and he came to the Basin after leaving the first fur trappers' rendezvous, in 1825. That first rendezvous was on Henry's Fork of the Green River, just above the south boundary of Wyoming, and it was apparently only a one-day affair, perhaps because the liquor supply was inadequate. Ashley chose the Basin route back to St. Louis for safety's sake, since he knew there was an Army expedition in the area which would afford protection from the Indians.[8]

On his trip back to St. Louis, Ashley left the rendezvous on July 2, 1825, with 50 men, headed for the Big Horn River; half of the group were to transport furs to the point of embarkation and then return to the mountains, while the rest would accompany the packs to St. Louis. On the way, a part of the group were attacked by the Blackfeet, but were fortunate to escape with only one man wounded, although all but two of the horses were lost. After waiting two days for additional mounts from the other men, they continued north across the Big Horn Basin to a point just below the Big Horn Canyon.

Ashley had 100 packs containing perhaps 3,200 beaver pelts that weighed a total of 9,700 pounds, worth $40-50,000 in St. Louis. When the work of loading the pelts for river traffic was completed, more than half the party left Ashley and returned to the mountains; the rest (a total of 24-28 men) proceeded with him down the river. They finally reached St. Louis on October 4, 1825. Ashley said that he had had the Big Horn explored from Wind River Canyon to the mouth of the river, and found it navigable for boats drawing three feet of water over the entire distance; this comment is simply inexplicable, and there is no way to reconcile the statement with the presence of the formidable Big Horn Canyon. Notwithstanding his favorable comment on the Basin, Ashley did not choose this water route for his return to St. Louis the following year, when he elected instead to go east by the Platte River route.[9]

---

[8]Ashley said there were 120 men at the rendezvous, and while James Beckwourth says there was liquor available, this commodity was not on Ashley's list of supplies, an omission that was corrected the following year. Fred R. Gowans, *Rocky Mountain Rendezvous: A History of the Fur Trade Rendezvous 1825-1840* (Provo, Utah, 1976), 12-14. Ashley was born in Chesterfield County, Virginia, about 1782; he died in Missouri, March 28, 1838. Harvey L. Carter, "William H. Ashley," in Leroy R. Hafen, ed., *Mountain Men and Fur Trade of the Far West*, (Lincoln, Nebraska, 1982), 79, 88.

[9]There are two opinions as to where the point of embarkation was, but Ashley said that he struck the river below the Big Horn Mountain, and he makes it clear that he did not mean Wind River Mountain, because he uses that term later in the same entry. Moreover, it does not seem logical that he would have tried to transport the valuable cargo by boat through the Big Horn Canyon.

Other trappers visited the Basin from time to time, as in 1829, when Robert Campbell, who was then 25, apparently trapped the Big Horn in the fall and spring before going to the trappers' rendezvous on the Popo Agie. The Basin claimed the lives of four of the trappers, who were apparently killed by the Blackfeet. In the fall of 1829, Milton Green Sublette, who was born about 1801, came north from the Popo Agie with 40 men, including Jean Baptiste Gervais and Henry Fraeb to trap the Big Horn and Yellowstone River country; they later rendezvoused at Pierre's Hole.[10]

Jedediah Smith and his men visited the Basin again, and in the process lost a hundred head of horses and mules in the deep snow on the mountains. They entered the Basin on the plains near the Stinking Water, and the group pronounced that place the "back door to that country which divines preach about." After caching their furs, the Smith party went on to meet Sublette. The following year, after Smith, Jackson and Sublette sold their interest in the trapping enterprise to the Rocky Mountain Fur Company, Smith brought his furs through the Basin from Pryors Gap, on the way to Wind River. A party under Samuel Tullock was sent to raise the cache they had made on the Big Horn River the previous December. In this party were Joseph L. Meek and a Frenchman named Glaud Ponto. While digging the furs out, the bank caved in on Meek and Ponto, killing the latter, whose body was then rolled in a blanket and pitched into the river. So much for the ceremony of burial in that savage era.[11]

In the fall of 1832, Zenas Leonard, then 23 years old, came to the Basin in a company of fifteen, on the trail of five horses that had been stolen by the Crows. At the time the horses were taken, the trappers were south of the Wind River Mountains, in the Shoshoni country. They followed the Crows north into the Basin, across the Owl Creek Mountains, and found the Indian village at the mouth of the Stinking Water. In this village was a black man, Edward Rose, who had first come west with Manuel Lisa, and

---

[10]Jedediah Smith gives the names of the four killed as Peter Spoon, Ezekiel Abel, Philip Adam and Luke Lariour; an enclosure gives the last name as J. Larime, and the assertion they were killed by the Snakes. Dale L. Morgan, *op. cit.*, 306, 341, 345. On August 30, 1830, Smith, Jackson and Sublette sold to another partnership consisting of Thomas Fitzpatrick, James Bridger, Milton Sublette, Henry Fraeb and Jean Gervais. Fred R. Gowans, *op. cit.*, 56, 67. Also, Dale L. Morgan, *op. cit.*, 304. Robert Campbell was born in Aughaklkane, Ulster, February 12, 1804, reached the United States in 1822 and went west for his tuberculosis. He died at St. Louis, October 16, 1879. Milton Sublette, younger brother of William Sublette, was born at Somerset, Kentucky; he died at Fort William (later Fort Laramie), April 5, 1837.

[11]Frances Fuller Victor, *The River of the West: The Adventures of Joe Meek* (Missoula, Montana, 1983), 79-80, 88, and Dale L. Morgan, *op. cit.*, 314.

stayed to live with the Crows. With the assistance of Rose and some "trifling presents," the horses were recovered. The Indians left their campsite when game became scarce, but the trappers remained until February, 1833, when they left to begin the spring hunt, going south over the Owl Creeks again.[12]

In 1833, the trappers again used the Big Horn River to transport their furs to St. Louis. After leaving the rendezvous on July 24, Fitzpatrick, Milton Sublette and Campbell travelled north to strike the Big Horn River. It was a diverse group. There was Nathaniel Jarvis Wyeth, born in 1802, whose work developing the New England ice trade would overshadow his involvement in the western fur trade.[13]

Along to test the curative powers of the West was Dr. Benjamin Harrison, the son of William Henry Harrison; the elder Harrison had paid $1,000 for his son's expenses, in the hope his drinking problem would be moderated; apparently the alcoholic antics of the rendezvous had not been reported to the father. Old Tippecanoe complained that the money had been spent in a "totally unaccountable" fashion. The younger Harrison, who was born in 1806, apparently did not impress his companions, for Wyeth said he was unreliable. Perhaps he felt the payment for his passage guaranteed him the right to avoid the menial chores of the journey. Nevertheless, his medical knowledge did prove useful.[14]

Also in the party was perhaps the Basin's most distinguished visitor to that point, Captain William Drummond Stewart, the younger son of a Scottish baronet, who would one day succeed to the title. Stewart, then 37, was born on an estate where the Birnam Wood of "Macbeth" was located, and was a veteran of the battle of Waterloo. He had left Scotland after some unfortunate personal troubles and had come west on the first

---

[12]Zenas Leonard was born March 19, 1809, in Clearfield County, Pennsylvania. John C. Ewers, ed., *Adventures of Zenas Leonard, Fur Trader* (Norman, Oklahoma, 1959), xvii, 51-52.

[13]Bernard DeVoto, *Across the Wide Missouri* (Boston, 1947), 29. Nathaniel Wyeth was born near Cambridge, Massachusetts, January 29, 1802; he died August 31, 1856.

[14]Benjamin Harrison continued to distress his family, for he was in Texas at the time of the uprising there in 1836, and was reported killed and his body "mangled" by the Mexicans. Actually, Harrison had been only slightly wounded and had escaped, but surrendered for lack of food after three or four days. The Mexican general was not impressed by his credentials, but did credit those of his father, and outfitted Benjamin with a horse, arms, money and a guide back to the Texans' lines. There he was again confined for a few days by the Texans, who surmised that someone so well equipped must be a spy. Benjamin Harrison died June 9, 1840. Freeman Cleaves, *Old Tippecanoe: William Henry Harrison and His Time* (New York, 1939), passim. Wyeth's comment on Harrison is in his letter to W. L. Sublette, February 23, 1834; nevertheless, he was gracious in forwarding Dr. Harrison's letter to old General Harrison, October 17, 1833, but limited his comments to a report of the son's good health.

of what were to be a number of journeys to the high plains. With Stewart was Antoine Clement, a half-breed Canadian, who was Stewart's companion and would one day return to Scotland with the baronet.[15]

Fitzpatrick and Sublette had 61 packs of beaver pelts, and Wyeth had 30. The trappers built bull boats, three for Campbell's 1,200 pounds of beaver, three for Bonneville and Cerre, and one large boat for Nat Wyeth, Milton Sublette and Wyeth's four assistants; it was eighteen feet long and five and a half wide, pointed at both ends, and was covered by the hides of three bull buffalos. Before they departed, Fitzpatrick and Milton Sublette negotiated with Wyeth one of the first contracts to be signed in the area, an agreement whereby Wyeth was to bring supplies to the 1834 rendezvous.[16]

We also know that trappers travelling with the Crows in the Basin in November 1834 participated in a fight with a band of Piegans. The Mountain Crows under Chief Long Hair were on a buffalo hunt, when one hundred or more Piegans were spotted nearby. Zenas Leonard watched the fight from a distance of 200 yards. The Piegans took advantage of a natural fortification, and the Crows were unable to dislodge them until the trappers led the charge on the enemy. James Pierson Beckwourth and Robert Meldrum were both present on this occasion, and Beckwourth may have led the charge on the Piegans, who were then routed.[17]

Beckwourth, whose name was probably originally Beckwith, was born in Fredericksburg, Virginia, April 26, 1798, according to his own account.

---

[15] Stewart was born at Murthly Castle on December 26, 1795, second son of Sir George Stewart, 17th Lord of Grandtully, and fifth Baronet of Murthly. In 1830, Stewart married Christina Stewart, who had just borne his son, George; it does not appear that the couple ever lived together. Mae Reed Porter and Odessa Davenport, *Scotsman in Buckskin: Sir William Drummond Stewart and the Rocky Mountain Fur Trade* (New York, 1963), 4, 17.

[16] Mae Reed Porter and Odessa Davenport, *op. cit.*, 70. Wyeth said the bull boat leaked "a little." "Correspondence and Journals of Captain Nathaniel J. Wyeth, 1831-6," Sources of the History of Oregon, I, 3-6 (Eugene, Oregon, 1899), 208. The contract with Wyeth was signed August 14, 1833. Leroy R. Hafen, *Broken Hand, op. cit.*, 132.

[17] Long Hair had signed the first Crow treaty with the United States, at the Mandan villages on August 4, 1825. The reports of the length of his hair, which he never cut, ranged from 9' 11" to 36'; it was combed and folded every morning by the Crow warriors. He died a few years before 1856. Ewers, *op. cit.*, 141, 144-57. Robert Meldrum was born in Scotland in 1812; he moved to Illinois in 1824 and then on to St. Louis, where he entered the Rocky Mountain fur trade. He may have had as many as six Indian wives, and at least one of these liaisons was solemnized by Father DeSmet. He died at Fort Union, July 10, 1865. Keith Algier, "Robert Meldrum and the Crow Peltry Trade," *Montana*, XXXVI, No. 3 (Summer, 1986), 41, and LeRoy R. Hafen, *The Mountain Men and the Fur Trade of the Far West*, VII (Glendale, California, 1969), 123.

At an early age, he moved to St. Louis with his parents, and he was apprenticed in the blacksmith trade. In 1824, he enlisted in General Ashley's Rocky Mountain party, but he reached the mountains only in the following year. He was inducted into the Crow nation, and since he was apparently a mulatto, it was easy for the Indians to imagine that he was really a long-separated member of their tribe.[18]

The battle with the Piegans cost the Crows about thirty killed and as many wounded, and the Piegans lost 69 killed. After the ritual mutilation of the dead and dying, the party moved off to the Nowood River, where the buffalo were numerous. When they later moved camp to the Big Horn at the Wind River Canyon, a party of hostiles tried to steal horses from them, and lost a "principal" chief in their unsuccessful raid, providing the Crows with another body to gloat over, before they moved on up the Wind River.

The fur trade era, supported by a faddish demand for the beaver hat, was colorful, but it lasted only for a few years. The heyday was the time of the annual rendezvous, the first of which was held by General William Ashley on Henry's Fork of the Green River in 1825, and the last was on the Green River in 1840. Thereafter, the remaining numbers of fur-bearing animals no longer would support the number of trappers who came for their pelts. With the passing of this phase, the Basin lapsed into a short period when its utility as a highway was tested.[19]

---
[18]Hiram Martin Chittenden, *The American Fur Trade of the Far West*, II (New York, 1935), 679ff. Beckwourth died in 1866.

[19]Fred R. Gowans, *op. cit., passim*.

CHAPTER III

Troopers and Teamsters

The era of the fur trappers was followed by expeditions of the Army. Most of these expeditions were peaceful explorations, not in pursuit of the enemy, and when the soldiers tried to bring wheeled vehicles with them, rather than merely ride horses, as previous visitors had, new difficulties arose. In the spring of 1860, Lieutenant Henry E. Maynadier tried to bring carts, ambulances and wagons into the Basin, and he had to abandon much of this equipment. Maynadier was a part of the expedition of Captain William Franklin Raynolds, which entered the Big Horn Basin as a part of the work that led to a detailed examination of the Yellowstone region.

Raynolds divided his command at Red Buttes, on the Platte River, and sent a detachment under Maynadier to enter the Big Horn Basin, with orders to rendezvous with the main command north of that region. On May 14, 1860, Maynadier left Raynolds, taking mules and some carts that could be abandoned if the territory proved too difficult for wheeled transport; in the group were 23 packers, herders and drivers, together with a topographer, a meteorologist, a physician and Paul Deval as guide. The group travelled west on the emigrant road to Independence Rock, which was reached on May 15, and at the mouth of the Popo Agie, Maynadier was joined by an escort led by Lt. John Mullan of the Second Dragoons.

By May 26, they were at the head of the Wind River canyon, and Maynadier turned to the right and ascended the mountains; after struggling through rugged country, the expedition followed a small stream back toward the river, expecting that the canyon would open to permit them to follow along the stream. This proved an unwise choice, because the passable stretch along the river was only about four miles long, at which point the canyon walls closed in once again, forcing the troops to climb back up to the rough terrain above the canyon.

For three days, they tried to haul their carts over the rugged land, and finally had to abandon all except the light ambulances and one wagon belonging to Lt. Mullans' escort. After passing beyond the canyon, they still could not find a ford to get across the river to the less broken land along the west bank. Their search for a ford was rendered more urgent by the fact the river was steadily rising from snow melt. Finally, they forded just north of the mouth of Nowater Creek, and on June 4 they were able to make seventeen miles in the easier region west of the river.[1]

The lieutenant saw the mouth of the Nowood, apparently from across the Big Horn, and commented that the Nowood was well timbered at its mouth but had no timber upstream. On June 5, after passing the mouth of the Nowood, the expedition turned northwest, following a lodge trail over a low hill, and struck the Gray Bull River. Their trials were not at an end, however; after crossing the Gray Bull, their next camp was without wood or grass, as they searched for the Stinking Creek, as Maynadier called it. Finally, they were pleasantly surprised when they abruptly came upon that river, hidden in a defile 70-80 feet below the plains.

This stream, usually called the Stinking Water until the Wyoming legislature gave it the more euphonius name of Shoshone, proved their most difficult crossing. On June 11, they tried to raft across, and failed, after which they tried to ford. The mules hitched to the ambulance were dragged out in the current and drowned, and all of the materials in the ambulance were lost, except for one box of stationery. The lieutenant sadly noted that he had ordered the men to place their weapons in the ambulance for safety's sake, and these were all lost. Finally, on June 15, the Maynadier expedition crossed the divide between Sage Creek and the Clark's Fork of the Yellowstone, leaving the Big Horn Basin. When Captain Raynolds submitted his report of the expedition, he commented that the Big Horn valley was "repelling in all its characteristics and can only be traversed with the greatest difficulty."[2]

---

[1]Lt. Maynadier does not identify the ford in his report, but the map accompanying the report shows its location.

[2]Maynadier claimed that no one had ever visited the head of the Clark's Fork, as it was "impassable to man or beast." The report of the expedition is found in Bvt. Brig. General William Franklin Raynolds, *Report on the Exploration of the Yellowstone River* (Washington, 1868). The report of First Lt. Henry E. Maynadier, 10th Infantry, begins at page 127. The 1901 legislature changed the name of the Stinking Water River to the Shoshone River.

Another reconnaissance of the Basin was that of Captain William A. Jones, who led a party to the area in the summer of 1873. Jones thought the climate was similar to the Wind River Valley, except that the Indians told him that the Basin was even windier than the Valley, a comment that sounds like deliberate disinformation on the Indians' part. He noted that the Basin was dry, and that the streams on the west slope of the Big Horns were rare, and "frequently dry." Consequently, travel in the area was "attended with much inconvenience." This laconic assessment clearly understated the difficulties.[3]

The Big Horn Basin was seldom the site for military engagements with Indians in the American West, simply because there were few non-Indian civilians or soldiers in the Basin during much of the time when hostilities were most common. We know that there were two engagements on Shell Creek in 1867, involving Company D, Second Cavalry, under the command of Captain David S. Gordon, in which four Indians were killed, but nothing more is known about these incidents.[4]

A more serious encounter occurred in the summer of 1874. In June of that year, the Sioux held a Sun Dance at their reservation in Dakota Territory, where they agreed to join with the Cheyennes and Arapahoes in a drive against the Wind River Shoshonis; when the three groups could not agree on the object of the raid, the Sioux and Cheyenne turned back, leaving the Arapahoes in their camp in the Big Horn Mountains. Several Shoshonis, including Chief Washakie's son Dick saw this camp and informed Captain Robert A. Torrey, then commanding Camp Brown, that hostiles were in the Basin.[5]

Camp Brown had no shortage of military rank at this moment, because General Philip Henry Sheridan and General Edward Otho Cresap Ord had just arrived. It was determined that the Army would engage the Arapahoes at once, and Company B of the Second U. S. Cavalry was detailed for that purpose. The company was under the command of Captain Alfred Elliott Bates, who was born in Michigan in 1840, had been admitted to West Point in 1861, and had received his captain's bars in 1869. The 63

---

[3] *Report Upon the Reconnaissance of Northwestern Wyoming, Made in the Summer of 1873 by William A. Jones, Captain of Engineers, U.S.A.* (Washington, 1874).

[4] The engagements were on October 26 and November 29, 1867. *Chronological List of Actions &c with Indians from January 15, 1837 to January, 1891* (Ft. Collins, Colorado, 1979), 30, 31. Captain Gordon was born about 1830, in New York.

[5] Hugh K. Knoefel, *Wyoming's Bloodiest Fourth of July* (Worland, Wyoming, 1969), n.p. Also, Virginia Cole Trenholm and Maurine Carley, *op. cit.*, 51, 239.

soldiers were accompanied by 167 Shoshoni Indians under Chief Washakie himself, and the combined unit left Camp Brown on July 1, 1874, marching at night at the suggestion of General Sheridan, who warned that the dust from the column would alert the hostiles if they marched during the hot summer day.[6]

The line of march was down the Wind River, past the head of the Wind River Canyon, then northwestward into the Big Horn Basin, where the Arapahoe village of 112 lodges was found in a ravine at the junction of Dead Indian Creek and Bates Creek. At 7:30 on the morning of July 4, Bates ordered the bugler to sound the charge. After the initial charge, the surviving Indians fled to a butte above the camp and opened fire on the soldiers, killing two and wounding three. The Army command then withdrew from the field, its ammunition nearly exhausted, and beat a hasty retreat to Camp Brown, to count casualties and write reports. Four enlisted men had been killed, and one officer and five men wounded. Bates reckoned that 26 hostiles were killed and 20 wounded. Captain Torrey, the commander at Camp Brown, chided Bates for not having won a decisive victory, and for his part, Bates complained that his Shoshoni allies had deserted him during the fight, although he complimented Chief Washakie. It was not an auspicious engagement.[7]

Wyoming's Clark's Fork Valley just north of the Basin was the scene of another engagement in the fall of 1878. Colonel Nelson Appleton Miles was in command of a small expedition to establish a wagon route and telegraph line west of the temporary Tongue River Cantonment, which would later be named Fort Keogh. In addition to the official purpose of his journey, Miles was obviously interested in visiting Yellowstone Park, for his entourage included five women and three children, including Mrs. Miles and their daughter Cecelia.

Unfortunately for the unofficial agenda, the expedition had no sooner reached the Park when Miles received word that a band of Bannocks were raiding through the Park region. To Miles, who had been complaining of the lack of promotion, this news presented an opportunity for recognition, and he quickly sent the civilians to Fort Ellis and led 75 soldiers and 75 Crow allies east.

---

[6]Trenholm and Carley, *op. cit.*, 240, and Knoefel, *op. cit.*

[7]The Arapahoes were able to save half their pony herd. Knoefel, *op. cit.* The casualty list is given in *Chronological List of Actions, &c., With Indians from January 15, 1837 to January, 1891.* (Washington, 1891), 57.

The Bannocks were on the Clark's Fork when Miles found them on September 3, and on the following morning he attacked them, killing eleven Indians and capturing 31; 200 horses were also captured. The Army casualties were light, but included Captain Andrew S. Bennett, who led the attack. Bennett Creek, a northern tributary of the Clark's Fork, is named for the captain.[8]

Although Lt. Maynadier had not been able to bring all of his vehicles through the Basin, his efforts suggested that a wagon road was possible. Gold discoveries northwest of the Yellowstone region in the early 1860's lent urgency to the search for a direct road through the Basin, which, if feasible, would shorten the route to the mines. There was a brief interval when it seemed that the Big Horn Basin might be a more direct and safer route to the new mining regions. The old mountain man, James Bridger, had mentioned the possibility of such a route west of the Big Horn Mountains, and in the summer of 1862, a party led by Edward Shelley, nephew of the famous poet, pioneered the route by taking three light wagons through the Basin.[9]

Shelley, who was born in 1827, and was still unmarried, would later succeed his cousin as baronet. He had been a captain in the 16th Lancers, and had enjoyed a colorful time during the Crimean War, when he was assigned to recruit and train irregular cavalry troops from the Ottoman Empire to be used as a counter to the Russian Cossacks. Although these so-called bashi bazouks never saw service against the Russians, their undisciplined style frequently got them in trouble with the regular troops of the allies.[10]

---

[8]Brian C. Pohanka, ed., *Nelson A. Miles: A Documenting Biography of His Military Career, 1861-1903* (Glendale, California, 1985), 116. Miles was promoted to brigadier general on December 15, 1880; he had been brevetted a major general in 1865 and again in 1867.

[9]Gold was discovered in the Deer Lodge Valley in 1860, at Bannack in 1862 and at Virginia City in 1863.

[10]Shelley, who was the eldest son of John Shelley, the poet's younger brother, was born on December 10 1827. In 1866, Edward Shelley married Mary Smythe, of County Cork, and he succeeded as the fourth baronet when his cousin, Sir Percy Florence Shelley, the poet's only son, died without issue on December 5, 1889. Edward Shelley also died without issue, September 17, 1890. The baronetcy had been created in favor of Sir Bysche Shelley on March 3, 1806. Sir Bernard Burke, *Peerage and Baronetcy* (London, 1930), 2021. The Shelley family adopted the additional name and arms of Rolls by royal license, May 19, 1917, after which time they were styled Shelley-Rolls. We know of the Shelley visit to the Basin from the report of the diary he kept, covering the period August 1861 to January 28, 1865. Herbert Oliver Brayer reported on the diary at a meeting of the Westerners, Chicago Corral, on December 17, 1956. *The Westerners Brand Book*, XIII, No. 11 (Chicago, January 1957), 81. Shelley became embroiled in the ensuing investigations of the British officers who commanded the Turkish irregulars.

Ned, as the Americans called him, had gone hunting in South America, Africa and on the frontiers of India and Afghanistan, and he had just spent four years in a leisurely journey around the world, sampling the excitement of the revolution in Mexico and the langorous beauties of the Hawaiian Islands, before stopping off to watch the assault on the Chinese in the Third Opium War. He was perhaps a classic example of the remittance man, for during those four years, he paid his expenses from remittances drawn on various branches of British banks. Shelley has been described as restless, vain, lustful and pugnacious, and perhaps each of those adjectives could be fairly applied to him at one time or other, but he formed close attachments to his many friends, who willingly spent much time with him when he met them in nearly every country he visited.

Shelley spent nearly a year in the American West, while the Civil War was in full scream, a time when British subjects were not particularly welcome in the north. Late in 1861, relations between Great Britain and the United States were extremely strained, as the result of the *Trent* affair, when an American naval vessel stopped the *Trent* and took off her two Confederate Commissioners, James Murray Mason and John Slidell. In the uproar that followed, feelings ran high on both sides of the ocean, and there was a good deal of criticism of Great Britain and British subjects in the United States.[11]

While J. Edward Wilkins, the British consul, was personally on good terms with American authorities, it was not a good season for British aristocrats in the north to maintain a high profile, and it is perhaps for this reason that we find no mention of Shelley in the St. Louis papers of the day. He enlisted Wilkins' help to obtain a pass from the American authorities to permit him to travel in the north (which presumably included the consul's standard admonition to observe "strict" neutrality), and when Shelley eventually left St. Louis for the west, Wilkins and his wife went with him.[12]

---

[11]Missouri Governor Hamilton R. Gamble mobilized the militia, requiring service from every able-bodied man on July 22, 1862, but it was possible for foreign subjects to obtain exemption from their consulates; the St. Louis papers reported that 448 British subjects obtained exemption certificates from the British consulate in that city in July, 1862, which further heightened Americans' ill feelings toward the British. *Daily Missouri Democrat*, May 16, July 23, 25, 1862.

[12]The usual pass issued at St. Louis permitted British subjects to travel throughout the Department of the Missouri, which at that time included the states of Missouri, Iowa, Minnesota, Wisconsin, Illinois, Arkansas and that portion of Kentucky west of the Cumberland River. Obviously, the journey Shelley was contemplating required a more liberal pass. Raphael P. Thian, Notes *Illustrating the Military Geography of the United States 1813-1880* (Austin, Texas, 1979), 74.

The Shelley party left St. Louis on May 16, 1862 by river steamer, and departed from Kansas City for the west on May 26. After a leisurely crossing of the plains, during which Shelley unsuccessfully tried to kill a buffalo with his revolver, they arrived in Denver on July 7, where they spent only two days before heading north to Fort Laramie.[13]

Shelley thrived on danger, and conditions on the Oregon Trail were certainly up to his standards. In April the Postmaster General suspended mail service on the trail, as the Indians were attacking the stage stations to stop the "paper wagons," as the natives called the mail coaches. In May a stage sent east from Salt Lake City to Deer Creek found that all livestock and other property had been destroyed or abandoned following an attack at the end of the previous month. Additional troops were now assigned to guard the mail, but in the meantime a warehouse in Julesburg was bulging with undelivered mail sacks and many other sacks were burned and cut open along the Sweetwater. In July, Ben Holladay moved the mail to the south to the so-called Cherokee Trail and abandoned 26 stations on the northern route.[14]

When Shelley and his party arrived at Fort Laramie, Wilkins and his wife left the party to return to the East, and Shelley continued westward on the Oregon Trail; on August 11 his group headed up the Platte with three light wagons and four or five teamsters and guides. When the party reached the fifth crossing of the Sweetwater, they left the Overland trail and headed north to the Popo Agie, which they followed down to the Wind River on September 3; they then marched north across the Owl Creek mountains into the Big Horn Basin.[15]

We do not know where Shelley learned of the route through the Big Horn Basin, but some inferences are possible. Since the Indians were openly raiding on the Oregon Trail, Shelley would also have been warned not to strike out east of the Big Horn Mountains, because of the same risk in that area. It has been argued that Bridger himself was the source of the information about the Basin route, and Bridger was in the area at the

---

[13]*The Rocky Mountain News*, July 8, 1862. We have little information about the members of the Shelley party, except for William Orcutt, who apparently joined the group in Denver.

[14]Ben Holladay visited Washington and secured the President's promise to protect the mail and to reimburse his costs; he was told to get the mail through. J. V. Frederick, *Ben Holladay: The Stagecoach King* (Glendale, California, 1940), 167-78.

[15]Wilkins was back in St. Louis by the first week in September. *Daily Missouri Democrat*, September 6, 1862. Shelley was at the fifth crossing of the Sweetwater on August 28 and on the Wind River on September 3.

time, scouting for Colonel William Oliver Collins; unfortunately, we do not know when or if they met.[16]

We know of Collins' whereabouts from the letters sent by his son, Lieutenant Caspar Collins, to his mother. During the time Shelley was at Fort Laramie, Collins and Bridger were on the Wind River, some miles to the west. By the time Shelley arrived at the Sweetwater crossing, he was very close to the Collins party, and may have met them there, although there is no written record of such a meeting.[17]

On September 21, the Shelley party crossed the Greybull River on the way north, and on the first of October, they paused and spent some time seeking a passable route out of the Basin. Herbert Brayer states that they crossed over to a south fork of the Yellowstone. Shelley eventually reached Fort Benton in the late fall, and he was back in St. Louis the following spring, on his way to Canada.[18]

While Shelley was no longer in the West, the news of his journey continued to reverberate there, and early in 1863, news of this new way to cross the dangerous northern range was reported in the Denver papers. *The Rocky Mountain News* of March 26, 1863 mentioned the route and also carried a letter by J. B. ("Buzz") Caven of Bannack, Idaho Territory, quoting Shelley to the effect the "he never saw a better mountain road" than the route through the Basin. The quote, if accurate, does not make a trivial comparison, for Shelley had earlier crossed the Andes from Argentina to Chile.[19]

Soon the new road would be tried again, although not with wagons. Prospectors were being drawn to the area that would soon be set apart as Montana Territory, and John Merin Bozeman, whose lack of success in prospecting had turned him to other ways to earn a living, was eager to

---

[16] According to the Fort Laramie post return for May, 1862, the first battalion of the Sixth Ohio Cavalry, under Lt. Col. Collins arrived at the fort on May 30, 1862. The *Daily Missouri Democrat* reported on July 30 that the overland mail had been resumed over the new route, and quoted Benjamin Holladay, who had the contract, to the effect that the new route was actually shorter by some 60 miles than the old one.

[17] The Postmaster General's order was dated July 11, 1862. Collins was at South Pass on June 30, and by August 13 he was on the upper crossing of the Wind River; in the intervening period, he had been west to the Green River. On August 31, they were camped at Independence Rock, and by September 20 they were back at Fort Laramie. Agnes Wright Spring, *Caspar Collins: The Life and Exploits of an Indian Fighter of the Sixties* (New York, 1927), 42, 119-32. Colonel Collins was the man for whom Fort Collins, Colorado was named, and his son is remembered in the name of Casper, Wyoming.

[18] Shelley reached Fort Benton on November 21, and he was in St. Louis by April 30, 1863.

[19] Bannack, later the first capital of Montana Territory, was in Idaho Territory at this time, as was most of Wyoming. The Caven letter was dated February 6, 1863.

guide them over a new route, which he reckoned would shorten the journey by 350 miles. Bozeman's objective was to open a road east of the Big Horn Mountains, but there were complications that made this infeasible on that first trip. Since Bozeman had not been in the West very long, his knowledge of western geography could not have been very extensive, so it is likely that John M. Jacobs contributed the greater knowledge of the area, and the story of the Shelley journey must also have reached their ears.[20]

In the spring of 1863, Bozeman and Jacobs came down to their appointed rendezvous on the overland emigration route just above Fort Laramie on the Platte River, to meet 89 men with 46 wagons. Apparently, Bozeman and Jacobs hired Rafael Gallegos, who was familiar with the area, to guide the train up the east flank of the Big Horns, as far as the Big Horn River; the two men from Bannack were then to take over for the remainder of the journey. On July 6, the train broke camp and began the journey up the eastern flank of the mountains. Two weeks later, while the train was camped on Lodge Pole Creek, they were visited by a band of about 150 Cheyennes and a few Sioux, who told them they could go no further.

Rafael and two other men carried a message back to Fort Laramie requesting a military escort, and while they waited for the reply, the train marked time, moving slowly back down the trail. Bozeman also quieted some unrest in the party over the relationship between a young woman who had left her husband on the North Platte and a young man named Beaumont by marrying the two; this apparently satisfied those who were discontented, although Bozeman was not authorized to perform a marriage ceremony, and in any case the jointure was bigamous. At the end of July the answer came back from the military at Fort Laramie that no escort could be spared, and the majority of the party then headed back down to the emigrant road, to make the long journey to the Montana mines via that route.[21]

Bozeman and eight other men then left the main party and headed over

---

[20] James McClellan Hamilton, *From Wilderness to Statehood: A History of Montana 1805-1900* (Portland, 1957), 167. Montana Territory was carved out of Idaho Territory, May 26, 1864, 13 *Statutes at Large* 86. Bozeman was born in Georgia in 1835. We do not know when John Jacobs was born, but a diarist in 1863 said Jacobs had spent 21 years in the west. In 1856, Jacobs settled with his Indian wife on the Beaverhead River and he died near Clancy, Montana in the winter of 1856-66. Susan Badger Doyle, "Journeys to the Land of Gold: Emigrants on the Bozeman Trail, 1863-1866," Montana, XLI, No. 4 (Autumn, 1991), 55ff.

[21] "Diary of Colonel Samuel Word," Contributions of the Historical Society of Montana (Helena, 1917), 66.

the Big Horn Mountains from the headwaters of the Powder River, entering the Basin on the east side from Ten Sleep Canyon. They had no wagons, and travelled only at night to avoid the Indians; the second night out, their pack horse fell into a deep ravine, and the supplies it was carrying were lost. They had reached the headwaters of the Clarks Fork before Bozeman was able to end a four day fast by killing an eagle. In this passage, Bozeman failed to travel the road east of the Big Horns that would later bear his name, but by going through the Basin he anticipated the competing route that would later be named for Bridger.[22]

In 1864, Bridger led a party over the trail that would be named for him. The train consisted of "nearly three hundred" persons, with 62 wagons, who started from Denver for the gold fields. Included in the train was The Rev. Learned Blackman Stateler, a Methodist minister, who left a record of the journey. The train was organized along military lines, and at the end of each day the wagons were circled to form a corral. The livestock were kept in this corral at night, and were grazed under strong guard outside the circle in the evening and again at daybreak. The train proceeded from Denver north to Fort Laramie, and from there westward over the Oregon trail to Red Buttes on the North Platte, where they turned north to follow Bridger's cutoff.[23]

Game, although not "abundant," was plentiful enough to supply them with meat, and the Statelers had brought a few cows from Kansas, which were sometimes yoked to pull the wagons, and they supplied the milk; the cream was "automatically" churned into butter by the jolting motion of the wagon. When one of the horses became disabled, Stateler hooked the wagon Mrs. Stateler was riding in behind the other, and in a "very steep place" the oxen pulling the lead wagon turned too sharply, pitching the second wagon down a precipice. The falling wagon turned over twice, throwing a stove and heavy boxes around the frightened woman, but it came to rest before it went over an even more "frightful" precipice. The action of the second wagon had also broken the axle of the lead wagon and thrown the horses down. To her husband's immense relief, the remark-

---

[22]George W. Irvin II and Mike J. Knock were with Bozeman. Burton S. Hill, "Bozeman and the Bozeman Trail," *Annals of Wyoming*, XXVI, No. 2 (October, 1964), 211. Bozeman's route through the Basin was, of course, different from Shelley's route the year before.

[23]The Rev. Learner Blackman Stateler was born July 7, 1811. When Stateler married Melinda Purdom in 1836, her father was opposed to her marriage to a preacher "with no home," and the concerns he had for his daughter's future were surely justified by this journey. The Rev. Edwin J. Stanley, *Life of Rev. L. B. Stateler, or Sixty-Five Years on the Frontier* (Dallas, 1907), 174ff.

able lady called out of the overturned wagon, "I am not hurt; save the team." Others in the train spliced the axle, and they were able to go on.[24]

To avoid Wind River Canyon, Bridger first went up Poison Spider Creek, northwest to the present location of Lysite on Badwater Creek, then north up Bridger Creek to cross over the Owl Creek Mountains to the head of Kirby Creek. He followed Kirby Creek to its mouth, where he crossed the Big Horn River. Before the train reached the Big Horn, there was a scare, when they found an Indian camp only a mile away from their position. The fear was that the Indians were Sioux, and the men took the best defensive positions they could find, while Bridger and a small unarmed group went off to the Indian camp. To their amazement, the Indians rushed up to Bridger, for they were Shoshonis, and Bridger was their friend.

The Big Horn River was swollen by spring runoff, and the wagons crossed on a ferryboat, built on the spot from trees they felled and cut up with axes and whipsaws; after crossing the river, the boat was then buried for the use of those following behind on the trail.

The next camp was on the west bank of the river, opposite the mouth of the No Wood River. The expedition then had to cross the dry hills in a single day's journey to the next water, in the Greybull River. Another dry march north brought them to the Stinking Water near the present site of Garland. The party then rested to wait the arrival of two additional trains following from the south. All three trains were together by June 18.

We have the diary kept by a member of the third train, Cornelius Hedges, then 34, who would later figure prominently in the history of Montana Territory. Born in Massachusetts in 1831, Hedges was a graduate of both Yale and Harvard, and before coming to the Rocky Mountain West, he lived for a time in Independence, Iowa, where he practiced law and edited the *Independence Civilian*. In the spring of 1864, Hedges and a number of others from Iowa headed west to prospect in Montana.[25]

---

[24]Stateler was married in Bowling Green, Kentucky, January 26, 1836. Stanley, *op. cit.*, 65.

[25]Hedges was born at Westfield, Massachusetts, October 28, 1831. At Yale, he demonstrated proficiency in Latin, Greek, "the theoretical parts of Arithmetic," and geography. In Montana, he first prospected in Alder Gulch, Virginia City, but then moved to Helena on January 16, 1865. He returned to Iowa and collected his wife, making the journey back to Helena by way of the first boat up the Missouri River in the 1867 season. He practiced law in Helena, and in 1872 was appointed as the first Superintendent of Public Instruction, serving six years in that office. In 1870, he was a member of the Washburn Expedition to the Yellowstone region, and he is credited with suggesting that the area be set aside as a park. Hedges died in Helena, April 29, 1907. Extensive material on Hedges is contained in the Montana State Historical Society files, Helena, Montana. Also, Ernest S. Osgood, "The Fiery Ordeal of Cornelius Hedges," *Montana*, XXV, No. 3 (Summer, 1975), 75.

When they got to the North Platte crossing at Fort Caspar, the Hedges party learned that the new Bridger Cutoff was the "rage" of the season. By the time their train reached its maximum size on June 5, there were more than 100 teams in it. On June 9, Hedges had his first glimpse of the snow-clad mountains marking the perimeter of the Big Horn Basin, and on the 11th they were camped beside the Big Horn, which Hedges was still calling the Wind River. The boat which Bridger had left for them was found, and in due course the entire train was ferried across, two wagons at a time.

After burying the boat again, the train followed the west bank of the river for two days, and then turned to make the dry run across the hills to the Greybull River. The teams began to give out on this stretch of the road, but on June 18 they were on the Stinking Water, and had joined the teams led by Bridger and John Jacobs. The three trains pushed on north, and were out of the Basin by June 23. Hedges had the sad experience of losing his wagon shortly after leaving the Basin; moreover, he was dismayed to arrive in Virginia City on July 10, only to meet some prospectors who had also been at the Platte crossing, and had arrived over the Bozeman Trail ten days earlier.[26]

Six more companies came up the Bridger Trail in 1864 (for a total of nine), in contrast with a total of only three on the rival Bozeman Trail for the same year. We have a diary kept by Major John Owen, who was with a group of about 20 wagons that Bridger led over the trail in September. Apparently, the old mountain man was not happy with his road, for he spent a number of days making revisions. Still, it was not an easy road, and Owen noted that he had seen the remains of "quite a number" of dead oxen.[27]

There was one other traveler on the Bridger Trail in 1864 who deserves mention, since he came back to settle in Wyoming. James Kerr Moore, who was to become the first post trader at Fort Washakie, used the trail when he first came west in July, although we cannot be certain which train he was with. Moore, who was born in Georgia, was then 21, and he had served the United States Supreme Court as a messenger for three years, coming away with a letter of recommendation that is rarely equalled: eight of the ten justices of the court personally certified to his faithfulness, dili-

---

[26]The portions of the Hedges diary dealing with the transit of the Basin are reproduced in Appendix A.

[27]The Owen trip commenced September 18, 1864. *The Journals and Letters of Major John Owen, Pioneer of the Northwest, 1850-1871* (New York, 1927), 311, et. seq.

gence, intelligence and good morals. In July 1864 Moore was in Omaha and paid $50 to join a wagon train for Virginia City, which crossed the Big Horn Basin on the Bridger Trail. He later returned to southwestern Wyoming before coming to Camp Augur in 1869 as the first sutler at that location.[28]

While Bridger's route was less troubled by Indian raids than Bozeman's route, it never caught on as a highway, because good water was scarce over much of the route, and the Big Horn Basin soon lapsed again into isolation; when Captain William Jones proposed having the Army build a shortcut to Montana which would pass through the northern Basin, General Philip Henry Sheridan called the idea "absurd." Nevertheless a portion of the old trail continued in use and eventually became a county road. In September, 1897, when Big Horn County was finally organized, the commissioners noted that the road between Basin City and Thermopolis was "practicably the old Bridger Trail."[29]

In 1865, General Patrick Connor led an expedition to build forts along the Bozeman Trail, and two years later a team sent to collect logs for construction ventured over to the west slope of the Big Horns, at the north end of the range, where they tried to float the logs they cut down the river through the Big Horn Canyon. Three men followed the logs in a boat, making what may have been the first such descent of the canyon. As an attempt to find a practical shipping route, the experiment proved a failure, and served only to underscore the storied inaccessibility of the Basin.[30]

If the Basin could not be a thoroughfare for travellers, there was still the chance it could be the home of a bonanza for some fortunate prospector, and soon these hardy souls arrived to test their luck.

---

[28]James Kerr Moore was born February 14, 1843, in Randolph County, Georgia. He served with the United States Supreme Court in 1857-60; the letter signed by the justices is dated April 16, 1864. Moore died in San Diego, January 30, 1920.

[29]*Annals of Wyoming*, XL, No. 1, and Big Horn County Commissioners journal, 29, September 7, 1897. General Sheridan's endorsement of Captain Jones' report was dated May 16, 1874, *op. cit.*

[30]Robert Beebe David, *Finn Burnett: Frontiersman* (Glendale, California, 1937), 200. Fincelius G. Burnett, who was one of the three men in the boat, was born April 8, 1844.

Judge William L. Kuykendall, an ex-Confederate who came West after the Civil War. He led the 1870 Big Horn Expedition, which came to the Basin to look for gold; Kuykendall rebuffed Army efforts to turn the expedition back.
Courtesy Wyoming State Museum.

CHAPTER IV

The Big Horn Expedition of 1870

It was inevitable that the gold fever that swept so much of the mountain West would also reach the Basin. Gold was not discovered in Wyoming until the 1860's, when the first strikes were made in the South Pass area, south of the Basin. In 1866 a large party of prospectors from Idaho and Montana led by Jefferson Standifer entered the Basin itself from the north, to prospect the western fringe along the front of the Absaroka Range; they found nothing of great interest.[1]

Then, in 1869, the year that Wyoming Territory was organized, an expedition was promoted to explore the Big Horn country, in search of the gold that was thought to be hidden in its rocks. This effort would not concern us here if it had succeeded in reaching the area originally planned, since the "Big Horn Country" of this expedition was clearly the region lying on the *eastern* slope of the Big Horn Mountains, in other words, in the Powder River Basin. Unfortunately, that area was reserved to the Sioux as a hunting ground, which was to cause a good deal of difficulty to the expedition, and ultimately divert it across the mountains to the Big Horn Basin itself.

Near the end of 1869, a meeting was held at the McDaniel's Theater in Cheyenne to organize an expedition to the Big Horn country. While members of the expedition would later be more than a bit ambiguous about what they considered the Big Horn country to include, William L. Kuykendall told the *Omaha Herald* that he "always" viewed the headwa-

---
[1] Robert A. Murray, "Miner's Delight, Investor's Despair. The Ups and Downs of a Sub-Marginal Mining Camp in Wyoming," *Annals of Wyoming* XLIV, No. 1 (Spring, 1972), 32-33.

ters of the Powder River as the objective for the expedition. Indeed, when he wrote his memoirs more than 40 years later, Kuykendall remembered that his objective was to use prospecting as a way to force the Sioux out of their hunting ground east of the Big Horns.[2]

The *Cheyenne Leader* reported that there were offers from Chicago and St. Louis to provision the party for four months, and the secretary of the territory assured the promotional meeting that the territorial government was trying to remove obstacles to the expedition. In the winter of 1869-70, preparations for the expedition went forward, and the governor of the territory and the chief justice were sent to Washington to assuage the concerns that were mounting in that quarter.[3]

The constitution of the association, which was published in the Cheyenne newspapers on Christmas Eve, set forth the purposes of the "Big Horn Mountains and Black Hills Exploring Expedition" as the exploring for gold, silver and other precious metals. While the total who might join the expedition was not limited, the stated minimum was 400 men in companies of 80 each, to provide sufficient protection against the Indian risks. Each member was to pay one dollar to join and fifty cents a month (but only until May 20, 1870), to cover the cost of advertising, stationery, hall rental and lights. Each member was to have a gun and at least one revolver, together with 500 rounds of ammunition for each gun and 250 rounds for each pistol; he was also to have four months' provisions. While it was not necessary for every member to bring a horse, the constitution required that there be at least 300 mounted men.[4]

The *Leader* continued to promote the expedition, saying that the cost of $150 to 200 per member was not more than any able-bodied man had in his pocket or could easily earn in a short time. While planning for the

---

[2] The first Meeting of the association was to have been at the Eagle Brewery Saloon on December 10, 1869, but it was postponed until the following night and moved to McDaniel's Theater. Kuykendall's letter was in the *Omaha Weekly Herald*, March 2, 1870. Also, Judge W. L. Kuykendall, *Frontier Days: A True Narrative of Striking Events on the Western Frontier* (n.p., 1917), 137.

[3] Governor John A. Campbell and Chief Justice John H. Howe left for Washington on December 21, 1869. The *Cheyenne Leader*, December 10, 11, 22, 1869. The governor's diary for this period casts little light on his thinking regarding the expedition. The entry for December 21 says simply, "Start with Judge Howe for the East, after arranging with Lee about appointments, &c." The governor's journey was not a hurried affair, and he stopped on the way to visit friends, including Mark Hanna in Cleveland, arriving in Washington in time for a reception with the President on January 13. He met the secretary of the interior and appeared before the Senate Committee on Indian Affairs. "Diary, John A. Campbell," *Annals of Wyoming* X, No. 2 (April, 1938), 70-73.

[4] *The Cheyenne Leader*, December 24, 1869.

expedition was going on, a disastrous fire swept through Cheyenne, which must surely have dampened the enthusiasm of some of the promoters.[5]

Recruiting efforts apparently were going slowly, even at the one dollar admission charge, and at a meeting in January, James McDaniel offered a $100 bill to pay the initiation fee for any men who joined at that meeting; ten new members immediately signed up, and Judge William L. Kuykendall reported that the association had 113 members—not 400, but still a respectable beginning.[6]

William Littlebury Kuykendall, who seems to have been the moving force behind the expedition, was a man who was accustomed to lead. Descended from a family of South Carolinians, he was born in Clay County, Missouri, in 1835 and he was appointed deputy clerk for the circuit court of Platte County on his seventeenth birthday. When it became obvious that Kansas would be erected into a territory, the Kuykendall family settled near Topeka, and young William raised a company of militia early in 1855, although that group did not see action in the troubles that followed. When the Civil War came, Kuykendall joined a Confederate company in Missouri as second lieutenant, and he saw action at the battle of Lexington, Missouri, in the fall of 1861; he was captured, paroled, and captured again and when the war was over he moved to Colorado, "nearly penniless and virtually in rags."[7]

In 1866, Kuykendall was in the freighting business in Denver, and the next year he moved up to Cheyenne, where he was named probate judge of Laramie County after that county was organized by Dakota Territory. He would later serve in the Wyoming territorial legislature, and in 1876 he organized another prospecting expedition to the Black Hills.[8]

At the end of January 1870, Kuykendall was elected captain of the first company, and by the middle of February, Nicholas J. O'Brien was elected captain of the second company. O'Brien, who was then 30, was deputy United States marshal in Cheyenne; born in Wexford, Ireland, he came to the United States in 1848, and when the Civil War broke out he served in the Union Army. He had built Fort Sedgwick on the South Platte, and his

---

[5]The fire struck Cheyenne just before noon on January 11, 1870. The proprietor of the Eagle Brewery, Charles Beno, was a key promoter of the association; his saloon was wiped out by the fire. *The Cheyenne Leader*, January 14, 17, 19, 1870.   [6]*The Cheyenne Leader*, January 22, 1870.

[7]Kuykendall married Eliza A. Montgomery in Leavenworth, Kansas, July 14, 1857; she died December 21, 1898. Kuykendall, *op. cit., passim*. Also George Benson Kuykendall, M.D., *History of the Kuykendall Family* (Portland, 1919), 201.

[8]William L. Kuykendall was born December 13, 1835; he died March 8, 1915.

knowledge of the Big Horn country stemmed from his service with General Patrick E. Connor's Powder River expedition in the summer of 1865. O'Brien said that miners accompanying the expedition found signs of mineralization along the eastern face of the Big Horns, on Crazy Woman Creek, Clear Creek and Piney Creek. Doubtless, this testimony gave a powerful impetus to the Big Horn expedition.[9]

No more companies were organized before the expedition was to get under way; the hopes for a minimum of 400 men had passed away. The *Chicago Tribune* reported that Col. Luke Murrin had been able to arrange transportation from Chicago to Cheyenne for $37 for association members—almost half the regular rates; the Chicago merchants were to contribute supplies and solicit other assistance for the expedition. There were other articles in the Philadelphia papers as well.[10]

Nevertheless, trouble was brewing in Washington. Even before the beginning of the year, complaints had been lodged with the President himself, and the Indian agent at the Whetstone Agency reported that the Sioux under his responsibility were unsettled by word of the pending expedition. On March 8 President Grant sent a routine letter to the Senate, calling attention to the need to appropriate funds for treaty obligations, and at the end of this letter, he referred to the Big Horn Expedition, saying, "Pains will be taken, and force used if necessary, to prevent the departure of the expedition. . ." By the middle of March, the *Omaha Herald* was repeating rumors that the expedition had been "squelched."[11]

The *Leader* reported that General Christopher Colon Augur had journeyed to Cheyenne to talk to the leaders of the expedition. General Augur, an imposing man with long white flowing sideburns, believed it would be cheaper to feed the Indians than to fight them, and he later reported that the leaders of the Big Horn Expedition had executed an "instrument," in which they agreed not to enter the reserved lands (i.e., the Sioux hunting ground). This was in fact so. On the day after Governor Campbell

---

[9] *The Cheyenne Leader*, January 31, 1870.

[10] *The Cheyenne Leader*, January 31, February 14, 1870.

[11] John B. Wolff of Washington, D. C. wrote to the President to complain about the expedition, on December 22, 1869, and again on April 30, 1870. Also, Captain DeWitt C. Poole, agent for the Whetstone Agency to Ely Samuel Parker, Commissioner of Indian Affairs, on February 23, 1870. Poole wrote to John A. Burbank, Superintendent of Indian Affairs, Yankton, on March 4, 1870. The Whetstone Agency was on the Missouri River at the mouth of Whetstone Creek, 18 miles from Fort Randall, Dakota Territory. Grant's March 8 letter included the comment, "I earnestly desire that if an Indian war becomes inevitable, the government of the United States, at least, should not be responsible for it." *Omaha Weekly Herald*, March 30, 1870.

THE BIG HORN EXPEDITION OF 1870

returned from Washington, General Augur had written a letter to him, stating categorically that the expedition could not go, and on the same day, the executive committee of the association sent the governor a letter in which they promised they would not "in any instance encroach upon Indian reservations or privileged hunting grounds;" the group met with him the next day.[12]

This sounded explicit enough, and the letter was forwarded to the President two days later. The governor also responded to the general by enclosing the association letter and blandly pointing out that the group had altered its original intention so as to meet the general's objection. The general's letter to the governor was also released to the press, and the *Leader* sadly reprinted it on March 23.[13]

However, the governor's true state of mind was revealed in another letter, also written March 23, to the Secretary of the Interior. After pointing out that Augur's letter had been published in the newspapers, he noted that the leaders of the expedition had given unequivocal assurances that they would avoid the Indian lands. Then he continued, "I do not believe that this committee of self constituted leaders can control their followers ....," and he therefore concluded that the expedition would probably trespass on Indian lands. But, he said, the Sioux were likely to go on the warpath the following summer, whether the Big Horn Expedition came north or not; he slyly suggested perhaps the presence of "say one thousand" armed civilians might even be of assistance to the beleaguered military forces in that eventuality.[14]

At a meeting on March 25, the three judges of the territorial supreme court addressed the expedition, each giving his solemn opinion that the purposes of the expedition were legal, but each also admonishing the gathering that nothing should be done against the will of the government. All of these public admonitions, together with the governor's letter to the Sec-

---

[12] General Augur wrote to John Taffe on January 23, 1871, "Bread and meat are the only things these Indians want—they say they have had enough talk." The governor returned to Cheyenne on March 20, 1870. Diary, *op. cit.*, 75. The letter from the executive committee of the association was dated March 21, 1870 and signed by Thomas D. Murrin, Charles Beno, L. F. Hathaway and H. Garbanati.

[13] The general also received a letter from the executive committee of the association, dated March 12, 1870 (the same day as the letter to the governor). In this letter, the leaders promised to confine their prospecting to the region which "lies without the Indian lands so far as they will be able to know the boundaries thereof." *Wyoming Tribune*, March 12, 1870.

[14] The Secretary of the Interior, J. D. Cox, sent Campbell's March 23 letter to the Secretary of War on March 31, 1870; it is not known whether it was distributed further.

retary of the Interior, may well have been intended to prepare official Washington for the very real probability that the expedition would cross Indian lands. Chief Justice Howe again went to Washington, and the secretary of the territory, General Edward M. Lee was also there; on April 7, he appeared before the House Committee on Territories, and he later reported that this committee was "in favor" of the expedition.[15]

Justice Howe wrote to General Sherman on April 14 that the expedition was to be permitted to leave, but on conditions that Sherman was to draft. The Howe letter was unnecessary, for Secretary Belknap had already written to the general, telling him that the expedition should not be permitted to trespass on Indian lands, and authorizing him to exercise his "own judgment" about accepting the leaders' pledge on the matter. On April 15, Sherman wrote to Sheridan that the leaders of the expedition must agree in writing not to trespass on the Shoshoni reservation, not to go north of the northern boundary of Wyoming, not to go east of the Big Horn Mountains, and not to expect any military protection.[16]

Actually, the military officers were personally sympathetic to the objectives of the expedition; indeed, General Augur called the treaty limitations "obnoxious" in his letter of March 21. Later, when the expedition reached Fort Steele, Colonel James S. Brisben sent word offering them any service, and when the party passed Camp Brown, the commander at Fort Fetterman wrote to Thomas D. Murrin to tell him that there were no Indians in the vicinity of the Big Horners.[17]

Early in April, the leadership of the expedition set the departure date for May 2, saying that 200 men were ready to go. The *Leader's* revised estimate of cost was now $75-$100 per man. Hopes in Cheyenne soared with a cryptic message from Chief Justice Howe (then in Washington again), "A great struggle, but finally successful. Expedition permitted. Instructions

---

[15] *The Cheyenne Daily Leader*, March 9, 14, 21, 25, 1870. Lee's visit to Washington is reported in the *Wyoming Tribune*, April 9, 1870. Judge Howe left on March 27, according to Campbell's diary; he had left the territory without official permission (which would later cause trouble), and the governor appointed Judge William T. Jones to serve in his absence. Diary, *op. cit.*, 74.

[16] William W. Belknap to General William T. Sherman, March 30, 1870.

[17] The general's report is contained in *House Executive Documents, 41st Congress, Third Session, Serial 1446*; it is dated October 25, 1870. The letter from the commander of Fort Fetterman is in the *Cheyenne Daily Leader*, August 2, 1870 and the report from Fort Steele is in the *Wyoming Tribune*, June 11, 1870. Kuykendall's memoirs contrast sharply with the view of the Fetterman commander; Kuykendall said that by the time the expedition reached the Sweetwater, there were Indians moving parallel to them "on both flanks," and he quoted the officers at Camp Brown as estimating they were "surrounded" by 1,000 Indians. Kuykendall, *op. cit.*, 138, 139.

THE BIG HORN EXPEDITION OF 1870

sent to Augur." The newspaper carried the call for bids for supplies to provision 400 men.[18]

When Howe returned, he reported that there had been three cabinet meetings on the subject, and that he had been threatened with dismissal for having left the territory without prior permission. These difficulties had apparently arisen because of a complaint by Church Howe, the United States Marshall in Cheyenne, and when word of it reached Cheyenne, a campaign was set afoot to have the marshal removed.[19]

By the middle of April, the *Tribune* could report that there were Big Horners in every hotel in the city. The departure date for the expedition was now moved to May 10, and for the first time the registration fee was set at $34 per man, to be used to defray the cost of provisions. For a time, recruitment picked up; on one day, forty arrived to join, and 14 men at the railroad roundhouse "struck" and joined the expedition. By the middle of May, ammunition had arrived for the 6-pounder Major John Talbot, a Cheyenne saloon keeper, had given to the expedition. Even so, when the governor reported to the Commissioner of Indian Affairs that the expedition was about to leave, he estimated that there were fewer than 150 men in it.[20]

By May 19, there were "about" 150 men and ten teams in camp near Cheyenne, but the pressure from Washington had caused the group to dissolve its original association and to reassemble into a mining expedition bound for the Sweetwater country. At least, that was the official word given out. For what may have been cosmetic effect, Thomas Murrin resigned as commander, and was replaced by Kuykendall; the *Tribune* said that Murrin would remain in the group to take charge of the artillery piece. All seemed in readiness.[21]

Trouble continued in Washington, and on May 12, the Secretary of the Senate asked the President to send to the Senate the information in his files on the expedition. At a cabinet meeting on May 13, the Secretary of

---

[18]*Cheyenne Daily Leader*, April 11, 15, 1870.

[19]The Tribune refers to the "affidavit man" as the source of difficulties in Washington, and then on May 7 makes clear that it was Church Howe who was responsible. Howe was a Republican, but opposed to the Campbell faction, and was at the time seeking the nomination for delegate to Congress, under the sponsorship of the Union Pacific Railroad. *Wyoming Tribune*, May 7, 1870.

[20]*Cheyenne Daily Leader*, April 15, 20, May 2, 12, 1870. The governor's letter to the commissioner of Indian affairs was dated May 11, 1870. Also *Wyoming Tribune*, April 16, May 14, 1870 and Kuykendall, *op. cit.*, 138. We do not know how Major Talbot came into possession of the cannon, which is assumed to have seen service in the Mexican War. *Bozeman Daily Chronicle*, June 27, 1973.

[21]The dissolution of the original association was reported in the *Wyoming Tribune*, May 21, 1870.

War was directed to have General Augur halt the expedition until the "contemplated" negotiations with Red Cloud were concluded. These orders went out the same day.[22]

The government was indeed contemplating negotiations with Red Cloud. The chief, whom Washington regarded as the leader of the "hostiles" among the Sioux tribes, had requested that he be permitted to visit the leaders in Washington; it is not clear whose idea this was, because Red Cloud later blurted out that he had been "sent" for. The request was seized upon by the so-called "peace party" in the east, as an opportunity to dampen the growing sense of hostility on the plains, and it was decided that the Sioux delegation could visit the nation's capitol.[23]

At a meeting on May 3, the cabinet made the decision to invite Red Cloud, and the word traveled back to the Indians in record time. It so happened that the son of Man-Afraid-of-His-Horse was at Fort Fetterman when word of the decision arrived; he left at once to inform his father (who was to be in the delegation) and Red Cloud. The response quickly came back to Fetterman that the chiefs would be at the fort on May 14, ready to go to Washington. It was this unexpectedly early response that apparently triggered the president's admonition that the Big Horn Expedition be held up.[24]

General John Haskell King at Fort D. A. Russell had the expedition virtually on his doorstep, and the men were chafing to be off; his response to his superiors was a work of art. He responded that the expedition had been abandoned; "in fact, it never could have started with any chances of success, being only 200 strong." Technically, he was correct, for the original Big Horn expedition had disbanded, but the general neglected to say that the most of the members had reformed themselves into a group whose stated objective was to mine the Sweetwater region.[25]

---

[22]George C. Graham to the President, May 12, 1870. Also, Secretary Belknap to General Townsend, May 13, 1870 and General Sherman to General Augur, May 13, 1870.

[23]At his meeting with the Secretary of the Interior, Red Cloud said, "From the word sent me I have come all the way to this house." James C. Olson, *Red Cloud, and the Sioux Problem* (Lincoln, Nebraska, 1965), 105. The request was relayed from Fort Fetterman to the Adjutant General on April 28, 1870, asking that Red Cloud, Man–Afraid-of-His-Horse and fifty warriors be permitted to visit Washington, and that General Smith be detailed as an escort. The delegation was reduced when the invitation was issued.

[24]Red Cloud left Fort Fetterman for Fort Laramie on May 18; there he met Col. John E. Smith, who was sent out from Washington to be the government escort. Because of concern over the treatment the Sioux might receive in Cheyenne, the party departed for Washington from Pine Bluffs, not Cheyenne. Man Afraid-of-His-Horse was unable to make the journey because of sickness. Olson, *op. cit.*, 94-97.

[25]General King's response was dated May 15, 1870. Olson, *op. cit.*, 95n.

THE BIG HORN EXPEDITION OF 1870   57

General Augur outlined the situation in his telegram to General Sherman on May 19. He started off by telling Sherman that Red Cloud and his party had arrived at Fetterman the day before. Then, he opened the subject of the expedition. "The Big Horn Expedition is abandoned," he said, adding, "About a hundred men who have incurred considerable expense in outfits wish to go to Sweetwater mines. Are there any objections?" Sherman replied the same day. "Good as to Red Cloud," he said. As to the Big Horn Expedition, Sherman did not object if they wanted to go to the Sweetwater mines, "as individuals, or in such manner as will not complicate Indian affairs, of which you are to be the judge." So the expedition could go.

The expedition got underway on May 20, 1870, but before leaving Fort D. A. Russell, the leaders executed an undertaking not to go in the neighborhood of the Big Horn Mountains, nor to trespass on the reservations; they referred to themselves as the "Big Horn Expedition," notwithstanding the assurances that were being reported about the abandonment of that expedition.[26]

By the time they reached Laramie there were 127 men in camp, but the party was overloaded, and some of the freight was going by rail to Rawlins Springs. The route had been altered to head northwest to Fort Steele, from whence it would strike north to the Sweetwater, so as to give the Sioux hunting ground a wide berth. While the *Leader* was continuing to sound somewhat optimistic, the *Laramie Daily Sentinel* emphasized that these changes had effectively disbanded the original Big Horn expedition and replaced it with a Sweetwater country project; according to the *Sentinel*, the new officers were elected because of dissension in the group.[27]

They were at Rawlins Springs on June 9, preparing to leave the following day. It was a year when the federal census was to be taken, and the census taker found most of the expedition still in camp at Rawlins Springs, so that we can identify more than a hundred of the participants. Although the organization had a somewhat military flavor, there was a decidedly lighter character there as well, for Charles Beno took along his eleven-year-old son Adolph, and Joseph Dyer's dog Ring would make the trip as well. There were three or four other teenagers, but the oldest man was 58, and the average age was nearly 30.

---

[26]The undertaking at Fort Russell was signed by William S. Kuykendall as commanding officer, and J. S. Farrar and William Wise, as commanders of the two companies.

[27]*Cheyenne Daily Leader*, May 19, 21, 27, 1870 and *Laramie Daily Sentinel*, May 19, 1870.

While the expedition was ponderously getting under way, and preparations were being made to send Red Cloud to Washington, still another group was being watched nervously by official Wyoming. On May 16, the Indian agent at Fort Bridger notified Governor Campbell that he was expecting Chief Washakie and his tribe, but thus far there was no word of them. Clearly, if the expedition did trespass on the Shoshoni reservation, it was desirable that the tribe not be there, and while we do not know whether the governor was conniving with the leaders of the expedition to have them cross the reservation, in his role as ex officio superintendent of Indian affairs in the territory, he certainly knew before the expedition departed that the Shoshonis were likely to be away from the reservation. Finally, on June 14, word came from Fort Bridger that the long-awaited Washakie and most of his tribe were camped near the fort. It had been a near thing.[28]

On June 22, the expedition left Atlantic City, after having rested there for two days, and paid lip service to the matter of visiting the Sweetwater mines; the following day it passed Camp Stambaugh, named for Lt. Charles B. Stambaugh, who had lost his life in an engagement near Miner's Delight only the month before. The expedition reached the Little Popo Agie River, thus breaking for the first time their solemn undertaking to avoid the Indian lands: the south boundary of the Shoshoni reservation was the divide between the Sweetwater River and the Popo Agie rivers. By the time they reached Camp Brown on June 24, they were well within the reservation.[29]

We have what appears to be an exact count of their numbers: there were 116 men. Of course, no difficulty arose from the Shoshonis, who were not around, and on June 26 the party headed north across the reservation. The Big Wind River was high, and the expedition had to build rafts to cross; Kuykendall later contended that they should be credited with pioneering this crossing of the river, which was later named Merritt's Cross-

---

[28]The governor advised the Commissioner of Indian Affairs that the Shoshonis were at Fort Bridger in a telegram on July 12, 1870.

[29]Charles J. Kappler, *Indian Treaties, 1778-1883* (New York, 1972), 1020. Lt. James Nicholas Wheelan, commanding Camp Stambaugh, reported that the expedition passed Camp Stambaugh on June 23 and Camp Brown on June 27. Lt. J. N. Wheelan to J. McB. Stembel, post adjutant at Fort Bridger, July 7, 1870. Camp Stambaugh was named for Lt. Charles B. Stambaugh, who was killed by the Indians near Miner's Delight on May 4, 1870. P. H. Sheridan, *Record of Engagements with Hostile Indians Within the Military Division of the Missouri, from 1868 to 1882* (Washington, 1882), 27.

ing, for the 1877 expedition led by General Wesley Merritt to intercept the fleeing Nez Perce Indians.

When the expedition headed north on June 26, an unidentified writer in South Pass passed that information on to the *Omaha Herald*, with the additional information that they were being guided by Dr. James G. Leonard, a miner from South Pass, who had promised to write from Camp Brown. Of course, Camp Brown was on the Shoshoni reservation, a clear indication that the expedition did not intend to observe the limits it had accepted in order to get permission to leave Cheyenne. This bit of news reached the ears of General Augur, and on the first of July he sent orders that the expedition was not to be permitted to venture further on the Shoshoni reservation than Twin Springs Creek.[30]

Augur's wire was sent to Fort Bridger to be forwarded to the South Pass region, but the telegraph had been down for six weeks and the telegram went out by mail to Lieutenant James Nicholas Wheelan, who was then commanding Camp Stambaugh. Wheelan was no stranger to Wyoming, for he had been with the escort for General Dodge when the city of Cheyenne was laid out in 1867, as the very first municipality in the Wyoming country.[31]

Major Robert S. LaMotte at Fort Bridger advised General Augur in Omaha that he feared the order to Lt. Wheelan would be too late, and sure, enough, the lieutenant responded on July 5 that he had received the copy only that day, long after the expedition had passed out of his precincts, and it was therefore "too late to act."

In Omaha, the general was under too much pressure to be put off by this response, and he wired back that if the orders arrived too late, it must be communicated to the expedition "somehow," and that military force should be used if required to bring them back. This order was in due course communicated to the lieutenant at Camp Stambaugh, who could see that the situation was becoming delicate, indeed. Lieutenant Wheelan, then 31, had been breveted a colonel in the Civil War for gallant and meritorious service, but in the postwar Army promotions were not coming so

---

[30]Dr. Leonard had been in the South Pass mining region as early as 1863. C. G. Coutant, *History of Wyoming and (The Far West)*, II (New York, 1966), 641. He was about 54 at the time, and was born in New York, according to the 1870 census. The letter from South Pass was signed "Enos," and was published in the *Omaha Weekly Herald*, July 6, 1870.

[31]Wheelan is in the ceremonial photograph taken with General Dodge and General Rawlins. Maury Klein, *Union Pacific: The Birth of a Railroad 1862-1893* (New York, 1987), 87.

fast; he had won his silver bars in 1866, and he might never make captain if he didn't handle this situation properly. Accordingly, on the 13th, he led 65 men and three officers north from Camp Stambaugh to follow the expedition, leaving only about 20 men and an officer at the camp.[32]

---

[32] J. N. Wheelan to R. S. LaMotte, commander at Fort Bridger. Wheelan explained that he took such a large part of his command because of fear that there were a large number of Indians following the expedition. James N. Wheelan was born in Pennsylvania but appointed from New York; he was promoted to captain December 15, 1873, to major March 7, 1893 and lieutenant colonel on June 9, 1899. Wheelan was enumerated with Captain David S. Gordon at Smith's Gulch on June 16, but obviously he was already on his way over the mountains at that time; as with so many census entries, the lieutenant's information on the list must have been provided by someone else.

CHAPTER V

Goldseekers in the Basin

On the evening of the 18th, while the Big Horn Expedition was twelve miles from the Greybull River, the detachment of troops from Camp Stambaugh overtook them. The story of the way in which their objectives of the expedition had changed since leaving Cheyenne is given in a letter from Major Daniel Curran dated August 1. He noted that when the expedition had crossed the Owl Creek Mountains on its way north, Kuykendall abruptly altered the course "due west," saying that he was as near to the Big Horn Mountains as he intended to go. In an interesting commentary on the solemn assurances they had given to General King at Fort Russell, Curran said that Kuykendall's course change was "contrary to all expectations," as it had been "generally understood" before leaving Cheyenne that they would prospect the western slope of the Big Horns.[1]

Now that Wheelan had found the expedition on the Greybull River, there then followed a ceremonial exchange of letters; Wheelan wrote to Judge Kuykendall under dateline of July 19, 1870, from "Camp Near Grey Bull, Wyoming Territory," and solemnly advised him that General Augur had ordered that the expedition not go beyond Twin Springs Creek. He then asked that this order be communicated to the men of the expedition and a response obtained.[2]

Kuykendall's reply was dated the same day, and it was not conciliatory. "Your communication of this date just received, no answer," he began.

---

[1] *Wyoming Tribune*, September 10, 1870. Daniel Curran, then 37, was born in Ireland.

[2] The July post returns for Fort Bridger show Companies B and D, Second Cavalry under the command of First Lieutenant Wheelan, with 106 enlisted men and 5 officers on detached scouting and escort duty in the vicinity of South Pass City and Miner's Delight. A sixth officer attached to Company B was absent on assignment at West Point: Alfred Elliott Bates, who later commanded the detachment involved in the Bates Battle in the Big Horn Basin, July 4, 1874.

Then he continued, "Allow me to say that whatever the objective point of the Expedition, when organizing in Cheyenne may have been, it is now settled on the above named river . . . with the intention of prospecting said stream. . . ." An anonymous diarist in the expedition noted that there was talk of joining the Crows rather than going back.[3]

The Judge's response was not calculated to soothe official Washington, but Lt. Wheelan had to make do with what he had. Without further ado, he led his troops back to Camp Stambaugh, which he reached on the 25th, taking with him the copy of his letter to Kuykendall and the response from the judge. In his report to Major LaMotte at Fort Bridger, Wheelan said blandly, "The enclosed correspondence will show that the Party have abandoned the idea of going to the Big Horn Mountains," a conclusion one can only infer from Kuykendall's failure to specify any objective beyond that of prospecting the Greybull River. Of the general's order to bring the expedition back if they had strayed too far north, he said not a word.

The expedition sent out two parties on prospecting errands, and Major Curran said that this effort by a party of only 20 men was to "satisfy all parties," although it was not expected the prospectors would find anything of interest. We have some additional information about the expedition's life on the Greybull River from an anonymous diary written by one of the participants, who apparently hired on to accompany someone on the expedition.[4]

The diarist noted that the prospecting party led by Kuykendall and William Wise went up the south fork, of the Greybull River, while Benjamin Dexter and his party went up the main stream. Joseph Dyer and another group went out to search for Charles "Irish Charley" McHenry, who had not returned to camp, but after two days' search it was assumed he had been eaten by wolves. McHenry's body was later found six miles from camp.[5]

---

[3] In his memoirs, written some years later, Kuykendall argued that Wheelan's orders only required him to intercept and return the expedition if they were "in or moving in the direction" of the Big Horn Mountains, and that Kuykendall therefore refused to move because they were moving away from the mountains. Kuykendall, *op. cit.*, 140. Wheelan's orders and Kuykendall's written response both contradict this argument.

[4] "Diary of a Member of the Big Horn Expedition, 1870, From the Region of Cheyenne, Wyoming, to Bozeman, Montana," July 20, 22. The diary is in the collections of the Montana Historical Society, Helena, Montana. The diary reports two prospecting parties, while Curran reports only one, but the sense of the two accounts is the same.

[5] William Wise was 40 at the time of the expedition. McHenry's body was finally discovered on August 5. He was from Cheyenne, where he had worked in Tim Dyer's French Restaurant.

A third party under Charles R. McLeland left camp on July 23, but we do not know where they were prospecting. While the prospecting parties were gone, the remaining members amused themselves by dividing themselves into baseball teams—the Gray Bulls and the Stinking Waters—and played the first baseball game in the Basin. (The Gray Bulls were victorious, 21 to 16.) A minor piece of good news was the return of Joe Dyer's dog Ring, half starved but otherwise well.[6]

The Dexter party returned on July 26, without any success to report, and without waiting for the return of the prospecting party led by Kuykendall and Wise, Dexter and a party of 27 men left camp, abandoning their wagons and heading north to "Lord only knows," as the diarist said; Curran, who was with this breakaway party, said it was agreed that the entire expedition would follow later.[7]

Two days later, Kuykendall and his men came in, having crossed back over the Wind River Mountains to reach the north branch of the Big Wind River, but they reported that there were "no prospects." The following day, those remaining in camp prepared to leave, 56 with six wagons going north to Montana, and the other 32 returning to Cheyenne; the count for the northern group did not include Dexter's party of 27, who had left earlier. According to Curran, this was the first division of the expedition, and he asserted that the split was initiated by Judge Kuykendall and others in the prospecting party. By August 18, Judge Kuykendall was back in Atlantic City with 31 other men.[8]

There were now two groups going north, taking with them the little cannon. The larger of the groups encountered a huge herd of buffalo, killed two calves and had a feast, "sufficient for any Son of a prodigal." This was the only wealth the Basin displayed for the goldseekers, although Curran said they saw some "float gold" on the Stinking Water. Although it was August, overcoats were in demand. As so many travelers in this country would comment, they were surprised on finding the Stinking Water flowing in its canyon; they had in fact expected to make a dry camp for the night when they came upon the river.

On the north side of the Stinking Water, they paused for a bit of

---

[6]Charles R. McLeland, 23, was the brother of the first postmaster of Cheyenne; with him in the party was another Cheyenne postal worker, Charles M. C. Jones, 25, and John C. Markle, 22, who was a tobacconist in Cheyenne.

[7]Dexter may have been Benjamin Dexter of Rawlings Spring.

[8]Curran's report is dated September 15, from Bozeman City, Montana. *Wyoming Tribune*, October 1, 1870.

prospecting, and then moved on to a tributary of the Clark's Fork, which they reached on August 14, and where Daniel Curran—traveling in advance of Dexter's party—found them. The next day, the two northern groups, consisting of the artillery piece and five wagons, together with 83 men, crossed the Clark's Fork, where they had a feast of trout. For the next week they prospected the Clark's Fork and its tributaries, and although the diary mentions "colors," there was not enough encouragement for them to continue. The bad luck perhaps shortened temper, for the diarist noted two men had a fight.

Dexter and a party of prospectors left camp on August 23 to prospect Sage Creek and the Big Horn Mountains—obviously seeking a partial redress of the wrong they felt Kuykendall had visited on them, but they had only gone two miles from camp when they encountered five Indians. Since the natives also had forty horses and mules, they assumed there was a larger party in the vicinity; the prospectors retired in good order and returned to camp, where they posted guard against the Indians.

On their way to the Bozeman Trail in Montana Territory, the remnant of the Big Horn expedition violated its agreement to avoid the Indian lands for yet a second time, when they crossed the Crow reservation; this time they encountered a large band of Crows and Bannocks near the Yellowstone River, and fired the cannon in the air. There was no hostile reaction from the natives, and in this respect they were more fortunate than two Bozeman prospectors, who were killed on one of the southern tributaries of the Clark's Fork earlier in the year.[9]

Dissension, which had plagued the expedition from the outset, continued in the group bound for Montana. At the end of August, a group of 13 men led by one of the few Texans, Charles Yarnell, 22, decided to strike off alone for Bozeman, and the diarist noted sourly, "No tears shed." Then a more serious accident befell one of the men, who was shot through the

---

[9]*Cheyenne Daily Leader*, August 23, 1870 and Big Horn Expedition diary, August 7, 1870. The diarist described the buffalo herd as "an hundred forty & four thousand buffalo." Also, *Wyoming Tribune*, September 10, 1870. The Crow treaty of 1868 contained the same language as the Shoshoni treaty, promising the Indians that unless authorized to do so, no one would be permitted to "pass over, settle upon or reside" in the territory set aside for a reservation. The Crow reservation covered all the area north of the Big Horn Basin, from the Yellowstone River on the west to 107° west longitude on the east. Kappler, *op. cit.*, 1008. Marvin J. Crandall and T. Dougherty were killed in the spring of 1870 near the forks of what is now called Crandall's Creek, apparently by young Crows. John K. Rollinson, "Historical sketch of Upper Clark's Fork of the Yellowstone and its Tributaries Within the State of Wyoming," *Annals of Wyoming*, XII, No. 3, 223-24.

lung; the diarist did not say whether he survived. On September 16, the northern group reached Bozeman.[10]

With the Bozeman group was the man who had given his name to the Comstock lode in Nevada, Henry Thomas Paige Comstock. He was born in Canada, and by the time of the Big Horn Expedition he was 55 years old. He had left Nevada in 1862 and wandered among the Oregon and Idaho mines, searching for another great lode and he was at Hamilton City, in the South Pass mining region, when the expedition passed through on its way to the Big Horn Basin. After his return to Bozeman, Comstock shot himself.[11]

Word of the events in the Basin filtered back to Cheyenne, and some of this information arrived ahead of the official military reports sent via Fort Bridger. The Omaha papers learned that Wheelan had returned without detaining the expedition, and there was talk in the Cheyenne papers that he had struck a deal for the expedition to stay in the mountains. The *Omaha Tribune* published an extract from a letter it had received from a member of Wheelan's party. The correspondent said that the expedition intended to prospect the Grey Bull, and he had the impression they would then break up and go to Montana or back to the South Pass region.[12]

It was for General Augur to put the official interpretation on what had happened in the Basin. In his report to the Secretary of War in October, the general complained that the expedition had broken its pledge to him, and that when he learned that they had entered the reservation, he had sent a troop of cavalry to "enforce their return." However, the officer in charge found the expedition in "very disorganized condition," and "on the point of dissolution," so that it was unnecessary to use the force he had authorized. Finally, the general noted that relations with the Indians had been "in no way" affected by the travels of the Big Horn Expedition.[13]

---

[10]Charles Eggleston, 21, who was born in New York, was shot by a gun "in Bishop's hands." William J. Bishop, 22, also born in New York, was one of the participants in the earlier fight recorded by the diarist.

[11]Bancroft gives Comstock's date of birth as 1820, but in the 1870 census of Wyoming he declared that he was 55. Comstock committed suicide September 27, 1870. Hubert Howe Bancroft, *History of Nevada, Colorado and Wyoming 1540-1888* (San Francisco, 1890), 98n.

[12]*Omaha Weekly Tribune*, August 13, 1870. The editor did not quote the letter in full, as was customary, perhaps to avoid identifying the writer. There were those in Wheelan's party who would not benefit by being publicly identified with the letter, including Dr. James T. Augur, 22, nephew of the general.

[13]"Report of Brigadier General Augur, Headquarters Department of the Platte, October 25, 1870," *House Executive Documents, 41st Congress, 3rd Session, Serial 1446.*

Nor was Lieutenant Wheelan's career damaged in any way; when President Chester A. Arthur came to Yellowstone Park in the summer of 1883, Wheelan, now a captain, was one of the couriers detailed to pass messages back and forth to the President between Shoshone Lake and Fort Ellis, Montana Territory.[14]

The little cannon that had been dragged all the way from Cheyenne to Bozeman was so have a lively life ahead of it. It is said to have been fired three times at Fort Ellis, to celebrate the expedition's arrival there, and then in 1874 it was used in another expedition prospecting for gold along the Yellowstone, and was fired on that occasion. The next year, the cannon sank in the Yellowstone when a flatboat capsized, but divers found it and recovered it, although they may have been more interested in the barrel of whiskey that was also on the sunken boat. With a restored carriage, it is now in the Pioneer Museum in Bozeman, but only after service in parades and a final firing by vandals in 1957. And so the story ends.[15]

Although most of the participants in the Big Horn expedition left in the fall of 1870, never to return, at least one came back. John Dwight Woodruff, who was 22 at the time of the expedition, eventually started the Embar ranch on Owl Creek. Born in Windsor, New York in 1847, Woodruff had come to Illinois with his family when he was only two years old. He developed a persistent cough, and came west to seek a cure. Woodruff drove a team on the way to Colorado in 1865, when he was 18, and in the clear air of the West the cough soon disappeared. He came to Wyoming in 1866, where he trapped and hunted, and he then served as guide to generals Sheridan and Crook when they selected the site for Fort Custer. After the events of 1870, Woodruff came back to Bozeman the following year to make his first cattle purchase. He was also a government scout during the Bates Battle in the Basin on July 4, 1874.

The Big Horn Expedition did not find gold in paying quantities, but there were later flurries of interest in prospecting, each of them doomed to a brief existence. The Basin would soon pass into the hands of a different sojourner—the cattleman of the open range—and while he was perhaps no more colorful than the trappers, teamsters and prospectors before him, his aim and outlook was very different from theirs.

---

[14]Thomas C. Reese, "President Arthur in Yellowstone National Park," Montana, XIX, No. 3 (July, 1969), 23.

[15]Helen, E. Fechter, "The Big Horn Gun," In *Celebration of our Past*, (Bozeman, Montana, 1993), 13-20.

The little cannon taken by the Big Horn Expedition from Cheyenne through the Big Horn Basin and then to Bozeman, in Montana Territory. The cannon is now in a Bozeman museum. *Courtesy Gallatin County Historical Society, Bozeman, Montana.*

If the Big Horn Basin was not to have a Leadville or a Virginia City, settlement would have to await the time when cattlemen or settlers could reach it with relative ease. The Yellowstone cordillera and the Big Horn and Wind River mountains also made travel difficult on the west, east and south, and as has already been noted, the Indian treaties of 1868 still left the Basin effectively encircled by the Indian presence: the Crow reservation was to the north, the Sioux hunting region was to the east and the Shoshoni reservation was to the south. The lack of rail connections to the north made approach from that direction more difficult than was the case for lands in the southern part of the territory, near the Union Pacific.

Some of these barriers around the Basin were in time removed. In the winter of 1875-76, the government ordered the Sioux to return to their reservations in Dakota; the deadline imposed by the order did not allow sufficient time for the word to be communicated to the Indians out on the plains, but it is not likely that the outcome would have been altered if more time had been allowed. In June of 1876, Brevet Brigadier General George Armstrong Custer made a foolhardy sally at an overwhelming force of Sioux that cost the lives of the entire group under his command, and in the aftermath of that defeat, the Sioux lost the war and their segregated hunting ground. The appropriation bill passed in August required that the tribe cede the Powder River hunting ground and the Black Hills in Dakota Territory as a condition for receiving additional appropriations, and the next month the deed was done. There was no longer an Indian presence in Wyoming east of the Big Horn Mountains.[16]

The Crow reservation had been established in 1868, entirely in Montana territory, and covering all the area west of the 107th meridian, between the Yellowstone River and the Wyoming line. The treaty establishing this reservation was signed only by the Mountain Crows, and the claims of the River Crows were left unresolved. Gold discoveries in the upper Yellowstone basin led to pressure to reduce the reservation, and in 1873 these negotiations were authorized by Congress; the subsequent negotiations did not produce an agreement.[17]

Then, in 1880, the Crows agreed to cede an area west of the Boulder River, and a right of way across the reduced reservation for the Northern Pacific railroad. This agreement, signed June 12, 1880, was only ratified two years later; the reduction of the reservation made it necessary to move the Crow Agency, which had at first been located in the west, near Livingston. In 1890 a second cession moved the western boundary eastward, necessitating another move of the Agency, then on the Stillwater River, to its final location on the Big Horn River. The net effect of these changes was that the Big Horn Basin could now be reached from the north without crossing Indian lands.[18]

An 1872 act of Congress had authorized the President to negotiate

---

[16]The Congressional ultimatum is contained in 19 *Statutes at Large* 192, August 15, 1876, and the cession agreement is in 19 *Statutes at Large* 254, September 26, 1876.

[17]On March 3, 1873, Congress authorized a commission to negotiate with the Crow tribe. Burton M. Smith, "Politics and the Crow Indian Land Cessions," *Montana*, CCCVI, No. 4 (Autumn, 1986), 29.

[18]The first Crow cession was signed June 12, 1880 and ratified April 11, 1882; the second cession was ratified October 15, 1892. *Ibid.*, 31, 34, and 22 *Statutes at Large* 42. The trend of shrinking the Indian lands was temporarily reversed in 1884 when the President set aside a reservation for the Northern Cheyennes in Montana, abutting on the Crow reservation, east of the 107th meridian. The 107th meridian was surveyed in 1891, and erroneously placed nearly a mile west of the actual location, creating a dispute between the two tribes. *The Billings Gazette*, June 19, 1992.

with the Shoshonis to secure the relinquishment of the south part of their reservation, where the mining settlement of Miner's Delight had been built. Felix Brunot, chairman of the board of Indian Commissioners, came to talk to Chief Washakie about an exchange of this land for land in the Big Horn Basin. The conversation with the chief is especially interesting, since the land the government was offering had in fact been Shoshoni hunting ground before they were driven west of the Wind River mountains. Nevertheless, Washakie refused to accept the trade, saying, "This land is good; that in the north is poor, and I think it belongs to the Crows. When you were at the Crows did the chief tell you to trade this land off?"[19]

Brunot replied, "I did not say anything to the Crows about it. It was none of their business. The land does not belong to them."

Washakie was not impressed. "The Shoshones think it belongs to the Crows," he said. In the end, the reduction of the reservation was achieved in exchange for $25,000 in cash, not Big Horn Basin land.

The first national park in the nation was created in 1872. Montana Territory had memorialized Congress to attach the upper Yellowstone area to Montana Territory, but no action was taken on that request. After the Hayden expedition returned from the Yellowstone region, Hayden, who was the geologist, recommended that a park be created.

There is some controversy over the question of priority in making the suggestion, but it seems clear that the interest of the Northern Pacific railroad in developing traffic in the regions tributary to its line, may have had a significant impact on the progress of legislation. It is also likely that the precedent of the Yosemite park was involved in the ultimate decision; in that case, the federal government had transferred the land for the park to the state of California, on the condition that the land could never be alienated from its public purpose. A number of those who supported the concept of a park in the Yellowstone region were from Montana Territory, and some of them seem to have had the Yosemite model in mind. Unfortunately, in this case the politics were awkward, since the bulk of the Yellowstone region was within the territory of Wyoming, and there was considerable reluctance to establish the precedent involved in a transfer of that area from Wyoming to Montana Territory.

It is perhaps for this reason that the concept of a national park was put forth as a way around the difficulty, for the Yellowstone legislation was

---

[19]The congressional authorization contemplated trading land north of the reservation for the area ceded. 17 *Statutes at Large* 214, June 1, 1872.

submitted by the delegate from Montana, and is apparently a redraft of the Yosemite enabling act. When the bill was considered in the Senate, Senator Cornelius Cole of California opposed it, saying that the natural wonders would not be interfered with by settlers; to this argument Senator Lyman Trumbull of Illinois assured his colleague that the law could later be repealed if it was "in anybody's way."[20]

As originally constituted in 1872, the park was rectangular in shape, and these original boundaries covered parts of four territories; it included a small part of the Shoshone River drainage in the western Big Horn Basin that lay inside Sweetwater and Uinta counties. Later revisions in 1929 and 1932 altered the boundaries to follow watersheds, and removed the park from the Big Horn Basin. Although the greater part of the park was in Wyoming, there was no entrance to it from that territory; the south entrance road was funded in 1892, and the east entrance was built after the railroad reached Cody in 1901.[21]

---

[20]In fact, repeal of the Yellowstone Park legislation was suggested in 1886. Aubrey L. Haines, *The Yellowstone Story: A History of Our First National Park*, I (Boulder, Colorado, 1977), 169-70, 324.

[21]The boundaries of the park were set so as to include certain natural features. Thus, the eastern boundary of the park was set on the meridian ten miles east of the most easterly point of Yellowstone Lake, the north boundary was on the latitude of the mouth of Gardiner's River, the south boundary was on the latitude ten miles south of the most southerly point of Yellowstone Lake, and the west boundary was fifteen miles west of the most westerly point of Madison Lake. 17 *Statutes at Large* 32, dated March 1, 1872. Most of the park was in Wyoming Territory, but these boundaries extended it into Montana on the north and northwest, and Idaho on the southwest; in addition, a small part of Dakota Territory lying west of Wyoming and south of Montana Territory was included in the park until it was attached to Montana Territory in 1873. 17 *Statutes at Large* 464, February 17, 1873.

CHAPTER VI

The Cattle Come

Once the risk from Indians had been reduced to a tolerable level, the cattle industry could bring their herds to the Basin, to take advantage of the grass that had heretofore been the sustenance of untold thousands of buffalo and other wild game. After the Custer debacle in the summer of 1876, the cattle could come; by this time the industry already was a force in Wyoming.

In 1871, there were enough cattle in Wyoming territory to cause a group of cattlemen to meet in Laramie to join together to obtain better freight rates for shipping their animals. This group called itself the Wyoming Stock Graziers Association, and the territorial governor was elected president, but the first significant organization of the stock growers began in 1873, when a meeting was held in Cheyenne to form a stock association. Mark Vincent Boughton was elected as the first president of this Laramie County Stock Association. In 1879, the Association authorized an executive committee to rule the industry and Thomas Sturgis took the reins as its powerful secretary, a post he would hold for eleven critical years; in the same year, the name Wyoming Stock Growers Association was adopted to signify the larger scope of the organization.[1]

The Association's reach was longer than that of the territorial government itself, and it has been noted that in 1885, one of the peak years for the Association, the budget of the Association was $52,796, while the territory itself got by with a budget of just over $38,000. The Association sent its inspectors to distant shipping points to make sure that its rules on

---

[1] The Albany County group met April 15, 1871; the Laramie County Stock Association met in the county clerk's office in Cheyenne on November 29, 1873. John Rolfe Burroughs, *Guardian of the Grasslands: The First Hundred Years of the Wyoming Stock Growers Association* (Cheyenne, 1971), 33, 54-55.

branding and documentation were observed, and the man who failed to heed their admonitions might well find he was not paid for the stock he sold. The inspectors, who numbered 25 at the zenith, enforced the laws against rustling, and they went wherever the trail led to get their men, whether it be to Dakota or Nebraska, or on the Indian reservations. The Association set the dates for the twice-yearly roundups, determined the areas that each would cover and appointed the foreman to be in charge. There were enough cattle in the Basin to justify a formal roundup for that region in 1883.[2]

Cattle entered the basin from the north, south and east. By the end of the 70's, there were sizable cattle operations on the other side of the mountains in these three directions, and it was only a matter of time before the burgeoning herds would push over the passes into the uncrowded ranges of the Basin. Perhaps the first cattle outfit in this region was the Two Dot Ranch of John W. Chapman. We can date Chapman's entry to northern Wyoming with precision, because he was scouting for a ranch location in the fall of 1878, at the time Colonel Miles fought his engagement with the Bannocks on Bennett Creek; Chapman was camped not far away, and visited the battleground on the day after the incident. The following year, Chapman, who was then 28 and unmarried, selected his cattle range on Pat O'Hara Creek, a tributary of the Clark's Fork River. While Chapman's range was not in the Big Horn River watershed, he was in Wyoming, and he is called the pioneer of cattlemen in northern Wyoming.[3]

After selecting his ranch site, Chapman made his way back to Oregon, traveling on the first leg of the journey through Yellowstone Park with the soldiers. The following year, he returned to Pat O'Hara Creek with a herd of Durham cattle from Oregon, but the old trapper had vanished, never to return. Chapman made his way back to Oregon again, and there he married Affie Chapman, who was no relative, in April 1881, and the couple spent their honeymoon on the trail back to Wyoming. Affie's two bache-

---

[2]Bill O'Neal, *Cattlemen vs. Sheepherders: Five Decades of Violence in the West 1880-1920* (Austin, Texas), 88, 90.

[3]Chapman was born in Springfield, Illinois, June 15, 1850, and journeyed to Oregon with his mother over the Oregon Trail. He died at Red Lodge, December 18, 1933. John K. Rollinson, *Wyoming Cattle Trails* (Caldwell, Idaho, 1948), 184-90. Pat O'Hara Creek was named for Pat O'Hara, a trapper who had worked for the American Fur Company, and had built a cabin on the creek.

lor brothers took up ranches near Chapman's location and brought in a number of sheep.

One of these brothers, Henry Chapman, was a small man and partially crippled, but this fact did not limit his capacity for trouble. In 1890, there was a dispute between Chapman and Albert de Caillet, regarding the illegal killing of deer by the latter, following which Caillet allegedly poisoned or shot some of Chapman's dogs. The next spring, the two men met on the prairie, both armed, and Chapman, who was on horseback, fired his Winchester, killing de Caillet's horse and breaking the Frenchman's arm. He shot twice more at de Caillet before riding away. Caillet was taken to Red Lodge, where he recovered from his injuries.[4]

Hank Chapman was involved in another shooting scrape with one of his herders in 1891. The herder, a man named Pierce, complained there were no spoons, and said he would not work for an outfit that didn't own at least half a dozen pewter spoons. This remark precipitated a quarrel and Pierce was shot, making it necessary for him to go to Red Lodge to recuperate. The *Picket* laconically prophesized, "It is not likely that any notice will be taken of the affair by the Wyoming authorities."[5]

John Chapman used the Roman Cross as a brand, but since he was not a member of the Wyoming Stock Growers Association, his brand does not appear in the early Wyoming brand books. Chapman later had a butcher shop in Red Lodge, in partnership with H. C. Provinse, and he also entered the banking business in Red Lodge, in partnership with W. F. Meyer and Paul Breteche. He sold his herd in 1897, to F. C. Valentine of Aurora, Nebraska.[6]

In 1879, Judge William Alexander Carter sent 3,800 head of Oregon cattle to the Lovell area; these were branded with two Roman crosses. Originally from Virginia, Carter had served in the army during the Seminole Indian War, and afterward was sutler at Fort Lauderdale, Florida. He went to California at the time of the gold rush in 1850, and in 1857 he came to Fort Bridger with Albert Sidney Johnston's army, sent to subdue the Mormons in Utah; in 1870 he was appointed sutler at the fort. In 1858, Governor Cuming of Utah Territory appointed Carter as probate

---
[4]*Buffalo Bulletin*, May 21, 1891, quoting the *Billings Gazette* of May 15.
[5]*Billings Gazette*, June 11, 1891.
[6]John K. Rollinson, "Brands of the Eighties and Nineties Used in Big Horn Basin, Wyoming Territory," *Annals of Wyoming*, XIX, No. 2, 65-66. In the summer of 1894, Chapman and Provinse agreed to operate the City Meat Market under Provinse's name. *Red Lodge Picket*, June 16, 1894.

judge of Green River County, Utah Territory, and he retained that position until this area was cut off from Utah territory and added to Wyoming in 1868.[7]

Carter accumulated his first cattle by trading fresh stock to emigrants on the trail for their worn out work animals. The grass on Carter's customary range was poor in 1878 and he apparently acted on the advice of his good friend Chief Washakie, who told him of the virgin range in the Big Horn Basin. Two thousand head of Oregon cows were sent to the Stinking Water in 1879, apparently the first outfit on that river. The judge was already an old man at this time (he died November 7, 1881), and his oldest son, also named William A. Carter, was placed in charge of the new ranch; he established the ranch headquarters about 17 miles south of the present location of Cody, at the north end of Carter Mountain. In 1883, a second drive of 2,000 head came up from southwestern Wyoming.

Peter McCulloch, who had gone to work for Judge Carter in 1869, was appointed the cow foreman for the ranch, a position he held until 1889. It was McCulloch who named Carter Creek and Carter Mountain for the judge; McCulloch Peaks are named for the foreman himself. In 1885, the Carter Cattle Company was organized, and Judge Carter's widow transferred the herds to it; the famous Bug brand was also adopted at this time. The Carter company escaped serious loss in the winter of 1886-87, but the "greater part" of the herd was lost the following winter, and the remainder was sold in 1889. The ranch was later sold to Col. William F. Cody.[8]

Another very early entrant to the Basin was Captain Henry Belknap, who is often mistakenly called an Englishman. Belknap was born in Massachusetts in 1826, which made him older than most of the men in this

---

[7]Carter was born in Prince William County, Virginia, on April 15, 1818. Harriet Orr said that President Grant Offered Judge Carter the appointment as Governor of Wyoming Territory, but he declined. Harriet Knight Orr, "Pioneer Culture when Wyoming was Young," *Annals of Wyoming*, XXVI, No. 1 (January, 1954), 35. Because of the ongoing controversy between the Mormons and the federally-appointed district court judges, the legislature assigned broad jurisdiction to the probate courts, where the judges were not subject to presidential appointment. Carter was therefore a very influential man in the area; he was also highly respected, and Dakota Territory named a county for him (the first Wyoming legislature changed the name to Sweetwater).

[8]*Ibid.*, 67. Peter McCulloch was born July 12, 1839, in Penningham, Wigton, Scotland. He came with his family to the United States in 1853, at the age of fourteen, and later served in the Civil War. He left the Big Horn Basin in 1896 and died April 17, 1925. Ester Johansson Murray, "'Short Grass and Heather:' Peter McCulloch in the Big Horn Basin," *Annals of Wyoming*, LI, No. 1 (Spring, 1979), 99-129. Also,William A.Carter (Jr.), to John K. Rollinson, September 14, 1941, John K. Rollinson, Cattle Trails of Wyoming, *op. cit.*, 304-306.

young country. He graduated from Harvard University in 1845, and then spent ten months testing the efficacy of hydrotherapy, an ancient form of medical care which had been revived in Austria in 1843. We do not know what Belknap concluded from this experiment, but he traveled about a good deal in the next few years, going to Michigan in 1846, taking a job the next year in a Boston counting room, before spending a year on a trip to Calcutta. Then it was to Ohio and a trip across the Atlantic to Europe, which would be repeated again in 1852.[9]

The outbreak of the Civil War brought experiences of a different sort, and Belknap served as a captain in the U. S. infantry, in company with men whose names would later figure in the Indian wars of the West. Belknap's commander was Col. Henry Beebe Carrington, and a fellow officer was William Judd Fetterman; it was Carrington who was in command at Fort Phil Kearny in 1866, when Fetterman and his unit perished at the hands of the Indians.[10]

Col. William D. Pickett, who had earned his rank in the Confederacy, said he first saw Belknap in the fall of 1882, when he had just arrived in the Basin with 1,000 cows. It is said that Belknap had come to the Basin to hunt, and returned the next year to start his ranch. Pickett's recollection of the beginnings of the Belknap ranch may be in error, for John Dyer, who was Belknap's foreman, recalled trailing the cattle to the Basin in the summer of 1880, and his statement is confirmed by other sources. According to Dyer, the cattle were trailed from Bozeman, south to the old Crow Agency at Benson's Landing, and then to the mouth of Pat O'Hara creek and into the Basin by way of Cottonwood Creek. Scouts went ahead of the herd and the wagons, choosing a route that the freight wagon and oxen could negotiate.

Belknap located his ranch on the South Fork of the Stinking Water, upstream from the Carter ranch, on a stream later called Belknap Creek and the herd was branded first with the F and after 1886 with the BN.

---

[9] A good description of the early history of the Belknap ranch is in a paper written by Sara Roberts, located in the Park County Historical Society archives, Cody, Wyoming, and much of what is written here is based on this paper.

[10] Henry Belknap was born in Boston, Massachusetts, September 7, 1826; both his parents were also born in Massachusetts. He died in Boston, January 21, 1909. His military service was in Company B, 18th U.S. Infantry, from May 14, 1861 to May 30, 1863. Fort Fetterman, on the North Platte, was named for Captain Fetterman, who was born about 1833; he died December 21, 1866. Colonel Carrington, who was born at Wallingford, Connecticut, March 2, 1824, was adjutant general of Ohio before the Civil War; he died October 26, 1912.

Peter McCulloch became foreman of the BN in 1894. The Belknap Ranch was purchased by an Englishman, Henry Algernon Cholmley Darley, who was then 29, in 1899. Darley sold the ranch to Victor G. Lantry in 1905.[11]

Belknap invested in Billings real estate, and in 1883 he erected two brick buildings there, the first permanent block in that city. He was also president and chief stockholder of the Billings Water-Power Company, which originally furnished water and later electricity to Billings.[12]

In 1878, Henry Clay Lovell made a scouting trip to Wyoming, and in 1879 he trailed two Kansas herds to the Basin. The herds were owned in partnership with Anthony L. Mason, of Kansas City, who provided financing for the Mason and Lovell operation. Lovell purchased five or more herds from eastern Oregon and eastern Washington Territory and located them on the Stinking Water.

Lovell was born in 1838 on a farm near Battle Creek, Michigan. He worked as a section hand on the Michigan Central Railroad, and later on a government mail train operating from Fort Dodge, Kansas, to Mexico City. He then went into the cattle business in northern Texas, Indian Territory and Kansas. It was during this period that he became associated with Anthony L. Mason, of Kansas City, who supplied capital for Lovell's operations.[13]

Lovell had his first headquarters south of the present location of the town of Manderson on the west side of the Big Horn River. The cleared fields at the site were noted by the government surveyors who were there in 1883. Lovell's headquarters did not remain long in this location, and after perhaps a year he moved to a tributary of Shell Creek known as Trapper Creek (named for the activities of Jack Copman, who had trapped there, beginning in 1881). Lovell moved his headquarters again, to the Five Springs area east of the present town of Lovell, but he retained the Trapper Creek location as a horse ranch, where he kept about 600 head of

---

[11] Darley was born at Aldby, York, on June 11, 1870 and educated at Charterhouse School. He died in 1945.

[12] *The Billings Herald*, May 19, 1883. Also, *Historic and Architectural Resource Survey, Billings, Montana* (Billings, 1981) and George Bird Grinnell, ed., *Hunting at High Altitude* (New York, 1913), 202. Henry Belknap died in Shelter Island Heights, New York, January 21, 1909. His will was probated in Yellowstone County, Montana, so as to distribute the Billings real estate. The electrical system of Billings was sold to Montana Power Company and the water system to the city of Billings.

[13] There is a story that Lovell was a member of Quantrill's guerrillas, but his name does not appear on the list of the guerrillas which was carefully compiled by Carl W. Breihan. Carl W. Breihan, *Quantrill and his Civil War Guerrillas* (New York, 1959), 166-74. Also, Willard T. Lovell to John T. Fuller, November 15, 1948.

William Clay Lovell, born in Michigan, trailed two herds of cattle from Kansas to the northern Basin in 1879, the beginning of the largest herd in the Basin. *Courtesy Wyoming State Museum.*

horses. Riley Kane, whose name was attached to the Kane post office on the Mason and Lovell ranch, was Lovell's foreman.

It is said that the Mason and Lovell operation was the largest in the Basin, and numbered perhaps 25,000 head (his son gave the total as 20,000 head); the range extended from the Pryor Creek region of Montana to Thermopolis in the south. In one account it is claimed that Lovell paid taxes in three counties in Wyoming, one in Montana and two in Dakota.

The Northern Pacific railroad, which had been marking time at Bismarck in Dakota Territory for ten years, finally overcame its financial difficulties and finished the main line into Billings in 1883. It was now a shorter trip to drive cattle north to Montana from the Powder River region or from the Big Horn Basin than to make the long trek south across Oregon Trail to the Union Pacific. Lovell is said to have made the first cattle shipment from the Basin on the Northern Pacific, a herd of 3,200 head of steers, shipped from Custer's Junction in the fall of 1883. Ed McNiely said that in the years 1882-84, Lovell shipped 5,000 head to the packing facility in Medora built by the Marquis de Mores.[14]

Lovell began irrigating land at the headquarters location, claiming a priority of 1884 for the ditch he took out on Willow Creek to irrigate 220 acres. Two years later, he made additional filings on Willow Creek and Five Springs Creek to irrigate 530 acres, and in 1895 Lovell made a small filing on Trapper Creek to irrigate 40 acres; the ditch was named the Willard, for his son. Lovell spent a fair amount of time in Billings, and in 1884 bought property in the city for a residence. He wound up his operation in 1896, when the remaining herd was trailed to Montana; Mason had died in 1892, and Lovell bought the land filings he had made.[15]

South of Lovell's operations was the range of George White Baxter's LU Ranch on Grass Creek, which was established in 1881. Born in Hendersonville, North Carolina, on January 7, 1855, Baxter was descended from a prominent Southern family; his uncle was Governor of Arkansas and his father was appointed to the federal circuit court of appeals. George Baxter graduated from West Point in 1877 and served in the Third Cavalry at the Spotted Tail Agency in Dakota and at Fort Washakie before he resigned from the Army in 1881.[16]

In 1881, Baxter came to Wyoming to go into the cattle business; he registered a brand jointly with Henry Belknap for a herd on the Greybull and Stinking Water, and the next year he registered the 7L and LU brands. A wealthy man, Baxter spent $150,000 on cattle to graze on his ranches,

---

[14]McNiely's recollection is in error, at least insofar as 1882 shipments are concerned, because the Medora facility was not completed until the fall of 1883. Ed McNiely, "A Short Sketch of the Life of Henry Lovell, from Boyhood to 1885," handwritten manuscript, American Heritage Center, University of Wyoming. For information on the Medora facility, see Donald Dresden, *The Marquis de Mores: Emperor of the Bad Lands* (Norman, Oklahoma, 1970), 40. Congress had authorized driving cattle across the Crow reservation in the law accepting the reduction of the reservation in 1882; the secretary of the Interior was to set the fees. 22 *Statutes at Large* 42, April 11, 1882. The first cattle shipments from Billings, in August 1883, were from Montana herds.

[15]One of the Billings deeds to Lovell was dated March 8, 1884. Yellowstone County clerk Deed Book A, 455. The Mason heirs conveyed to Lovell on January 4, 1896. Johnson County Book 2, 30. Lovell died in Portland, Oregon, March 2, 1903. Willard T. Lovell to John T. Fuller, November 15, 1948.

[16]George Baxter's father, John Baxter, supported the John Bell ticket for the presidency in 1860, and sided with the Union during the War; President Hayes appointed him to the sixth circuit court of appeals in 1877. George Baxter was educated at the University of Tennessee and the University of the South before entering the U.S. Military Academy.

including the LU. He was also the manager of the Western Union Beef Company, which succeeded to the EK ranch in the Powder River Basin, and owned a number of other ranches in Montana, Texas and Wyoming. Baxter left Wyoming in 1900, and the LU brand was acquired by the LU Sheep Company, which was incorporated in 1899 by Jay L. Torrey, David Dickie and Jacob Price.[17]

Baxter was only 31 when President Cleveland appointed him territorial governor in 1886, making him the youngest territorial governor. Unfortunately, there were complaints that he had illegally fenced large tracts of the public domain scattered among the 30,000 acres of railroad land he had purchased in 1884. Baxter had erected fences, but only after he had obtained legal advice in Wyoming and from his father that his action was legal. Before he was permitted to take the oath of office, he was required to state that he had no illegal fences, and on the strength of his assurance, he was permitted to qualify on November 11.

Nevertheless, when the President learned of the fences, he asked for Baxter's resignation, which the governor said he would send. Whether Baxter actually resigned is unclear, because he later was requested to apply for leave from the office for the period from December 5 through January 24, 1887, the date when Governor Moonlight took office. In 1888, a Wyoming case declared that fencing of the sort Baxter had erected was legal, and Baxter then went to see President Cleveland. He claimed that the President was very sympathetic, and offered another federal post, but Baxter insisted that he be named governor of Wyoming, which the President refused to do.[18]

Baxter served in the territorial legislature and was a delegate to the con-

---

[17]The 7L and LU brands were registered in Sweetwater County on May 22, 1882. The Western Union Beef Company's home ranch was the 7D of Fort Stockton, Texas; the company also owned the Cross Half Circle at Brush, Colorado, the 4P in the Platte River Valley, the Double Mule Shoe in Texas, and the Sandstone at Ekalaka, Montana. Meta Osborne, "John Alexander Osborne," *Annals of Wyoming*, XIV, No. 4 (October, 1942), 316.

[18]On December 5, Baxter wired L. Q.C. Lamar that his resignation would be forwarded "immediately," but when the Treasury inquired regarding the status of his salary, Baxter was requested to ask for leave during the period December 5, 1886 to January 24, 1887, and his request was then approved on March 17, 1887, thus giving Baxter 74 days of tenure as governor. The story of Baxter's 1888 visit with the President is from Baxter's letter of June 2, 1888 to Judge Howell E. Jackson, who had replaced his father on the Sixth Circuit Court of Appeals in Nashville. Early in 1888, the Wyoming district court, construing an 1885 statute, declared that fencing of the checkerboard sections was legal, so long as the fences remained on the patented sections; this holding was confirmed by the Wyoming Supreme court the following year, although it was overturned in 1895. U.S. *vs.* Douglas-Willan, Sartoris Company, June 6, 1889. 22 *Pacific Reporter* 92.

stitutional convention in 1889, where he introduced the woman suffrage provision, saying, "I believe in it because . . . it is right; because it is fair; and because it is just . . . ." He ran unsuccessfully for the governorship in 1890 and in the spring of 1892, Baxter was one of the prime movers in the Johnson County Invasion. He moved to Denver in 1895, where he served on the capitol building commission before moving back to Tennessee. Upon retirement in 1914, he moved to New York City, where he died in 1929.[19]

If John Chapman was the first to bring cattle to this northern region of Wyoming, his priority over the first entrants to the southern Basin was slim. In the spring of 1878, the government let a contract for a herd of 500 head of cattle to be brought to the new Shoshoni reservation, and a team set out from Camp Brown to buy the cattle and drive them back. Fincelius G. Burnett, who had just resigned as farmer for the reservation so that he could take the cattle contract, had the backing of James Kerr Moore, post trader at the Camp, and Captain Robert A. Torrey, commander of Camp Brown. With him on the trip to Montana was John Dwight Woodruff, who wanted to buy a herd for himself; Chief Washakie detailed four Shoshoni scouts to choose a return route for the herd.

Born in Windsor, New York, in 1847, Woodruff and his family had moved to Illinois when John Dwight was only two years old. He developed a persistent cough, and came west to seek a cure; he drove a team for one Gardner on the way to Colorado in 1865, when he was then 18 years old. The cough soon disappeared, and Woodruff came to Wyoming in 1866, where he trapped and hunted. Woodruff served as a guide to generals Sheridan and Crook when they were selecting the site for Fort Custer; he was a government scout during the Bates Battle, July 4, 1874.[20]

The cattle purchased in Montana met the Shoshoni scouts at the Yellowstone and were trailed south across the Crow reservation, up Pat O'Hara Creek, and over the divide to the Stinking Water, then down the

---

[19]In 1903, Baxter returned to Knoxville, Tennessee, where he became a bank director. He died in New York City from a gastric hemorrhage, November 18, 1929. The *New York Times*, December 19, 1929. Also, *Natrona County Tribune* (Casper), September 21, 1899 and "A Memorial to the Members of the Constitutional Convention of Wyoming," *Annals of Wyoming*, XII, No. 3 (July, 1940), 181.

[20]Woodruff married Josephine Doty in Chicago on March 14, 1883; she died in 1920. Woodruff died June 6, 1925. Tacetta B. Walker, *Stories of Early Days In Wyoming: Big Horn Basin* (Casper, 1936), 45-53, 56.

John Dwight Woodruff, whose cabin in the southern Basin was certainly one of the earliest built in the Basin, if not the first. *Courtesy Wyoming State Museum.*

old trail along the west side of the Basin to Owl Creek. The drive reached Owl Creek on October 5, 1878, where Woodruff stopped with his cattle, while the contract herd was trailed south over the Owl Creek Mountains to the reservation. This was the beginning of the Embar outfit, named for the M Bar brand, which had been registered by James Kerr Moore in 1877.[21]

The Embar range was originally on Jakey's Fork of the upper Wind River, where Moore and Torrey had their headquarters for a joint herd they managed under a six year contract they signed in 1878. Moore ran the business, and each had a half interest in the herd. The original foreman was Nelson Yarnell, who had been an Army scout, but Moore fired him before the partners moved their female stock to Owl Creek in 1880, after their range on the Wind River become overgrazed. Thereafter, the

---

[21]James K. Moore registered the M brand in 1873 and on September 21, 1877, he registered the M–brand. The latter brand was transferred to Robert A. Torrey on September 23, 1881.

partners' range was Upper Wind River, Cottonwood Creek and Kirby Creek, with Jacob Price as foreman.[22]

On Owl Creek, Woodruff built the first cabin in the Basin, a 12x20 foot structure with a sod roof and dirt floor and tiny two pane windows. Woodruff also added sheep to the operation in 1878, when he purchased an Oregon flock. In the meantime, In 1881, Woodruff sold his share of the Embar to Captain Robert A. Torrey, who had apparently also acquired Moore's share, as well.[23]

Torrey was later joined in the operation by his brother, Colonel Jay L. Torrey, who had been the author of the Torrey bankruptcy law. The Torrey brothers sold the sheep and stocked the range with Oregon cattle. They also raised horses, which they sold for use on streetcars, and later to the British government for military service in the Boer War. In 1890 Col. Torrey hired William P. Duncan to build the first frame house on the ranch; the hands called it the White House.[24]

On the east side of the Basin, John Luman, who was then living in Lander, brought a herd of Idaho cattle to Paintrock Creek in 1881. Luman's range was on Cottonwood Creek and on the Nowater, with a horse range on Paintrock Creek. At 43, Luman was older than many in that era of the young entrepreneur; born in Virginia, Luman had been in Kansas in the early days of that territory and in Colorado in the Pikes Peak days, before going to work for Judge Carter at Fort Bridger. A "squaw man," Luman was proud of his Indian wife.[25]

---

[22]The partnership agreement between Moore and Torrey is summarized in notes of James Kerr Moore, Jr., son of James Kerr Moore, in the possession of Mrs. Evelyn Bell, Cody, Wyoming. Moore discussed the matter of replacing Yarnell as foreman, and also the need to move the female stock to Owl Creek in a letter to Torrey, dated June 19, 1880. James K. Moore letterbook, also in Mrs. Bell's possession.

[23]Captain Torrey took command of the 13th Infantry at Fort Washakie on May 26, 1871. Post returns, Fort Washakie, June 10, 1871. Although Moore's 1878 contract with Torrey had a six year term, Moore was already offering to sell his interest to Torrey in the fall of 1878. James K. Moore to Captain R. A. Torrey, August 20, 1878, James K. Moore letterbook, in the possession of Mrs. Evelyn Bell, Cody, Wyoming. In partnership with his brother, Edward Day Woodruff, John D. Woodruff became a sheep rancher of considerable importance on the reservation; his wool clip in 1888 was said to total 150,000 pounds. Edward Norris Wentworth, *America's Sheep Trails*, (Ames, Iowa, 1948), 320.

[24]The White House burned in 1931. Dorothy Buchanan Milek, *Hot Springs: A Wyoming County History* (Basin, Wyoming, 1986), 24, 29-30; and The *Clipper* (Lander), August 19, 1898.

[25]Luman was born in Jackson County, Virginia in 1838; in 1854 he was in Douglas County, Kansas, and in 1859 he was in Colorado. After his work with Judge Carter, Luman returned to Colorado for seven years of mining and prospecting. By 1872, he was back in Wyoming, with 200 head of cattle from southern Colorado, for a range on Sybille Creek. In 1876, he sold the Sybille operation to Swan and the next year he went to Montana, but was back in Lander in 1880. Bancroft interview with John Luman, by George H. Morrison.

In 1881, Worden P. Noble of Lander had a herd on Ten Sleep Creek, branded with the WP brand, which he had registered in 1877; Noble is said to have been the first to stock that area. Noble was born in Sackett Harbor, New York, in 1847 and came to Fort Laramie in 1866 as a bookkeeper for Jules Ecoffey. In 1868 he went to South Pass City for a year, where he was a merchant serving the gold mining region. Noble then became a contractor for the government at Camp Stambaugh for seven years, and by 1879, when he was elected to the territorial council on the Democratic ticket, he was said to be the largest government and Indian contractor in the territory. Later, he turned to stock raising.[26]

In 1883, Noble sold the WP herd to Horace Plunkett for $153,000, who placed it in his partnership with Henry J. Windsor and John C. Coble. When that operation liquidated in 1888, the WP passed on to the Bay State Land and Cattle Company, which was then preparing to move its herds from the Nebraska Panhandle to Wyoming. The Bay State had started up in Nebraska in 1873, and at one time had virtual control of the range on the south side of the North Platte in the Nebraska Panhandle. When the Nebraska range became crowded, the Bay State sent 10,000 steers to Montana's Judith Basin, but 20,000 head of she stock was moved to the Big Horn Basin in 1888, where the Bay State operated until 1898.[27]

---

[26]John Rolfe Burroughs, op. cit., 150, Cheyenne Daily Sun, March 29, 1881, Ichabod S. Bartlett, History of Wyoming (1918), 163 and Cheyenne Daily Sun, November 8, 1879. The WP brand was registered in Sweetwater County on November 10, 1877.

[27]The original corporation established in 1877 was called the Evans-Jackson Livestock Company of Council Bluffs, Iowa; the name changed to Evans-Mead in 1882, and later in the same year it became the Bay State Livestock Company. The corporation was liquidated in Omaha in 1898. The Bay State ranch passed into the hands of Roe Emery, who sold it to George Saban. After Saban was found guilty in the Spring Creek raid of 1909, he transferred the ranch to his father in law, W. T. Whaley. Vera Saban and Earl L. Hanway, "Bay State Marked an Era," Annals of Wyoming, LIV, No. 2, (Fall, 1982), 67-71. Horace Plunkett met Jack Donahue in the late summer of 1888, when the latter was moving Bay State herds into the Basin. Plunkett diaries, August 6, 1888.

Some of the French contingent in the northern Basin, posing in front of the Shield Ranch headquarters; Paul Breteche is second from left and Rene Vion is at far right.
Courtesy William Agricola.

CHAPTER VII

Fleurs-de-lis Along the Stinking Water

The foreign aristocrats who came to work and to play at the cattle business held themselves apart from the rest of society in the Basin and their neighbors returned the favor; Otto Franc, for example, although an aristocrat himself, simply ignored his French neighbors in his diary. Perhaps his actions are understandable, considering the recent war between Germans and French in 1870.

Franc had established his range on the western side of the Basin, as one of the first ranchers there. His name was Otto Franc von Liechtenstein, and he had come to New York from Wiesbaden, in Hesse-Nassau, in 1866, when he was twenty years old; he was following his two older brothers, Carl Augustus Franc and Carl B. Franc, who had pioneered the importation of green bananas to New York, and were shortly to monopolize that trade for a time. Otto immediately joined the firm as the New York salesman, and stayed in the banana importing business for eleven years, until his health began to fail.[1]

---

[1] Otto Franc was born August, 1846, according to the 1900 census of Big Horn County, Wyoming; he became a naturalized citizen before the Court of Common Pleas in New York County, New York, October 14, 1872. The certificate is in his desert land entry file in the National Archives. Carl Augustus Franc was a steward on an early Pacific Mail ship on the run from New York to Colon (then in Colombia); he experimented with bananas as a delicacy for his passengers. In June 1864, he bought six bunches of green bananas and imported them in New York, earning a profit of more than 1000%. He then quit his steward's job and devoted all his efforts to the banana business; after Otto arrived, the brothers dominated the New York banana trade for three summers. Their plantations were later established in what is now the Panama Canal Zone (at that time part of Colombia). Charles Marson Wilson, *Empire in Green and Gold: The Story of the American Banana Trade* (New York, 1947), 26, and Frederick Upham Adams, *Conquest of the Tropics: The Story of the Creative Enterprises Conducted by the United Fruit Company* (New York, 1914), 35.

Otto Franc (the three brothers abandoned the use of "von Liechtenstein") then went west in 1877 to seek some improvement in his health. It was on this trip that he first saw the Greybull River country, and determined to establish a cattle ranch there; in 1879 he purchased 1,200 Oregon and Utah cows, and brought them to the Wood River country, where Franc adopted the famous Pitchfork brand to mark them. The main ranch house, with adobe walls eighteen inches thick, was built in 1880.

Late in 1886, the Morgan Franc Cattle Company was organized in New Jersey with a capital of $750,000; the company included Otto Franc and his brothers, Charles Augustus Franc of New York City and Carl B. Franc of Brooklyn. Sources are scarce regarding the involvement of Franc's relatives in the Wyoming operation, but we do know that Otto Franc's brother, Charles Augustus Franc, came to visit the ranch in the fall of 1884, and his nephew, Albert March, came from Germany to visit his uncle, in the summer of 1897.[2]

Franc adopted the style of some of the other large ranchers, spending at least a part of the winter in more pleasant climates; although he spent the winter of 1883 with his relatives in Brooklyn, he seems to have preferred California as a winter home. In 1898, he and E. H. "Skew" Johnson, the livestock agent for the Northern Pacific, spent two months at Catalina Island, where they fished. The two men brought back some mounted specimens, which they donated to the Billings Club. Franc took up the patriotic causes of his newly-adopted country, and when feelings were running high at the time of the Spanish-American War, he offered to donate a horse to the American cause.[3]

The Pitchfork spread grew larger, but it was not a great financial success. Moreover, Franc became increasingly nervous following the events of the cattlemen's invasion of Johnson County in 1892, according to John W. "Josh" Deane, who said Franc employed Deane to sleep in his room as a guard. Otto Franc died on the ranch, November 30, 1903, as a result of an apparent accident with a shotgun, and when his brothers probated his estate, they found that Franc owned 1,920 acres of patented land and over

---

[2]Charles Augustus Franc was accompanied by H. E. Zinsser of New York, in August, 1884. *The Billings Herald*, August 30, 1884. Albert March, who lived in Charlottenburg, Germany, was a large earthenware manufacturer. *The Billings Gazette*, June 22, 1897.

[3]Johnson later joined the XIT ranch in Texas. *The Billings Gazette*, March 15, May 13, 1898. Also, *The Billings Herald*, November 1, 1883.

17,000 acres of state leases, plus a large range on federal lands; there were over 2,000 head of cattle, of which about 1,500 were mature animals - not a great many more than he had first purchased in 1879. The ranch was very large in area, and it was heavily mortgaged, making it difficult to sell. In due course, the entire Pitchfork operation was sold to Louis B. Phelps, who had bought up the mortgages on it, for $85,000, of which nearly $49,000 represented the sale of the land. After deducting nearly $50,000 to pay the debts, the two sisters of Otto Franc received about $18,500 each.[4]

We know little about the small group of French nobles in the north, because of the lack of records left by them. Fortunately, we have the chatty letters written by Victor Arland, and they do give us some tidbits about the noblemen, since Arland was much taken with titles. For his part, Arland ignored others of his countrymen, quite as completely as Franc did.

The French presence in the north end of the Basin began with Victor Arland, who came West to prospect for gold and stayed on in the Big Horn Basin, where he established two ranches and sold them to his countrymen. These ranches, known as the Crown and Shield outfits, for the brands they used, attracted a number of Frenchmen, who wanted to try their hand at the cattle business, either as workers or investors.

Victor Arland came to America in 1870, when he was about 22 years old; he traveled to Mexico and Louisiana in 1872 and worked in Grafton, Illinois, for a time in 1874, where he planted grapes, berries and fruit trees; in 1875, he went to the Black Hills to prospect for gold. We have a description of Arland from Camille P. Dadant, who said he was athletic and fearless, but had a very pleasant, beardless face. Both Arland and his partner, John F. Corbett, were single, although Arland told Dadant that

---

[4]As with many early deaths, there were rumors of foul play in connection with Franc's accident, but Deane refused to do more than recite the known facts. Charles Lindsay, "John W. Deane, Wyoming Pioneer," *Annals of Wyoming*, IX, No. 3 (January, 1933), 749-50. Otto Franc's two brothers were the executors of his will, which was dated October 30, 1895; his two sisters were named to share the estate equally. The first section of the will modestly directed his executors to bury him "decently, . . . with proper regard to my station and condition in life and the circumstances of my estate." Phelps paid $17.50 each for the 1,524 mature animals, and $8 each for the 637 calves. The mortgages that Phelps purchased were all executed January 10, 1899. Franc had two $10,000 policies on his life, but each of them had loans outstanding against them. Letters testamentary were issued to the executors on February 26, 1904, and the final decree in the probate was issued May 9, 1906. The will and related documents are found in probate file No. 81, Big Horn County clerk of court.

he would like to inspire a "tender passion" in some Frenchwoman of 25-30 years of age.⁵

In September, 1880, Arland came to Trail Creek with his partner, John F. Corbett, and built a ranch there for another cattleman, who did not complete the deal with him. Since Arland had spent $200 of his own money on the project, he wanted to sell it, and until he was able to make the sale, he was compelled to live there.

We do not know if Arland knew about Moreton Frewen's hunting operations across the Big Horns in the Powder River Basin, but in any case, he set about to do for the French aristocracy what Frewen was doing for the British, providing a base camp on his Big Horn Ranch where aristocrats could come and hunt. In the process, he created what may have been the first mercantile establishment in the Basin. Soon, he boasted that he was surrounded by "big bugs," and he was also receiving American guests from New York, Chicago, Philadelphia and "other places."⁶

In the summer of 1882, Arland was visited by two Frenchmen who had served in the Franco-Prussian war; both would later enter the cattle business in Montana. The Baron de Bonnemain, who was born in 1851, had come to New York after the war, and after his hunting trip determined to take up a cattle ranch which by 1883 was running 3,200 head of cattle and 700 horses on a range of 32 sections in Montana. G. Weis took up a smaller ranch on the Musselshell, and was running 850 head there. In 1884, Arland entertained the Viscount de Bonchamps and the Count de Heursel for hunting trips in the mountains, and business was brisk enough for him to complain that he got little rest, since Corbett spent much of his time on the road.⁷

---

⁵In the Black Hills, Arland camped outside the Spotted Tail Agency because of tension at the agency arising from the dispute between the government and the Sioux which led to the Custer debacle in 1876. We infer Arland's age from the description of Camille P. Dadant, who said he was about three years younger than Arland; Dadant was born April, 1851, according to the 1900 Illinois census for Hancock County, which would give Arland an approximate birthdate of 1848. Also, typescript of remarks by C. P. Dadant, dated May, 1925 and letter, Victor Arland to Camille Dadant, August 25, 1885, in the Arland Collection, Buffalo Bill Historical Center, Cody, Wyoming; hereinafter cited as the Arland Collection.

⁶Victor Arland to Camille Dadant, March 1, August 20, October 18, 1882. Arland Collection.

⁷Hubert Howe Bancroft, *History of Washington. Idaho and Montana 1845-1889* (San Francisco, 1890), 737-38. The Bonchamps family had been ennobled in 1666, and Charles Melchior Artus, Marquis de Bonchamps, served as a volunteer in the American Revolution; he later was a leader in the Vendean uprising in 1793. In the battle at Cholet, he was killed, but before dying, he ordered that the prisoners be spared. A later marquis led the Bonchamps expedition to Africa in 1897-98. The young vicomte Jules de Bonchamps who came to Wyoming was 29 when he landed on the S.S. *Canada* on June 3, 1884. His home was at the Chateau d'Ouizy (Calvados). Antoine Bachelin-Deflorenne,

After a bridge was built over the Stinking Water in 1883, Arland moved to within about three miles of the new bridge, where he built a store, a saloon and a restaurant; with the related outbuildings, the place had the appearance of a village, which Arland said had earned the local name "Vickburg." When the government established a post office at his location, it received the name Arland. A traveler noted that there was also a coal mine at Arland, which provided an unlimited quantity of the best coal.[8]

The Marquise de Mores came on a hunting trip in 1885, and killed four bears "by herself," which Arland regarded as good advertising for his business. The marquise was the daughter of Louis A. von Hoffman, a New York banker, and her husband, the Marquis de Mores, was son and heir of the Duc de Vallombrosa. De Mores was an avid hunter in his own right, and he reported that on a tiger hunt in India in 1888, his group, which employed 70 elephants, killed 22 tigers, of which two represented his personal kills, but of his wife, who often galloped across the prairies with an eagle feather in her hat, he said, "She ... is a better shot than I am."*

The marquis had a ranch and slaughterhouse at Medora in Dakota Territory, and sales outlets in New York. In the summer of 1883, de Mores' Northern Pacific Refrigerator Car Company was advertising in the *Herald* for slaughter cattle in 500-1,000 head lots, and in fall of that year, the marquis visited Billings, intent on extending his operations to that city. Late in the year he agreed to build a slaughterhouse and an ice house large enough to hold 1,000 tons of ice northeast of the city. The Billings merchants raised contributions to provide him with the necessary 120 acres. Optimism for the project was high, and the following spring it was reported that 6,000 head would be slaughtered at Billings that year.[9]

Unfortunately, there were delays with construction, and in the fall of 1884, the marquis admitted that operations would have to wait for the next season. In October the subscribers to the land grant met to consider what to do with the money the marquis had returned to them; the Billings operation was dead. The marquis' Medora operations also failed, and

---

Etat Present de ia Noblesse Francaise (Paris, 1884), 323. Also, Victor Arland to Camille Dadant, July 24, September 6, 1883, October 6, 1884 and August 25, 1885, Arland Collection.

[8]Arland post office was established November 10, 1885. Daniel Y. Meschter, *Wyoming Territorial and Pre-Territorial Post Offices* (Cheyenne, 1971), 8. Also, Henry A. Kirk, "Sixty Days to and in Yellowstone Park," *Annals of Wyoming*, XLIV, No. 1 (Spring, 1972), 16.

*Arnold O. Goplen, "The Career of Marquis de Mores in the Bad Lands of North Dakota," *North Dakota History*, XIII, Nos. 1, 2 (Jan.-Apr. 1946).

[9]*The Billings Herald*, October 13, December 8, 1883.

when Count Jean de Hedouville visited them in 1887, the buildings were in poor repair; de Hedouville wrote that the marquis had spent a million dollars on his "foolish" enterprises, confirming the western criticism that the French knew nothing about "colonization."[10]

The marquis returned to France after his meat slaughtering business failed, but he continued to return to the West from time to time. While his ranching and slaughterhouse businesses were centered in Dakota, he was no stranger to Wyoming, for in 1888 he was developing a mining prospect on the east side of the Big Horn Mountains.[11]

Arland's establishment was a lively place, and in addition to the a dance hall, there was a house of ill repute operated by Arland's friend, Rose Williams. In 1888, Arland himself shot and killed "Broken Nose" Jackson at a George Washington birthday dance Arland was hosting. Jackson threatened Arland, and when he returned to make good his threat, Arland shot him. The following day, a coroner's inquest was held by Otto Franc, and Arland was acquitted.[12]

The next Frenchmen to establish a permanent operation in the northern Basin were the du Dore brothers, Count Jean-Yvan Barbier du Dore and his brother, Viscount Gustave-Marie Francois Barbier du Dore. Count Du Dore had traveled extensively in Europe, Asia and Africa and was on a hunting trip in the West with his brother in 1881, when he became impressed by opportunities in the cattle business "in the neighborhood of the Rockies," as Arland put it.

Du Dore was searching for a ranch location when he heard that Arland was living on Trail Creek, on the western side of the Big Horn Basin. He came over to the Trail Creek ranch, and purchased it for $600 (Arland proudly noted that this was the amount he had been asking for it). The ranch was originally conceived as a company involving the du Dore brothers, with the Baron de Bonnemain and a Mr. Bustard, who was "a big capitalist," (at least in Arland's eyes). De Bonnemain, of Maine, France, first came to the Basin in the summer of 1882, and that winter he was in California, where he owned vineyards. He came to the Basin again in each of

---

[10]Jean de Hedouville to Louis Marie Leonce de Campigneulles, November 14, 1887, in the de Hedouville collection, in the possession of William Agricola, hereinafter the de Hedouville collection.

[11]*Billings Weekly Gazette*, June 14, 1888 and *Big Horn Sentinel*, September 22, 1888.

[12]Otto Franc mentions the shooting and the inquest in his diary, February 22, 23, 1888. The incident is described in Bob Edgar and Jack Turnell, *Brand of a Legend* (Cody, 1978), 62.

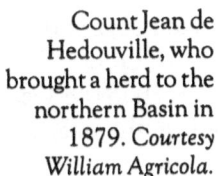
Count Jean de Hedouville, who brought a herd to the northern Basin in 1879. *Courtesy William Agricola.*

the two subsequent years, and on his third visit, in 1884, he became interested in investing in the cattle business.[13]

The Trail Creek ranch was stocked with about 1,200 Oregon cattle and branded with the Crown brand, the foreman was M. C. Tracy and operations were supervised by Paul Breteche, another Frenchman. Paul Breteche was born about 1856 and had been in the Basin at least since 1884, when he would have been 28; Jean de Hedouville called him an intelligent and serious young man. He was still single when he came to Wyoming, and in the summer of 1891 he married Florestine Daveau, who was of French parentage, but was the adopted daughter of a family in Brooklyn. A daughter was born to the Breteches in California during the

---

[13]The story of the sale to du Dore is found in Arland's letter to Camille Dadant, of Hamilton, Illinois, March 1, 1882, Arland Collection. Du Dore's father was the second son of Jacque-Rene Barbier du Dore, who had commanded the French royal army of the West and was ennobled in 1818. The family seat was near Nantes, at Chateau du Dore, in the commune of Montrevault (Maine-et-Loire). Jean-Yvan married Louise de Romons on May 19, 1885, and they had four children. Vicomte A. Reverend, *Les Familles Titres et Anoblies aux* XIXe *Siecle: Titres, Anoblissements et Pairies De la Restauration 1814-1830,* I, (Paris, 1974). Also, *The Billings Herald,* August 25, 1883, June 21, 1884.

1892-93 winter, but died in the fall of 1893 and is buried in the Trail Creek cemetery.[14]

Breteche invested in other ventures in the West, including a private bank in Red Lodge and a pair of butcher shops in Red Lodge and Billings; the latter were apparently an effort to achieve increased profits from forward integration in the cattle business. Since the French in the West were generally aware of what their countrymen were doing in the area, it is likely that Breteche was influenced in choosing this venture by the example of the Marquis de Mores, who was also butchering cattle at his location at Medora, in Dakota Territory and had property in Billings, Montana. Whatever the impetus for the investment may have been, the butcher business was not profitable for Breteche and it was sold to Florence Breteche in August 1893.[15]

At first, Arland was delighted with the deal he had made with the du Dores, and boasted, "We are going to have a little French colony here." But soon his enthusiasm died, for Count du Dore proved to have a difficult disposition. When the count proved to be a "real brute," his partners decamped, leaving the brothers alone with an investment of $25-30,000.[16]

A second ranch owned by the French was located about five miles north of du Dore, on Cottonwood Creek; this ranch was also purchased from Arland, who received $400 for it. The Shield ranch, named for its brand, was purchased by Count Robert-Antoine-Adrien de Mailly-Nesle, who was born in 1856; it was stocked with about 1,000 head of Oregon

---

[14]In the summer of 1884, the du Dore brothers and the Comte de Mailly were in Billings on their way to Huntley to pick up 1,200 head of cattle for the ranch on the Stinking Water. *The Billings Herald,* June 7, 1884. The *Gazette* reported that Breteche was to be married in New York on June 27, 1891. Breteche was 34 when he landed from the *La Champagne* from Havre on February 26, 1890 according to the passenger lists. See also, *Daily Gazette,* September 29, 1887 and June 1, 1891. The Breteche ditches from Trail Creek have a priority of June 1, 1884; final proof was established by Abram C. Newton in 1905. Files of the State Engineer. In the fall of 1893, Breteche and his wife went to California for the winter, and returned with their infant daughter the following January. *Red Lodge Picket,* October 8, 1892, January 28, 1893. Breteche reported to de Hedouville that their daughter died September 5, 1893. Paul Breleche to Jean de Hedouville, September 17, 1893. De Hedouville collection.

[15]The butcher shops were a partnership with Harry E. Ashelby, a Billings rancher. In 1895, Breteche joined John W. Chapman and William F. Meyer, a Red Lodge lawyer, in a private banking business in Red Lodge, under the name Meyer, Chapman and Breteche, which received a state charter in 1912; it operated as the First Security Bank and later the Montana Bank of Red Lodge. Fred H. Allen was the first cashier of the private bank. William F. Meyer came to Montana in 1882 and was elected to the state house of representatives in 1894; he was later a state senator. *Red Lodge Picket,* October 15, 1892.

[16]Victor Arland to Camille Dadant, December 20, 1883, Arland Collection.

cattle. If du Dore was overly concerned with the loftiness of his social position, the de Mailly family was, indeed, a family entitled to a certain amount of pretension. It was a very eminent knightly family in France, and was ennobled as comtes de Mailly in 1744 and as marquises de Mailly-Nesle; they were also princes of Orange.[17]

Apparently, de Mailly had originally planned to have du Dore manage his cattle, but after a quarrel with the latter, he placed them in the care of Rene Vion. In the summer of 1884, the count and Vion executed a contract in Billings which set forth the terms under which the latter would manage the ranch. De Mailly had purchased 1,000 head of cattle for 140,000 francs, and he was to supply the funds for the operation; Vion was to receive half the profits, after the recovery of de Mailly's investment. The contract was to run for a bit over six years, and Vion was bound to spend at least seven months of each year on the ranch.[18]

Paul A. A. Cottu also had come to live on the ranch for nearly a year in 1884-85, learning the cattle business, and by 1888 he was cooking for Vion. The only one of this French community to acquire land, Cottu received a patent for 320 acres from the U. S. government in 1898, but by the time the patent issued, Cottu had already disposed of the land to Richard Ashworth.[19]

In 1887, de Mailly returned to the ranch, and on that occasion he told the *Gazette* that no cattle had been sold from the ranch in the past three

---

[17]The sale of the Shield ranch to de Mailly probably was in 1884; both Paul Cottu and van der Ruy visited the ranch with de Mailly in the fall of 1885, and Cottu was there on a visit in 1889. Victor Arland to Camille Dadant, October 6, 1884 and August 25, 1885, Arland Collection and *Billings Gazette*, December 12, 1889. De Mailly was born April 18, 1856, second son of Ferry-Paul-Alexandre de Mailly, the 16th marquis; he died August 10, 1897, and was succeeded by his oldest son. The territory of Nesle was erected into a comte by Louis XI in 1466; the fourth count was created a marquis in 1548; their titles were confirmed by Louis XIV in 1701. Reverend, *op. cit.* Count Robert's first marriage was in October, 1879, to Marie-Anne-Clarisse de Goulaine, daughter of the Marquis de Goulaine. After a divorce, he married the second time in London, to Jean de Reszke. Marquis de Ruvigny, *The Titled Nobility of Europe* (London, 1914), 1072. Also, Paul Breteche to Jean de Hedouville, July 6, 1888, the de Hedouville collection. De Mailly was joined in the ranching venture by a Dutch nobleman, the Baron van der Ruy.

[18]Rene Vion was born about 1853; he was 33 when he landed in New York on the *St. Laurent* on March 18, 1886, according to the passenger lists for New York arrivals. In 1885 Vion made a preemption claim in the area. The contract with de Mailly, which is dated July 1, 1884, was to run from July 1, 1884 to November 1, 1890. Written entirely in French, it is filed in Miscellaneous Book A, 413, Yellowstone County clerk.

[19]The patent to Cottu issued December 1, 1898; the conveyance to Ashworth was dated October 22, 1897 and recites that Cottu, who was unmarried, sold the land for $1,000.

years, and he expected to find a "goodly" number of steers ready for sale. Whether he was satisfied is not recorded, but unless the Shield outfit was very lucky in the winter of 1886-87, one must assume he was disappointed. The Shield outfit did make a shipment in September, but we do not know how many head were involved, although the Gazette story said it was "several carloads."[20]

The proceeds Vion received from cattle sales must have been meager, for the partners were discussing liquidation in the fall of 1888. Then in June 1889 the Billings Gazette carried the story that the French syndicate which owned the de Mailly operation had given power of attorney to Henry G. Williams of the Hurlbut Land and Cattle Company to take possession of the Shield ranch from Rene Vion. Later stories gave the information that Vion had mortgaged the operation to "parties in Billings" for $7,500. Finally, the truth appeared that, in fact, the investors received nothing, simply because there was no money to pay them. At the conclusion of this investigation, the Shield operation was purchased by Paul Breteche, and Vion returned to France, leaving debts behind him.[21]

Another member of the French ranching group was Jean Marie de Hedouville, a younger son of Count de Hedouville, whose family were confirmed as comtes de Hedouville in 1815. De Hedouville had served in the French army during the Franco-Prussian war in 1870, and he was taken prisoner at Sedan. He had come west as early as 1879, and had intended to make his first investment in cattle in 1886, but the purchase was not completed in that year, which happily avoided the losses of the 1886-87 winter; his horses on the ranch survived the winter well.[22]

The small herd of Oregon cattle de Hedouville had purchased over the winter were finally delivered to Huntley at the beginning of June 1887,

---

[20]On his second visit to the ranch, de Mailly came to New York from Havre on the Normandie, landing August 3, according to the passenger list; in 1887, he was on the La Bretagne, also from Havre, which landed in New York, July 11, 1887. Vion realized $2.90 per head from the sale of the cattle. Daily Gazette, July 22, September 14, 29, 1887.

[21]Williams was superintendent of the OZ operation of the Hurlbut Land and Cattle Company, whose range was on the Tongue River, but would shortly move to the Crow reservation in southern Montana. The transfer to Breteche was apparently in December, 1889. The Billings Gazette, June 20, 29, August 22, December 12, 1889. Breteche wrote de Hedouville in the summer of 1889 that he was going to demand money from Vion, and he wrote again the following spring, giving the information that Vion owed the bank of Bailey and Billings $300 and as much to John W. Chapman. Paul Breteche to Jean de Hedouville, June 25, 1889, March 17, 1890, de Hedouville collection.

[22]In a letter to his cousin Leonce in May, 1887, de Hedouville reminded Leonce of the route they had taken to the West in 1879. Jean de Hedouville to Leonce de Campigneulles, May 31, 1887, de Hedouville collection.

and the count, who was then 38, came to meet them, in the company of Viscount Gustave du Dore, who was then 31, and Baron A. de Klopstein, 34, who had come along to view the country in the West. The Atlantic crossing had been a bad one, for they were on board the steamer *La Champagne* when it collided with the *Ville de Rio Janeiro* off the French coast, and a number of people were drowned. The passengers had to be transferred to the *La Bretagne* for the trip to New York.[23]

Rene Vion and R. Camille de Beyssac came up from the ranch to meet the group at Huntley, where the herd were branded with the MO brand, and then trailed to the Crown Ranch, where they were to be placed on the range. De Hedouville paid du Dore a dollar per head per year for this privilege. Since the Clark's Fork was still swollen by snowmelt, the herd was trailed up Pryor Creek, through Pryor Gap to Sage Creek, and thence to the ranch. On the first night out, they camped near the Crow chief Plenty Coups, who was in a teepee, and much impressed the French with his bearing and hospitality. The rest of the journey was relatively uneventful, although one cow and a calf died, while three other calves were born; they also had to kill a large rattlesnake that had been attracted by the warmth of their bedrolls, and they learned to fold their blankets to thwart such unwanted attention.[24]

Breteche now owned the Shield brand and was running the Crown brand, as well as the smaller herd under the MO brand of de Hedouville, and one of his major problems was acting as intermediary among the several parties, who often made extreme demands. In the fall of 1890, Breteche shipped 275 three- and four-year-old steers from the Shield and Crown brands, but only 6 for de Hedouville. Apparently, these results did not satisfy de Hedouville, as he began looking for a buyer for his herd in the fall of 1892.[25]

---

[23]Jean Marie de Hedouville was born May 10, 1849; he died in 1931. De Klopstein was from an old Lorraine family who had been ennobled in the Holy Roman Empire; their French barony was granted on May 30, 1870. The ages for du Dore and de Klopstein was taken from the passenger list of the *La Bretagne*, which docked at New York from Havre on May 19, 1887.

[24]The original herd entrusted to du Dore apparently consisted of 168 heifers and 7 bulls; 18 calves were branded for him in the spring of 1887, according to the contract signed by the two men on October 30, 1887. The heifers apparently were purchased for $24 each, as this was the loss he attributed to the one that died. In the spring of 1888, 35 calves were branded for him. Interestingly, de Hedouville apparently failed to discern the French roots of Plenty Coups' name, and in his letter spells the name phonetically as "Plenty Cuse." Jean de Hedouville to Leonce de Campigneulles, July 11, 1887. De Hedouville collection.

[25]Total sales for de Hedouville in 1890 were 14, including heifers; 51 were sold the following year and 23 in 1892. Paul Breteche to Jean de Hedouville, August 27, 1890, September 8, December 15, 1892. De Hedouville collection. The MO brand was registered in Fremont County on May 10, 1886.

In the summer of 1890, Albert L. de Caillet, who had come to Wyoming with de Hedouville in 1887 to look for opportunities in the ranching business, bought the Shield outfit from Breteche for $700, and in the fall of that year, Breteche and de Caillet purchased George Wise's herd and divided it between them. De Caillet now had a cattle operation of some size, but he did not have an easy relationship with his neighbors in Wyoming.[26]

In 1890, Hank Chapman quarreled with de Caillet over his deer poaching, and in the spring of the following year the argument flared up again; this time Chapman shot the Frenchman, although he recovered. De Caillet also ran afoul of the authorities in Yellowstone Park, who took his rifle from him. Although de Caillet was regarded as a protege of Paul Breteche, their relationship did not keep de Caillet from suing the butcher shop partnership of Harry E. Ashelby and Paul Breteche in 1893, to recover the value of 300 head of cattle. The suit claimed that 300 head of cattle were missing and that Ashelby and Breteche had taken them, but this was denied by the two defendants and when witnesses proved scarce, de Caillet had to abandon the case. In the spring of 1895, de Caillet wound up his Wyoming affairs and returned to his lumbering interests in Florida.[27]

In the summer of 1892, Breteche complained that the departure of de Caillet the previous year had left him short of money. The following year Breteche sold 1,500 head of cattle to Richard Ashworth, which was the first time he reduced his investments in the West. That fall, he also shipped all of the Crown cattle except for 2,000 head, giving the poor condition of grass as the reason.[28]

Still another Frenchman was in the region as early as 1889. Louis de la Brosse, whom the *Gazette* called a friend and comrade of Paul Breteche, was in Billings in the fall of that year and in the fall of 1890 he was cooking for de Caillet. When de Hedouville was looking for a buyer for his herd, Breteche suggested he sell to de la Brosse, but the latter was not interested in buying. De la Brosse did not buy herds, but he did invest some money on mortgages in the north Basin.[29]

---

[26]Paul Breteche to Jean de Hedouville, July 11, August 27, 1890. Also, Jean de Hedouville to his cousin, Louis Marie Leonce de Campigneulles, October 24, 1891. De Hedouville collection. De Caillet used the S anchor and WL brands.

[27]*Red Lodge Picket*, August 19, November 4, 1893, May 26, 1894. The lawsuit against Ashelby and Breteche was filed October 3, 1893 and dismissed by the plaintiff March 13, 1894, apparently as the result of a settlement between the parties. Case No. 671, Yellowstone County district court.

[28]Paul Breteche to Jean de Hedouville, June 28, 1892. De Hedouville collection. Also, *Red Lodge Picket*, October 7, 28, 1893.

[29]Paul Breteche to Jean de Hedouville, August 10, 1890. De Hedouville collection. De la Brosse

Since the nonresident owners all seemed to be interested in selling, Breteche proposed that he buy their herds for his butcher shop operations in Billings and Red Lodge, paying them in proportion to the size of their respective operations. For de Hedouville, this would have involved a sale of 561 head, according to Breteche's book count calculations, which used a 2% allowance for losses. In the summer of 1894, Breteche and de Hedouville contracted for the former to buy the latter's herd for $6,000, plus a percentage of any excess realizations from butchering.[30]

When de Hedouville wrote in the fall of 1894 to ask payment of the override percentage, Breteche gave the pained response that there had been no excess proceeds, and in fact he had lost money on the transaction. He claimed that he was able to locate only 300 head, not the 561 on the books. Breteche closed out his cattle operations and returned to Nantes, France, where he died in February 1897.[31]

Arland, who had been the nucleus of the French settlement, did not live to see this disintegration of the little French community, and for him the western adventure ended on an especially sad note. His health was declining, for reasons he did not specify, and by the summer of 1889, Arland was intent on liquidating his business. Unfortunately, this was not to be. On the afternoon of April 24, 1890, Arland visited Red Lodge, and after supper was "circulating" in the town, taking in the sights, in the company of Lum Wilson and John Dyer; the latter was the foreman of the Belknap cattle "pool." At around midnight the three men were in the Gem Saloon of John S. "Fat Jack" Dunivin, when Arland was shot through the heart by someone standing outside a rear window.[32]

In spite of swift action on the part of Dyer to have the murder investi-

---

loaned a total of $725 on two mortgages in 1896; they were released in 1907, after he had returned to Paris.

[30]Paul Breteche to Jean de Hedouville, December 15, 1892. De Hedouville collection.

[31]Du Dore sold the Crown ranch to Abram C. Newton who moved on the ranch late in 1895 to spend the winter. *Red Lodge Picket*, December 7, 1895. David Smethurst acted as administrator for the probate of Breteche's estate in Carbon County, Montana in 1903. At that time, there were three mortgages held by Breteche that had been paid and needed to be released on the public records. There are two 1909 mortgages recorded that were payable to Florence Breteche of Nantes, France. See Mortgage Deed Book 1, Big Horn County, 53, 56.

[32]In the spring of 1890, the Fremont Cattle Company pooled its herds with those of S. A. Wilson and Captain Belknap, forming the so-called Belknap pool; the foreman was John Dyer. *Billings Gazette*, May 8, 1890. The patrons in the saloon examined the rear of the premises and confirmed where the killer had stood; they also gave the newspaper the information that the killer had gone to Frannie Swail's place after the incident. Dr. F.R. Musser examined Arland, but could do nothing for him. *Red Lodge Picket*, April 26, 1890.

gated, Frank Lendon, who was initially arrested for the crime, was subsequently released, and the coroner's jury gave its verdict of gunshot wound by person or persons unknown; poor Victor Arland was buried in a grave in Red Lodge, never able to stir the tender passions of some French lady, as he had once hoped. The mystery of his killing was never solved, and the following month, when a coal miner near Red Lodge was found shot with over $400 cash on the body, the *Picket* complained that there was "too much promiscuous shooting" in the area.[33]

Arland had a safe, where it was expected "thousands of dollars" in gold would be found, but when it was opened, it was empty. The town of Arland struggled on for another seven years, but it did not thrive under Corbett, and in 1894 the Arland post office was replaced by Wise, Wyoming, named for the rancher, George A. Wise. In the spring of 1893, A. J. McCray purchased Corbett's road ranch on the Stinking Water, and Corbett moved to Meeteetse two years later, where he died in 1910.[34]

The French were often contentious with their non-Gallic neighbors, as in the case of de Caillet's troubles with Hank Chapman, and they often also quarreled among themselves. Du Dore apparently never mastered the art of accommodation with his partners, and the fact that Vion was summarily dismissed may suggest a personality flaw there, as well. Breteche said that Vion and his partner Joe Cline conspired to steal cattle from George Wise and Breteche sniffed that Vion preferred the "riff-raff" to his own countrymen. We find only one account which credits the French noblemen with good will, in the story of a Republican rally in the fall of 1884, when the du Dore brothers and their friends entertained the gathering with French songs and snatches of tunes from operas.[35]

Whether the unfavorable incidents are sufficient to establish a pattern

---

[33] *Red Lodge Picket*, May 31, June 7, 1890. Breteche "supposed" that Lendon was the "assassin." Paul Breteche to Jean de Hedouville, May 25, 1890, de Hedouville collection.

[34] Arland told Dadant that he was going to liquidate the business in his letters of June 23 and November 10, 1889, Arland Collection. The murder of Victor Arland is reported in the *Billings Gazette*, May 1, 1890. At the instance of John Dyer, William Lendon was arrested on suspicion of murder because he had testified against Arland at the time of the Jackson shooting inquest in Wyoming; the sheriff later released Lendon for lack of evidence. The Arland Collection has a notation of uncertain source which incorrectly gives Arland's death as December 1889, and the further information that Lendon was a friend of "Big Nose" Jackson, whom Arland had killed, supposedly after a quarrel over a woman. See also Bob Edgar, *op. cit.*, 67 and *The Buffalo Bulletin*, April 20, 1893. Corbett moved to Meeteetse in 1895, where he died in 1910. Northern *Wyoming Daily News*, June 19, 1992.

[35] Paul Breteche to Jean de Hedouville, November 22, 1888, de Hedouville collection. Also, *The Billings Herald*, November 8, 1884.

is open to question, but it is worth nothing that two of the other well-known French ranchers in the West also had difficulties with their neighbors. The Marquis de Mores got on so poorly with his neighbors in Dakota, that a concerted effort was made to run him out of the country in 1883; when he defended himself, one of his opponents died, and the marquis was tried three times for the killing before he cleared himself. The marquis' life ended tragically in another violent incident, for he was assassinated by natives in North Africa in 1896. Another Frenchman in the West, Baron Edmond de Mandat-Grancey, who had the Fleur de Lis horse ranch in Dakota, was quick to respond to provocation. He recounted with glee the occasion when he tossed a drunken cowboy into an empty horse stall after the hapless hand came into the stable looking for the "cursed French Baron."[36]

In spite of their arrogance, the French did not build pretentious headquarters for their operations, perhaps because they did not spend a great deal of time on the ranch. Jean de Hedouville made a sketch of the headquarters at the Shield ranch, a one-story affair which had two private bedrooms at one end, one for the owners and one for Rene Vion; a room for the cowboys at the other end of the building; and a kitchen and other necessary work space between. By contrast, Moreton Frewen, over on the Powder River, built a large house with a 40-foot hall for entertaining and a mezzanine where musicians could entertain guests.

De Hedouville originally intended to settle in Wyoming, but he customarily came to the ranch in the summer and spent the winter in Florida, and when the ranching operations did not prove highly profitable, he made his permanent home in Florida. In 1891, de Caillet spent the winter in Florida with de Hedouville.[37]

There are few remaining reminders of the little French enclave in the Big Horn Basin, but one of them is Breteche Creek, a tributary of the North Fork of the Shoshone River, named for Paul Breteche.

---

[36]Galiot Francois Edmond de Mandat-Grancey was born June, 1842 and died in 1911. He first visited Dakota in 1883, and it was on July 4 of that year that the incident with the cowboy occurred. Keith Cochran, ed., *Buffalo Gap: A French Ranch in Dakota, 1887* (n.p., 1981), i-iii, and Edmond Baron de Mandat Grancey, *Cowboys and Colonels: Narrative of a Journey Across the Prairie and Over the Black Hills of Dakota* (Lincoln, Nebraska, 1984), 189.

[37]In the summer of 1891, de Caillet spent over a month in Yellowstone Park, and he was in Billings in late October, before going to Florida for the winter. The count apparently chose Florida as his permanent residence on the urging of Count James L. Nugent, who was also living there. The Nugents were of Irish extraction and descended from the barony of Delvin. *Billings Gazette*, October 29, 1891, and journal of Jean de Hedouville; de Hedouville collection.

CHAPTER VIII

The Union Jack on Canyon Creek

The first British ranches in northern Wyoming were on the east side of the Big Horns, in the Powder River basin. The pioneers in those ventures were the Frewen brothers, Moreton and Richard, who started their Big Horn Ranche in 1879, following a hunting trip to Wyoming the previous fall. This operation, which used the 76 brand, was later incorporated in England as the Powder River Cattle Company, Ltd. Moreton Frewen also operated a sort of hunting camp for British aristocrats, and his guest book bore the names of a number of British peers.

Most of the British cattlemen in the Big Horn Basin were located in the southern area, east of the river, but there were some in the north, as well. Captain Henry Belknap was instrumental in advising his good friend, Richard Ashworth, to take up ranching in the Basin. Ashworth, who was born about 1856, had been in the West in 1881 and approached Horace Plunkett, younger son of Lord Dunsany, about having Plunkett manage a ranch for him in Wyoming; nothing developed from that conversation. The following year, Ashworth, in partnership with James C. Johnston, established the Hoodoo ranch, first on the Greybull River and later on Upper Sage Creek, using the Double Mill Iron brand; late in 1893, he purchased 1,500 head of cattle from Paul Breteche.[1]

Ashworth, who was a bachelor when he came West, brought with him from England some of the trappings of the British aristocracy, as when he imported a pair of Scottish fox hounds, and his ranch headquarters was

---

[1] Richard Ashworth, then 25, with his brother Walter, 18, landed at New York on April 26, 1881, according to the passenger list of the *Gallia*.

impressive enough to be called Ashfordville by the cowhands. Nevertheless, he was well liked by his American neighbors, which was not the case for his countrymen in the Powder River country, where feelings against them were "very strong," according to the Johnson County sheriff in 1881.[2]

Ashworth's partner, James C. Johnston, was another Englishman. When the Swan Land and Livestock Company fired Alexander H. Swan as U. S. manager of the company, Johnston was hired for two months to supervise the count of the Swan herds, which had been purchased on the basis of book count. At the end of this assignment, Johnston was briefly considered for the manager's job, but did not receive an offer because of unstated "personal habits" and the fact that the Ashworth and Johnston operation had not been successful. These considerations apparently did not damage his long term prospects, since Johnston became manager of The Prairie Cattle Company in 1890, and the ultimate revenge on his detractors in the Swan Company came when he was elected a director of that company in 1912 and became chairman three years later.[3]

Ashworth's manager was Wilfred Jevons, whose life ended tragically. Jevons was sufficiently attracted to the American West to become a naturalized citizen of the United States; he married Grace McKeown in 1894, and in the same year they bought Ashworth's interest in the Picture Frame ranch. Then in 1895, Jevons shot himself at Arland following a "social" game of cards with Dr. Johnson, the dentist; it is said that the incident arose from his infatuation with a young woman who also worked for Ashworth. Jevons, whose family came from Manchester, England, was 35 at the time of his death, and his widow was only 18; she was the beneficiary of a $10,000 life insurance policy with New York Life Insurance Company. John Dyer took Jevons' position with Ashworth.[4]

The Ashworth operation apparently involved investments from other

---

[2]Plunkett diaries, September 6, 1881. The roof of the Ashworth headquarters building was blown off in a storm early in 1884. *The Billings Herald*, February 23, 1884 and *Daily Gazette*, May 6, 1887. Frank Canton, who was no enemy of the British, was puzzled at the animus shown them, particularly the Frewen brothers. Frank M. Canton to Thomas Sturgis, November 11, 1881, Wyoming Stock Growers Association collection, University of Wyoming.

[3]In 1887, Johnston said he had been with Ashworth for five years. Finlay Dun to Swan headquarters, Western Range Cattle Industry Study. Also John Clay, Jr., *My Life on the Range*, 200.

[4]*Red Lodge Picket*, October 7, 1893, March 17, 1894, April 6, 1895 and *Billings Gazette*, February 23, 1895. Jevons was born March 10, 1858 and shot himself February 17, 1895; he was naturalized in the summer of 1881. *Carbon County Journal*, June 13, 1881. The jealousy motive for Jevons' suicide is given in Bob Edgar and Jack Turnell, *Brand of a Legend* (Cody, Wyoming, 1978), 81, but A. A. Anderson has a thinly disguised version of the story in his autobiography, where he identifies Jevon's wife as the woman in the case, with Ashworth himself as the other man. Anderson, *op. cit.*, 79.

members of the Ashworth family, and we can infer that it may not have been profitable, for early in 1896 a Helena lawyer came to the ranch to take possession on behalf of Richard's father; Richard was to continue to operate the ranch under the lawyer's supervision. Nevertheless, family relations were not so strained as to prevent Richard's brother Oliver from spending the summer on the ranch in 1898. Richard Ashworth died on a boat in the Mediterranean, under circumstances said to have been "mysterious."[5]

In the southern part of the Basin, the British outfits headquartered in the Powder River Basin sent herds to the range across the Big Horns; one such example was the EK ranch of Horace Plunkett, who arrived in the Powder River Basin in the fall of 1879, when he was 25. Plunkett came west for his health, and he fretted about his physical condition throughout his life. He was 5'10" tall and weighed only 132 pounds; plagued by diarrhea when he became overtired, he often had trouble sleeping, and spending a night on the ground, with only a blanket separating his bony hips from the gravel underneath, was a painful experience. Plunkett's projects in Wyoming were as diverse as those of Moreton Frewen, and he was involved in ranching down on the Laramie Plains, a huge irrigation project, the electric light company in Cheyenne and speculation in railroad lands.[6]

The EK ranch was originally a partnership between Horace Plunkett and Alexis Charles Burke Roche, unmarried and 25, son of Lord Fermoy. Roche stammered, but a more annoying trait was his tendency to ignore the feelings of others, while insisting on respect for his own. Although Alexis had been in the household of the Viceroy of Ireland before coming West, he had not attended "public" school, as Horace Plunkett had, and the latter thought this lack of training for the life of a gentleman explained why he lorded it over the stable boys.[7]

---

[5]N. J. McConnell of the Helena firm of McConnell, Gunn and McConnell came to take possession of the ranch. *Red Lodge Picket*, February 20, 1896. Also, *Billings Gazette*, June 24, 1898.

[6]Horace Curzon Plunkett was born October 24, 1854, third son of Baron Dunsany. He was knighted in 1903 and died March 26, 1932. The Plunkett & Roche partnership began October 15, 1879. Plunkett diaries, August 26, 1881. The Ione Cattle Company had a number of contracts to buy land from the Union Pacific Railroad; it was a venture involving Plunkett and E. S. R. Boughton. The Wyoming Development Company had a huge irrigation project, and it involved a number of key political figures, including Governor Hoyt, Francis E. Warren, Judge Joseph M. Carey, and the banker Morton E. Post.

[7]Alexis Roche was Gentleman at Large in the household of the Duke of Marlborough when the duke was Lord Lieutenant of Ireland. In 1889, after he had left the West, Roche married Lucy Maude Groschen, eldest daughter of the Chancellor of the Exchequer. Horace Plunkett attended Eton, one of the most famous of the great English public schools, which were really private schools. Plunkett diaries, August 31, 1884, May 22, 1887.

The Plunkett and Roche partnership had other investors, including Alexis' brother Edmund Roche, 20, and Edward S. R. Boughton, 21, son of a baronet. We do not know when the EK began sending cattle into the Big Horn Basin, but at least by 1883 Alexis Roche had built a cabin on Little Canyon Creek, and by the summer of 1885, they regarded the Nowater as their winter range.[8]

In 1886, the EK and NH ranches were combined with other properties to form the Frontier Land and Cattle Company, with a capital of $1.5 million and some 18,000 head of cattle; Plunkett was named president, with a salary of $3,000 per year. The EK partners were shareholders of the new company, and there were some new investors, although not so many as Plunkett would have liked, for most of his neighbors on the range declined to join. Andrew Gilchrist joined the company, bringing with him his ranch on Crow Creek, near Cheyenne.

Gilchrist was older than Plunkett; he was born in Ayrshire, Scotland in 1841, a descendant of the old covenantors, and he had been in the Life Guards, the senior regiment in the British Army, but, alas—as Plunkett noted in his diary—he had only served as a private. He was married in Scotland before coming to Connecticut in 1870; he came west to Greeley, Colorado, in the same year and five years later he was ranching in Wyoming, and by the time Plunkett met him, he had built up a "considerable" fortune from nothing.[9]

Another Frontier shareholder was young W. D. "Beau" Watson-Smythe, grandson of Robert Watson, the legendary "Old Master" of hounds at the Meath hunt, back in Ireland. Beau Watson first came to Cheyenne in the spring of 1885, and the trip north to the Powder River was his first experience at camping in the open. Nevertheless, he quickly adapted to the new environment, and soon was working for Johnny Pierce on the WP outfit in the Big Horn Basin. Watson was to become Plunkett's most trusted employee, and Horace said on one occasion that sending Beau to look after matters permitted him to be in two places at once; yet the young man was slow to approach a point of social equality with

---

[8] Alexis Charles Burke Roche was born July 28, 1852, and Edmund Burke Roche was born in 1859; their older brother Edward had succeeded their father as Baron Fermoy in 1874. Edward Shuckburgh Rouse Boughton was born in 1858. Plunkett slept in the Roche cabin on Little Canyon Creek in June 1883. Plunkett diaries, June 5, 1883; also, July 17, October 13, 1884, June 9, 1885. Hugh Cullen agreed to invest 1,000 pounds in Plunkett & Roche, and Thomas Leonard put in 4,000 pounds. Plunkett diaries, January 11, 14, 1882.

[9] Plunkett diaries, May 9, 1883 and Bancroft interviews, University of Wyoming.

Horace, despite the fact that the Watsons were supposed to have been distant relatives of the earls of Rockingham.[10]

One of Plunkett's other ranching partnerships was one he organized in 1882 with Henry J. Windsor and John C. Coble, both of whom also later became shareholders in the Frontier company. This partnership had cattle on the Nowood as early as the spring of 1883, and they later spent $153,000 to acquire the WP herd of Worden P. Noble, which was ranging on Ten Sleep Creek; that herd was placed in the hands of John Pierce as foreman. Late in 1883, Thomas Sturgis approached Plunkett to get him to dispose of $500,000 of Union Cattle Company stock in England, giving Horace a share in management and a 5% commission, payable in stock. When Moreton Frewen gave up his managership of the Powder River Cattle Company, Plunkett reluctantly took over that task as well, to protect his own extensive interests nearby.[11]

Plunkett's operations in the Basin did not immediately prosper. In the fall of 1883, he came over to the Basin to observe the steer gathering, and found the WP cattle were not fat, although the numbers showed up well. The following year, he brought some bulls for the WP outfit from Gilchrist's Crow Creek ranch; in the spring 1885 roundup, the situation was a bit more encouraging, for Plunkett saw no dead cattle on the Nowater range, which he rode over thoroughly. Conditions on the Powder River were even more crowded than in the Basin, and in that same summer Plunkett agreed with Windsor to send their steers from the Powder River to a new range on the Upper Nowood; the steers were sent over to the Basin a month later. The following spring there were also cattle from the Powder River company in the Basin.[12]

The fall gather in 1885 was poor, land titles were proving hard to get, and the price of beef was down in the spring of 1886. Plunkett came over to the Basin in the summer of 1886 to round up more cattle to be sent to Alberta for the Powder River company, having failed to find enough across the mountains.[13]

Plunkett was given to wide swings of opinion on people and his rela-

---

[10]Elizabeth, Countess of Fingall, *Seventy Years Young* (Dublin, 1991), 198-200. Also, Plunkett diaries, May 22, 24, June 8, 1885, and July 4, 1887.

[11]Plunkett agreed to manage the Powder River Company on condition that it be liquidated. Plunkett was also partner with Morstom Tibbetts in the partnership of Tibbetts & Co. Plunkett diaries, April 21, 1886.

[12]Plunkett diaries, September 9, 1883, May 8, 1884 and June 9, 10, 27, 29, 1885.

[13]Plunkett diaries, September 27, 1885, April 28, June 17, 1886.

tionships with his partners were often stormy. In the fall of 1885, Pierce told Plunkett that Windsor had inflated the brand tally, but Horace later accepted Windsor's assurance to the contrary, and the incident did not end their business relationship. In the spring of 1887 Plunkett fired Alexis Roche, who had been associated with him for eight years, because Roche's relations with the neighbors were so poor the latter refused to cooperate with him on the range. Plunkett's choices in foremen were uniformly bad on the Powder River range, although he had a high regard for, and a good relationship with, Johnny Pierce, who ran the WP outfit in the Big Horn Basin.[14]

The foreign aristocrats often had enough money to try new ideas, and Plunkett was no exception. He began to worry about overcrowding on the range at least as early as the fall of 1884, and the next year the Frontier company acquired a facility for winter feeding located north of Omaha at Herman, Nebraska, in an effort to reduce the risk of winter losses. Plunkett visited the facility in the fall of 1885, and sent young Watson-Smythe there to look after the books. Although he thought the feeding operation was going well the following spring, by fall it was apparent that the facility, which was being run by Gilchrist, had lost $250,000 in less than a year; while Horace was contemplating this, a prairie fire worsened the situation by burning pastures and threatening to wipe out the haystacks. The Herman facility was transferred to Windsor when the Frontier company was broken up in 1886.[15]

Although Plunkett and his business associates had substantial operations in the Basin, they never actually lived there, and instead crossed the mountain from time to time to look after matters there. Indeed, even when he was on the Powder River, Plunkett favored the relative luxury of the Bar C ranch headquarters of Peters and Alston in preference to his own accommodations on the EK and NH ranches, or the Frewen's big house on the 76 Ranch of the Powder River company. The trip to the Big Horn Basin was a long one, frequently in freezing weather, even when the ranges below were under summer sun. Plunkett complained that to live in Wyoming, one should have both winter and summer clothing at all times.

---

[14]Plunkett diaries, September 27, 1885, May 9, 21, 1887. Plunkett had to fire Jack Donahue and Phil du Fran, while "Roach" Chapman fled the scene after he was arrested for horse stealing. In the summer of 1886, Horace fired Nate Champion for lack of work, and that unfortunate man would die six years later at the time of the cattlemen's invasion of Johnson County.

[15]Plunkett diaries, August 25, 1884, November 2, 1885 and April 19, September 14, November 4, 1886.

On his last trip to the Basin in the summer of 1888, a hailstorm hit the region, and stones bounced six feet in the air and killed chickens; the same storm also struck across the mountain, where it killed a colt and a calf on Crazy Woman Creek.[16]

Plunkett followed the usual pattern of the foreign rancher, going home to Ireland for the winter and returning in the spring. Although he spent a good deal of time in Wyoming, Plunkett claimed not to have any interest in the country, except for business. His great passion was fox hunting, and when he was in County Meath, he would ride out nearly every day during the hunt season, for a total of more than thirty hunts each year. Most of the other owners of the large ranches left the range for at least a part of the winter. Otto Franc and Paul Breteche preferred California, where Franc went fishing off Catalina Island, and Breteche and his wife went to Alameda. Jean de Hedouville lived most of the time in Florida, and Albert de Caillet also went there, where he had lumber interests. Like Plunkett, Ashworth and James Winn went home to Britain, while the other French counts went to France. For some, such as Otto Franc, the winter trip was a matter of only a few weeks, while the French counts seldom came back to the West before midsummer.

Another of Plunkett's close associates did maintain a ranch headquarters in the southeast Basin. This was the Big Horn Cattle Company, using the Bar X Bar brand and managed by Algernon James Winn, third son of Lord St. Oswald. Winn, born in 1861, was a close friend of Moreton Frewen, and as early as the fall of 1880, Frewen tried to devise a way to induce Jim Winn to come to Wyoming, and in the summer of 1882, when Frewen was in England visiting Nostell Priory, the Winn family seat, the family asked him to write their son Jim and invite him to join the cattle industry in Wyoming.[17]

In 1882, Horace Plunkett also saw Jim Winn, whose sister was about to marry to one of Plunkett's cousins (causing Winn to call Horace his "cousin on toast"). The two men settled on the plan to purchase Worden P. Noble's Ten Sleep herd, splitting it two-thirds for Plunkett and one-third

---

[16]There were still hailstones on the ground 24 hours after the storm. Plunkett diaries, July 27, 1888.

[17]Some have erroneously assumed that the Big Horn Cattle Company was Frewen's operation. Frewen diary, July 20, 1882. Winn was born January 12, 1861. His father was created first baron St. Oswald on July 6, 1885; he was a member of parliament and had been a Lord of the Treasury. L. G. Pine, *Burke's Peerage* (London, 1953), 1159. Also, Moreton Frewen to Clara Jerome, October 9, 1880, Frewen Collection.

for Winn. Plunkett made the deal with Noble in January 1883, for $153,000, buying the herd in a partnership with Windsor and Andrew Gilchrist, but Winn was unable to raise his share of the money. Winn finally got his own herd later in the year, as Frewen bought a trail herd from one Fisher at $33 per head and another from Clark and China on Montana's Sun River (for $34 per head). To cement his position in Wyoming society, Winn joined the Cheyenne Club in 1883, and in the same year he joined the Wyoming Stock Growers Association.[18]

When Plunkett came across the mountains to visit the spring or fall roundup, or simply to ride over the range, he always stopped to see Jim Winn. In the summer of 1885, he came over to inspect the Nowater country, and spent some time with Winn, discussing what could be done to hold the range against settlers. Although he did not commit these plans to his diary, he was soon back in the Basin, bringing a surveyor to lay out claims under the Desert Land Act. The temperature was 87° on Ten Sleep Creek, making the task of finding survey corners a hot one, and Horace took a bath in the ice-cold creek.[19]

When the Union Pacific was the only railroad in the region, the cattle from the Big Horn Basin were trailed south over the mountains for shipment, but after the Northern Pacific reached Montana, the ranchers in the north end of both the Powder River Basin and the Big Horn Basin trailed their cattle north to shipping points on that railroad. Another alternative became available after the Northwestern reached Douglas; then the outfits in the southern part of the Powder River Basin trailed south to that shipping point, and they moved their stock from the Big Horn Basin east over the mountains to join the herds to be shipped over the Northwestern. After the Cheyenne Northern built north from Cheyenne, the ranchers bound for the Powder River Basin often used that railroad as far north as Wendover, before taking the stage for the remainder of the trip.[20]

On this trip Plunkett was joined by a stock inspector, of the "cool dark devil type," with a careless sleepy manner which belied the energy which his calling obviously demanded. The country was also "infested" by Indi-

---

[18]In 1883, Laura Sophia Priscilla "Bea" Winn was married to Lord Cloncurry, who in turn was descended from the barons Dunsany. Plunkett diary, December 12, 13, 1882, January 15, May 8, 1883 and October 31, 1889. Also, Frewen diary, May 12, 1883, Cheyenne Club membership list and Wyoming Stock Growers Association applications, American Heritage Center, University of Wyoming.

[19]Plunkett diaries, June 11, 15, July 20, 1885.

[20]Plunkett diaries, June 28, 1885.

ans, and a Cheyenne brave asked Plunkett to "mend" his rifle, but Horace avoided the task by saying "No savvy." The Cheyenne was not convinced this was so, pointing to the camp blacksmith and saying "Hot man savvy!"

Sometimes the rigors of life on the range was at least a match for the skills of the young aristocrats. In the summer of 1883, Winn came to Plunkett's EK ranch with Clement Finch, younger brother of Lord Aylesford, and with Plunkett they set out to join the roundup in the Nowood country, guided by Robert Stewart. They spent the night in Alexis Roche's cabin, but after searching in vain for the roundup for five days, Plunkett nearly drowned while crossing the swollen Ten Sleep creek, at which point Winn abandoned the search and left Plunkett to go on alone. Plunkett then hired Eugene Frank Sykes, a young trapper in the Basin, to guide him, first to Shell Creek and then to the mouth of the Nowood, a journey which necessitated a crossing of that stream, also swollen by spring runoff. Plunkett's horse, still unrecovered from his experience in the Ten Sleep, rolled over in the Nowood and drowned, so that Plunkett had to complete the six miles to the roundup on Sykes' horse.[21]

Although Plunkett did not comment on Frank Sykes, this trapper and guide was born in Michigan, and when Plunkett met him he was about 27 years old. Sykes was an irascible character who seemed to enjoy frightening people, and kept his own private blacklist of those who had offended him in some way. He carried a long barrel .44 pistol that protruded an inch or two beyond his holster, which he used to threaten people who offended him, but it was apparently seldom fired, for the cartridges in the cylinder were corroded when he died, although the left side of the barrel was shiny from rubbing against his buckskins.

A short man, Sykes was perhaps not over five feet six, but he was stout and muscular, and the loss of an eye in an accident in the Big Horns gave him a truly fearsome appearance. He came to the Paint Rock country about 1882, and he had at least one Indian wife; in 1888 he married Minnie May Forshee, who was then only 16. Their only child soon died, and by 1890, she had left his "bed and board;" Minnie died in the fall of 1894, and Frank buried her outside the limits of his small ranch, because she, too, had got on his blacklist. Sykes moved from the Paintrock area to a small ranch on the Montana line near Sykes Springs, a tributary of Crooked Creek. There he pastured a few animals and tanned hides; on "tanning days," he stripped down to a breechclout or less, and posted a

---
[21]Plunkett diary, June 4, 5, 10, 12, 1883.

sign at the gate warning visitors to stay away. Although he seems not to have had many friends, the girls in the area answered advertisements in his name, so as to swell the mail volume of the fledgling post office.[22]

The Wyoming Stock Growers Association meeting in the fall of 1885 tried to reduce costs in the industry by reducing the scale of wages and abolishing the free board system on the range. Plunkett had taken a lead in these discussions, and all winter the disgruntled cowboys on the range talked of shooting him. When Horace returned to the Basin the following spring, only Johnnie Pierce was cordial to him, although nobody apparently tried to shoot him.

Winn's foreman for the Big Horn Cattle Company was Milo Burke, and Frank Bull was the so-called ranch keeper. Winn hired Frank Spicer Ainsworth, who had been trapping in the mountains, to build a house on Canyon Creek, as headquarters for the ranch. Horace Plunkett visited Winn's ranch in the summer of 1884 and remarked that the house was on a "lovely site by the waterfall of Canyon Creek," but the roof was still not finished. According to Ainsworth's description, the house was to have large rooms, with carpet on the floors and a total of seven fireplaces. Winn insisted that only "first cut" logs be used, and finding the necessary timber caused construction to proceed slowly; when young Frank Bull and his new bride arrived late in the fall of 1883 to go to work, the house was still not ready to be occupied. They moved into one room the following March; it was a spartan life for Mrs. Bull, who is said to have been the first white woman to live in the Basin. Winn enthusiastically told Frewen that he wanted to build a telephone line over to the 76 ranch, a distance of 60 miles (Frewen already had a telephone between his 76 ranch headquarters and the Powder River crossing), but this ambitious project never bore fruit.[23]

At first things on the Bar X Bar seemed to go well, as Winn told the *Gazette* that he had 27,000 head of cattle on the range, and could produce

---

[22]Eugene Frank Sykes was born in Michigan, about 1856, and he and Minnie May Forshee were married March 7, 1888; Minnie died September 29, 1894, according to a postscript Frank wrote on an unmailed letter she had written, which is in the possession of Mrs. Ivan Tippetts, Lovell, Wyoming. The Bonanza *Rustler* of June 14, 1890 carried an advertisement in which Sykes disclaimed responsibility for his wife's debts. There are several references to Sykes' Indian wife or wives, perhaps the most detailed being that of Clyde Barndt of Bridger, Montana, who gave an interview to Mrs. Clark Burrell of Lovell, Wyoming, on March 13, 1961, in which he claimed there were two Indian wives.

[23]Frank Bull was born February, 1855, in New York, and Milo Burke was ten years younger, born in Nebraska in January, 1865, according to the 1900 census for Big Horn County, Wyoming; Ainsworth was born in Iowa, in April, 1857. Plunkett diary, June 9, 1884 and Moreton Frewen to Clara Frewen, July 16, 1883.

a four-year-old steer for $4; it is likely that this report was considerably inflated. Winn said he had sold 1,200 head in the fall of 1885 for $27 a head and the next spring, he was able to report that he would ship 500 head of cattle, and that they had been able to put up 180 tons of hay cut from ranch land; nevertheless, the calf crop was only fair. In 1886, Burke, acting as Winn's agent, filed an appropriation on the Winn Ditch from Ten Sleep Creek to irrigate 880 acres, and in 1888, Winn filed on the Perfection Ditch, also from Ten Sleep Creek, to irrigate 500 acres.[24]

Although the Indians were not actually hostile, they came to the Basin to hunt and beg for cattle to eat. In the summer of 1884, the Shoshonis were in the Nowood country at roundup time, and surprisingly they did not ask for what Plunkett called their "usual 5th portion," but an Arapaho band came to beg, and claimed they were only killing buffalo, but that the Shoshonis had killed two of Winn's cattle, whose brand they described. In the fall of 1885, Winn complained that 75 families of Crow Indians were camped nearby, killing cattle.[25]

In the fall of 1884, there was an accident involving one of Winn's friends that gave a name to one of the tributaries of Ten Sleep Creek, and set in motion a story that still circulates in the West. That fall, Gilbert Henry Chandos Leigh, a young member of the British parliament and eldest son of Lord Leigh of Stoneleigh Abbey, came to the Frewen ranch in the Powder River country for a hunting trip, before continuing west to San Francisco to meet his brother Dudley. With Leigh was William Henry ("Willy") Grenfell, former member of parliament from Salisbury, who later gave a detailed account of the incident. Both men were good friends of Frewen, but the latter had left his ranch for Cheyenne on September 17. Leigh and Grenfell were guided by Robert Stewart, a well-known guide from the area, and they took with them a cook and a number of men.[26]

---

[24]*Cheyenne Daily Sun*, August 21, 1885, *Democratic Leader*, October 14, 1886 and *Daily Gazette*, April 12, 1886.

[25]Plunkett did not credit the Arapaho story, which he attributed to the enmity between the two tribes, who were now forced to share the Wind River Reservation. Plunkett diaries, June 5, 1884.

[26]Leigh, son of the second baron Leigh and the daughter of the Marquess of Westminster, was born September 1, 1851, and educated at Harrow School and Cambridge University, where he received the M. A. degree in 1878. He was elected on the Liberal slate from South Warwickshire in 1880. He was unmarried at the time of his death, so that the barony later descended on his brother, Francis Dudley Leigh. Frewen and Leigh had been in Acacia Lodge together. Frewen heard of the accident while he was in Cheyenne, on September 24, 1884. Grenfell was born October 30, 1855. He was elected to parliament from Salisbury in 1880, and on several other occasions after that. He was raised to the peerage as Baron Desborough of Taplow in 1905. L. G. Wickham Legg and E. T. Williams, eds., *The Dictionary of National Biography, 1941-1950* (London, 1959), 328.

They crossed from the Powder River country by way of the headwaters of the Tongue River and made camp on Ten Sleep Creek. It was Leigh's custom to hunt alone, and on September 12, the day before he was to leave Wyoming, he left camp at sunrise, saying he was going to kill an elk. When he did not return in the evening, the men at the camp were concerned, and the following morning they rode down to a nearby ranch (probably Winn's), to inquire if Leigh had spent the night there. On learning that he had not been seen at the ranch, five men searched for him; his horse was found two miles from camp, with Leigh's coat tied on its back. No further trace of him was found, and the search went on daily for a week; on September 21, the searchers found Leigh's hat nearly three miles from camp, and then finally the body, located behind a rock eighty feet high, some 300-400 feet down the canyon from the rim. The skull was fractured and the legs broken.

Grenfell retraced Leigh's steps from the camp on the creek below. The canyon's walls were sheer at this point, with no ledge extending lower than 100 feet from the ground, so that the only access to the top was a mile and a half up the canyon. Leigh had climbed to the top and then followed the rim of the canyon downstream; he was on foot and apparently returning to his horse when he fell. At the point where he fell, the rim of the canyon shelves quickly, and was very slick, the ground covered with loose stones.

The body was placed on the trunks of two trees that had been lashed together, and in this fashion was carried the 25 miles back to Frewen's ranch on the Powder River. The remains were then taken to the railroad at Rock Creek, and early on the morning of October 6, the coffin started east in the company of Francis Dudley Leigh, younger brother of the dead man. The funeral was held in England on October 22, 1884, and Frewen was back there for the occasion, sending a wreath from Gillie's western friends and a card saying, "From western Ranchemen, in memory of the friend of many campfires." The Buffalo photographer, M. D. Houghton, was commissioned to photograph the site of the accident for Leigh's relatives.[27]

The Wyoming capacity for legend-making then took over. It was said that the weather was so bad when Leigh's body was found that he was kept

---

[27]Grenfell's account is in most respects in agreement with the story in the *Big Horn Sentinel*, October 11, 1884. *The Warwick and Warwickshire and Leamington Gazette*, October 18, 1884. Also, Horace Plunkett diary, October 6, 1884 and Frewen diary. Houghton returned from photographing the accident site in the canyon at the end of October. *Big Horn Sentinel*, November 1, 1884.

Gilbert Henry Chandos Leigh, for whom Leigh Creek is named, fell to his death in Ten Sleep Canyon in 1884. *Courtesy Wyoming State Museum.*

frozen in the back room of a cabin until spring. The true story, which we have given here in full, was also reported in the *Big Horn Sentinel*; it is, of course, far less colorful. The place from which Leigh fell is now marked by a monument purchased by Horace Plunkett and erected by Robert Stewart, and the little creek below is now named Leigh Creek.[28]

An effort to drive cattle from the Powder River range to Canada to relieve the overcrowded Wyoming ranges did not materialize soon enough to prevent the losses of the 1886-87 winter, when 75% of the cows and 50% of the steers on the Powder River range perished. When Plunkett visited the roundup in June, there were only two wagons working, where ten had been required before. Eerily, the few survivors he saw included some of the old animals he had brought on the range in 1880.[29]

---

[28]*Big Horn Sentinel*, October 11, 1884. The funeral is reported in the *Warwick & Warickshire and Leamington Gazette*, October 25, 1884. The frozen body story is often repeated, and is found in Paul Frison, *First White Woman* (Basin, Wyoming, 1969), 21. The *Big Horn Sentinel* reported on July 11, 1885 that the monument to Leigh would be erected "soon," and on October 17 it reported that Stewart had returned from doing so.

[29]Plunkett diaries, July 2, 1887.

Most of the Frontier company assets were distributed among the shareholders in late October 1886. After the disaster that was the winter of 1886-87, Plunkett met with Thomas Sturgis, who was now proposing a giant cattle trust, patterned after the Standard Oil Trust, and including the Chicago packing interests of Nelson Morris. Plunkett immediately seized upon this as a way out of his distressing financial situation, and Jim Winn also proposed to commit the Big Horn Cattle Company herds to the trust. In spite of its prestigious backers, including the governor of Colorado and Richard G. Head, manager of the old Prairie Land and Cattle Company, the trust never attracted enough cattle to make it a success. In the spring of 1888, after Sturgis' Union Cattle Company had failed, Richard Head and George W. Baxter confided to Plunkett that the trust was nothing more than Sturgis' scheme to rescue the Union Cattle Company. When Plunkett stopped at the trust offices in New York on his way West, he found Sturgis had been "dethroned."[30]

For all the misfortune, there were still some cattle on the range, for the 1888 spring roundup in the Basin found 700 WP calves to brand, but the big outfits were winding down their operations. Seeing the handwriting on the wall, Johnny Pierce asked Plunkett if he could apply for the foreman's job on the EK, which was now run by the cattle trust, and Horace regretfully let him go, thereby losing one of his few good choices for foreman. John Garrison was given the WP job.

Plunkett met Jack Donahue, onetime foreman of the EK, and learned from him that Donahue was on his way to fetch another herd to the Basin for the Bay State outfit. This seeming reversal of the pattern of decline for the large operations was explained by that company's efforts to overcome the overcrowding of its Nebraska ranges by transferring its herds to the Basin.[31]

Plunkett saw Winn in London in early 1887, and Winn was then hopeful that his ranch could be sold to Sir John Lister-Kaye, an English baronet. Lister-Kaye, tall, blond and blue-eyed, with a "fine sandy moustache," had made some money in ranching in Canada, but his penchant for exotic ideas rivaled that of the frenetic Frewen, and in fact Plunkett had earlier sold him the Canadian holdings of Frewen's former company, the

---

[30]The cattle trust had 218,934 head (excluding calves and bulls) committed to it in 1888, and this total had declined by 50,000 to 164,472 the following year. Gene M. Gressley, *Bankers and Cattlemen* (Lincoln, Nebraska, 1966), 264-65. Also, Plunkett diaries, January 21, May 24, 26, 1888.

[31]Plunkett diaries, July 4, August 4, 15, 1888.

Powder River Cattle Company. Unfortunately for Winn, the often erratic Lister-Kaye did not buy the Big Horn Cattle Company, and when Winn and Plunkett visited the range in June, the headquarters had already been abandoned; Burke was discharged as foreman in the fall of 1887 and replaced by Charles Carter.[32]

The company was not without assets, for the 1888 assessment list for Fremont County shows 1,950 head on the rolls, valued at $21,900, and the rolls of Johnson County showed 100 head of horses and 2,000 cows valued at $25,500. In the summer of 1888, Winn disposed of the remaining cows for $22.50 and the beef animals for $28.50, delivered at Rock Creek. Frederick George Samuel Hesse, Frewen's old foreman on the Powder River range, reported in September, 1888 that Winn had gone to Cheyenne to get another job; the hay on the ranch was sold to the Bay State Company. Finally, in 1893, Winn disposed of the remaining property to Fred G. S. Hesse, for 800 pounds sterling. Winn, still unmarried, died on August 7, 1894.[33]

Plunkett disposed of his share of the Tibbetts & Company partnership in the Basin for shares in the Frontier company held by Charles Wyndham-Quin, a cousin of Lord Dunraven. In the fall of 1887, he burned papers "by the bushel" as he prepared to abandon his American cattle ranching ventures. Geoffrey Millais, son of the painter, photographed the ranch headquarters as a memento. In Cheyenne, there was a party at the Cheyenne Club to say goodbye.[34]

---

[32] Book D, Johnson County clerk, 263, 632-33 and Plunkett diary, March 22, June 20, 1887. Lister-Kaye, born in 1853, was from a distinguished English family; his brother-in-law was Lord Mandeville, eldest son and heir of the Duke of Manchester. Both Lister-Kaye and Mandeville had married American heiresses who were sisters, the daughters of Antonio Yznaga del Valle of Ravenswood, Louisiana. Edward Brado, *Cattle Kingdom: Early Ranching in Alberta* (Toronto, 1984), 263. W. A. Richards noted Burke's dismissal in a letter to his brother Arthur, February 22, 1888 and Plunkett said Carter was the new foreman in his entry of October 4, 1887.

[33] The 1888 Fremont County assessment figure is from the *Fremont Clipper* (Lander, Wyoming), July 19, 1888; the same article lists 1,925 head for Horace Plunkett's Frontier Land and Cattle Company, valued at $21,175. The Johnson County assessment is from the *Big Horn Sentinel*, July 14, 1888. The deed to Hesse was dated April 12, 1893; it gives Winn's residence as 9 Billiter Square, London; Hesse, who had been Frewen's foreman in the Powder River country was then living in Omaha, a reluctant exile from his Johnson County properties as a result of his involvement in the Johnson County War of 1892. American Heritage Center, University of Wyoming. Also, F. G. S. Hesse to F. A. Kemp, September 4, 1888, F. G. S. Hesse to A. J. Winn, January 27, 1890, F. G. S. Hesse letterbooks, in possession of Fred E. Hesse. Also, Plunkett diaries, July 7, 1888.

[34] Charles Frederick Talbot Wyndham-Quin was born in 1864; his mother was the sister of Lord Mayo, who was also connected by marriage to Horace Plunkett's family. Plunkett diaries, October 19, 1887.

In the aftermath of the winter of 1886-87, there were fewer of the foreign aristocrats in the Basin, although some appeared from time to time after that. After his father died in 1889, Horace Plunkett came less often to America, because the fortune he had inherited now demanded his attention in Britain, and he no longer felt pressure to make his fortune in the West. Still, a few remained, as when Cecil Clifton and Harold Arthur Lowther came down to the Big Horn Basin from their Northfield ranch near Roundup, Montana, in the fall of 1895, "looking up sheep;" two years later, Lowther left for British Columbia, on his way to the Klondike.[35]

[35]Lowther was a cousin of Lord Lonsdale and Clifton was a younger son of Lord Grey de Ruthyn, but would unexpectedly succeed to the barony in 1912. The partners were still acquiring land in Montana in 1903 and 1904. *The Billings Gazette*, November 9, 1895. Cecil Clifton was born January, 1862 and died in 1934. *New York Times*, May 23, 1934. The deeds to Clifton and Lowther are recorded in the Fergus County clerk's office, Roundup, Montana. The baron Grey de Ruthyn had the hereditary privilege to bear the sovereign's golden spur at the coronation. Harold Lowther was born in 1864. He made the trip to British Columbia in the company of the Billings city clerk (one Herford). *The Billings Gazette*, November 23, 1897.

CHAPTER IX

The End of the Range Cattle Era

In the summer of 1883, when the Northern Pacific was considering a subsidy for the bridge over the Stinking Water, Charles Wilson was sent from St. Paul to the Big Horn Basin to guage the commercial significance of the cattle ranches there. Wilson listed herd sizes for the operators in the Basin, and these numbers were later published in the Billings *Post* and the *Herald*, giving us an early view of the size of the cattle operations in the Basin in that year.[1]

The largest herd was that of Mason and Lovell, at 12,000 head, followed closely by Captain Robert E. Torrey (10,000) and by Otto Franc and Windsor & Plunkett, (each with 7,000), and William A. Carter, John Luman and Harvey Booth (each with 6,000). C. W. Wright on Wind River and George W. & J. A. Baxter were each listed at 4,000, and Captain Henry Belknap's total was given at 3,000, while Richard Ashworth & James C. Johnston were listed at 2,000 head. The list was completed with 800 head for George Wise & Livingston on Meeteetse Creek and 600 head for Speed Stagner at the Hot Springs on the Big Horn; the *Post* article admitted that there were other smaller herds. If the totals are reasonably accurate, the Big Horn Basin could not have held more than 100,000 head at this time, and in fact the *Herald* gave the total as 55,600.[2]

By 1885, cattle operations in the Big Horn Basin and other areas tributary to Billings made it possible for that city to take first place in Montana

---
[1]*Post* (Billings, Montana), March 31, 1883 and *The Billings Herald*, June 2, 16, 1883. The two newspapers give slightly different lists, but they are in general agreement.
[2]Speed Stagner was born about 1848, in Kentucky, according to the 1880 census.

cattle shipments; nevertheless, this was the high water mark of the industry, for bad times were close at hand. In the spring of 1886, the *Gazette* reported that a big influx of herds was expected in the Owl Creek and Nowood country that season, but also noted that cattle in Custer and Choteau counties (Montana) were weak and thin; those west of the Big Horn and south of the Musselshell were in better shape. Overcrowding was obviously taking its toll.[3]

The winter of 1886-87 has been blamed for the demise of the range cattle industry, and it is true that the industry as it had existed before that winter was gone after the spring thaw finally came, but it is an exaggeration to claim that weather alone did this to the industry. The ranges were overstocked and the stock were thin and weak before the cold weather came. Cattle prices had dropped in 1885, and were even lower the following year. By November 1886, the Chicago cattle market was "demoralized," and the *Gazette* speculated gloomily that the season for shipping would be the smallest in the history of Billings. The actual results were not that bad, and the cattlemen did ship more animals in 1886 than the year before, but the price was $10 to $15 per head less than 1885, which in turn had been $10 on the average below 1884.[4]

Even though forage was poor, cattlemen assumed that the price slide would not continue, and held large numbers over the winter, in the hopes of reaping the benefits of an expected price increase. Conditions were made worse by the fact that fall rains came too late to generate grass growth, range fires struck a number of sections, and wolves and coyotes were especially plentiful.[5]

Then the snows came, heavy enough to delay the Pacific Express on the Northern Pacific by as much as six hours, and one record says that it snowed nearly every day in the months of December, January and February. Cowboys marooned for months in remote cabins, often lacked sufficient supplies. There are few contemporary records which are detailed enough to given the full story. Otto Franc kept a diary in which he made nearly daily notations on the weather. His record shows the first snow fell

---

[3]The *Daily Gazette* (Billings) for January 4, 1886 gives total 1885 shipments as 15,587 head from Billings, with Mingusville (the future Wibaux) in second place with 6,856, and Miles City a poor third with 2,657. Also *Daily Gazette*, April 20, 23, 1886.

[4]The Northern Pacific shipped 83,000 head from Montana and western Dakota in 1886, as compared with 73,000 head in 1885. *Daily Gazette* (Billings), November 16, 1886.

[5]Parmly Billings Library clippings from the Three Forks, Montana, *News*.

at the Pitchfork ranch on September 15, but there were days in which the temperatures rose and there was thawing; nevertheless, by November 21, he made the ominous entry, *"Deep snow everywhere."*[6]

The diary does not give a picture of the suffering on the range, but on January 30, 1887, three Crow Indians visited the ranch and told Franc that there were dead cattle in the Sage Creek basin, and on February 4, Franc wrote, "More cattle come up from below & have to be driven off." Obviously, the cattle were not finding feed on the range.

The suffering was not confined to the animals, and Victor Arland wrote in March that several people had frozen to death, including two only fifteen miles away from his store. In one such case, Otto Franc recorded the discovery of the body of one Oldis in Kyle's cabin on February 10, but it was February 16 before the body had thawed sufficiently to bend the arms and place it in a coffin; poor Oldis was finally buried on February 18.[7]

It was weirdly ironic that the *Gazette* noted some cattlemen had consulted Madam Sampson, a "prophetess" at Miles City, who assured them that their losses in the coming winter would not be "unusually heavy." But Madam Sampson was wrong, even though the newspapers kept a strange silence through most of the winter. Then, in February, the postmaster at Albright, Montana, in Custer County said, "Foremen of the big cattle companies are sitting by the stove and only stir out to go to town or report to their employers or the editors, 'All is well on the range,' while cattle are dying by the thousands." When the long-awaited chinook arrived in March, a Miles City editor wearily wrote, "At the risk of a great setback, we cannot refrain from a third and last call. Springtime has surely come, gentle Annie."[8]

The weakened animals on the overcrowded range had died in great numbers that winter, and the carnage cast a pall over the Montana Stock Growers meeting the following April; losses in Montana were estimated at 50% in Yellowstone and Musselshell counties, and almost as bad in the Judith Basin. Arland at first estimated the losses in the Big Horn Basin at not more than 15%, but the following year, he revised that estimate to

---

[6]The Otto Franc diaries are in the Buffalo Bill Historical Center, Cody, Wyoming.

[7]Victor Arland to Camille Dadant, March 26, 1887, Victor Arland collection, Buffalo Bill Historical Center, Cody, Wyoming.

[8]*Daily Gazette* (Billings), December 1, 1886. The February, 1887 quote is from the *New York Times*, February 17, 1887. The March, 1887, quotation is from the Parmly Billings Library clippings.

"close to 50%," and he thought losses for the ranchers in Montana and the rest of Wyoming were in the range of 60%-90%. John Luman branded only 400 calves in the spring of 1887, as against 3,000 the year before.[9]

In spite of the losses on the range, prices still continued to fall, one shipment in the fall of 1887 bringing only $2.50 per cwt., and all through the year 1887, the mighty fell. Morton E. Post was still in the banking business, and he wrote plaintively to his wife in May, "how... does one go about foreclosing an entire community?" In October, Post himself was drawn into the maelstrom as his own bank failed. One indication of the size of losses was the 1888 assessment rolls for Fremont County, which fell from $1,203,576 in 1887 to $843,647 the following year; the number of cattle assessed dropped from 86,260 in 1887 to 74,390 the following year. For Johnson County, the assessed value of horses and cattle dropped from $2,886,333 in 1886 to $2,097,111.50 the following year. Although these two counties covered more area than the Basin, these numbers imply a 22% loss in assessed value for a large part of northern Wyoming.[10]

Although the losses were large, there was still room for the western love of a good story, as the *Gazette* reported that in the Judith country, where conditions were said to have been so bad that one cow died "on top of a house." The editor opined that the snow must either have been "tolerably deep," or the house "not very high."[11]

When the cattlemen first arrived, their ranches were not encumbered by specific boundaries; their operations were almost wholly on the public domain, and they moved about as range conditions and the size of their herds dictated. They seldom made an effort to acquire title to anything other than the land and water rights for headquarters locations and the occasional hay meadow. Indeed, the Wyoming Stock Growers Association overwhelmingly defeated a proposition to offer the grazing land for sale to the cattlemen; the investment would have been too large. Later,

---

[9] Victor Arland to Camille Dadant, March 26, 1887 and March 12, 1888, Victor Arland Collection, Buffalo Bill Historical Center, Cody, Wyoming. David John Wasden, *From Beaver to Oil A Century in the Development of Wyoming's Big Horn Basin* (Cheyenne, 1973), 116. Byron Wickwire said that Luman sold out for only $12,000. "Life Story of 'Kansas' Wickwire, as told to A. W. Coons."

[10] The banking firm of Morton E. Post & Co. failed following the failure of its West Cliff, Colorado bank on October 10. *The Cheyenne Daily Sun*, October 11, 1887. The Post quote is from a letter Morton E. Post to Amelia Post, May 23, 1887. Gene M. Gressley, *Bankers and Cattlemen* (Lincoln, Nebraska, 1966), 144. The Fremont County 1888 assessment is from the *Fremont Clipper*, August 23, 1888. Johnson County assessments are from the *Big Horn Sentinel*, February 4, 1888.

[11] *Daily Gazette*, May 25, 1887.

after the "die-out" of 1886-87, the survivors commenced to file on more land to give their outfits a dependable situs for their operations.

The very feature which made the free range industry so profitable ultimately proved its undoing, for even the awesome authority of the stock growers association could not keep others from using the free range and overcrowding it. Although the early ranchers did not fence except in the vicinity of the railroad, where owned ranges were checkerboarded with public land, the government made it clear in 1885 that the public lands could not be fenced.

With no fences to keep out the herds looking for feed, the overcrowded ranges soon spilled their problems onto neighboring regions, and there were few bright spots in this dreary picture. When the first hard winter struck the overcrowded ranges, the weakened animals died in great numbers, and the range cattle industry was mortally wounded. It would recover only under a different economic system, one where at least the core of the range was owned by the rancher, and finally the federal lands could be leased for grazing under the Taylor Grazing Act. The new cattle industry was now a long term industry that required heavy capital investment, and it would never again generate the high returns some of the early free range outfits had realized.[12]

In the aftermath of the winter of 1886-87, the weakened industry blamed more than overcrowding and the weather for its condition, and the bitterness the big outfits felt against the rustler faction finally had a focused expression in the events of 1892. Although not a part of our story, the invasion of Johnson County by the cattlemen threw a shadow across the Basin.

There are few extant records which describe feelings in the Basin at the time of the Johnson County invasion by the cattlemen in the spring of 1892, although it is clear that the time was not without passion on both sides. The big operators in the Basin were certainly aware of the events building up across the mountains from them, and on March 2, 1892,

---

[12]The Taylor Grazing Act, named for Congressman Edward T. Taylor of Colorado, was effective June 28, 1934; it created a system of rentals for the public lands, and laid down a system to regulate grazing use. 48 *Statutes at Large* 1269, and Wesley Calef, *Private Grazing and Public Lands: Studies of the Local Management of the Taylor Grazing Act* (Chicago, 1960), 52. A British royal commission in 1881 reported that cattle raising on the plains of the Rocky Mountain west had earned more than 33 per cent annually in the preceding ten years; some of the early outfits did even better than this average. Lawrence M. Woods, *British Gentlemen in the Wild West: The Era of the Intensely English Cowboy* (New York, 1989), 53.

Otto Franc recorded in his diary that he was leaving for Billings to attend a meeting of the stockmen of northern Wyoming, to consider ways to "protect ourselves against rustlers." He returned to the ranch on March 12, but did not commit to writing the conclusions of the Billings meeting. A second meeting was held at Baxter's LU ranch on March 20, but again we do not know what happened there. Then there was no further mention of the subject, and on April 8 and 9, when the invaders were already in Johnson County, Franc's entries dealt with the weather: ". . . the Red Lodge stage cannot run."

In the middle of March, *The Big Horn County Rustler* in Bonanza wrote a very guarded comment, saying that there were "vague hints" that the big stockmen were intending a "war of extermination" against the "so-called rustlers." The *Rustler* said that the rumors bore the mark of "having been inspired by certain knowledge based upon authentic information." But the editor said no more.[13]

George B. "Bear George" McClellan was 29 in the spring of 1892, and he was working for W. A. Richards on the west slope of the Big Horns. McClellan was in Casper buying provisions for the ranch when he learned that a force of armed men were on their way to the Powder River; he briefly considered and rejected the idea of trying to warn his friends in the Powder River country about the invading army. The following morning, the news of the invasion was a widespread topic in Casper.[14]

McClellan then faced the task of returning to Red Bank while the countryside was in an uproar, and although he was advised to wait for tempers to cool, he decided to leave for home. Three days later, he was safely at Lost Cabin, where "all was excitement," since the papers carrying the news of the invasion had just arrived from Cheyenne. Back at the ranch, McClellan was met by a messenger from Spring Creek, asking him to come over there, which he did; he found "twelve or fifteen of the boys, . . . some, if not all, of them, had been interested in rustling, more or less," to use his remarkably ambiguous description.

The delegation at Spring Creek wanted McClellan to go back over the mountain to the Powder River country to learn what was happening; presumably he was chosen for the task because he was not on the cattlemen's

---

[13] *The Buffalo Bulletin*, March 17, 1892.

[14] McClellan was born in Simcoe, Ontario, on October 18, 1862. He went to Kansas with his parents in 1868 and came to the Basin in 1883. He served as state representative in 1907 and as state senator, 1909-15 and 1931-33. He died at his ranch, October 18, 1934. "Stories by 'Bear' George B. McClellan," *Annals of Wyoming*, XXVI, No. 1 (January, 1954), 39-49; McClellan's biography is at 105.

THE END OF THE RANGE CATTLE ERA   123

blacklist. There was still heavy snow on the mountains, and McClellan was not eager to make the trip, which could only be accomplished on snow shoes or skis, but the men urged him to go, and at length he agreed, on condition that one of their number should accompany him. It fell to the lot of Tom O'Day to make the journey with Bear George.

Thomas O'Day, sometimes called "Peep," was later described by the Pinkertons as a dark-skinned man, "quarrelsome and a heavy drinker." McClellan was less specific about O'Day, saying that O'Day had some fine qualities, "and some not so fine." He added that when O'Day got drunk, he wanted to fight McClellan, just to prove he could "whip" the formidable Bear George. O'Day, who was then living on Bridger Creek, had not yet joined the famous Wild Bunch, who later robbed the bank at Belle Fourche, South Dakota in 1897; in this affray, which yielded the gang only $97, O'Day was arrested.[15]

McClellan and O'Day mounted showshoes and McClellan carried a five foot snowshoe pole that sometimes proved too short to reach down through the snowdrifts to solid ground. The two spent the night on the mountains, and after reaching the other side got horses for the trip on to Buffalo. A traveler on the road gave them news of the siege at the TA ranch, and they proceeded to that place, where they found "the whole country had turned out...," and everybody was armed: "Every mother's son of them had his gun and some of them two or three." McClellan had a laconic evaluation of the dispute between the two factions: "there was cause on both sides."

The two men went on to Buffalo, where they spent the night, and then began the trek back to the Basin. The next night was spent at Charles W. Morgareidge's ranch on the Middle Fork of the Powder River, where they were welcomed and given lodging after the nervous rancher learned their identities. The return journey over the mountain was made the more difficult for McClellan by partial snowblindness, but in due course they brought the news to Spring Creek.

The *Red Lodge Picket* speculated that the Montana stockgrowers would

---

[15]O'Day was to hold the horses for the Belle Fourche bank robbery on June 26, 1897, and his horse shied, leaving him with only a clergyman's mule to attempt his escape. This animal balked, and O'Day went to jail at Deadwood. James D. Horan, *Desperate Men: Revelations from the Sealed Pinkerton Files* (New York, 1949), 203-204. O'Day was next captured on the Big Horn Mountains with 23 stolen horses on November 23, 1903. Alfred James Mokler, *History of Natrona County 1888-1922* (New York, 1923), 327. Also, Doug Engebretson, *Empty Saddles, Forgotten Names: Outlaws of the Black Hills and Wyoming* (Aberdeen, S. D., n.d.), 173.

launch a coordinated attack on northern Wyoming in support of their Wyoming colleagues, and in May, 1892, after the invasion, there was a meeting at Owl Creek among those settlers who were concerned that an invasion might be mounted on their side of the Big Horns. Resolutions of solidarity with the anti-cattle faction were passed, and the group resolved to resist any similar invasion in their country. Early the following month, the situation had cooled enough so that the editor in Buffalo could write off the expected invasion of the Basin as a rumor.[16]

There were two killings in 1892 that grew out of the dispute between so-called rustlers and the big cattlemen, but they were not directly connected to the events across the mountain. In the fall of that year, the small stockmen mounted a roundup of their stock south of the Greybull River, and with that roundup were Jack Bedford and David A. "Dab" Burch, 26 and 30 years old, respectively, both of whom had been under surveillance by Association cattle detectives during the summer of 1892. Burch came to Wyoming from Missouri, and had gained a certain notoriety in 1889, when he fought a duel with "Pistol Billy" Rogers at Baxter's LU ranch; on that occasion, both men were wounded, but both later recovered, although Rogers died of tuberculosis soon afterward.[17]

The route of the roundup in the fall of 1892 was south from the Greybull, across the badlands to the Big Horn and up that stream to Fifteen Mile Creek, then up Fifteen Mile to Buffalo Basin, and east of Tatman Mountain to the place of beginning. On the first night of the roundup, three stray saddle horses came into the roundup, and although the foreman insisted they be cut out and left behind, Bedford and Burch wanted to take them along and advertise them as strays. On September 27, after the roundup had ended, John L. Seaman, a rancher on the Nowood, swore out a complaint for the theft of two horses on September 19 by Bedford and Burch, and a warrant for their arrest was issued. The trial was set before Walter W. Peay, justice of the peace, on October 1, at Peay's place on the lower Nowood River.

---

[16]The Montana Stock Growers Association passed resolutions in support of the invasion on April 21. *Red Lodge Picket*, April 16, 23, 1892. The committee appointed by the Owl Creek group consisted of Edmund Cusack, George M. Sliney, Banjamin Hanson, M. Brown, J. D. McCulloch and S. D. Close, with S. P. Warden as secretary. The *Fremont Clipper*, May 27, 1892. Also, *The Buffalo Bulletin*, June 9, 1892.

[17]Jack Bedford was born near Dallas, Texas, and came up the trail in 1890, after which he worked for the Mason and Lovell ranch. David A. Burch was born in Missouri and came to Wyoming in 1888 and settled on Owl creek, where he ran horses until the spring of 1892, when he moved to Otto. Bob Edgar and Jack Turnell, *op. cit.*, 73 and Tacetta B. Walker, *op. cit.*, 173.

At the trial were the two defendants, five witnesses, and three stock detectives, one of whom, John T. Wickham, worked for the Pitchfork ranch. After the trial, Seaman asked that the case be dismissed, because he no longer believed the horses had been stolen. As the defendants were preparing to return to Otto, a dispute arose between Bedford and H. B. Peverly, another of the stock detectives, and Bedford threatened to horsewhip Peverly. The two men were parted, but Peverly lodged a complaint against Bedford and Burch for disturbing the peace "by commencing a row, making threats and drawing revolver and a loded [sic] pistol." When Bedford and Burch rode back toward the crossing of the Big Horn River, they were met by the three stock detectives, who had a new warrant for the arrest of Bedford and Burch.[18]

Joseph Rodgers, the third stock detective, volunteered to take the two men back to Peay for a hearing, and the other witnesses from Otto then left. At the Peay place, Peay fined each man $10, and when they refused to pay, he remanded them to the county jail in Buffalo. Rodgers tied the men's feet under their horses, and tied the horses together. He asked permission to spend the night at the Seaman ranch at Bonanza, and this was granted. Seaman, Rodgers and the two prisoners then departed for Bonanza, and the other two stock detectives rode north and turned east past the Oyer C. Morgan place and then crossed the river to intercept the group bound for Bonanza.[19]

At Bonanza, the two stock detectives told Seaman they had decided to take the prisoners back to Peay and withdraw charges; Seaman thereupon left the prisoners with them. After Seaman's departure, the two men were shot. The bodies were discovered by Perry Townsend, who reported the incident to Peay.[20]

There was apparently a considerable uproar over the killings, but the news did not occupy center stage in the Buffalo papers. A small item appeared on October 12, reporting the deaths, but giving no details, and late in October there was an ironic comment that the deputy at Warren knew the assassins, but that Johnson County could not afford to prosecute anymore cattlemen (referring to the trial then pending in southern Wyoming for the Johnson County invasion).

---

[18]Edgar and Turnell, *op. cit.*, 74. The charge against Bedford and Burch is found in the Justice Court Docket Book, Johnson County.

[19]*Ibid.*, 74.

[20]Townsend buried the men on the bluffs, where they remained until the following March, when the bodies were removed to Otto. *Ibid.*, 75.

On November 10, the *Bulletin* reported that "Dab" Burch's father and brother in law had visited the Basin, and that his father had taken Burch's saddle home with him. Then silence prevailed, and when the county attorney of Johnson County swore out an information against Rodgers, Wickham and Peverly on November 28, charging them with first degree murder, this action was not reported at all in the *Buffalo Bulletin*.[21]

By December, Otto Franc was concerned that his man Wickham was being threatened with prosecution; Joe Rodgers, who may well have fired the shot that killed Bedford, was now also working for the Pitchfork. On December 16, Franc tersely noted in his diary, "... I sent Wickham off somewhere where the rustlers won't find him." His concern continued to mount, and in March, his foreman brought some disturbing news from the *Rustler*. Unfortunately, we do not know what that news was, but it caused Franc to leave the very next day, taking Rodgers with him to Billings; while he was gone, a sheriff's posse visited the Pitchfork looking for Rodgers. When Franc returned, he noted, "... I have provided for the safety of Joe Rogers [sic] and Wickham during my absence."[22]

The Johnson County officials had maintained a distinctly low profile in the prosecution of the three men. There was still surprisingly little information in the public press, and while some of this may have been attributable to editorial bias, it is also possible that when Johnson County was ready to proceed, it did not want to tip off the cattlemen. Why the sudden activity now? The explanation lies in the changes that had taken place in state politics. Following the Johnson County invasion, the Republicans were soundly defeated in the 1892 election at the state level, and the man elected to the governor's chair was a Democrat, the colorful Dr. John E. Osborne, who had been the man to skin Big Nose George a decade earlier.

When Governor Osborne was firmly in office (he had climbed through the window of the governor's office to ensure a "fair" canvass of the election results), the time was ripe for Johnson County to pursue the Burch and Bedford affair. It then became apparent that Franc's efforts on behalf of his men had not fully protected them. On April 29, 1893, the Johnson county attorney made a formal request for the extradition of the three fugitives from Montana, and on the same day the Johnson County sheriff wired Fergus County Sheriff Willliam D. Deaton in Lewistown, Mon-

---

[21] *The Buffalo Bulletin*, October 12, 27, November 10, 1892. The case is Joseph Rodgers, et. al., Case No. 245, Johnson County.

[22] Franc mentions the matter in diary entries of December 5 and 16, 1892, March 19, 20, 30, 1893.

tana, requesting that Wickham be arrested there. Sheriff Deaton arrested Wickham on May 1.[23]

In Cheyenne, the extradition request from Johnson County was promptly honored by Governor Osborne, under date of May 4, and the next day the sheriff in Buffalo wired Sheriff Deaton that he expected the papers "today;" two days later, another wire to Lewistown said the deputy had started from Montana "with requisition."[24]

This disturbing news reached the ear of Otto Franc, and he promptly departed for Helena, where he signed a petition to the Montana Supreme Court asking for the release of Wickham. On May 11, William Young Pemberton, the chief justice of the Montana Supreme Court, issued an order directing District Judge George R. Milburn in Billings to hold a hearing on May 16 for a writ of *habeas corpus* for Wickham.[25]

The next day, Montana's Lieutenant Governor Alexander C. Botkin, who was then acting governor of that territory, wrote Wickham's attorney apologetically, saying he did not feel he could deny the order for Wickham's extradition, even though he said deputy John D. Hopkins had admitted that the arrest warrant for Wickham was "bogus." Nevertheless, Botkin said that he had urged Governor Osborne to have Wickham conveyed to Clearmont by train, and by posse for the remaining 30 miles to Buffalo; it appears that Osborne agreed to this routing.[26]

Lt. Governor Botkin did comply with Governor Osborne's request,

---

[23]"I want Wickham arrest [sic] hold for requisition and writ." C. M. Devoe to W. D. Deaton, April 29, 1893.

[24]C. M. Devoe to W. D. Deaton, May 5, and A. G. Bennett to W. D. Deaton, May 7, 1893.

[25]Otto Franc's petition was dated May 10, 1893. Chief Justice William Young Pemberton was born in Nashville, Tennessee on June 1, 1841 and educated in Missouri; he came to Virginia City, Montana, in 1863, and was elected chief justice on the Democratic ticket in 1892 and commenced serving January 2, 1893. He died in Excelsior Springs, Missouri, August 26, 1922. Tom Stout, *Montana, Its Story and Biography*, I, (Chicago, 1921), 435. George R. Milburn, a Democrat, was born in Washington, D. C., November 15, 1850, graduated in law from National University in Washington, and was named special Indian agent in November, 1882; in 1884, he built the new Crow Agency in Montana. In 1889, he was elected district judge for the seventh district, and was reelected in 1892. *Progressive Men of the State of Montana* (Chicago, n.d.), 313.

[26]Alexander C. Botkin was born in Madison, Wisconsin, October 13, 1842, and graduated from the University of Albany, New York, in 1866. From 1868 to 1876, he worked for the *Chicago Times* and the *Milwaukee Sentinel*, and in 1878 was appointed as U. S. Marshall for Montana Territory. In 1892, he was elected lieutenant governor of Montana. *Progressive Men of the State of Montana, op. cit.*, 1640. The route agreed upon between the two governors was on the Oregon Short Line south to the connection with the Union Pacific, then east to the connection with the Burlington, and then by way of the Burlington to Clearmont, Wyoming, where the posse would meet them. Alexander C. Botkin to O. F. Goddard, May 12, 13, 1893.

and on May 13 he issued an order to any sheriff, deputy or constable in Montana to arrest Joseph Rodgers, James [sic] Wickham and John Peverley. The extradition request reached the sheriff in Lewistown on May 15, and on May 18, he delivered Wickham to Billings for the hearing that had been directed by Chief Justice Pemberton. Once the case was in the hands of Judge Milburn, matters were easier for Wickham, who was represented by Orpheus Fletcher Goddard, a power in the Montana Republican party.[27]

Goddard told Judge Milburn that the extradition request was faulty on four grounds. First, he said the information executed by the Johnson County attorney did not state facts sufficient to convince the court that a crime had been committed. Second, he said that the man claiming to be the John D. Hopkins named by the Wyoming governor as his representative to receive Wickham was in fact known in Wyoming as "Johnny Dee," and was therefore not the person identified in the request. Third, the information charged a James Wickham, not John T. Wickham, and the latter was therefore not the man charged with the crime. Finally, Goddard said the request should be denied because Wickham could not be safely conveyed to Buffalo. He pointed out that Hopkins had ignored the routing agreed upon by the two governors, and had instead placed Wickham in a wagon, intending to take him via Billings to Fort Custer and then by stage to Buffalo.[28]

The judge accepted all of the arguments advanced by Goddard, although perhaps the last was the most telling, for the judge seized on Hopkins' disregard for the Montana governor's orders as endangering Wickham's life by taking him to a place where "it is notorious that law does not prevail." In an order dated May 26, Judge Milburn ordered that a writ of *habeas corpus* should be issued for Wickham, but stayed it for two weeks to permit further referral to the governor and the Supreme Court of Montana. The excited crowd from the courthouse then watched as the Yellow-

---

[27]We are told that Goddard was called Oscar in his childhood, but as an adult he was O.F.

[28]O. Fletcher Goddard was born in Troy, Iowa, January 20, 1853; he studied law under his uncle and came to Billings in March, 1883, where he practiced law. Goddard was county prosecuting attorney and district attorney during the territorial period, and he was also attorney for the Chicago, Burlington and Quincy railroad and a director of the Montana Coal and Iron Company, which operated the Bear Creek coal mine; he also owned several irrigated ranches in Yellowstone County. A "true" Republican, he was said to have had the power to deny the Democrats a senatorial seat from Montana. Tom Stout, *op. cit.*, II, 211.

stone County sheriff raced to overtake the Wyoming deputy; the race was won by the Montana lawman.[29]

The first indication in the Wyoming press that all of this was afoot was in an item in the Laramie *Boomerang*, which quoted a "dispatch" from Buffalo, to the effect that "Peaveler" was to be picked up. Then, a Lander item of June 2 reported the arrest of Wickham in Billings, and the writ to secure his release. A more complete report from the *Billings Gazette* was quoted in the *Buffalo Bulletin* of June 8, 1893.[30]

Wickham was free, and we hear no more about him, but there was at least one further lingering effect of the Wickham affair. In the spring of 1894, Governor Osborne of Wyoming refused an extradition request from Montana, saying, however, ". . . I beg leave to reassure you that my action in this matter has not been prompted by a desire to retaliate for the discourteous treatment received at the hands of Montana's Chief Executive at the time a requisition was made by me for the delivery of a Wyoming criminal. . . ."[31]

In the aftermath of the Johnson County invasion, yet another colorful character came to the Big Horn Basin to live. He had enjoyed a varied career, and was the editor of a newspaper that unabashedly endorsed the position of the big cattlemen until just before the Johnson County invasion. The manner in which he then changed sides is an interesting story.

Asa Shinn Mercer was born in Illinois in June, 1839, and went to Washington Territory as a surveyor for the government in 1861; the following year he became the first president of the University of Washington. In 1863, Governor Pickering appointed him commissioner of immigration for Washington Territory, with the responsibility to stimulate immigration to that territory. Mercer went east to bring twelve schoolteachers to the West; they all got married, according to his later account, and the following year he hired three hundred more. From Washington Territory, Mercer went to California, where his first son was born in 1872, and then to Oregon, where he built the first grain wharf at Astoria and shipped grain to the east in sailing vessels; he sent the first cargo from Oregon to Liverpool.

---

[29]In the Matter of the Application of John T. Wickham for a Writ of Habeas Corpus, District Court, Yellowstone County, Montana. The order was dated May 26, 1893, and filed July 10, 1893. Also, *Red Lodge Picket*, May 27, 1893.

[30]*The Clipper* (Lander), May 26, June 2, 1893.

[31]John E. Osborne to John E. Rickards, April 14, 1894. *The Billings Gazette*, April 14, 1894.

Mercer then started his newspaper career with the *Oregon Granger,* in Albany, Oregon. In 1876, he left Washington Territory and moved to Texas, where he started a number of papers; at one time he is said to have owned all except one of the newspapers between Decatur, Texas, and the New Mexico line, including the *Texas Panhandle* at Mobeetie, the *Cross Timbers* at Bowie, the *Wichita Herald* and the *Vernon Guard* at Vernon. While attending a livestock meeting in Dodge City, Kansas, in the spring of 1883, he met S. A. Marney of the *Texas Live Stock Journal,* which was published in Fort Worth. Marney suggested they form a partnership to publish a newspaper for the cattle industry in Cheyenne, where the cattle industry was thriving.

Mercer purchased the necessary equipment in St. Louis, at a cost of something over $3,000 and also advanced the money for Marney to scout the territory. The first issue of the *Northwestern Live Stock Journal* was published on November 23, 1883. The newspaper was successful enough to draw acid comments from its competitors in Cheyenne. In the spring of 1884, Mercer gave Marney a half interest in the newspaper, on the understanding that the latter would spend his time on the road soliciting advertising for the newspaper.[32]

This arrangement soon broke down, as Marney developed an appetite for the office affairs of the enterprise, where he had installed his brother in law, Frank J. Burton, as bookkeeper. When Mercer fired Burton and hired one Trimble as his replacement, the partners came to blows. The altercation soon spread to the entire Mercer family, and climaxed when Mrs. Mercer struck down the unfortunate Marney with a majolica spittoon. Mercer paid a fine for his involvement in the fracas, but the partnership was at an end, and Mercer bought Marney's interest for $2,000.

Mercer carried on the *Journal* alone until 1887, when he transferred the newspaper to the Northwestern Live Stock Journal Publishing Company, which had as its secretary Thomas B. Adams, who was then also serving as secretary of the Wyoming Stock Growers Association. This association was apparently amicable, with no public evidence of discontent until the fall of 1892, after the Johnson County invasion.

The *Journal* did not criticize the invasion until July 7, three months after it occurred. It may well be that Mercer had by this time intended to turn the *Journal* into a Democratically-aligned general circulation newspa-

---

[32]Charles Hall, "Asa S. Mercer and 'The Banditti of the Plains:' A Reappraisal," *Annals of Wyoming,* XLIX, No. 1 (Spring, 1977), 53-64.

per. In August, Mercer attacked John Clay, Jr., the powerful cattleman who was then living in Chicago. Clay had ducked allegations of involvement with the invasion by noting that he was abroad at the critical times, and Mercer said Clay was "Too great a coward himself to shoulder a musket and fight."

Then Mercer fired a broadside at the cattlemen. In the issue of Sunday, October 16, 1892, readers were greeted by the confession of George Dunning, one of the paid gunmen in the invasion, in the form of an affidavit sworn to on October 6. The Democratic party ordered 24,000 extra copies to distribute throughout the state, and if it did not determine the election, it certainly made the campaign more exciting. John Clay now responded to Mercer's August attack on him by filing a libel action in Chicago. When Mercer went to that city for the World's Fair, he was served in the Clay case, but the case was put over until November 6, and apparently subsequently dropped.[33]

The Republicans and the cattlemen tried to prevent the distribution of the edition, by obtaining service on an old 1891 judgment against Mercer; although the regular edition of 1,400 copies had already gone out to the regular subscription list, they were able to close the *Journal* down for two weeks, and the 24,000 extra copies were confiscated. Whether for that reason of some other, the *Journal* was finished as a business enterprise; its last issue was apparently published not later than July, 1893, for in that month the plant was leased to J. D. Hurd of the *Evanston Register*, to bring out a weekly.

The following year, Mercer published the book for which he is chiefly remembered in Wyoming, *The Banditti of the Plains, or the Cattlemen's Invasion of Wyoming in 1892: [The Crowning Infamy of the Ages]*. The manuscript was finished in February, and the book was published in August by the *Rocky Mountain News* in Denver, and at the time its editor was attempting to exert influence over Democratic politics in Wyoming; those early copies sold for one dollar. There grew up the legend that the cattlemen suppressed the book by legal action and by seizing and burning the copies, but there is no apparent basis in fact for that story, even though copies of the first edition are now rare.

Mercer's book failed to guarantee him a place in Democratic politics, and in 1896 the family moved to a homestead in the Big Horn Basin, near

---

[33]Helena Huntington Smith, *The War on Powder River: The History of an Insurrection* (Lincoln, Nebraska, 1966), 272 *et seq.*

Hyattville. Nor did he warm to the cattlemen who were once his friends. In 1900, the Wyoming congressional delegation were advocating the cession of the federal lands to the states, so that they could then be leased to the stockmen. Mercer rose up against this proposal, saying that it would "wipe out the real population of the state," presumably referring to the homesteader. Mercer died at Hyattville, August 24, 1917.[34]

Already in 1891, old Colonel Ijams had said of Wyoming, "There are too many people here now—too many people and not enough cattle," and when Otto Franc was in Omaha in 1900, he said, "Ours used to be a great cattle country, but it is mostly sheep now...."[35]

---

[34]Mercer wrote to the *Wyoming Derrick*, which was also opposed to the leasing proposal, on the grounds it would limit the opportunity to patent the federal lands. *Wyoming Derrick* (Casper), March 1, 1900, and *Cheyenne State Leader*, July 31, 1917.

[35]*Wyoming Derrick* (Casper), October 18, 1900.

CHAPTER X

The Frontier Spirit

The Big Horn Basin was remote, as we have said, and even without the intervention of outlaws and others of violent disposition, life was harsh. In the summer of 1886, George Gordon, one of the cowboys working for the Frontier Cattle Company, fell under his horse and broke his right leg above the knee, as well as suffering internal injuries. Doctor Watkins had to journey from Buffalo to treat him. When Horace Plunkett came to help his "best and oldest" hand, he found that Gordon's recovery was not materially assisted by the presence of a room full of cowboys, all smoking, and two "fast" ladies from the "Hog Ranch" on Spring Creek, which Phil du Fran had opened earlier in the year.[1]

There was a good deal of wildlife in the Basin in those days, some quite dangerous. George B. McClellan earned his nickname, "Bear George," for his wealth of bear stories, and he killed 23 of the great beasts in the Big Horn Mountains in the fall of 1885; on one hunting trip he dispatched seven silver tip grizzlies. When John Corbett found Philip Henry Vetter dead in his cabin near the Grey Bull River, his arms lacerated and deep gashes in his stomach, it was at first feared that he might have been murdered. Then two slips of paper were discovered, with Vetter's handwriting on them.[2]

---

[1] *Big Horn Sentinel*, July 31, 1886 and Horace Plunkett diary, July 28, 1886. Before coming to Wyoming, Phil du Fran, "a Frenchy and a little Indian," according to Mari Sandoz, had been foreman for the Durfee and Gasman ranch in Nebraska. Mari Sandoz, *The Cattlemen* (Lincoln, Nebraska, 1958), 195-96. Horace Plunkett hired Phil du Fran as foreman of the EK ranch on August 6, 1884, after Jack Donahue resigned, but fired him on May 31, 1885 for incompetence; du Fran was city marshall in Buffalo just before he opened his road ranch on Spring Creek. *Big Horn Sentinel*, May 29, 1886, and Plunkett diary, August 6, 1884, May 31, 1885.

[2] "Stories by 'Bear' George McClellan," *Annals of Wyoming*, XXVI, No. 1 (January 1954), 39ff.

The first paper gave instructions to his friend Jacob, adding, "I have gone down the river after bear." The second paper, written later, gives the story in brief, painful strokes. "I am awfully hurt. I had ought to go to Franc's, but cannot stand it, I am hurt eternally [sic]. Oh, how I bleed! I am smothering. If I had not gone down after supper after the bear, I would be all right. I must lie on the bed. Oh, God have mercy!" The coroner's inquest found his rifle in the willows near the river, two empty shell casings nearby and one shell jammed in the chamber. His hat was fifty feet away.[3]

Mountain lions were also a risk. In the spring of 1889, the three sons of Dow Waln had an encounter with a mountain lion. The boys, 7, 9 and 11, investigated a noise in the barn near Paint Rock Creek and were attacked by the mountain lion they found inside; the eleven-year-old set upon the big cat with a club and it escaped, later to be killed by Mr. Allen. At the end of 1892, one of Wesley Newton's sheepherders was attacked by a lion, and his life was only spared by the efforts of the faithful sheepdog, who lost his own life in the encounter. The lion measured eight feet from the head to the tip of his tail.[4]

Wild animals were not the only dark spirits afoot, and the county seats which were the centers for law enforcement were all on the far side of the mountains. Nevertheless, there were some representatives of the law in the Basin. Johnson County maintained a deputy in the Basin; Thomas R. Adams, foreman for the Big Horn Cattle Company, held the post at first, and when he left the Basin to take another position, Ed Lloyd replaced him. Walter W. Peay, who lived on the lower Nowood, was for a time justice of the peace for Johnson County. His docket book has survived, giving us a view of the frontier justice dispensed in his court.

Peay handled both civil and criminal cases, and the first civil case in his court, in the summer of 1885, was dismissed when the parties refused to pay the justice fees and mileage costs. Then, in 1891, Mrs. Todd sued Minnie Whittington for five dollars and received a judgment in her favor, and the defendant, who had been represented at the trial by W. S. Collins, evidently considered his services inadequate, for he was forced to sue his client for his ten dollar fee.[5]

---

[3]Vetter was born in Woodstock, Virginia, on February 7, 1855, and came to Wyoming ten years before he was killed. The Vetter story is told in a September 23, 1892 report to *The Montana Vociferator* (Red Lodge), September 28, 1892. Vetter was apparently killed September 1. According to Bob Edgar, he was buried by Corbett and John Gleavers, on the river bank near his cabin.

[4]*Red Lodge Picket*, January 7, 1893.

[5]Albert W. Welch *vs.* James Rose, filed July 29, 1885. Rose was accused of cutting hay on Welch's land. Also, Mrs. M. E. Todd *vs.* E. Minnie Whittington, June 18, 1891. Justice Court Docket, Johnson County.

In the fall of 1884, Johnson County Sheriff Canton himself was in the Basin looking for a men who had rustled horses and mules from Hyatt. The suspect was Harry Anable, formerly of Billings, who had been fired by Hyatt, and was thought to have retaliated by running off Hyatt's stock. The sheriff's investigation bore fruit, for Harry Anable and Jack Knight were arrested in the No Wood country by deputy Tom Adams, who brought them to Buffalo to stand trial; both men received sentences of three years at the prison in Joliet.[6]

In the fall of 1885, Sheriff Canton and stock inspector Gross brought Teton Jackson in from the Paint Rock country and charged him with horse stealing. Jackson, who had built a cabin and put up hay to winter his stolen stock, was also wanted in Blackfoot, Idaho, and in Lander; the Idaho case against him must have been the stronger one, for he was given up to be tried in that jurisdiction, where he was convicted of grand larceny.[7]

Later in the same year, Gross, acting as both cattle inspector and deputy sheriff, brought back to Buffalo the body of George Stevens, alias "Big George" and "Red Cloud." Stevens was shot by Gross for horse stealing and refusing arrest. With Gross was Frank Lamb and 14 head of stolen horses. The two men had been living in a cabin on Spring Creek, and at daybreak Gross, Dave Hart and Billy Burnett surprised them in bed; when Stevens protested, he was shot. Stevens, who had formerly worked for a number of big cattle outfits, was also wanted in Custer County, Montana, on a similar charge. Lamb, who was then only 21, claimed to be a native of Genesee, Idaho; early the following year, he was sentenced to six years in the penitentiary. Frank Bell, a third member of the "Big George" gang, was later captured at Lander by Ed Lloyd, the Johnson County deputy in the Paint Rock area; Bell was also wanted in Miles City for horse stealing.[8]

In 1888, Henry (Hank) Gorman was killed by Daniel V. Bayne. Gor-

---

[6]Tom Adams left his position with the Big Horn Cattle Company in June, 1885, to become the foreman for the Morton E. Post ranch in the southern part of the territory. *Big Horn Sentinel*, January 10, September 27, December 13, 1884, June 13, 1885. The Anable matter apparently involved Hyatt before he came to the Paint Rock country from Buffalo; the *Big Horn Sentinel* of November 22, 1884, noted that the new grocery store of Hyatt & Landis had opened in Buffalo.

[7]Teton Jackson was convicted of grand larceny on November 1, 1885, in the district court for Bingham County, Idaho. *Big Horn Sentinel*, October 17, November 7, 1885.

[8]Lamb was released from prison on April 11, 1890. Elnora L. Frye, *Atlas of Wyoming Outlaws at the Territorial Penitentiary* (Laramie, Wyoming, 1990), 284. *Big Horn Sentinel*, December 5, 26, 1885 and January 2, 1886.

man had been the "terror" of the Basin for some time, and in the spring of 1888 he shot into Hyatt's store, and then went on to Bayne's ranch, where he assaulted Bayne and "one or two" others. Bayne shot him with his Winchester, but the editor of the *Sentinel* emphasized that he was given a "proper" burial. In due course the killing was ruled justifiable.[9]

A strange incident occurred in the spring of 1891. Oyer C. Morgan, who lived on the lower Nowood River a few miles above its junction with the Big Horn, came to Bonanza to report that James McDermott and his four year old son had been shot at the Madden ranch south of Bonanza.[10]

The conflict started with a disagreement between McDermott and his wife, apparently over an alleged affair between McDermott and another woman, one Helen Martin. Mrs. McDermott left the McDermott place and went to the Madden ranch, three quarters of a mile away, taking another child (a girl) with her. Late in the day, Tom Madden went to see McDermott about the difficulties, and McDermott warned him that if his wife did not return he would "clean up the whole outfit of you." Madden returned to his own ranch, and shortly saw McDermott coming toward his house, carrying little Phil wrapped in a heavy blanket.[11]

Madden advanced to meet McDermott, and according to Madden's story, McDermott was carrying a revolver. When Madden aimed his own weapon at McDermott, McDermott held the boy up in front of him, so that Madden's bullet struck the boy and went beyond to strike McDermott himself. Little Phil died of the wound and was buried shortly thereafter.[12]

This story was bad enough, but it was shortly to become more bizarre. Early in May, McDermott had recovered sufficiently from his injury to ponder revenge. He wrote to John J. Tatman, a rancher who had settled on the Greybull River in 1886, telling the rancher that he and Madden had once stolen a herd of Tatman horses and driven them to Nebraska; he claimed that he had been a reluctant accomplice of Madden. When Tatman came to Bonanza in response to the letter, Mrs. McDermott confirmed the main elements of the story, but claimed that McDermott had

---
[9]The Gorman killing was reported in the *Big Horn Sentinel*, March 17, 1888; the disposition of the case was reported on April 7.
[10]The shooting occurred March 30, 1891. *The Buffalo Bulletin*, May 14, 1891.
[11]*The Buffalo Bulletin*, June 18, 1891.
[12]*The Buffalo Bulletin*, April 16, 1891.

been the ringleader, and had kept all the proceeds from the sale of the stolen horses.[13]

As a sort of bonus disclosure, Mrs. McDermott also volunteered the information that she and McDermott had repeatedly robbed U. S. mail sacks and had in fact seen a letter in which Tatman had sent money to the county clerk. *The Buffalo Bulletin* reported that Madden had "skipped," but was expected to testify in the case under promise of immunity. To complicate matters still further, McDermott was next charged in justice court with negligence in connection with his son's death.[14]

The mail robbery story immediately caused a stir, because a man named Swift had been accused of taking $120 from the mails in 1888, and had been forced to make restitution to Cassel H. George, the sender of the money. Now, Swift claimed he had been innocent all along, which prompted Sam Hyatt to challenge Swift's story, saying the man had confessed, both to the post office detective and to Hyatt himself.

McDermott's negligence trial was finally heard in Buffalo on June 15. Madden was there to testify, having turned himself in to the Fremont County authorities, where he was admitted to $1,000 bail. Madden, who said he was 29, admitted meeting McDermott in 1880, in Sioux City; he said he met Mary McDermott in Glendinning, Montana. When Mary McDermott testified, she said that McDermott threatened her because she told Madden of McDermott's affair with Helen Martin. When the testimony was completed, McDermott was released on the negligence charge, and immediately arrested again, for robbing the mails. In July, James McDermott, Thomas Madden and John Kearny were indicted in Fremont County for horse stealing.[15]

Convicted on the charge of stealing $100 from the mails, McDermott was confined to jail, where he continued to complain about the stories being published about him, contending that it was not true that he and Madden were cattle rustlers. He admitted that Madden liked horse flesh, but denied that the man had ever stolen a cow: whether this distinction mattered to anyone who heard about it, we cannot know. Madden was

---

[13] Meanwhile, the horse stealing "confession" elicited a letter from Hyattville saying that the managers of the Bay State outfit expected to save "several hundred" dollars each year from the breakup of the gang of horse thieves. *The Buffalo Bulletin*, May 21, 1891.

[14] *The Buffalo Bulletin*, May 7, 1891. The case of Wyoming vs. James McDermott was filed May 9, 1891. Justice Court Docket book, Johnson County.

[15] The sheriff of Meagher County, Montana also wanted McDermott for a murder committed near Neihart, Montana, in 1884. *The Buffalo Bulletin*, May 14, June 18, July 23, 1891.

convicted and sentenced to seven years with hard labor in the penitentiary for horse stealing.[16]

McDermott's troubles continued, and in the spring of 1892, his land was sold for nonpayment of taxes; the following summer, two travelers from Billings spent the night in the house he had owned, which was then abandoned. In December, he swore out a complaint against Peter Madden and Mary McDermott for cohabiting in a state of adultery, but this case was dismissed when he did not appear to testify. Early the following January, McDermott sued Peter Madden and Mrs. McDermott for selling his cattle while he was absent. This long-running saga continued in 1893, as McDermott returned to the Basin, where Mrs. McDermott and her daughter were now living with Peter Madden (Tom Madden was then confined to the penitentiary). When McDermott appeared at the Madden ranch, Madden opened fire on him, and McDermott shot Madden, killing him. He then took his wife and went to Bonanza, where he turned himself over to the authorities. In November, a jury acquitted McDermott for the killing of Peter Madden.[17]

It is perhaps fitting that we should have some permanent reminders of these incidents. A long dry gulch flowing south into the Nowood River just east of McDermott's farm is now known on the maps as McDermott's Gulch, and just to the south of his farm and across the river, McDermott's Butte rises 400 feet above the river bottom, as a silent witness to those violent days.[18]

William A. Gallagher, a tall, lean cowhand with a drooping mustache and a severe temper, was working for Paul Breteche in the fall of 1892,

---

[16] *The Buffalo Bulletin*, August 20, 1891. Although he is consistently referred to as Tom or Thomas Madden in the press, Madden's prison records show his name as John. Madden was born in Brunswick, Maine. While in prison, he was disciplined in the "dark cell" for talking in line and for taking part in a mutiny in which the warden was beaten; Madden was shot during the latter incident. Elnora L. Frye, *op. cit.*, 121-22.

[17] *The Buffalo Bulletin*, April 28, 1892 and January 5, November 23, 1893. The case of Wyoming vs. Peter Madden and Mary McDermott was filed December 29, 1892. Justice Court Docket Book, Johnson County. The crime of cohabitation in a state of adultery was introduced by the first territorial legislature and carried a penalty of a fine not exceeding $200 and not more than six months in jail, with each offence adding the same penalty; the last territorial legislature cut the penalty to a fine of not more than $100 and three months in jail, and eliminated the separate offense feature. Also, *The Weekly Times* (Billings), July 29, 1893.

[18] McDermott's farm was located on the north side of the Nowood River, in the northwest quarter of Section 4 and the northeast quarter of Section 5, Township 49 North, Range 91 West of the Sixth Principal Meridian. The mouth of McDermott's Gulch is in the northeast quarter of Section 4, and McDermott's Butte is in the northwest quarter of Section 9.

when he trailed 600 head of cattle into Montana. Gallagher and his friends went into Red Lodge, where they shot up George Hubbard's saloon and received a $50 fine and three months in the Livingston jail. This lapse may have cost Gallagher his job with Breteche, for soon he was working on the Palette Ranch for A. A. Anderson, who rated Billy an exceptional horseman and roper. When Anderson paid him off, Billy demanded $75 more than Anderson was paying him and threatened Anderson when the excess was not paid.[19]

The threat against Anderson did not bear fruit, but more serious problems for Billy arose early in 1894. He had developed a fondness for Belle Drewry, one of the denizens of Rose Williams' house of ill repute at Arland, and on March 15 they were together at the ranch where Gallagher was working. Also there were two other hands, William Wheaton and William "Blind Bill" Houlihan. Wheaton, who was born in Tawilla City, Utah, was then 23 and single. In the course of the afternoon, Billy Gallagher began to quarrel with Belle about a bill of sale, and threatened to strike her, when Wheaton intervened. Gallagher than drew his pistol and for the next hour or so kept the other three in the room at gunpoint, periodically "clicking" the pistol, according to Belle's later testimony before the coroner's jury.

Gallagher finally permitted Belle to leave the house, and soon he sent Blind Bill out to saddle his horse. Gallagher and Wheaton then walked to the stable, and at some point Wheaton was able to draw his own pistol and shoot Gallagher. Although both Wheaton and Belle were charged with the offence, only Wheaton was tried, and he received eight years in the penitentiary for manslaughter. Although the testimony agrees that Gallagher was quarrelsome and savage, Wheaton also had his rough side, for he had a confrontation with a guard in 1896 and tried to burn down the prison broom shop two years later; the warden opposed a petition for pardon, and Wheaton was forced to serve out his term.[20]

Slick Creek, a dry watercourse that enters the Big Horn River from the east below Worland, took its name from an incident in August of 1895, when William J. Ewing, a New Mexico sheep shearer, was attacked where the road crossed the creek. Ewing was then 30 years old, and had been

---

[19]Abraham Archibald Anderson, *Experiences and Impressions—The Autobiography of Colonel A. A. Anderson* (Freeport, New York, 1970), 77.

[20]Wheaton was sentenced July 15, 1894. The State of Wyoming vs. William Wheaton, cases 182 and 187, Fremont County. Although most of the ranchers in the area signed a petition for his pardon, Governor W. A. Richards did not act on the petition.

working for the Noble sheep outfit; he had accumulated what one story says was $350 in gold and two cashier's checks. He suffered from rheumatism, and had gone to the hot springs for ten days; it was on the return trip from Thermopolis to Montana that he was ambushed. At the time of the ambush, Ewing was using the road that crossed to the east side of the river at Owl Creek, and went up Kirby Creek before turning northwest across the badlands.[21]

The ambush occurred at the place where the road dropped down into the dry creek, a location twenty miles from habitation in either direction. There a masked man ordered Ewing to throw up his hands, and without waiting for a response, he shot Ewing in the left arm below the elbow, the bullet passing across his stomach and lodging in the right arm. Ewing's horses then bolted, and headed south over the road they had just come; although the ambusher followed, firing several times, he did not venture close enough to get within range of the Winchester Ewing had in the wagon. Despite his serious wounds, Ewing was able to steer the team back across the 35 miles to Henry Sherard's saloon at Andersonville, just across the river from the "Old Town" of Thermopolis, at the mouth of Owl Creek.

Andersonville, which was named for Charles W. "Badland Charley" Anderson, and his brother, Ed, consisted of a restaurant, a house of ill repute and a saloon, was actually older than the "Old Town" across the river; it was a hangout for outlaws from the Hole in the Wall, across the divide to the east. At this place, Ewing's wounds were attended to by Ed Farlow, who was at the time also tending the gunshot wound his brother Zeke had received earlier at a dance in these lively precincts.[22]

Albert "Slick" Nard rode into Andersonville soon after Ewing arrived, and there he was accused of the crime, based on Ewing's story of the incident. Ewing remembered that the gunman's Winchester had a broken carrier block, so that the shells had to be fed into the chamber by hand; Nard was found to be carrying such a weapon. Moreover, Nard was using ammunition that had been cut off after being molded, to lighten the weight of the load, and the bullet extracted from Ewing bore the same

---

[21] *Weekly Profile* (Worland, Wyoming), December 31, 1970. The assault occurred on August 8, 1895. State vs. Albert Nard, Case No. 300, Johnson County.

[22] "Life Story of 'Kansas' Wickwire, as told to A. W. Coons," typescript, University of Wyoming, and the account of Ed Farlow, in the Wyoming State Archives. Also, *Fremont Clipper*, August 16, 1895 and Tacetta Walker, *op. cit.*, 149.

Albert "Slick" Nard, whose 1895 attack on William J. Ewing at the place where the road crossed a dry creek, gave his nickname to Slick Creek. Nard subsequently received 14 years in the penitentiary for his deed. *Courtesy Wyoming State Museum.*

marks. Finally, the scene of the ambush bore evidence of the track of a horse with a broken hoof, and Nard's horse had such a hoof. Nard tried to construct an alibi, but these pieces of evidence convinced the lawmen; it also convinced some of the local settlers, who were "considering seriously" whether to save Johnson County the expense of a trial.[23]

The perpetrator of the offense was a young man of 28 years, who had earned his nickname for his cattle and horse rustling. Nard is said to have been a cowboy for the Bar X Bar, and he had been on the other side of the law only three years earlier, when he was paid for killing Jack Bliss, a notorious desperado who had escaped from the Fremont County jail in May 1892.

Apparently, Nard had at one time been a partner of Bliss, but later broke with him and was hired by the Wyoming Stock Growers Association to apprehend his former partner. Bliss had an $1,800 price on his

---

[23]Dorothy G. Milek, *The Gift of Bah Guewana: A History of Wyoming's Hot Springs State Park* (Thermopolis, Wyoming, 1975), 19.

head, he made his way to the South Fork of the Stinking Water, where he lived by looting miners' cabins. Deputy Sheriff Joseph Irey and his posse found Bliss on June 4, in a stone fortress, where he was shot.[24]

There was some question whether Nard actually earned his bounty money, because there were some who contended that Nard killed an innocent man and brought back his scalp and two ears as evidence that Bliss was dead. At the time of the Bliss affair, Nard was living at Lander with his wife, Jennie, who was the sister of John Hollywood, bar owner at Thermopolis, but after Jennie divorced Nard, he came to the hot springs, where he was doing chores for the McGraths at the time of the assault on Ewing.[25]

After the Ewing incident, Nard was charged on November 7, 1895, with shooting with intent to commit murder, and was convicted after a jury trial and sentenced to fourteen years in the penitentiary, leaving his name to enhance the creek where the ambush occurred.[26]

There was no shortage of such incidents. As late as 1894, the *Fremont Clipper* editorialized on the feud then going on between the outlaws in parts of Johnson County and those in parts of Fremont County, apparently referring to those in the Basin living on both sides of the river. The immediate reason for the comment was the robbery of Dr. E. C. Enderley's Inter-National Pharmacy in Thermopolis by three masked men, an incident in which Enderley's face was cut when he resisted; he was forced to open the safe containing $1,300. Jake Snyder, of Red Lodge, one of the robbers, was shot and later captured. While making their escape, the thieves had trouble with their horses; the unruly steeds, spooked by the

---

[24]*The Red Lodge Picket* gave the names of the men with Irey as Dave Shock, B. Benbrook and S. Bernard; the last is apparently Slick Nard. *Red Lodge Picket,* June 11, July 2, 1892.

[25]There was a James Otis Bliss, who used the alias Dick Carr, who appeared in Buffalo shortly after Jack Bliss was supposedly killed, and this Bliss robbed a Wells Fargo stage in Rawhide, Nevada, in 1908. The Fremont County prosecutor argued that there were others who saw Bliss' body, and they would not have been deceived by a substitution. *Fremont Clipper,* December 13, 1895. Byron F. "Kansas" Wickwire said that Nard had been a Bar X Bar cowboy. Also, Tacetta B. Walker, *op. cit.,* 172. Nard married Jennie Hollywood in Johnson County, June 24, 1888; she was then 16. She married J. Frank Warner of Hyattville in 1897.

[26]The account of the Bliss escape in 1892 is given in the *Fremont Clipper,* May 20, 1892; his killing is recounted in the *Cheyenne Daily Leader,* June 14, 1892. According to the prison records, Nard was married, 5' 8" tall, stocky, with light brown hair and gray eyes; he was born in Texas, and his card in the file tersely states that he had no religion and no education. Nard was sentenced in Johnson County on November 16, 1895, and was released March 12, 1907, after having been credited with two years, 8 months and three days of good time. Records of the Wyoming State Penitentiary, Rawlins, Wyoming. Also, *Wyoming State Journal* (Lander, Wyoming), August 17, 1917.

gunfire, bucked the loot from their riders' pockets. The *Clipper* editor opined that the outlaws should be taught respect for the law or driven out.[27]

In the spring of 1896, the Lander *Clipper* noted that cattle stealing was "on the decline" perhaps in part because rustlers were finding it difficult to find someone to post bond for them, but as late as the summer of 1897, the *Billings Gazette* spoke of a "veritable reign of terror" in the area newly organized as Big Horn County, over the whole region from Basin City east to the Hole in the Wall. In the latter location, a gang was holed up under the leadership of Tom O'Day, a former cowpuncher whom the *Gazette* described as a "merry, light-hearted Irish boy." At the hot springs, where the new townsite had not yet been laid out, a group of masked men held up a card game in the only gambling house, taking all the money on the table and in the pockets of those present.[28]

The new town of Thermopolis continued to be troubled by the rougher element. John Hollywood, saloon keeper in Thermopolis and brother-in-law of "Slick" Nard, beat Frank Sayles, foreman of H. P. Rothwell's Padlock ranch, over the head with a six-shooter early in 1899; Sayles died shortly after the attack, perhaps because he was left unconscious and uncared-for in a back room. The argument may have been over Sayles' bar bill at the Hollywood establishment, or perhaps it had to do with a spree of shooting that left several Thermopolis establishments without windows or lights. Hollywood was charged with murder, and W. S. Edgell and Stanley Miller were charged as accessories.[29]

Nevertheless, the law tried to assert itself, and the following month, Justice J. S. Kerr fined Fred Waln for drawing a gun at a dance at Hubbard's dance hall, and threatened to punish others for similar offences. When John Hollywood's bartender went down the street and fired three shots in derision of the court's ruling, he too was arrested, given six months in jail and fined $100.[30]

---

[27]*Fremont Clipper* (Lander), November 30, 1894 and Dorothy G. Milek, *The Gift of Bah Guewana*, op. cit., 21. Also, *The Billings Gazette*, December 15, 1894.

[28]*The Billings Gazette*, June 15, 1897 and *The Clipper* (Lander), March 6, 1896, August 6, 1897.

[29]*Natrona County Tribune* (Casper), January 12, 19, 1899. John Hollywood was born May, 1867, in Scotland; he came to the United States in 1871, and had been married to his wife Nina for only three years in 1900, according to the 1900 census.

[30]Hollywood's bartender was Charles Chanler; he called out "Rats" when the justice sentenced Waln, and then went to Smith & Slane's saloon and fired three shots in front. *The Clipper* (Lander), January 13, February 3, 1899.

Following the winter of 1886-87, the preeminence of the cattle industry declined, as we have already noted, but the sheep industry withstood the weather reasonably well. The conflict between the two livestock interests became serious by 1893 and 1894, when there were several raids on sheep camps in Converse County, and in the Henry's Fork region of southwest Wyoming. In 1897, the conflict reached the Basin, and in the southern part of that region the cattlemen set a deadline ranging from Kirby Creek to Ten Sleep, and the sheepmen were warned not to cross north of the line.[31]

Then, in 1902, two bands were rimrocked in the Wood River country southwest of Meeteetse, and the next spring raiders attacked a sheep camp between Thermopolis and Meeteetse, clubbed and shot 200 sheep belonging to William Minick and assassinated Minick's brother Ben. The source of the shell casings found at the site was identified, and three men were arrested in July of 1903, but no convictions resulted.

The violence continued in 1904, when Lincoln A. Morrison, a prominent sheep rancher, was assassinated on Kirby Creek. On Trapper Creek, an entire band belonging to Jess D. Lynn was rimrocked, and even though there were persistent rumors of the identity of the perpetrators, no arrests were made. In the late summer of 1905, 4,000 sheep were shot, clubbed and dynamited, and a team of horses were killed on Shell Creek by raiders who struck a bank owned by Louis Gantz; the dogs were tied to the sheep wagons before the wagons were burned. Again, no legal action was taken.

The climax of all of this warfare was on April 2, 1909, when a band belonging to Joseph Allemand and Joe Emge was struck by seven raiders, who killed the sheepmen and two of their herders, burned the wagons and killed more than two dozen sheep. The band of about 2,500 had been trailed from Worland to Spring Creek, across a deadline marked by a plowed furrow.[32]

In contrast with the former atrocities, the public reaction to the Spring Creek raid was intense. The newly-formed Wyoming Wool Growers Association offered a reward of $1,000, the county association offered an additional $1,000, the National association offered $2,000, and rewards from

---

[31]O'Neal, *op. cit.*, 92, 96.

[32]Two herders were spared by the raiders, and they later testified for the prosecution at the trial. O'Neal, *op. cit.*, 132, 138. Joseph Emge was born in Indiana in January, 1863, according to the 1900 census of Big Horn County, Wyoming.

the county and Allemand's brother brought the total reward money to $5,500. Funds were available to hire superb legal talent to assist the young Big Horn County Attorney, Percy W. Metz. This action proved decisive, for the cattlemen did not spare expense in their own defense.[33]

Tensions ran high, and soldiers from the state militia were camped in Basin for a time. A grand jury was convened, and the prosecutors maintained steady pressure on the witnesses, looking for a weak link; one witness shot himself after his first day's testimony. Three key witnesses were spirited out of Wyoming for safekeeping, and in due course, prosecution lawyers Edward Elmer Enterline and William L. Simpson had negotiated a plea bargain with Albert Keyes and Charles Farris, who were given immunity in exchange for their testimony against the rest. The grand jury issued indictments against the seven men in the raid.[34]

The defense successfully challenged the fairness of the jury roster prepared by the county officials, but the ploy backfired, for the new roster badly diluted the cattleman representation in the fast-growing county and replaced their influence with that of homesteaders, and the result did not favor the defendants. The trial in November heard the testimony of two of the raiders, and ended in the conviction of Herbert Brink, followed by guilty pleas from the remaining men. The foreman of the jury was William H. Packard, a beekeeper, who was also the bishop of the Burlington ward of the Mormon church and a key leader of the Burlington colony. While Packard was a farmer and not a stockman, he had had an unfortunate experience with cattlemen the first spring he was in the Basin, when he found his cow with a fine calf, bearing the brand of another rancher. In any case, the choice of Packard as foreman was no help for the cattlemen.[35]

---

[33]The Wyoming Wool Growers Association was formed in April, 1905, although there had been county organizations earlier. O'Neal, op. cit., 126. Percy W. Metz, who was 25 in 1909, was the son of Judge William S. Metz, of Sheridan, who had been the judge of the fourth judicial district in 1895; at the time of the trial in Basin, the district was under Judge C. H. Parmalee of Buffalo. Percy Metz was assisted in the prosecution by William L. Simpson of Cody and Edward Elmer Enterline of Sheridan. The defense team included Judge Joseph L. Stotts of Sheridan, who had been the fourth district judge in 1897-1906.

[34]William Garrison left Basin after his first day's testimony before the grand jury, and went to the Voss farm south of Manderson, where he wrote two notes and then killed himself. The indictments were issued against Herbert Brink, Edward Eaton, Albert Keyes, Charles Farris, Tommy Dixon, George Saban and Milton Alexander. O'Neal, op. cit., 142.

[35]Lowene Packard Saxton, The Packard Legacy (Sacramento, California, 1992), 161-62. Packard was 58 at the time of the trial.

On November 15, the charges against Charles Farris and Albert Keyes were dismissed for their services to the prosecution, and they were given safe conduct out of town. The other five men left five days later on a circuitous train trip to Rawlins that took them north to Montana, then southeast to the Union Pacific in Nebraska, and thence west to Rawlins.

The convictions in the Spring Creek raid were an effective springboard for the career of Percy Metz, who became the first judge of the Fifth Judicial district, but of much more importance was the stamp of the process of law that was finally placed on the sometimes lawless society of the Big Horn Basin.

CHAPTER XI

The Old Counties in the Basin

Soon after the Big Horn Basin came under the American flag as a part of the Louisiana Purchase in 1803, the area was included in the District of Louisiana, the first of the territories to be erected by the federal government for the new area. These territories created counties to serve their settled areas, but the Wyoming country and its Big Horn Basin generally was ignored as a sort of unsettled appendage. There were no permanent habitations in the Basin before John Dwight Woodruff built his cabin on Owl Creek, and no settlers for a local government to serve. This was the situation during the period under the District of Louisiana (1804-05), Louisiana Territory (1805-12) and Missouri Territory (1812-1834).

In 1834, the eastern part of the Missouri Territory was attached to the Michigan Territory and the huge remaining area east of the continental divide was set aside as Indian Territory, in one of many efforts to set aside land where the Indians could be moved away from the more desirable regions where white settlement was advancing. There was no local government in Indian Territory for the next twenty years, until the need to build the transcontinental railroad gave rise to pressures to erect governments in the area set aside for the Indians.

The principle of a large insulated Indian Territory was soon shunted aside. The Kansas-Nebraska Act of 1854, which played such an important role in the events leading to the Civil War, created two territories from the former Indian Territory, Kansas Territory and Nebraska Territory; the latter territory included the Big Horn Basin. A year earlier, Congress had authorized the president to negotiate the extinguishment of Indian title in the territory, and much of the more desirable eastern region was freed up by the time the Kansas-Nebraska Act passed. The acting governor of Nebraska Territory set the capital at Omaha City, on the Missouri River, and the early days of the territory were marked mostly by land speculation in its eastern regions. A number of counties were created by the legislature, including two in the Wyoming country, but neither of these counties reached up into the Basin.[1]

Dakota Territory was organized from the Minnesota and Nebraska territories in 1861, in order to provide government for the unorganized part of the Minnesota Territory that had been detached when the State of Minnesota was admitted to the Union in 1858. Dakota Territory was also given the northern part of the Wyoming country, including the Big Horn Basin, but the lawmakers at Yankton concentrated on the eastern part of the territory, and did nothing with their western reaches. When gold was discovered in Idaho in 1862, Idaho Territory had to be created; this occurred in the following year, and that part of the Wyoming country formerly attached to Dakota and Nebraska was now attached to the new territory.[2]

The legislature of Idaho territory proceeded to carve up its geography into counties, including two created early in 1864 that covered the Big Horn Basin: Ogalala County and Yellowstone County. The seat of the former was temporarily set at Fort Laramie, which would have been a formidable journey if anyone had been living in the Basin at the time and needed to go to the county seat. There is no indication that either county was ever organized, for in the spring of 1864, Montana Territory was created, and in that act the Wyoming country that had been included in Idaho Territory was once again attached to Dakota Territory.[3]

---

[1]Nebraska Territory was created on May 30, 1854, with latitude 40° as the southern boundary and the continental divide as the western boundary. 10 *Statutes at Large* 277. On January 6, 1860, the Nebraska legislature created Wilson County and Morton County in the Wyoming country; the seat of the latter county was at Platte City, which was not within the county boundaries. *Laws, Joint Resolutions and Memorials Passed at the Sixth Session of the Legislative Assembly of the Territory of Nebraska* (Nebraska City,1860), 139-40.

[2]Dakota Territory was created March 2, 1861; the capital was at Yankton. 12 *Statutes at Large* 239. Idaho Territory was created March 3, 1863, and included all of the Wyoming country. 12 *Statutes at Large* 808. The Idaho capital was originally at Lewiston, although it was moved to Boise City in 1864. L. Milton Woods, *Wyoming Country*, op. cit., 154, 161.

[3]The first session of the Idaho Territory legislature established Ogalala County and Yellowstone County, effective January 16, 1864. Ogalala County was all of the territory south of 45° and east of longitude 108°, while Yellowstone County included all the area west of Ogalala and east of the Rocky Mountains which had not been included in the other counties. L. Milton Woods, *Wyoming Country*, op. cit., 163. Longitude 108° passes west of Worland and east of Greybull and Basin. The shift of the Wyoming country from Idaho to Dakota Territory was effective May 26, 1864, 13 *Statutes at Large* 86.

Dakota Territory did not immediately erect counties in Wyoming, but discovery of gold in the South Pass area in the 1860's forced the issue. The first mining district was organized in 1865, and soon there were enough settlers in the South Pass region to force Dakota Territory to create Laramie County, early in 1867. This huge county included most of what is now Wyoming, including all of the Big Horn Basin; the seat was fixed at Fort Sanders, near the present location of Laramie. Late in the same year, Laramie County was reduced by the creation of Carter County out of the western section; the eastern rim of the Big Horn Basin remained in Laramie County, and the western section was then in Carter County. Carter County was named for Judge William Alexander Carter, then the probate judge of Green River County, Utah; its seat was South Pass City. Early in 1868, the Laramie County seat was moved to Cheyenne, which had been laid out by the Union Pacific railroad the previous year, at the point where construction stopped for the winter.[4]

The arrival of the railroad in 1867 brought more people to the Wyoming country, and increased pressure for more counties. So great was the influx in the South Pass mining region and along the railroad that the Wyoming country had enough people to overwhelm political control by the eastern power center of Dakota Territory along the Missouri River. In the summer of 1868, Wyoming Territory was created by Congress, with the full blessing of the older territory, but the new territory could not be organized because of the ongoing controversy between President Johnson and the Republican-controlled Congress, and Dakota Territory had to continue to try to govern its unwanted western regions.[5]

Late in 1868, the Dakota legislature created Albany County, with its seat at Laramie City and early the next year Carbon County was cut off the western edge of Albany, with Rawling's Spring as county seat. The latter county included the eastern rim of the Big Horn Basin that had been in Laramie and later Albany counties. Meanwhile, in the interval before Wyoming Territory could be organized and removed from Dakota jurisdiction, Laramie and Carter Counties actually cast a majority of the votes

---

[4]Laramie County was created by the Dakota legislature on January 9, 1867 and Carter County was created December 17, 1867; Laramie County was reconstituted and its seat moved, effective January 3, 1868. L. Milton Woods, *Wyoming Country, op. cit.*, 157-59. The area remaining in Laramie County after Carter was created would have included Ten Sleep. Fort Sanders was established June 23, 1866.

[5]Wyoming Territory was created July 25, 1868. President Johnson nominated officers for Wyoming Territory, but they were not confirmed by the Senate, and organization of the territory had to await the arrival of President Grant the following year.

in Dakota Territory's 1868 election, creating a real risk in the vote for delegate to Congress.[6]

When Wyoming was organized in 1869, the new territory had four Dakota Territory counties, and the Big Horn Basin was divided between Carter and Carbon, with one county seat at South Pass City, and the other down on the Union Pacific railroad, at Rawling's Spring.

There was a fifth organized county within the boundaries of Wyoming Territory, Utah Territory's Green River County; because of the controversy over polygamy in Utah, prejudice in Congress against that territory was so strong that Utah laws were not permitted to carry over to the new territory and, the western strip, which also included a small area from Idaho Territory, came into Wyoming Territory unorganized.

The first Wyoming legislature created Uinta County from the unorganized strip, and, like the other four counties, its boundaries extended north to the Montana line. The Uinta County seat was placed at Merrill, a townsite near Fort Bridger, but the next year the seat was moved to Evanston, and Merrill thereafter disappeared from the Wyoming map. The first Wyoming legislature also changed the name of Carter County to Sweetwater County, and in 1873 its county seat was moved to Green River, on the railroad. Thus, Uinta County included the tiny part of the Big Horn drainage west of Sweetwater County; all of the counties in the Big Horn Basin had seats along the railroad in the southern part of the territory, which would have been a great inconvenience to the Basin, if there had been any living there to suffer from it.[7]

The first Wyoming territorial legislature in 1869 memorialized the federal government to secure the elimination of the Sioux hunting ground in the northeast corner of the territory. The Sioux were finally excluded from

---

[6]Albany County was created December 16, 1868 and Carbon County was created on January 9, 1869. L. Milton Woods, *Wyoming Country, op. cit.*, 157-59. The total vote for Dakota Territory delegate in 1868 was 4,597, of which Laramie and Carter counties accounted for 3,101, spread among several candidates.

[7]The first legislature also changed the spelling of the Carbon County seat to Rawlin's Springs. The springs were named by General Grenville Dodge for General John Aaron Rawlins, who commanded the troops protecting the railroad construction crews in 1868. General Rawlins died in 1870, at the age of 38. Uinta County was created December 1, 1869; its eastern boundary was the meridian of 33° west of Washington, or approximately longitude 110° 3' 25". *General Laws, Memorials and Resolutions of the Territory of Wyoming, Passed at the First Session of the Legislative Assembly, Convened at Cheyenne, October 12, 1869* (Cheyenne, 1870), Chapter 34, 37. The Sweetwater County seat was moved effective December 9, 1873. *Organic Act and General Laws of Wyoming, Together with the Memorials and Resolutions Passed by the Third Legislative Assembly, Convened at Cheyenne, November 4, 1873* (Cheyenne, 1874), Chapter XXXVIII.

this area following the Custer debacle in 1876, and by then the legislature in 1875 had already created two counties to cover that area. Pease County, the westernmost of the two, was named for Eugene L. Pease, of Uinta County, who was president of the territorial council that session; it included the northern part of Carbon County and that part of Sweetwater County as far west as the Big Horn River. Four years later, Pease County was renamed to honor Edward Payson Johnson, a Cheyenne attorney, who had been elected to the Council in September, and died before the legislature convened. The change of name did not hasten organization of the county, and the area continued to be administered from the county seats down on the railroad.[8]

The opening of the Powder River Basin brought a surge of activity there, and that basin now began to fill with ranches (other settlers were not far behind); the Frewen brothers established the 76 ranch on the Powder River in 1879 after visiting the area following a hunting trip the previous year, and they had neighbors on that range in the same year. Their ranch headquarters was in the north end of Carbon County, and in the fall of 1880, Moreton Frewen found it necessary to go to Rawlins to conduct some legal business; he expected it would take him ten days to cover the 200 miles to the county seat and back.

By 1881, the town of Buffalo had been laid out and the territory could organize the two counties that the Wyoming legislature had erected in 1875. An election on April 19, 1881 placed the Johnson county seat at Buffalo, a settlement which started up in 1879 on Clear Creek, near the new Fort McKinney.

In the years that followed, those who lived in the eastern Big Horn Basin faced an arduous journey east over the Big Horn mountains to Buffalo, the seat of Johnson County. The road crossed over from Buffalo to the store Samuel Washington Hyatt had opened on Paint Rock Creek. From Hyatt's store the road went down to cross the Nowood at Bonanza,

---

[8]The long memorial asking for the opening of the route through the Powder River country is Chapter 99 of the 1869 laws, *op. cit.* Pease County was created December 8, 1875; the name was changed to Johnson on December 13, 1879. *The Compiled Laws of Wyoming* (Cheyenne, 1876), 199, and L. Milton Woods, *op. cit.*, 177 and Burton S. Hill, "Buffalo—Ancient Cow Town, A Wyoming Saga," *Annals of Wyoming*, XXXV, No 2 (October 1963), 125-30. Edward Payson Johnson was born August 21, 1842, in Greenbush, Ohio. He served with the 93rd Ohio Volunteers in the Civil War, after which he graduated from Michigan University in law (March, 1867). Johnson opened a law office in Denver, and then moved to Cheyenne. He died October 3, 1879. Robert C. Morris, *Collections of the Wyoming Historical Society*, I (Cheyenne, 1897), 337. Also, Moreton Frewen to Clara Jerome, October 1, 1880, American Heritage Center, University of Wyoming.

and on to the old ferry at Alamo, on the Big Horn, where it connected with the old Bridger Trail. The journey into the Basin from the south was no better, for when W. A. Richards settled in the Red Bank area in 1888, he wrote that the trip to his ranch from the stage at Rongis was four days' drive "in good weather."[9]

The Wind River Reservation was reduced in 1872 to exclude the area where Lander now stands, and in 1884, the northern part of Sweetwater County was cut off and erected as Fremont County, with Lander as the seat. At a meeting in the spring of 1884, the commissioners of Fremont County recognized the existence of their road into the Basin, and designated the road from the North Fork of Owl Creek to Stinking Water as a county road. This road commenced at the wagon crossing on the South Fork of Owl Creek, then proceeded to the North Fork of Owl Creek, to Cottonwood Creek, Grass Creek, and down Grass Creek to Baxter's LU Ranch, then over to Gooseberry Creek at McDonald's Ranch, then up Gooseberry six miles, and over to the Greybull River. From the Greybull River, the road went to Meeteetse Creek, over to Sage Creek and then to the Stinking Water at the wagon crossing.[10]

Before there was a county seat inside the Basin, still a third county was created with some Basin land inside its boundaries. In the 1888 legislature, the Johnson County council member (who lived in Sheridan) succeeded in obtaining a division of Johnson County. When originally created, Sheridan County included all of the northern part of Johnson County and extended to the Big Horn River, as well.[11]

The new county was bitterly contested by the Buffalo residents, and the editor of the *Sentinel* gleefully quoted the Omaha *Bee's* assessment of the legislature that had created the new county: "After wrestling sixty days

---

[9]W. A. Richards to Milo Rowell, March 5, 1888, American Heritage Center, University of Wyoming. When the Lincoln Land Company surveyors were in the Manderson area in 1907, they located on their maps the point at which the old ferry crossed the Big Horn River at Manderson; it was near the southwest corner of the SW¼SE¼, Section 25, Township 50N, Range 93W. Lincoln Land Company townsite files, Manderson, Wyoming.

[10]Virginia Cole Trenholm and Maurine Carley, *op. cit.*, 230-32 and proceedings of a special meeting of the commissioners, Fremont County, May 6, 7, 1884. Fremont County was established March 6, 1884. *Session Laws of Wyoming Territory, Passed by the Seventh Legislative Assembly, Convened at Cheyenne, January 10, 1882* (Cheyenne, 1882), 66. The Wind River Indian reservation was reduced to exclude all of the reservation south of the North Fork of the Big Popo Agie River, effective September 26, 1872. L. Milton Woods, *Wyoming Country, op. cit.*, 108.

[11]The bill creating Sheridan County was passed over the governor's veto and became effective March 9, 1888. *Session Laws of Wyoming Territory, Passed by the Tenth Legislative Assembly, Convened at Cheyenne, on the Tenth Day of January, 1888* (Cheyenne, 1888), 218.

with the gravest of problems and the poorest of whiskey, the Wyoming legislature has adjourned to meet no more." A lawsuit contested the validity of the act creating Sheridan County and two other counties, because the enabling act had been passed a few days beyond the sixty-day limit of the legislature; a temporary injunction was issued, but when the matter was set for hearing in Cheyenne, Chief Justice Maginnis dissolved the injunction.[12]

This should have ended the dispute, but in Johnson County, the diehards opposing county division were able to get the Sheridan County question scheduled for hearing at the June term of the probate court in Buffalo. At that trial, Judge Micah Chrisman Saufley, who had just replaced Judge Blair in the district, made a number of strange statements in the course of his opinion. First, he declared that when Judge Maginnis had acted on this matter he was outside the district, so that he was without jurisdiction and his ruling was therefore invalid. Then Judge Saufley went on to examine the matter of the legislative action after the legal sixty-day term. He concluded that the legislature began its session on January 10, 1888 and that the act in question was passed on March 10, 1888, observing dramatically, "The body is just as dead the minute that breath has left, as after a year has elapsed."

It would seem that the judge was about to wipe out Sheridan County. But then, he took another turn in the legal road. He reasoned that since the restraining order of Judge Maginnis was invalid, it could not be lifted; moreover, since Sheridan County had already been organized, its officers could not now be restrained from organizing.[13]

This curious opinion is even more curious if we consider what had happened in Cheyenne the preceding month. The proponents of Sheridan County had hurried to the Supreme Court in Cheyenne to stop the Buffalo proceedings, and the Supreme Court concluded on June 12 that the probate court of Johnson County did not have jurisdiction over such matters. This was half a month before Judge Saufley came to Buffalo to hear that case. The opinion of the Supreme Court was written by Justice Samuel T. Corn, and it is not surprising that Chief Justice William L. Maginnis concurred, but it is surprising that the second concurring justice in Cheyenne on that day was Micah Chrisman Saufley. In any event,

---
[12]Judge Maginnis refused to impeach the legislative record which stated that the act was passed during the sixtieth day; he dissolved the injunction on April 21. *Big Horn Sentinel*, April 21, 1888 and *Cheyenne Daily Leader*, April 20, 21, 1888.

[13]*Big Horn Sentinel*, July 7, 1888.

Sheridan county remained as it had been organized, with its seat at Sheridan.[14]

The Big Horn Basin now had one county seat for the area west of the river, which could be reached across the mountains at Lander, while for the area east of the river, the county seat was across the mountains at Buffalo—or perhaps across the mountains at Sheridan. There were now functioning county governments for the Basin, but it was a chore for anyone living in the Basin to reach a county seat.

Good transportation was a luxury in many parts of Wyoming, and it should be remembered that the last stage line in Wyoming, in service from Casper to Lander, only suspended service in 1906. The Basin was more remote than other parts of Wyoming; indeed, it was the coming of the railroad to the Basin that made it possible to reach markets outside the region, so that intensive farming finally could be practiced in the area.

Once the Northern Pacific reached Billings, that location was closer to the northern ranches than Fort Washakie or Lander, but the Stinking Water was a formidable barrier. In the spring of 1883, Otto Franc wrote to *The Billings Herald* to solicit help in bridging the river; he sent Captain Henry Belknap and Col. W. D. Pickett to Billings to plead the case. By fall, the Billings Board of Trade had agreed to provide $500, and the Northern Pacific was also to contribute $500, if the ranchers could raise the balance, which was then assumed to be $1,000; soon there was a story that Frederick Billings would personally contribute $100 to the bridge. Franc promptly responded that the balance could be raised in Wyoming. The bridge was accordingly built that year, at an apparent cost of $5,000.[15]

After the bridge was built, the easier roads extended north into Montana; in 1885, the Meeteetse stage line from Billings was advertising a schedule departing every Monday after the arrival of the Pacific Express in Billings, with stops at Bruckman (near Laurel), Red Lodge, Dillworth, Corbett and Meeteetse. The return stage left Meeteetse every Friday. The editor of the *Big Horn Sentinel* in Buffalo fretted that the businessmen in Billings were conspiring to take the trade in the Basin to that city and he urged Johnson County to improve transportation.[16]

---

[14]The Wyoming Supreme Court case is A. J. McCray vs. Henry Baker, et. al., decided June 12, 1888, 18 *Pacific Reporter* 749.

[15]Otto Franc's first letter was dated April 9, 1883. *The Billings Herald*, April 28, August 4, September 22, 1883. The first bridge washed out in June, 1887, and a ferry was pressed into service until it could be replaced, a bit further upstream; this second bridge was in use until 1907. *Northern Wyoming Daily News*, June 19, 1992.

[16]Virginia Cole Trenholm, ed., *Wyoming Blue Book*, II (Cheyenne, Wyoming, 1974), 520-27.

THE OLD COUNTIES IN THE BASIN   155

Some governmental actions were taken to improve communication; Johnson County built a bridge over Ten Sleep Creek late in 1887, and let bids for two bridges to cross the Nowood River in the Mahogany Buttes canyon the same year. A new wagon road along the Nowood from Bonanza to Broken Back Creek shortened the distance by about ten miles, but it opened only in 1888. In April of that year, the road from Paint Rock Creek to the Big Horn River was made a county road.

The inadequacy of mail service was the subject of unending complaints throughout the Basin. Before the government instituted mail service, John W. "Josh" Deane set up a private mail route in the Basin in the late seventies, using a route from Fort Washakie over the Owl Creek Mountains to the Embar Ranch, then up the Greybull River and north to the Shoshone. Deane was born in Pennsylvania in 1856, and when he was fifteen, ran away from home to work on the western cattle trails. When this work brought him to Wyoming, he heard of the gold discoveries at Atlantic City and determined to go there, which he did in 1873. On the way to the diggings, Deane fell in with a band of Cheyennes, who left the lad with a romantic perception of the natives. He foolishly turned his pony in with their horses, only to learn in the morning that pony, saddle and outfit were gone. Deane spent five months with the Indians, but when he chanced to see the marks of hobnailed boots on a trail, he nearly cried with relief at this sign of a white man.[17]

Deane drove bull teams carrying materials to build the new Fort Washakie and also carried dispatches for government troops. On one mission from the Wind River to the Yellowstone for the troops in the spring of 1876, Deane got his first view of the Big Horn Basin, crossing north over the Owl Creek Mountains. Later in the decade, he established his own private mail route into the Basin, delivering mail to miners, who paid a flat rate for letters and newspapers, and to deliver the mail they were sending out. When the cattlemen arrived, they became customers, also. His route then ran from Fort Washakie to John D. Woodruff's Embar ranch, then up the Greybull River, across the Stinking Water and on to the Stillwater in Montana.

On one such journey, Deane met George Marquette for the first time. He was near the head of Sage Creek when he heard the strains of "Arkansas Traveler," and proceeded to a crude tent, where the bearded trapper was playing the fiddle. Deane said that he contributed some spirits

---

[17]Deane was later mayor of Meeteetse. He died in Meeteetse, June 13, 1930. Charles Lindsay, "John W. Deane, Wyoming Pioneer," *Annals of Wyoming*, IX, No. 3 (January, 1933), 743-751.

he had along in his outfit, which improved the music. Marquette, who was born in Ohio in January, 1841, had served two enlistments in the Civil war and had trapped on the eastern slopes of the Big Horns before coming to the Basin. He established a ranch at the forks of the Stinking Water and also often performed at ranch and saloon dances in the area.[18]

The first post office in the Basin, called Franc, was established on the Pitchfork ranch on April 6, 1882; it was moved to the Wilson ranch on Meeteetse Creek the following year, and its name was then changed to Meeteetse. In January, 1888, a new post office at Lovell's ranch was authorized, with Josiah Cook as postmaster. The post office department advertised for contractors for a mail route from Corbett, on the Billings-Meeteetse stage line, to Hyattville, via Bonanza. A second contract was issued for service from Bonanza to Red Bank, where Mrs. W. A. Richards had already been appointed postmistress.[19]

Mail service for the Basin was inaugurated from Meeteetse in July of the same year, but the east side of the river was not reached from this point until later in the fall. Still, complaints continued, and at the end of 1889, it was said that mail from Billings to the Basin took ten days to two weeks, and during the winter, some people saw no mail for 30 days. In the spring of 1894, the Otto *Courier* complained that the April 7 issue of the Red *Lodge Picket* did not reach Otto until May 3. Daily mail from Red Lodge to Meeteetse, Fenton, Burlington, Otto, Basin City, Alamo, Bonanza and Hyattville did not finally commence until July 1, 1898, and a week later the Lander *Clipper* noted that Basin City, Otto and Meeteetse were rejoicing over daily mail.[20]

---

[18]The Marquette ranch was purchased by Wesley H. Newton in 1892; he later sold it to his brother, Abram C. Newton. *Red Lodge Picket*, November 19, 1892, November 25, 1893. Marquette's Civil War service was in the 5th Missouri Cavalry and the 11th Minnesota Infantry.

[19]The name of the Franc post office was originally spelled "Frank," but the name was changed to Franc on September 15, 1882, and to Meeteetse on June 14, 1883. Daniel Y. Meschter, *op. cit.*, 11, 14.

[20]The post office contracts were advertised in April, 1888. Government mail service was inaugurated from Meeteetse to Bonanza, to Spring Creek, to Red Bank and to Lost Cabin in the fall of 1888. Fremont Clipper, August 9, 1888. Also, *Big Horn Sentinel*, October 8, 1887 and January 28, April 7, 14, 1888. The 1889 comments were quoted from the *Rustler* in the *Billings Gazette*, December 12, 1889. Also, *Billings Gazette*, August 3, 1897, *Red Lodge Picket*, May 12, 1894 and *The Clipper* (Lander), July 8, 1898.

CHAPTER XII

Water and a Governor from the Basin

By the time county organization came to the Big Horn Basin, there were already some people settling permanently along the streams, preparing to try to wring a livelihood from the harsh environment which the area presented. To do so, it was necessary to take water from the streams and use it to irrigate the land, for the natural precipitation was on the order of seven or eight inches per year, and two or three of that might fall in a single torrential rainstorm that would roar across the bare soil and carry tons of soil to the rivers below.

The eastern part of the United States had adopted the common law of riparian use, so that the settlers along the banks of streams were entitled to the use of the water in them. In the West, it was necessary to take the water from the streams and convey it for long distances to the place where it could be used; obviously, the riparian rules would not do for this region. As a consequence, a system of appropriation grew up in the west, where it was made use of in the mining regions and in the new agricultural regions that relied on irrigation.

The appropriation system recognized that there would not be enough water to irrigate all fertile land in the area, and therefore adopted the principle that the first use was the one to be favored, followed by later uses until all of the water had been used. Of course, the runoff in the streams in the spring of the year was much heavier than at other times, so that it was not unusual for the junior rights to be without water in some seasons, while there might be more than they could use in the spring.

The federal courts had long recognized and applied the West's appropriation doctrine; in the mining law of 1866, a provision was inserted to guarantee access to water for the purpose of mining, agriculture, manufacturing and other purposes. Instead of writing a new set of federal water laws, Congress adopted local customs, laws and decisions of the courts as the controlling rule for water rights, and in 1870 this provision was explicitly extended to all public lands and all patents granted for public lands. Thus, local customs, laws and decisions of courts prevailed, even against the United States and its grantees on the public domain.[1]

A lead case on the subject was a case involving Wyoming water. The dispute involved William Albert Morris, whose daughter gave her name to the town of Frannie. Morris was born in 1847, in Fort Wayne, Indiana, and the family came west over the Oregon Trail in 1851. Morris came to the Basin in 1886, and in 1888 he took a "possessory" right on Sage Creek, a tributary of the Shoshone River, to irrigate his 160 acre farm. Sage Creek rises in Montana, and in due course settlers in that territory attempted to appropriate the water of Sage Creek under the laws of Montana. Morris litigated the issue in the federal courts, and eventually the case of Bean vs. Morris became a landmark decision for the principle that the appropriation doctrine is still valid even where the stream flows from another state or territory.[2]

Wyoming Territory set up its own system of appropriation in 1886, when the legislature directed that anyone claiming an appropriation on any stream in Wyoming should file a statement with the clerk of the district court before September 1, 1886. The clerk of court was designated as the repository for such filings and all future appropriations, and the courts were given the authority to adjudicate them. The Big Horn River and its eastern tributaries were placed in district No. 5, while the western tributaries of the river were in district No. 8.[3]

This system remained in force until the first state legislature gave the administration of water rights to the state engineer; this legislation also

---

[1] The act of July 26, 1866 provided: "Section 9. Whenever by priority of possession, right to use of water for mining, agricultural, manufacturing or other purposes, have vested and accrued and the same are recognized and acknowledged by the local customs, laws and the decisions of courts, the possessors and owners of such rights shall be maintained and protected." 14 *Statutes at Large* 251. The act of July 9, 1870 extended Section 9 to all public lands and all patents granted or preemptions or homesteads allowed. 16 *Statutes at Large* 217.

[2] 55 *Lawyers Edition* 219-21, decided May 28, 1911.

[3] Chapter 61 of the 1886 session laws was effective March 11, 1886. *Session Laws of Wyoming Territory, Passed by the Ninth Legislative Assembly, Convened at Cheyenne, on the Twelfth Day of January, 1886* (Cheyenne, 1886).

WATER AND A GOVERNOR FROM THE BASIN   159

placed the Big Horn River and its tributaries in district No. 3. The oldest priorities in Wyoming are for two 1862 diversions from Black's Fork of the Green River and one from the Bear River for the old Myer ranch near Fort Bridger, in the southwest corner of the territory. These ditches were taken out when the area was still included in Utah Territory.[4]

The first state engineer was Elwood Mead, who had been territorial engineer since March 31, 1888. Mead pioneered what eventually would be called the Wyoming System, with centralized records of appropriations for all streams. When he took office, Mead found some streams badly over-appropriated, with some appropriations of the same stream distributed through several counties. By establishing the standard of one acre-foot per seventy acres, Mead was able to reduce the over-appropriation and spread the water more fairly among the potential users.[5]

A further complication was introduced by the presence of the Indian lands. It was very uncertain what, if any, water was to be allocated under the appropriation system to the reservations which the Indians had received in the old treaties. Much of the Rocky Mountain West was divided up in the treaty summer of 1868, and the Wind River Reservation in Wyoming was one of those erected at that time. That reservation sits athwart the Wind River, which is the name the Big Horn masquerades under before it passes through the Wind River canyon. While the treaty creating the reservation clearly contemplated that the Indians should take up agricultural pursuits, it is not by any means clear how the negotiators expected to deal with the water question.

The issue was squarely faced in a Montana case involving the Fort Belknap Indian reservation which was decided by the United States Supreme Court in 1908. The reservation, which lay along the south side of the Milk River, had been carved out of the great Blackfeet reservation in 1888 and set aside for the Gros Ventre and Assiniboine Indians. As early as 1889,

---

[4]Chapter 8 of the 1890 state legislature's session laws was effective December 22, 1890. *Session Laws of the State of Wyoming, Enacted by the First State Legislature, Convened at Cheyenne on the Twelfth Day of November, 1890.* (Cheyenne, 1891). The office of territorial engineer was created in 1888, but the legislature left the filing of water rights with the courts; the first and only territorial engineer was Elwood Mead, who took office March 31, 1888. Mead was also the first State Engineer. Virginia Cole Trenholm, *Wyoming Blue Book,* II (Cheyenne, 1974), 166. The Myer appropriation from the Bear River was taken out May 1, 1862 and the Black's Fork appropriation was taken out by Edgar N. Carter for the Carter No. 4 ditch and the Carter No. 5 ditch. *Tabulation of Adjudicated Water Rights of the State of Wyoming, Water Division Number Four* (Cheyenne, 1968), 69, 103.

[5]James R. Kluger, *Turning on Water with a Shovel: The Career of Elwood Mead* (Albuquerque, 1992), 20.

the Indians commenced diverting the water of the Milk River for domestic purposes and for irrigation, and in 1895 they made diversions to cover a total of 30,000 acres.[6]

Following the reduction of the great Blackfeet reservation in 1888, settlers took up the former reservation lands upstream from the Fort Belknap reservation and began appropriating the water of the Milk River to irrigate those lands, which were patented in 1895, 1900 and 1903. As a consequence of these upstream appropriations, Indians on the reservation first began experiencing water shortages in 1905. The superintendent on the reservation took the matter to the U. S. Justice Department, which responded with an action to enjoin upstream appropriation of the water so as to permit the Indians to irrigate their lands.[7]

When the matter finally reached the United States Supreme Court, that court observed that the land retained by the Indians on the reservation was "practically valueless" without irrigation, and concluded that Indians intended to reserve the necessary rights to use the water for irrigation. Moreover, the court also held that the transfer of jurisdiction over the water from Montana Territory to the State of Montana did not alter the reservation of water, since the United States government had the power to retain that reservation when the state was created.[8]

Following the precedent of the Winters case, the Wyoming courts concluded that the Indians had intended to reserve 500,000 acre feet of water from the Wind River and that this reservation of water should have a priority of 1868, which was the date of the treaty with the Shoshoni Indians, even though the Indians had not appropriated water under the territorial and state systems. This conclusion was upheld by the United States Supreme Court.[9]

---

[6]The Blackfeet reservation was established August 17, 1855, 11 *Statutes at Large* 657. The agreement approved April 15, 1874 provided for a somewhat reduced but still large, reservation for the Gros Ventre, Piegan, Blood, Blackfeet and River Crow Indians. Both of the larger reservations included what later became the Fort Belknap reservation. 18 *Statutes at Large*, 28. The reduction which established the separate Fort Belknap reservation was dated May 1, 1888, 25 *Statutes at Large* 113.

[7]Winters, et. al., vs. United States, 143 *Federal Reporter* 740 (Ninth Circuit Court of Appeals, February 5, 1906) and 207 *United States Reporter* 564.

[8]Lloyd Burton, *American Indian Water Rights and the Limits of Law* (Lawrence, Kansas, 1991), 21. The defendants in the Winters case were Henry Winters, John W. Acker, Chris Cruse, Agnes Downs and others. Winters, et. al. vs. United States, 207 *United States Reporter* 564.

[9]Winters vs. United States, 207 U. S. *Reports* 565. The Shoshoni treaty was dated July 3, 1868 and ratified February 26, 1869. 15 *Statutes at Large* 673. The Wyoming Supreme Court decision is *In re Rights to Use Water in Big Horn River*, 753 Pacific 2nd 76 (1988), affirmed by the United States Supreme Court in 109 *Supreme Court* 2994 (1989).

William Alford Richards, elected governor of Wyoming in 1894, the first governor to be elected from the Big Horn Basin. *Courtesy Wyoming State Museum.*

The government surveyors were in the southern part of the Basin in the summer of 1882 and 1883, laying out the townships and ranges, and in 1884 William Alford Richards came to the Big Horn Basin to do some surveying for the big ranches located on the west slope of the Big Horn Mountains, notably the WP outfit of Worden Noble. Thus began the Basin's connection with the first man to be chosen as governor of Wyoming from this area. Richards later settled on a ranch at Red Bank, and was elected governor of Wyoming in 1895 (his sixth cousin, DeForest Richards, followed him as governor).[10]

Richards was born at Hazel Green, Wisconsin, on March 9, 1849, the second of three sons; his father was from New York, and the first of the Richards to come to America had landed at Plymouth Rock in 1630. He joined the Union Army in September, 1863, with his older brother, Alonzo Van Ness Richards, driving an ambulance, since he was only fourteen at the time, and could not enlist. He returned to Wisconsin in the

---

[10]Alice McCreery and Tacetta B. Walker, "Wyoming's Fourth Governor - William A. Richards," *Annals of Wyoming*, XX, No. 2 (July, 1948), 99-130.

spring of 1864, and worked on a farm there. After graduating from high school in Galena, Illinois, he prepared to go west to Omaha in 1869.

While in Nebraska, Richards had worked on a government survey team, making surveys of the public lands in Nebraska. In Omaha, he met Harriet Alice Hunt, who was to become his wife. During 1873 and 1874, Richards and his older brother, Captain Alonzo Richards, worked on the survey of the south and west boundaries of Wyoming, and after concluding this work, he went back to Nebraska, where he continued surveying. On December 28, 1874, he married Miss Hunt in Oakland, and in 1877 he was elected county surveyor of Santa Clara County, California. In 1881, Richards went to Colorado Springs, in an effort to recover from an illness which had been diagnosed as consumption, and then became the surveyor of El Paso County.

After completing the surveying work he had contracted to do in the Basin in November, 1884, and before he departed for home, Richards visited the lands along the Big Horn River, located some of the federal survey corners, and ran several miles of survey lines on both sides of the river, near the present location of the city of Worland. He clearly had been thinking of a large irrigation project, because he noted in his diary that these lands were the sort he wanted for his "scheme" to divert water from the Big Horn River.

Richards returned to Colorado Springs, and he organized the Big Horn Ditch Company, which was incorporated late in 1885 with a capitalization of $17,020; the seven directors (who did not include Richards in their number) were from Colorado Springs. Based on Richard's plan for this ditch, 20,000 acres were filed under the Desert Land Act by various people on February 11, 1885. The group included the sheriff of El Paso County, the city clerk of Colorado Springs, the school superintendent, a hotel keeper and a grocer; there were also participants from Denver and California.[11]

The project was merely a land development project, as the filers did not even expect to go to the Big Horn Basin to irrigate their lands; indeed, the group signed a contract to pay Owen Thomas Gebhart ten cents per acre to perform enough irrigation to qualify the land for final proof. Gebhart,

---

[11]The seven original directors were John A. Himebaugh, David B. Fairley, Alvan A. McGovney Frederick G. Rowe, John J. Corum, Milo Rowell and Arthur G. Draper; all except McGovney filed on lands on the Colorado Flats, and McGovney later purchased the section filed on by William L. Swift. The office of the company was Colorado Springs. Big Horn Ditch Company incorporation, filed July 11, 1885, Miscellaneous Book A, Johnson County, 278, 279. Also, W. A. Richards to David Loban, January 31, 1888, American Heritage Center, University of Wyoming. The occupations of some of the participants are given in the *Big Horn Sentinel*, June 29, 1889.

who was then about 26, had met Richards in Colorado in 1883; he later published the *Basin City Herald*. Richards did the surveying work for the ditch, and expected to be paid for this work, but when the total cost of the project ran over the expectations of the board of directors in Colorado Springs, Richards had difficulty collecting for his final billing.[12]

By January, 1888, Richards was complaining that the ditch company members were "considerably dissatisfied," chiefly because the General Land Office was now insisting that the filers have personal knowledge that their lands had been irrigated. The trip from Colorado Springs to the Basin entailed a long day on the train, and then a day on the stage to Rongis, on the Sweetwater. From Rongis to the Basin was four days' drive in good weather, and Richards estimated that the requirement of a personal visit to the Basin added $200 to the cost of each full section.[13]

Richards' original filing for the ditch estimated that it would be twenty-six feet wide at the headgate and extend north for eighteen and a half miles, but when it was completed the dimensions were more modest. Gebhart began construction on the ditch in June, 1885, and it was finally finished by the middle of June, 1888. In the meantime, Richards had filed his own homestead in the Red Bank area along the western slope of the Big Horns and was contemplating buying 500 head of cattle from M. Burke and Sons. Richards also secured the Red Bank post office for the ranch.[14]

The construction work went well, without injuries to the workers, although it was difficult and expensive to get lumber for flumes; after Hyatt established a sawmill on Paint Rock Creek, the work could be finished. The completed ditch was twelve feet wide for the first eight miles, reducing to eight feet, and finally six. Gebhart and his men were now supposed to demonstrate that water could be brought on the land, but by August 4, they quit work because the water level in the river had fallen below the headgate.[15]

---

[12]Owen Thomas Gebhart was born in Urbana, Ohio, in January, 1860, and he came to Colorado in 1883. In August, 1896 he established the *Basin City Herald*. *The Midwest Review*, VII, No. 2 (February, 1926), 54.

[13]*Ibid.*, and W. A. Richards to Milo Rowell, February 7, 1888 and W. A. Richards to Hardin C. McCreery, June 19, 1888, American Heritage Center, University of Wyoming.

[14]*Basin Republican-Rustler*, December 9, 1982. M. Burke of Omaha was a widow, and her sons were partners in the ranching business. Milo Burke had been discharged as foreman of the Big Horn Cattle Company in November, 1887. W. A. Richards to Arthur Richards, February 22, 1888, American Heritage Center, University of Wyoming.

[15]W. A. Richards to Frederick G. Rowe, June 19, 1888 and W. A. Richards to Hardin C. McCreery, August 4, 1888, American Heritage Center, University of Wyoming.

To deal with this new crisis, Richards proposed that the ditch be deepened, which would cost $3,000 and sacrifice two or three parcels at the upper end of the project. He thought it should then be possible to divide up the land and sell 140 claims of 160 acres each. Nevertheless, the added cost was more than the long-suffering members would bear, and the project lay dormant for a number of years. Patents were issued for the land in 1890 and 1891, but the water rights for the ditch were never formally adjudicated. The *Fremont Clipper* sourly commented that even at high water, the ditch would not carry enough to irrigate 40 acres, yet the Colorado group had proved up on 10,000 acres of land. Actually, the editor was mistaken: the patents finally totaled more than 14,000 acres.[16]

Richard's ditch does not appear in the listing of appropriations from the streams of Wyoming, because it was not a successful appropriation of the water, and the ditch was abandoned after irrigation was demonstrated as the federal law required. The earliest territorial priorities on the Big Horn River and its tributaries are from Owl Creek and its North Fork, for the Owl Creek Livestock Company and the Embar Cattle Company, both with a priority of 1880, before Big Horn County was created. All of the earliest filings were on the smaller streams flowing into the Big Horn, because these streams were easier to divert than the deep-flowing river was. Thus, there were diversions on East Timber Creek, a Greybull River tributary, in 1881, and on Marquette Creek, a Shoshone River tributary the following year. Only in 1888 was there a successful diversion of the Big Horn River by Charles Pfeiffer, and even then his ditch was what the oldtimers called a "high water" ditch; lands irrigated under the Pfeiffer ditch were later consolidated into the Fritz Ditch, with a headgate nearly six miles further up the river.

Even though the task of moving earth was accomplished with horses and black powder blasting, and the landowners had limited capital, there were some surprisingly ambitious engineering projects. In 1897, Walter W. Peay devised a scheme to irrigate his homestead south of the present town of Manderson, located in a bend on the east side of the Big Horn River, between that river and the Nowood River, a short distance to the east. Peay concluded that the best way to irrigate the tract was from the

---

[16]Richards visited the ditch on June 11 and 12, 1888 and gave a progress report to McCreely. *Basin Republican-Rustler*, December 9, 1982, W. A. Richards to Milo Rowell, March 5, 1888 and W. A. Richards to Hardin C. McCreery, June 19, 1888, American Heritage Center, University of Wyoming Also, *Fremont Clipper* (Lander), September 7, 1892. Patents were issued for 14,671.97 acres; two members of the group did not complete proof. The Big Horn Ditch Company's charter was revoked in 1923.

Nowood, but that stream followed closely under some cut banks just upstream from his property, so that if he took his ditch from the west side of the Nowood, he could not get upstream far enough to give his ditch the elevation it needed to serve the land.

Peay solved his dilemma by taking the ditch from the east side of the Nowood, then crossing that stream with a flume. This Contention Ditch was to serve a total of 198 acres; work commenced on October 1, 1897, but the flume was swept away by the Nowood and time for completion was extended to September 30, 1903. Shortly thereafter, the State Engineer signified receipt of notice of completion. In the course of time, the Big Horn River cut across the oxbow where Peay's land was located, so that the area once served by the Contention Ditch is now on the west side of the Big Horn River.[17]

Richard's operation at Red Bank was more lasting than the Colorado Flats venture. In 1887, his family joined him at the Red Bank Ranch, and the following spring the furniture was brought from the railroad at Casper over 170 miles of primitive roads, but at last Mrs. Richards' square Chickering grand piano was in place, hauled up by Richards himself. Richards entered into local politics, and was elected as county commissioner for Johnson County in 1886, but in 1889 he was appointed Surveyor General of Wyoming by President Harrison, and the family once again moved to Cheyenne, leaving the Red Bank Ranch in the hands of George "Bear George" McClellan.

Richards continued a lively interest in the Basin, and was a moving spirit in the formation of the Red Bank Telephone Company, with seventy miles of line and thirty subscribers. He also tried his hand at town lot speculation in the new town of Warren, where he bought fifteen lots from Joe DeBarthe in the fall of 1890. Richards lost his position as surveyor general in 1893, when Cleveland was once again elected, and the Richards family moved back to Red Bank. In 1894, he was nominated for governor on the Republican ticket, and in the election that fall was elected.[18]

---

[17]The ditch was to be 6,289 feet long, and had to be flumed across the Harmony Ditch (a 30 foot flume), as well as the Big Horn River (a 178 foot flume). The ditch was surveyed August 24 & 25, 1897, by W. W. Peay, who seemed not to be troubled by the fact that he was also the principal beneficiary of the survey (the lands of E. R. Converse were also served). The priority of permit No. 1572 is September 3, 1897; eventually, 20 acres were proved up under the ditch. The point of diversion was later changed to the Harmony Ditch, presumably to avoid the first flume mentioned above. *Tabulation of Adjudicated Water Rights of the State of Wyoming: Water Division Number Three* (Cheyenne, Wyoming, 1964), 75.

[18]The deed from Joe DeBarthe to William A. Richards was dated August 15, 1890; Richards paid $500.

It is not surprising that the Basin, which was for so long a remote frontier of Wyoming, would not be the home of many of the leaders of the territory and state. Richards was the first resident of the Basin to reach the governor's office; as the fourth governor of the state, he succeeded John Osborne, who had been elected in the Democratic victory that followed the Republican eclipse brought on by the events of 1892. Richards was inaugurated January 7, 1895.[19]

Considering his high interest in irrigation projects, it was fitting that Wyoming received its donation of land under the Carey Act during Richard's term as governor. This was the era when there was much agitation for cession of the remaining federal land to the states. The railroads controlled by James J. Hill were particularly interested in the idea, as a way to promote large scale development in the area where they had land grants; this theme was discussed at irrigation congresses in 1891 and 1893, and the idea was endorsed by the Land Commissioner in his report in 1891. At the urging of Elwood Mead, Senator Francis E. Warren introduced a bill in 1891, calling for the cession of the federal lands to the states, with the funds to be devoted to irrigation facilities.[20]

Nevertheless this grand design did not materialize; instead, Joseph M. Carey, who was then chairman of the Senate Committee on Public Lands sponsored the Carey Act, which offered the western states up to 1,000,000 acres each, to be distributed to actual settlers who could reclaim the land. Carey had introduced the legislation in 1892, but it failed to pass at that time; it finally passed Congress in 1894.[21]

The Wyoming legislature accepted the grant of the Carey Act lands in February of 1894 and the State Board of Land Commissioners set up the machinery to administer the act. The Carey Act failed to live up to the expectations of its partisans, and in the first five years after its enactment, only Wyoming had developed land under its provisions; three years later,

---

[19]Richards was not the only governor to come from the Basin. Frank C. Emerson, who had been state engineer after his tenure as superintendent of the Lower Hanover Canal Association, was twice elected as governor, serving from January 3, 1927, until he died in office, February 18, 1931. Milward L. Simpson, the first graduate of the University of Wyoming to be elected governor, served from January 3, 1955 until January 6, 1959.

[20]Kluger, *op. cit.*, 22-23.

[21]The Carey Act passed Congress on August 15, 1894 and was signed by the President on August 18, 1895. The state board met April 2, 1895 and approval was given on September 14, 1895. James D. McLaird, "Building the Town of Cody, George T. Beck, 1894-1943," *Annals of Wyoming*, XL, No. 3 (April, 1968), 75-77. Also, Roy M. Robbins, *op. cit.*, 328.

only 11,321 acres had been patented. While only one of the ten eligible states was able to patent a majority of the million acre total, Wyoming eventually patented more than 200,000 acres under the Carey Act.[22]

It was fitting that Richards should be the governor to authorize the organization of Big Horn County, which he did in 1896; the county was finally organized the following year. Also during Richard's term, and perhaps a mark of the passing of the wild phase of the state, was the enactment of a law making killing of buffalo a felony, punishable by a prison sentence. Nevertheless, all of the trappings of civilization had not yet arrived, for when the next legislators added a crime for breaking into locked buildings, they took care to add "out house" to the list of structures so protected. The 1897 legislature also accepted the cession of the square mile including the hot springs at Thermopolis and in the same year sugar factories were given a ten year tax exemption, on condition that they process beets grown in Wyoming, if available. This incentive proved inadequate to attract new investment immediately, and the first sugar factory was not built until 1915, when Holly Sugar Company built its Sheridan plant; this action was followed by two 600 ton per day plants in the Basin, Great Western Sugar Company's Lovell plant in 1916 and the Wyoming Sugar Company plant in Worland the following year.[23]

At the end of his term, Richards declined to be a candidate, either for governor or United States senator, and on March 4, 1899, President McKinley appointed him assistant commissioner of the General Land Office; four years later he became commissioner. On October 27, 1903, Mrs. Richards died, and in 1907, W. A. Richards returned to Wyoming and the Red Bank Ranch for a time; the following year he was appointed State Tax Collector. He died July 25, 1912.[24]

---

[22]By 1958, Idaho had patented 617,334 acres under the Carey Act, and Wyoming had patented 203,311; two of the ten eligible states, Washington and Arizona, failed to patent any land under the Act. Paul W. Gates, *History of Public Land Law Development* (Washington, D. C., 1968), 650-51.

[23]The Carey Act lands were accepted effective February 14, 1895. The law making killing buffalo a crime was approved the same day. The Wyoming Historical Society was created February 16, 1895. *Session Laws of the State of Wyoming, Enacted by the Third State Legislature, Convened at Cheyenne on January 8, 1895* (Cheyenne, 1895), 69, 166. The locked building law was approved February 8, 1897, and the hot springs cession and the sugar factory tax exemption were approved February 24, 1897. *Session Laws of the State of Wyoming Passed by the Fourth State Legislature* (Cheyenne, 1897), 29, 77, 78.

[24]Richards was responsible for devising the lottery plan used in distributing public lands in the Indian Territory (now Oklahoma).

A gathering of early Big Horn County officials in front of
Hyatt's store in Hyattville. Colonel William D. Pickett is
No. 14 and Samuel W. Hyatt is No. 10.
Courtesy of Milton Hyatt.

CHAPTER XIII

Before Big Horn County

Before regular mail service was established in the Basin by the Post Office, the ranchers and a few other residents in the north end of the region hired their own carrier, who brought letters and small parcels up from Fort Washakie. The man who performed this work was John William Deane, whom everyone called "Josh." Born in Phoenixville, Pennsylvania, in 1856, Deane came to Wyoming in 1873. His story is one of those adventures that characterized the young men who came to the West in that era.[1]

At the age of fifteen, Deane obtained the money to leave home by filching three ten dollar bills his mother gave him to pay the grocery bill. With his friend Eddie Post, Deane struck out "west," riding on freight cars. At Indianapolis, an incredible stroke of luck gave them the money to extend their journey; while standing in front of a bank, the two boys witnessed a robbery, and when they told the authorities where the robbers had gone, there was a magnificent $100 reward for their troubles. Josh used part of his $50 to send a bank draft to his mother to replace the bills he had taken from the grocery money, and then the two were off to Kansas City.

From Kansas City, Deane went to Dallas, where the Santa Fe railroad was under construction, and got a job on the construction gang. It was here that he noticed first hand the activities on a cattle ranch near the railroad; when he asked for a job, the foreman suggested he join a cattle drive to the north that was making ready to leave. After he learned to ride a horse, Josh made a number of drives with this Texas outfit, but he left this work at Ogallala, Nebraska, and soon fell in with an Indian hunting party.

---

[1]Deane was born February 28, 1856, according to the obituary written after his death on June 13, 1930. In 1929, he completed his autobiography, which was edited by Dorothy Lindsay. The typescript of *The Mayor of Meeteetsee: The Autobiography of John W. Deane*, is dated July, 1930 and is in the Meeteetsee, Wyoming, museum.

Deane's first experience with the Indians was a sad one, for he turned his pony out with theirs, only to find it gone in the morning. He stayed with the Indians all winter, and in the spring they moved toward the South Pass region. One day, Josh was walking some distance from the Indian village when he saw the marks of hobnailed boots, and almost cried at this sign of a white man. He trailed the boot prints to a trapper's camp, and the trapper took him to Atlantic City; he learned that a new military post was to be established, and he secured a job driving a freight rig to bring supplies to this post, which would be named Camp Brown. Later, he became foreman working on a freight operation owned by John Arnold and James K. Moore, but quit when Moore reduced his wages from $75 per month to $60.

In 1876, Deane realized his ambition to become a government dispatch carrier, for which he received $125 per month. He carried dispatches chiefly among Forts Steele, Fetterman, Bridger and Washakie. In this connection, Deane related a story which we cannot verify. Shortly after the middle of June, Colonel Mason, who was commanding Fort Washakie, sent Deane to the army camp in the Rosebud country. Deane selected a Shoshoni, Niogen Doget, to accompany him.

When Deane rode north across the Owl Creek Mountains, he saw the Big Horn Basin for the first time. He crossed to the river and then followed it north to Sheep Canyon. They had to swim the Stinking Water, and then crossed the Pryor range to reach the Big Horn River below its canyon. They found Major Marcus Reno's camp on the Little Big Horn River, and could see signs of the battle that had just been fought. He was ordered to stay clear of the battleground, but after receiving dispatches to take with him, Deane proceeded to the north of Reno's position, where he saw the site of Custer's battle; he even identified the general himself, who was still unburied.

Soon after his return from the Little Big Horn, Deane began his private mail route to serve the cattlemen and trappers in the northern Basin. There was considerable flexibility in Deane's contract terms. John D. Woodruff subscribed, paying $20 per month, contracting for mail and such merchandise as could be delivered on a pack horse. George Baxter, at the LU ranch on Grass Creek contributed $10 per month. On Meeteetsee Creek, Deane met Otto Franc, who agreed to subscribe when he returned from Oregon with his cattle. At the head of Sage Creek, he met George Marquette, who was interested in the mail service, but had little money; Deane refused his offer of beaver pelts, and promised free delivery if Marquette would play the fiddle for him. Colonel Pickett wanted a guarantee of weekly delivery, but when Deane could not give it to him, subscribed anyway.

When the prospectors on Deane's route moved their camp, they would leave the forwarding address in a can buried at the edge of the campfire and marked with a peg. Although the route was profitable for Deane, its success called forth the services of the government, which established a regular mail route from Fort Washakie to Corbett and Meeteetsee. Deane continued to serve the route, working for the government.

Even before Big Horn County was created, the Colorado Flats in the southern part of the Basin had already been patented, although there were apparently no actual settlers living on the land. Even though Richards' irrigation project on the Big Horn had failed, there would soon be more than a few actual settlers along the river. We have a view on life in that early period from the reports of several junkets to this remote region by newspaper editors of the day.

The north end of the Basin was visited by Shelby Eli Dillard of Red Lodge, when he branched out from his work as editor of the *Red Lodge Picket* to start up a quarterly called the *Stinking Water Prospector* in the summer of 1891. The name of the paper indicates his effort to serve what appeared to be a new mining region, and in his first issue Dillard reported on a trip he had taken to the South Fork of the Stinking Water. Traveling by team and buggy, Dillard and his party (who are not otherwise identified) spent the first night out of Red Lodge near the Bear Creek coal mines; they passed the house of Sam Taggart just before coming down into the Clark's Fork valley. At the mouth of Bennett Creek on the Clark's Fork, they encountered the first group of gold miners, who claimed to have found the yellow metal, but not in paying quantities.[2]

After a stop to visit Z. Thomas Brown at his place on the Clark's Fork, the party finally came to the first "habitable" point, the "immense" sheep ranch of Thomas and James Hogan, on Paint Creek. They then proceeded to Pat O'Hara Creek, where they crossed the ranches of bachelor brothers Henry and Andrew Chapman, with their miles of fences and well-built residence house, sheds, stables and corrals. Dillard said that the Chapmans had 600 head of horses, including a "few" thoroughbreds, 500 head of graded cattle and 4,000 sheep. The ranches produced 1,000 tons of hay.

---

[2]The first issue of the *Stinking Water Prospector* was June 24, 1891, and this may have been the only issue.

Further up the same creek was the "model" ranch of John W. Chapman, brother-in-law of Henry and Andrew. John had a luxurious residence, where the party spent the night, surprised to find such a place so far from a city. John Chapman had 1,300 acres of deeded land, all under fence, producing 1,800 tons of hay. There were also 1,200 fine graded Hereford cattle and several hundred of inferior grade, 1,000 horses, including an imported stallion which cost $1,000 and a Percheron Chapman had raised which Dillard said "eight hundred dollars could not purchase."

After leaving the comforts of the Chapman ranch, the party rode south across the divide to Cottonwood Creek, and on the way were reminded how near they were to the wilderness, when they saw six coyotes chasing a monster grizzly bear. On Cottonwood Creek they met a man whom Dillard called Count Albert Chioles, the first of that rank Dillard had ever seen. Dillard expressed the opinion that the count with his book's horses, dogs, guns and rod got more out of life in Wyoming than he ever experienced in "wicked" Paris, but we do not know what response, if any, the count had to that point of view.[3]

The next place of interest was the ford on the Stinking Water, where Dillard and his group had the same difficulties many a traveler before had experienced, to the point that they feared losing their lives, to say nothing of a $1,000 team. After the crossing was finally negotiated, the party went to the ranch of George Marquette, on the creek named for him, and there they again spent the night. Unfortunately, the musical Marquette was missing, and only John Freeman was there to welcome the guests; we do not know whether Marquette's "ornery" bench-legged dog was home at the time.[4]

The first stop on the following morning was at the ranch of Captain Henry Belknap on Belknap Creek, which flows north into the South Fork of the Stinking Water. Belknap had some 1,500 acres, with 14,000 head of cattle and 2,000 head of horses, a "fine" residence with a lawn on a grassy knoll and "cozy" cottages for the employees. That night they camped out on Rock Creek, where they caught "a basket" of mountain trout. The next morning they forded the South Fork below William McLaughlin's ranch and arrived at Cabin Creek by noon, where they followed western tradi-

---

[3]There were counts in the region, but the name of the so-called count whom Dillard met is a puzzle; the probability is that he was Albert L. de Caillet.

[4]The Marquette name also graced a post office, which had only recently been established.

tion by moving into to a house where the owners were away. There, for most of two days, they prepared their packs for the final stage of the journey to the mines, some seven miles away, which could only be reached by horse.

The party spent three days at the mines, and then returned to their buggy on Cabin Creek. On the way back, they again stopped at Marquette's place, and this time George was at home, and eager to entertain them on the organ, while McLaughlin played the fiddle and Freeman the banjo. Their next camp was on Alkali Creek, where there was a survey party for the B & M Railroad under the leadership of Edward Gillette. Dillard was astonished to find that of the sixteen men, fully eight were "instrumentalists" who entertained them through the evening.

Further south, on the west side of the river, there were few permanent settlers, and a three week trip by the editor of the *Fremont Clipper* in the spring of 1888 gives us a view of that area. J. W. Thompson was living at the mouth of Owl Creek, and had made some "improvements" on his land there; at the mouth of Fifteen Mile Creek a Mr. Birdsley was in camp, but this may not have been a permanent settlement. At the mouth of the Nowood was William J. Shafer, another Union Army veteran, who came to the Basin from Lander in the fall of 1887 to take up a homestead on the Big Horn River. He had built a cabin on the east side of the river, in Johnson County and would later plat the town of Alamo on the west side, opposite the mouth of the Nowood River.[5]

There were a few more settlers on the east side of the Basin. An editor from Buffalo, who made a journey to the hot springs in the northeast corner of the Wind River Reservation in the fall of 1888. The springs on the east side of the river in Johnson County were not accessible by wagon, and to reach them it was necessary for the party from Buffalo to go down to the river and then cross over to the county road in Fremont County. The road from Buffalo to Paint Rock was good all the way, according to this account, except for a "long hill" on the east side of the mountain. The distance from Buffalo to Winn's Bar X Bar ranch was 65-70 miles, and from there it was a further 20-22 miles to Hyatt's store, which was shortly to become Hyattville; there the party found good fishing.

Samuel Washington Hyatt, then 50, was another of the transplanted southerners who had come west after the Civil War. He was born in North Carolina, and had moved to Texas at the age of 19; when the Civil

---
[5]Shafer served in the 58th Illinois Infantry.

War came, he enlisted for two years as an infantryman in the Confederate army. In 1884, he came to Buffalo, where he opened a store and two years later he came to the Basin. Hyatt and a son by his first marriage laid out the town of Hyattville in 1887 and in the summer of 1888, Horace Plunkett said the whiskey served at Hyatt's store was the "deadliest;" another asserted the elixir would put out a campfire.[6]

From Hyatt's store to Taylor's place at Bonanza was 12 miles, and the road was again said to be good; about four miles above Bonanza on the No Wood was James McDermott's place, which would be the scene of much sorrow some years later. McDermott's garden was watered by an overshot water wheel with five gallon cans on each paddle, a temporary arrangement until ditches from the river could be made ready.

Bonanza was platted in 1888 by Albert A. (Pap) Conant, born about 1817, a veteran of the Civil War, who had first visited the Basin as a prospector in 1872. The editor in Buffalo reported in 1886 that the sage brush at the townsite grew twelve to fifteen feet high.[7]

The first successful exploitation of oil in the Basin did not come until 1906, with the opening of the Garland anticline, but the Bonanza boom was the first of many false starts. Although the story in the Buffalo newspaper does not mention the excitement surrounding Bonanza's oil boom, the equipment to commence drilling was already on its way. Two ten-horse teams and one eight-horse team brought the machinery for the Big Horn Oil Company venture organized by Winfield S. Collins, and with them were eight families totalling perhaps 25 people. Men were dispatched to the mountains to cut timber to be fashioned into timbers at Hyatt's sawmill. By the middle of October, the rig was assembled and had drilled 150 feet. Unfortunately, the development stalled, and the following May

---

[6]Hyatt was born in North Carolina, April 2, 1838. He was married four times, and had a total of seven children; his son, William Lee Hyatt, was the son of the first marriage. On November 27, 1890, he married his fourth wife, Elizabeth Calhoun, and another son, Samuel C. Hyatt, was the only child of that marriage. S. W. Hyatt died October 23, 1903. *Progressive Men of the State of Wyoming* (Chicago, 1903), 551. Although biographies commonly list him as a captain or colonel, his Confederate service record from Company A of the 16th Texas Infantry shows his highest rank as sergeant. The plat for Hyattville was filed by Samuel Washington Hyatt and William Lee Hyatt on September 7, 1889. Before this date, Hyatt's advertisement of this era commonly spell the name of the settlement "Hyattsville." Also, Horace Plunkett diary, July 4, 1888.

[7]Conant was "nearly" 68 when he died early in May, 1905. He was born in Oneida County, New York, and when he was seventeen he moved to southern Michigan with his parents. He served in the 3rd Michigan Infantry, and was in the first battle of Bull Run; he was wounded at the battle of Fair Oaks, May 31 and June 1, 1862. After the war, he came to Dakota and Wyoming territories as a prospector. The *Cody Enterprise*, May 11, 1905 and the *Big Horn County Rustler*, May 4, 1905. Also, *Big Horn Sentinel*, August 28, 1886.

Joseph DeBarthe, born in Connecticut, started the Basin's first newspaper, Bonanza Rustler, in 1889. Never in one place for very long, DeBarthe left the following year. *Courtesy Wyoming State Museum.*

the *Billings Gazette* reported that the oil operation was at a standstill, although the promoters were hopeful for activity during the summer. Visitors from Billings were shown the oil springs in the summer of 1893, but although the residents could burn the oil in their lamps, the promoters had not found the source of the seep. The little boom town had a justice of the peace (W. J. Shafer) and a visitor reported that the building to house the new Bonanza *Herald* promoted by Isaac C. Wynn of the *Fremont Clipper* was "nearly complete."[8]

Bonanza did get its newspaper, the first in the Big Horn Basin, but it

---

[8]*Big Horn Sentinel*, September 15, 22, October 13, 1888, *Billings Gazette*, May 9, 1889, and *The Weekly Times* (Billings), July 29, 1893. Isaac C. Wynn was born in Scioto County, Ohio, October 20, 1830. After serving in the Army, he came back to Ohio, where he served in appointive governmental positions for eleven years; in 1880, he resigned and moved to Teller, Colorado, where he remained three years. He came to Lander in July, 1884, and established the *Mountaineer* on January 1, 1885, which he sold in May, 1887, after which he started the *Clipper* in September of the same year. He disposed of the *Clipper* in September, 1893 and moved to Los Angeles, where he remained until the summer of 1895; he then returned to Lander, and bought the *Mountaineer*, which he was editing when he died in May, 1897.

was not to be the *Herald*. In the spring of 1889, Joseph DeBarthe, who had worked in Lander for Wynn's bitter competitor, the *Wind River Mountaineer* for two years, ordered the equipment for the *Bonanza Rustler*, and it commenced publishing from Bonanza on June 1, with a fulsome description on the new town. A. A. Conant had given two lots to DeBarthe for the newspaper, and the building it was housed in was 20 x 20; it sat not fifty yards from the No Wood river, and the Big Horn Oil Company derrick was immediately in front of the building.[9]

DeBarthe, who was born in Connecticut in 1854, had been apprenticed to a Wilkes Barre, Pennsylvania, newspaper at the age of 14, and in 1887 he came to Denver for his health. He had lived in eight different places in the twelve years before he came to Denver, and he was not a man to remain in one place for long. He stayed at the *Rustler* only until the fall of 1890, when he went to Buffalo, to establish the *Buffalo Bulletin*, which issued its first number October 9, 1890. At Buffalo, he was editor for a year and a half, a period that included the Johnson County invasion by the cattlemen; during this time DeBarthe concentrated on touting the vast resources of Wyoming and its bright future, and ignored the festering conflict between cattlemen and rustlers out on the range, despite the fact that cattle were the only private industry in the county. Early in 1893, DeBarthe started the *Free Lance* in Buffalo; Will D. Edgar was the publisher.[10]

Back in Bonanza, The *Rustler* was acquired by William A. Richards, who employed Thomas F. Daggett as editor; Daggett had come to Bonanza the year before to work for DeBarthe. Apparently, Daggett and DeBarthe had similar editorial views, because during the events of the Johnson

---

[9] A copy of the first issue survives in the Fremont County Library in Lander. See also, *Big Horn Sentinel*, April 20, 1889. The *Rustler* proved to be a wandering newspaper. After its beginnings at Bonanza, it was moved to Otto, then about 1896 back across the river to Hyattville before finally settling in Basin about 1900. Lola Homsher, *Guide to Wyoming Newspapers, 1867-1967* (Cheyenne, 1971), 9; also *Billings Gazette*, June 13, 1889.

[10] DeBarthe and C. M. Lingle purchased the *Big Horn Sentinel* from C. H. Parmelee on October 9, 1890 and converted it to the *Buffalo Bulletin*. Vance Lucas, "Buffalo Newspapers," *Buffalo's First Century* (Buffalo, Wyoming, 1984), 164. Also, The *Clipper*, February 3, 1893. In the summer of 1896, we read that DeBarthe and his associates had made a rich gold strike near Sheridan, but we hear no more about this supposed Bonanza. The *Clipper* (Lander), June 5, 1896. DeBarthe was born in Granby, Connecticut, March 29, 1854 and married Harriet Simonds on May 17, 1875. From Buffalo, DeBarthe went to Sheridan, where he published the *Sheridan Enterprise* and from Sheridan he went to St. Joseph, Missouri; after he left Sheridan, he no longer lived with his wife, who remained in Buffalo. He died in Marion, Ohio, May 6, 1928. Cora M. Beach, *Women of Wyoming*, II (Lusk, Wyoming), 308. A review of his tenure at Buffalo is found in Helena Huntington Smith, *op. cit.*, 139-47.

County invasion, both the *Rustler* and the *Buffalo Bulletin* were accused of "openly" advocating the cause of the "cattle thieves," to the disgust of the editors at the papers aligned with the other side of that controversy. We do not know whether editorial policy impaired the financial strength of the *Rustler*, or whether it was true that it was only DeBarthe's absence from Bonanza that caused the paper to suspend publication for a time in 1893.[11]

After fording the Nowood at Bonanza, another 15 miles brought the Buffalo travelers to the ferry on the Big Horn, about three miles above the mouth of the No Wood, near the location of Lovell's first ranch headquarters. This was the old ferry that had been operated by Richard Sullivan, a dangerous character who went about armed with both a pistol and rifle and was regarded as a "wholesale" rustler by the Wyoming Stock Growers Association detectives. Operating from his remote location in a large cottonwood grove by the river, he was said to be stealing horses, and then driving them west to Idaho by way of Teton Pass.[12]

By the time the Buffalo group arrived here, Sullivan had decided to leave the country, and the ferry had been sold to Jerry Sheehan, who was in operation on that location in the fall of 1888; Sheehan in turn disposed of it to Perry Townsend in the fall of 1891. The editor noted wryly that on the east side it was difficult to get horses on the boat, and on the west side it was almost impossible to get them off, although he said the ferry was "good" when there was someone to operate it. Nonetheless, the ferry service was essential, since the river could not be forded except at low water; conditions improved in the fall of 1891, when Perry Townsend took over the old Sullivan crossing and launched a new 40 foot ferryboat.[13]

Once across the river, the Buffalo party were in Fremont County, and one senses a chauvinistic air in the criticism of the roads there. The editor

---

[11] *Billings Gazette*, March 10, 1892. On July 29, 1893, the Billings *Times* commented that the *Rustler* "does not issue during [deBarthe's] absence;" on September 8, *The Clipper* (Lander) carried an item welcoming the *Rustler's* resumed publication.

[12] In a report dated October 15, 1887, George B. Henderson, the stock detective, detailed Sullivan's horse stealing operation, and this was confirmed by another letter dated June 21, 1891, from John David, manager of the Fremont Cattle Company in Meeteetse. Wyoming Stock Growers Association collection, American Heritage Center, University of Wyoming.

[13] The Sullivan ferry was purchased from Sullivan and Kearney in 1888 by Jerry Sheehan, and by the fall of 1891, Townsend was running the ferry. The Townsend ferryboat was 18 feet wide. *Fremont Clipper* (Lander), August 8, 1888 and *Buffalo Bulletin*, October 8, 1891, June 23, 1893. Townsend, who lived south of Shafer, also conceived a project for a ditch on the west side of the Big Horn, upstream from Alamo; the Townsend ditch had a priority of January 8, 1891.

complained that the county road ran from half a mile to three miles from the river, so that camping places affording access to the stream were rare. Gooseberry Creek was about thirty miles upstream from the ferry, and although these sources do not mention them, others testified to "untold quantit[ies]" of gooseberries along its banks. The hot springs were another 30 miles south, and there were no ranches or stores near them. The Buffalo group found no trout in the Big Horn, but plenty of flat fish and catfish ranging from three to twelve pounds.[14]

The Buffalo party did not see W. J. Shafer, since they crossed the river south of his ferry. John R. Harris and Henry Burdick had taken up locations near Shafer, and in 1888 Harris had nearly 40 acres of oats planted and "several" acres of alfalfa. Shafer later filed on the land that became the townsite of Alamo and platted the town; he also operated the ferry across the river at this point. Alamo got its post office on May 26, 1890, and also had a newspaper, the *Alamo Argus*, which was published by Will D. Edgar until he moved it to Otto as the *Otto Mascot* in 1892. Unfortunately, someone burned the *Mascot* early in the same year, and the following year, we find Edgar in Buffalo, as publisher of the *Free Lance*, edited by Joe DeBarthe.[15]

Further south was the first German colony, a small group of farmers who selected land just north of the Colorado Flats. The first to arrive was Charles R. Pfeiffer, whose Pfeiffer Ditch to divert water from the Big Horn River has a priority of April 15, 1888, the oldest on the main stem of the Big Horn River. He would later be joined by the Vosses and their relatives and inlaws.[16]

At the south end of the county was Thermopolis, the old town just outside the reservation at the mouth of Owl Creek; its name was apparently chosen by Dr. Julius Schuelke, of Lander. Thermopolis did not have a post

---

[14]The trip by the Buffalo party was reported in the *Big Horn Sentinel*, August 18, 1888. It apparently consisted of Owen Simmons, Robert Bennet, Hugh Evans, Henry Leighton, Frank Thomas, J. D. Seibert and F. C. Eldred, according to a listing in the *Sentinel* of August 11, 1888. On July 19, 1892, a party led by Henry A. Kirk picked gooseberries on Gooseberry Creek and made gooseberry jam from them. Henry A. Kirk, "Sixty Days to and in Yellowstone Park," *Annals of Wyoming*, XLVI, No. 1 (Spring, 1972), 15.

[15]Otto had another newspaper, the *Otto Courier*, which was started by Lou Blakesly at the end of 1893. *Fremont Clipper*, October 22, November 19, 1887, May 24, 1888, *Basin Republican Rustler*, July 14, 1883. Also The *Clipper* (Lander), February 3, 1893 and *Red Lodge Picket*, January 8, 1892, October 14, 1893.

[16]1880 census, Lake County, Colorado. In the 1880 census, Pfeiffer gave his age as 28, which would have yielded a birthdate of 1852.

office at the beginning, and the mail for the area was delivered at Torrey, a post office run by Jennie Cusack, on Ed Cusack's ranch, two miles up Owl Creek from the old town of Thermopolis. There was a ferry across the river at the old town; it was operated by Jack Shafer and Neil Cunnington. Shafer was son of the the proprietor of the Alamo ferry, William J. Shafer.[17]

Thermopolis had a newspaper, the *Big Horn River Pilot*, which unfortunately ceased publication late in 1895 for a time, when its editor, E. T. Payton, was committed to the insane asylum at Evanston; he was released and made his way back to Thermopolis, but his disorder recurred in the spring of 1898. Finally, he made the best out of a bad situation and began writing in the *Pilot* about his observations at the asylum.[18]

Thermopolis could not be located at the hot springs until after the final reduction of the Wind River Reservation. Owl Creek was the north boundary of the Wind River Indian Reservation, so the south end of the Basin lay inside the reservation. As early as 1891, efforts were made to secure the cession of the area around the hot springs, but an agreement reached with the tribes in October, 1891 was not accepted in Washington. Further impetus for a cession arose after William A. Richards, a rancher from the Basin, was elected governor, and in 1896, James McLaughlin was given the task of negotiating the purchase of the springs.[19]

On April 21, 1896, the Arapahoes, represented by Chief Sharp Nose, and the Shoshonis, represented by the venerable Chief Washakie, agreed to sell a parcel ten miles by ten miles from the northeast corner of the reservation for $60,000. The agreement was signed by 273 representatives of the two tribes. For Washakie, then 98 years old, this would be his last

---

[17] *The Clipper* (Lander), June 12, 1896.

[18] E. T. Payton was committed to the asylum in October and released the following month, to go to Rapid City, where his mother and brother lived. He then returned and took up his old job, but in May, 1898, Frank Snaveley brought him back to the jail in Lander. The following week, he returned to Thermopolis, and in February of the following year began writing about his experiences at the Evanston asylum. Unfortunately, the newspaper was not a financial success, and the editor reported that in 1898 it took in $30.18 less than expenses; "We have been trying to figure out how it is kept running," the *Clipper* commented laconically. *The Fremont Clipper* (Lander), October 11, November 8, 1895. Also, *The Clipper* (Lander), October 22, 1897, May 20, 27, 1898, February 3, June 9, 1899.

[19] Early in 1896, the secretary of the interior promised Congressman Frank W. Mondell that government representatives would start for the reservation in two weeks, to inquire into the possibility of buying the hot springs; Major John McLaughlin, Indian inspector, was given the task, and he arrived in Wyoming in April. He promptly left for the hot springs, taking three representatives from each tribe with him. *The Clipper* (Lander), February 21, April 10, 1896.

signing with the government, closing a period of 63 years, which began with the Fort Bridger treaty of 1863, in which the government set aside most of southwestern Wyoming for the Shoshonis.[20]

Although the Indians had agreed to the cession, it was still necessary to secure the appropriation from Congress, and that action was by no means assured. Frank W. Mondell introduced the bill, which would have created the area as a National Hot Springs Reservation, but the Senate refused to create the Reservation, and also balked at paying for the hot springs if they were to be given to the State of Wyoming. Colorado's Senator Henry Moore Teller insisted, not without logic, that the State should pay for the land if it was to receive the springs. Finally, Teller partially relented and gave Mondell twenty minutes to draw an amendment accepting the ten miles square and ceding one square mile to the state. Mondell, working without any survey information, drafted the mile square reservation by centering it on the main spring; the amendment was in Teller's hands within the time limit. With this change, the bill passed Congress on June 9, 1897.[21]

After the agreement with the Indians opened settlement in the ten mile square in the northeast corner of the reservation, Thermopolis moved south to the point across from the hot springs, deserting the old town in September, 1897. In the two weeks after the ceded area was completed, there were some 80 persons living at the new townsite, in 50 tents and houses, although the road from the old town was still difficult.[22]

While the recitation of settlers' names in these stories does not amount to a large number, there must have been enough others in the area to give rise to the call for more polling places for the fall elections, the suggested points being the new town of Otto and Lovell's old ranch headquarters on the Big Horn, upstream from the mouth of the Nowood. When the Fremont County polling places were finally set, there was one at Otto, one at Lovell's post office on the Stinking Water and one at Sullivan's ferry on

---

[20]Washakie was born in 1804, or thereabout (some say as early as 1798); his father was of the Flathead tribe. His first treaty signing was July 2, 1863, at Fort Bridger. He died February 20, 1900; Chief Sharp Nose died July 12, 1901. Grace Raymond Hebard, *op. cit.*, 48, 279, 289 and 18 *Statutes at Large* 685. Also, *The Clipper* (Lander), April 24, 1896.

[21]The boundary of the mile square reservation begins half a mile east of the "principal hot spring," then extends half a mile north, a mile west, a mile south, a mile east, and half a mile north to the point of beginning. 30 *Statutes at Large* 62, Approved June 7, 1897. Also, Dorothy G. Milek, *Bah Guewana*, *op. cit.*, 41.

[22]*The Clipper* (Lander), October 22, 1897.

the Big Horn; the editor of the *Clipper* estimated that there would be 50 votes at Otto, 10 or 15 at Lovell, and 25 at Sullivan's ferry. In Johnson County, there were polling places at the school house on the Paint Rock Creek, Taylor's store at Bonanza, the Bar X Bar on Ten Sleep Creek, Gill's ranch at Mahogany Buttes and at William Robinson's ranch on Spring Creek. In the election, 35 votes were cast at Paint Rock, 17 at Bonanza, 27 at Ten Sleep, 26 at Mahogany Buttes, 22 at Shell Creek and 43 at Spring Creek. The editor complained that the Basin vote was "light."[23]

---

[23]*Fremont Clipper*, May 24, August 2, 16, 1888, and *Big Horn Sentinel*, October 6, November 10, 1888.

Colonel William Douglas Pickett, who earned his commission under the Confederacy and came West after the Civil War. He is rightly called the father of Big Horn County for his efforts to secure the enabling legislation for the county from the last territorial legislature. *Courtesy Wyoming State Museum.*

CHAPTER XIV

Counties Inside the Basin

The father of Big Horn County was Col. William Douglas Pickett, a true son of the old South who had served with distinction in the Confederate army. Pickett was born in Alabama on October 2, 1827, the youngest child of a Virginia Pickett family. He received his education at Transylvania University in Lexington, Kentucky, where he was trained as an engineer and when he was only nineteen he joined a party of surveyors who were to survey a colony in northwestern Texas. While there, Pickett and his seven year old sorrel horse joined the Texas Rangers, serving a year in the Mexican War, although the service of his unit consisted of duty on the northwestern frontier, as protection against the Comanches.[1]

The Rangers played a colorful role in the Mexican War, and although General Zachary Taylor has often been quoted as saying they were "too licentious to do much good," he often gave them the most difficult assignments, and when he was ordered to release any Ranger he could spare, he did not release a man. The unit Pickett served in was the Texas Mounted Volunteers, raised by John Coffee Hays, as colonel and Peter Hansborough Bell as lieutenant colonel. Hayes took five companies south to join General Taylor in June, 1847, and Bell was left with the rest of the command, including Pickett's unit, to perform frontier duty in the north.[2]

After the Mexican War, Pickett returned to his home in Kentucky, where he worked as a civil engineer on the railroads of that state and on the Memphis and Ohio, in Tennessee. He joined the Confederate army

---

[1] Pickett's service record from the Mexican War shows service in Captain William Fitzhugh's company of Bell's Regiment of Texas Mounted Volunteers from February 2, 1847, to February 2, 1848. He received a U.S. pension for this service.

[2] Frederick Wilkins, *The Highly Irregular Irregulars: Texas Rangers in the Mexican War* (Austin, Texas, 1990), 61, 146.

after the outbreak of the Civil War, claiming to have been "about the first" citizen of Tennessee to do so, and was shortly assigned to the staff of "Old Reliable," Lt. General William Joseph Hardee. There he served as assistant inspector general and became one of Hardee's "indispensables," rising to the rank of lieutenant colonel. After the fall of Atlanta, Hardee asked for the command of the army in Florida, South Carolina and Georgia and Pickett followed him to that command.[3]

When General William Tecumseh Sherman destroyed the buildings within his fortified lines in Atlanta, Pickett received the refugees ejected from the area, about 500 "women and children and a few old men," and saw the hardships of those people. While Sherman has been noted for his march to the sea, his later campaign swing north through the Carolinas was a much more difficult undertaking and, if possible, left even more devastation in its wake. Pickett saw this operation first hand, and his recollection of it was forever inflamed thereafter.[4]

Sherman cut himself off from supply lines and relied on foragers to feed the army and its livestock, destroying what they could not use. All too often, foraging quickly degenerated into looting parties, as foragers stripped the countryside of those valuables that struck their fancy. When Sherman moved north through the Carolinas, Pickett was almost continuously in front of him, and could often see the smoke from the fires of nearly every farmhouse in a forty-mile swath that formed the path of Sherman's army. The troops also fired the pine forests, creating a black pall that spread over the Carolinas. When Sherman reached the Cape Fear River at Fayetteville, North Carolina, Federal supply boats could then reach him again, and they foolishly brought oats for the animals, instead of the shoes that were desperately needed; the Army officers scornfully offered to send back a load of corn from the booty the foragers had obtained. Pickett was paroled with General Joseph Eggleston Johnston's army in North Carolina in April 1865, after Johnston failed in an effort to link his army with that of Lee.[5]

---

[3]Nathaniel Cheairs Hughes, Jr., *General William J. Hardee: Old Reliable* (Baton, Rouge, 1965), 116, 250. Pickett received a captain's commission from the governor of Tennessee on April 15, 1861 and he joined the staff of General Hardee on September 2, 1861, was promoted to lieutenant colonel March 10, 1864 and was paroled April 26, 1865. Pickett's second cousin, George E. Pickett, led the famous charge at Gettysburg. See Stella Pickett Hardy, *Colonial Families of the Southern States of America*, (Baltimore, 1981), *passim*.

[4]*Confederate Veteran*, XIV, No. 7 (July, 1906), 295, and No. 9 (September, 1906), 397. Also, *Cheyenne Sun*, January 14, 1890.

[5]John G. Barrett, *Sherman's March Through the Carolinas* (Chapel Hill, N. C., 1956), 135.

After the war, Pickett returned to work for the Memphis and Ohio, which needed to be rebuilt after the ravages of the war. He resigned from this job in 1873 and went to Bismarck, in Dakota Territory, where he occupied himself hunting around the headwaters of the Missouri for the next seven years. Pickett first saw the Big Horn Basin in September 1879 and returned there the following year. It was Pickett's recollection that there were only three residents in the entire Basin in the fall of 1880, Carter, Belknap and Franc. Pickett spent the 1881-82 winter in Bozeman and in the summer of 1882 he was back on the Greybull River again; the following spring he settled at the mouth of Pickett's Creek, a tributary of the Greybull River, where he began raising Herefords, which were branded with the Ram's Horn brand (also called the Double Reverse J).[6]

Although Pickett apparently got along well with most of his neighbors, there was at least one notable exception: Abraham Archibald Anderson, owner of the Palette Ranches on the Greybull River. Anderson, who was born in 1847, had studied art in Paris, and maintained a studio in New York City. He first came to Wyoming about 1896, bringing with him a letter of introduction to Col. Pickett. Despite the introduction, Pickett and Anderson did not get on well, although we only have Anderson's reason for the difficulty between them.[7]

Anderson located his own Palette Ranches, named for the artist's palette, above Pickett's, and built a studio there. Soon, he was titillating the denizens of the area with his artistic talents, aided by female models, supposedly imported from Paris. He submitted a painting, *A Woman Taken in Adultery*, to the national jury for the Chicago World's Fair in 1893, but it was rejected, and Anderson's protests were unavailing. Nevertheless, the painting, which had won a medal in the 1889 Paris Salon, was subsequently hung in the French section of the exhibition, but there it was ordered covered by a crimson cloth because it was "too immoral" for exhibition. There were others who were critical of his art, for when he painted the portrait of William A. Richards, the latter refused to accept it, although the painting was later given to the State of Wyoming.[8]

---

[6]George Bird Grinnell, ed., *Hunting at High Altitude* (New York, 1913), 11-14. Pickett received two U. S. patents in 1889 and 1890.

[7]Anderson's studio in New York was located at 57 West 58th Street. He came to Wyoming with his friend, John Claflin, of New York.

[8]Anderson apparently located his ranch at least by June, 1893, which was the date of his water appropriation; he purchased 160 acres from Edward B. Glanagan on October 23, 1897. Anderson wrote his autobiography in 1933, but there are numerous factual lapses in it. Also, *Revisiting the White City: American Art at the 1893 World's Fair* (Washington, 1993), 90, 120n.

Anderson continued to make news, as when he brought an "outing wagon" of his own design to the West in the summer of 1896, and after the turn of the century, as when Prince Albert of Monaco was a visitor at his ranch. He became interested in the conservation of forests, and when the Yellowstone Forest Reserve was set aside by President Theodore Roosevelt, Anderson became the first superintendent, a position he held until 1906, and which afforded him the scope for continued controversy.[9]

In 1888 Pickett was elected to represent Fremont County in the house of representatives in the 1890 legislature. Pickett was now in a position to work for a county in the Basin, but unfortunately, his efforts soon became entwined with the movement to admit Wyoming Territory as a state. This movement gained momentum in early 1888, when Joseph M. Carey, the Wyoming delegate in the House of Representatives, introduced a bill in Congress to admit Wyoming. The Carey bill and another in the Senate went nowhere in 1888, nor did three other bills introduced the following year. Back in Wyoming, Governor Francis E. Warren took the initiative by calling an election for a constitutional convention, and this convention met on September 2, to begin work drafting a constitution for the state.

When the convention first considered the matter of county division, M. C. Barrow proposed that no new county could be created unless the new county and the remaining portion of the parent county should each have at least $3 million in assessed valuation. Under these rules, a county would have to have at least $6 million in assessed valuation to divide, and in 1889, only Laramie County could have been divided; indeed, five of the ten counties that were organized in 1889 had less than $3 million in assessed valuation.[10]

This proposal touched off a spirited debate in the convention. The movement for lower restriction was led by H. A. Coffeen, a merchant from Sheridan. Sheridan County had been organized the year before, after a bruising battle with Johnson County, and it still did not have a courthouse. There was a good deal of needling from the other delegates over Sheridan County's parsimony, especially the case of an alleged murderer who had not been tried, because the county did not want to pay the

---

[9]*Red Lodge Picket*, June 10, 1893, July 25, 1896. Anderson was appointed superintendent of the forest on July 1, 1902.

[10]In 1889, the total assessed valuation in the territory was $31.4 million; Laramie County led the list with $7.9 million and Sheridan was the smallest with $1.2 million. *Report of the Governor of Wyoming to the Secretary of the Interior, 1889* (Washington, D. C., 1889), 660. The governor's report, which was dated October 15, noted that the totals were incomplete.

cost of a term of court. The county division proposal was referred to the sixth standing committee, which had members from each county in the territory, and that committee reported back in a week, with a $2 million limit for both the new county and the remaining parent, a limit apparently authored by John M. McCandlish of Buffalo.

The committee also proposed that both the new county and the remaining parent have at least 1,500 inhabitants before the new county could be organized. Before 1888, the question of how large the population of a new county had to be was decided at the time each county was created. Thus, the act creating the counties of Crook and Johnson (originally named Pease) permitted organization when there were 500 electors in each county. The general appropriation bill of 1888 enacted a general provision for organizing counties, in which the population requirement was set at 300 electors.[11]

When the committee report reached the convention's committee of the whole, most of the debate centered on the assessed valuation limitation, and two Laramie county delegates made a strong effort to increase it, first to $3 million, then $2.5 million; both efforts failed, but the debate suggested the possibility of an alternative. Meyer Frank of Crook County agreed that $2 million assessed valuation was enough for a new county, but not enough for the parent county, with indebtedness to fund. William C. Irvine of Converse County seized on this idea and proposed that the remaining parent county must have at least $3 million, and this amendment was accepted.[12]

Pickett realized that organizing a county for the Big Horn Basin would be much more difficult if the territory was admitted as a state with such a constitutional provision, and he lobbied to get the limitations reduced by the convention, but without success. The territory could still take action before the constitution became effective, and Pickett now turned his attentions to the legislative arena. There, he was opposed chiefly by Johnson County, which was adamantly opposed to the formation of a new county in the Basin. Johnson County's financial condition was "pitable [sic]," to quote its own delegate to the constitutional convention. It had

---

[11] Pease County and Crook County were created December 8, 1875. The general appropriation bill of 1888 was passed over the governor's veto on March 9, 1888.

[12] Crook County, which had only $2.3 million in assessed valuation, would shortly be divided by the creation of Weston County, and Frank may have been seeking some additional protection against that possibility. It is not clear whether Frank realized that the constitution also required that existing debt be apportioned to the new counties.

just built a new courthouse, and its warrants were sometimes refused by the banks. Sheridan County actually favored the new county as a means to eliminate an expensive and inaccessible area and Fremont County represented the swing consideration.[13]

Events now speeded up. The constitutional convention in Cheyenne adjourned September 30, after approving the limitations on county formation and organization. In Washington, on December 9, 1889, Orville Platt introduced yet another bill in the Senate to admit Wyoming - the third for that year - and on the eighteenth, Joseph M. Carey introduced HR 982 in the House. Pickett spent Christmas week negotiating a compromise with the leaders of Fremont County to secure their support for a new Big Horn County. This plan would make it possible for the new county to be organized with 300 electors and $1.5 million assessed valuation, provided that the surviving portions of Fremont and Johnson counties each had at least $1.6 million in assessed valuation. Pickett was able to draw the boundaries of the new county with the help of William A. Richards, who was then surveyor general for Wyoming; a slight adjustment was made to accommodate the wishes of Fremont County.[14]

Pickett introduced the Big Horn County bill in the Wyoming house of representatives, to cut off the western part of Johnson and Sheridan counties and the northern part of Fremont County. While the bill was working its way through the legislature, two bills to admit Wyoming were actively being considered in Congress, and Pickett knew that if statehood came too soon, the new county would be doomed. Pickett's efforts were opposed in the territorial Council by George T. Beck, who represented both Sheridan and Johnson counties. Beck privately acknowledged that it was desirable to create a county in the Basin, but felt obliged to oppose Pickett's bill because of strong opposition among his constituents. It was only after Pickett agreed to amend his bill to delay organization of Big Horn County until after February 2, 1892 that Beck permitted the Big Horn County bill to become law, effective March 12, 1890.[15]

Carey's bill to admit Wyoming as a state passed the U. S. House of Rep-

---

[13]*Journals and Debates of the Constitutional Convention of the State of Wyoming* (Cheyenne, 1893), 302.

[14]Sheridan County lost only a small area to Big Horn County, and no language was inserted to protect the assessed valuation of that county.

[15]*Progressive Men of Wyoming* (Chicago, 1903), 897. Weston County was also created on March 12, 1890; these were the last counties created by Wyoming Territory. In the spring of 1883, Pickett filed a water right on Pickett's Creek to irrigate 45 acres. *Park County Enterprise*, February 4, 1910.

resentatives on March 26 and the Senate on June 27; it was signed by President Harrison on July 10. The restrictive county organization provision remained in the Wyoming constitution, but Pickett assumed that it did not apply to an existing county, such as Big Horn, even though it was unorganized.

The boundaries of the new county contained nearly all of the Big Horn Basin. The northern part of the western boundary was inside the Yellowstone Park reservation, and it abutted on the eastern boundary of Uinta County, as that county was described in 1869. Big Horn County included the northern part of Fremont county as far south as the Wind River Indian reservation, and the eastern boundary approximately followed the crest of the Big Horn Mountains to the Montana line. Only the new town of Thermopolis and that portion of the Big Horn River drainage included in the Wind River Indian reservation was outside the new county; this area would be picked up by Hot Springs County when it was created in 1911.

Pickett thought that his deal with Fremont County to delay the organization of Big Horn County until after February 2, 1892, would ensure that the county could be organized without opposition after that date. Nevertheless, when efforts were made to organize the new county, it was the commissioners of Fremont County who brought an action to enjoin the county organization, claiming that Big Horn County was now subject to the constitutional limitation. At the beginning of 1895, the Wyoming Supreme Court ruled on the controversy; although it easily found that Big Horn was a county, created by the 1890 act, it also ruled that this unorganized county was now subject to the rules of Section 2, Article 12 of the constitution, which had become effective before it was organized. The organization of the county was therefore enjoined, since it had too few inhabitants.[16]

It was left for Governor William A. Richards, himself a rancher from the Basin, finally to act to organize Big Horn County, and he issued commissions to the newly appointed commissioners under a letter dated June 27, 1896; the county was declared organized on January 4, 1897.

When DeForest Richards and Fenimore Chatterton ran for the office

---

[16]One of the questions raised in this case was whether Sheridan County, which was created in 1888, and extended into Big Horn County, had to have $3 million in assessed valuation; the Court answered this question in the negative. Board of Commissioners of Fremont County vs. Perkins, et. al. 5 *Wyoming Reports* 166, decided January 5, 1895.

of governor and secretary of state in 1898, they had to conduct most of their campaign by buckboard. To deal with the Basin, Richards sent a team of mares to Hyattville to await their arrival from the south. The two politicians came into the Basin over the Owl Creek Mountains, on a road which was too steep for the mules to pull the buckboard with the men on board, so Richards walked behind, while Chatterton led the mules; the two men arrived in Thermopolis generously dyed by the red dust of the road. The bridge over the river had been washed out by the spring flood, so the good citizens of the town could press their case for a replacement.[17]

The campaign trail then led north to Basin, following the west side of the river, and Chatterton said there was not a house between the two towns, forcing them spend the night camped on a sand bar. After an evening's speaking and dancing, they went the next day to Cody, where the two men separated, Chatterton taking the mail carrier's buckboard to deliver a speech in Meeteetse, while Richards stayed to massage the political temperament in Cody. Another forty miles took them to the Burlington colony, and the next day they arrived at Hyattville, where they exchanged mules for horses and drove over the mountains to Sheridan.[18]

The organization of Big Horn County kicked off the competition for the county seat. The Mormon settlement near Burlington provided voting strength to the nearby town of Otto, which had been platted by Frank S. Wood in 1888; it was the home of two newspapers, the *Courier*, owned by Hal and Lou Blakesley, which had started publication in 1889 and the *Rustler*, recently moved from Bonanza. Otto was clearly the senior town in contention, although there were other candidates, including Alamo, although the latter must have been a distinctly long shot.[19]

Opposing the Otto initiative was the new town of Basin City, which was the creature of Winfield S. Collins. Born in Champaign County, Ohio, on March 30, 1848, Collins graduated from agricultural college as

---

[17]The steel bridge was built in 1902.

[18]Fenimore Chatterton, *Yesterday's Wyoming: The Intimate Memoirs of Fenimore Chatterton* (Denver, 1957), 53-57.

[19]*The Billings Gazette* noted on May 2, 1889 that Otto would soon have a newspaper. W. E. Coutant, who was highly critical of the Basin City editorializing against Otto, boosted the idea of Alamo as county seat. The *Fremont Clipper* (Lander), November 15, 1895. Also, *Basin Republican-Rustler*, December 16, 1982.

a civil engineer in 1870. In 1877, he began the study of law in Springfield, Illinois, and was admitted to the bar there; he then moved to Nebraska, where he became a county surveyor. Collins then moved to Wyoming, first to Fort Fetterman (in 1885) and then Douglas. In the fall of 1887, the *Fremont Clipper* reported that Collins and Col. Ligier were surveying a ditch 19 miles long to irrigate 40 sections from the Big Horn River. The following year, Collins came to Bonanza, having organized a group from Nebraska in an effort to develop the oil fields there. The oil development ultimately failed, but for a time there were high hopes for Bonanza, which was surveyed by Collins when the town was platted.[20]

When Collins saw that Big Horn County was to be organized, he planned to move to the county seat, which he assumed would be Otto. This town had been platted and named by Frank S. Wood, the former surveyor of Fremont County. When Collins tried to buy lots from Wood, they could not make a deal, and Collins angrily drove off to set up his own town on the Big Horn River. The town of Basin City was platted on the public domain under the federal townsite laws. Otto's newspaper advantage over Basin was sharply reduced when the *Paint Rock Record* moved to Basin, where it was rechristened the *Basin City Herald*; it began publication under the new masthead on August 24, 1896, under the direction of O. Thomas Gebhart and Joseph Magill.[21]

Magill, was born in County Tyrone on January 25, 1848, and was educated for the priesthood at Armacat, Ireland, and also in Rome. When his health failed, the doctors suggested he come to the American West, and on September 8, 1886, he arrived in Cheyenne directly from Ireland. In Lander, he met Dr. Julius Schuelke, who told him of the hot springs on the Big Horn; Magill visited the springs, and was later employed as a cowboy on the Embar Ranch before he accepted the job as editor of the *Basin City Herald*.[22]

The scene was now set for a county seat battle that has earned itself a place in numerous accounts of journalism in the West. At one point, the

---

[20]Collins died in Basin, November 11, 1916. *Fremont Clipper* (Lander, Wyoming), November 19, 1887, July 19, 1888 and *Basin Republican-Rustler*, July 1, 1971.

[21]We do not know what price Wood was demanding; his 1888 advertisement offered town lots for sale at $25 for a corner, $15 for an inside lot. *Progressive Men of the State of Wyoming* (Chicago, 1903), 789, Lylas Skovgard, *Basin City* (Basin, Wyoming, 1988), 7 and *Fremont Clipper* (Lander, Wyoming), April 5, 26, 1888.

[22]Magill also worked on the *Omaha World-Herald*. Tacetta Walker, *op. cit.*, 143.

editor of the *Courier* referred to Joe Magill of the *Herald* as "A low lived, brainless coward, biggest lying coward that ever breathed the breath of life, halfwitted cur, brainless pup, skunk and poor fool."[23]

All of this was without avail, because the Otto campaign ran afoul of the new settlement of Cody, the brainchild of George T. Beck of Sheridan, son of a Kentucky senator. Beck had tried his hand at politics, but failed to secure the appointment as Wyoming governor at the time that President Cleveland needed to appoint someone to replace the disgraced Baxter. In the spring of 1894, Beck assembled a surveying party which included the Wyoming state engineer, but also included Horton S. Boal, who was married to the daughter of Col. William F. Cody. After a trip through the Basin, enthusiasm for the area ran high, and eventually Cody and Beck formed the Shoshone Land and Irrigation Company; the town was platted in February, 1896.

While Cody could not hope to claim the county seat for itself, it could draw enough votes to give the election to Basin City, and that is what happened. The voters gave 481 votes to Basin, 420 votes to Otto and 243 to Cody. In the aftermath of the battle, Otto lost the *Rustler*, which moved to Hyattville. The *Red Lodge Picket*, which had supported the northern contenders for in the contest, opined that "Basin City, like the man who bought the elephant, has the county seat, but does not know what to do with it."[24]

This comment may have been sour grapes, but even a supporter of the new county seat had to admit it was "pretty much an open prairie." Nevertheless, Basin continued to grow, and the *Basin City Herald* said that the ornamentation on the white-washed walls of the county's "palatial shack," consisted of cornices and scrolls that were "works of art," in a style that blended arabesque and rococo. In 1898 the first bank chartered in the Basin was organized there, the Big Horn County State Bank, with Willis J. Booth as president, and David L. Darr as cashier. Darr, who was born in Illinois, had come to Basin City in August. It was winter when the bank started up, and the freighter charged with the task of bringing a thousand

---

[23]While the quoted item is perhaps the best known of this sort, frontier editors were often colorful. The Lander *Mountaineer* had the following to say about the efforts of I. C. Wynn, editor of the *Fremont Clipper*, to secure subscriptions in the Basin: "Brother I. C. Wynn, the prehistoric pump who removes the bilge water from the Lander *Clipper*, recently sent out a bundle of subscription blanks into the Nowood country asking for a $1,000 bonus for establishing a $300 newspaper at Bonanza...." Quoted in the *Fremont Clipper*, April 26, 1888.

[24]*The Clipper* (Lander), October 15, 1897, and *Red Lodge Picket*, November 28, 1896.

silver dollars to the bank found himself snowbound on the road. He marked the keg "horseshoes," and left the rig in the snow, while he sought shelter at a nearby ranch; the money was still there when he returned.[25]

As population grew, so did agitation for more counties. C. F. Robertson, who was the first mayor of Worland and secretary of the Hanover Land and Irrigation Company, lobbied three successive legislatures to give the Worland area a county, but that effort failed. The first successful effort to divide Big Horn County was in 1909, when bills were introduced in the legislature creating Park County from the northwestern corner of Big Horn, and Hot Springs in the south, including all the area presently within Washakie and Hot Springs counties. In February, the Park County bill passed; the name of Hot Springs was changed to Washakie and under that name the second bill also passed. On February 20, Governor Bryant B. Brooks signed the bill creating Park County, but he returned the Washakie County bill without his signature.[26]

The governor noted that the proposed Washakie County had an assessed valuation of $1.25 million, which was less than the minimum required by the state constitution; the shrunken Big Horn County after removing Park and Washakie would have only $2.2 million in assessed valuation, which was also less than the constitutional requirement. He therefore permitted Park County to be organized, because it had sufficient valuation, and the rest of Big Horn County would have enough assessed valuation if Washakie County was not taken from it. It should be noted that the legislature had anticipated this difficulty by delaying the effective date of the Washakie County bill until September 7, 1910, so that assessed values could grow enough to satisfy the constitution, but the governor would not accept the assumption of future growth.[27]

---

[25]The Big Horn County Bank received state charter No. 9, dated December 20, 1898. The bank closed May 15, 1922. David L. Darr was born on January 7, 1856, in Ipava, Illinois. He moved to Nebraska, and was the cashier of a bank at O'Neill, Nebraska, before coming to Wyoming. L. Milton Woods, *Sometimes the Books Froze: Wyoming's Economy and its Banks* (Boulder, Colorado, 1985), 56, 147, 172 and Ichabod S. Bartlett, *History of Wyoming*, II (Chicago, 1918), 121. Also, *Red Lodge Picket*, December 5, 1896.

[26]The north boundary of Hot Springs county (renamed Washakie) was set at the twelfth standard parallel. One of those supporting this first Hot Springs County was none other than Charles H. Worland. *Thermopolis Record*, December 16, 1906, January 9, 1909.

[27]Section 2, Article XII of the Wyoming constitution required that new counties have an assessed valuation of at least $2 million, and that the surviving parent county have a remaining assessed valuation of at least $3 million. The total assessed valuation of Big Horn County at the time of this legislation was $5,522,959.43; the area erected into Park County had a valuation of $2.019 million. *Thermopolis Record*, February 27, 1909.

So it was that Park County was created, giving it more than half of Big Horn County. The Big Horn County commissioners challenged the constitutionality of the Park County statute and this action delayed organization until the Supreme Court of Wyoming could rule on the question. Park County was finally organized January 9, 1911, with its seat at Cody, which overcame a strong challenge from Powell, the former Camp Colter.[28]

In the eleventh legislature, two bills to create new counties from Big Horn were introduced in the senate at the beginning of 1911. On January 13, Patrick J. Sullivan, a sheep rancher from Casper, introduced S. F. 3, a bill to create Hot Springs County from the south end of Big Horn County, and on the following day, George B. McClellan, the senator from Big Horn County, introduced S. F. 7, a bill to create Hanover County. The committee of the whole changed the name of Hanover County to Washakie, to honor the great Shoshoni chief, who had died in 1900. Both measures passed the legislature and were signed by Governor Carey on February 9, 1911.

Hot Springs County included the southern part of Big Horn County, a small area in the southern part of Park County and also received from Fremont County that part of the southern Basin included within the Wind River Indian Reservation. Just north of Hot Springs County was Washakie County, which received what was left of the southeastern corner of Big Horn County. Hot Springs County was organized January 6, 1913, with its seat in Thermopolis and Washakie County was organized the same day, with its seat at Worland.[29]

The 1911 legislation also gave Park County the north end of Yellowstone Park, which had been in Uinta County since 1872, so that Park County now included a large area outside the Big Horn Basin. Even without its 900,000 acres or so in the Park, Park County was the largest county in the Basin, with 3,332,480 acres, followed by the shrunken Big Horn

---

[28]*Wyoming Compiled Statutes*, 1910, Chapter 81, Section 1031, Lucille Nichols Patrick, *The Best Little Town by a Dam Site, or Cody's First 20 Years* (Cody, Wyoming, 1968), 138, and Virginia Cole Trenholm, ed., *Wyoming Blue Book*, II (Cheyenne, Wyoming, 1974), 524. The Supreme Court upheld the Park County statute in Board of County Commissioners of Big Horn County vs. Woods, et., al. 18 *Wyoming Reports* 316, February 10, 1910.

[29]In a law effective February 21, 1911, the legislature also redescribed the Big Horn County boundary in terms of sections and ranges. *Session Laws of the State of Wyoming, Passed by the Eleventh State Legislature Convened at Cheyenne on the Tenth Day of January, 1911* (Laramie, Wyoming, 1911), 7, 9, 103.

County, with 1,990,400 acres; Washakie has 1,434,240 acres and Hot Springs is the smallest of the four Basin counties, with 1,296,000 acres. Together, the four counties cover 8,053,120 acres; this total includes the Clark's Fork drainage in the north of Park County, but we can infer that the Big Horn Basin as a geographical unit covers about eight million acres.[30]

---

[30] Virginia Cole Trenholm, ed., *Wyoming Blue Book*, II (Cheyenne, Wyoming, 1974), 520-27. The 1911 legislature gave the southern part of Yellowstone Park to Lincoln County. Also, Viola McNealey, "The Seven Days of Hanover County," *Annals of Wyoming*, XLII, No. 1 (April, 1970), 44-46. Of course, there never was a Hanover County, because its name did not survive the legislative process.

William Frederick Cody, an early scout for the Army who became a flamboyant Wild West showman. Cody's fame extended far beyond Wyoming, but he contributed much to the development of the northern Basin.
Courtesy Wyoming State Museum.

CHAPTER XV

More Than a Wild West Show

The ranchers who survived the disastrous 1886-87 winter correctly perceived that they could no longer build a successful enterprise on the basis of free government land. It was now necessary to have some reliable means of controlling access to grazing lands; before the passage of the Taylor Grazing Act in 1934, this meant that the land would have to be acquired in fee. So it was that the cattlemen began lining up to file on the public lands, and they began to make other uses of it. In the summer of 1897, Otto Franc had 35 men working on the Pitchfork with plows and scrapers, leveling the land to raise a purported 12,000 tons of hay. Soon farmers would join the cattlemen in this sort of work.

Of course, it was not possible to secure title to the government land until the survey had been completed. The land district for Wyoming was authorized early in 1870, and the area near the railroad was being surveyed in 1870; the perimeters of the territory were surveyed beginning in 1873, but the government survey contractors did not reach the Basin until 1882. Once the townships had been laid out it was possible to file on the land under a variety of land laws. The first land office was in Cheyenne, and in 1876 a second office was established in Evanston, which covered all of Uinta County and most of Sweetwater County.[1]

At this point, all lands west of the Big Horn River were included in the Evanston district, while most of the land east of the river was still in the Cheyenne district—but the trek from the Basin was a formidable undertak-

---

[1]The Cheyenne office was authorized February 5, 1870, and opened August 10, 1870; the Evanston office was authorized August 9, 1876, and opened August 13, 1877.

ing in either case. Although Congress never did place a land office within the Basin, it authorized a land office at Buffalo in 1887, and this office went into operation in the spring of the following year; for those in the western part of the Basin, authorization of the Lander office in 1890 was of some help. Although the journey to make filings and submit proofs still entailed a trek over the mountains, it was considerably shortened. The cattlemen now took advantage of the new situation, and at the end of the eighties there was a substantial increase in filings on government land by the ranching industry.[2]

These early filings did not account for a large acreage, and any significant influx of population would have to await the large-scale promotions for settlement of farm land. As we have seen, the Colorado Flats promotion did not result in immediate settlement, although the land did go to patent. In the north of the Basin, other efforts were more successful. The man for whom the city of Cody is named was born in Iowa, lived a number of years in Nebraska, was already a man of fifty by the time he came to the Big Horn Basin, and is now buried in Colorado. Yet the name of William Frederick Cody is more permanently entangled with events in the Big Horn Basin than it ever can be in those other places.

There is much hyperbole in the stories about Bill Cody, but the truth is colorful enough. Born in LeClaire, Iowa on February 26, 1846, Bill Cody was a mere boy of eleven when he first came west on a wagon bearing supplies for the Army's Utah Expedition of 1857, and on this trip his wagon was captured by the Mormons under Lot Smith. The next year he was in the west again, headed for the Colorado gold fields. During the Civil War, Cody for a time served in the Kansas volunteer cavalry, but the rank of colonel he carried through his mature years came not from the military, but from Nebraska Governor John M. Thayer. In the spring of 1887, before Cody departed for England with his Wild West Show, Governor Thayer appointed Cody his aide de camp with the rank of colonel.[3]

---

[2]In a letter to Milo Rowell, February 7, 1888, W. A. Richards noted that there would be a new land office in Buffalo, but that funding for it was not yet in place. The Buffalo office was authorized March 3, 1887, and opened May 1, 1888. The Lander office was authorized April 23, 1890; it took in the area including Meeteetse and the western settlements soon to be made on the Stinking Water, upstream from the present location of Cowley and Lovell.

[3]Lot Smith and his insurgents burned three supply trains and forced the expedition to halt for the winter, a hundred miles short of its Utah destination. Nellie Snyder Yost, *Buffalo Bill, His Family, Friends, Fame, Failures and Fortunes* (Chicago, 1979), *passim*. Governor Thayer had also served as the second governor of Wyoming Territory, March 1, 1875, to May 29, 1878.

After the war, Cody found work scouting for the military in the West, and by the end of 1871 he was certainly one of the best known hunting scouts in the West; in one eight-month period in 1867-68 he had killed 4,280 buffalo to fill a contract with a construction contractor for the Kansas Pacific. It was therefore no surprise that he was detailed by General Phil Sheridan to provide scout services for the spectacular hunt to be conducted in January, 1872, for the third son of Tsar Alexander II, the Grand Duke Alexis. The grand duke, who would celebrate his twenty-first birthday while on the hunt, was a handsome blond blue-eyed young man, over six feet tall, with huge hands and feet, who captivated American women. Cody's job was to ensure that the grand duke would kill enough buffaloes.[4]

This was the stuff movies are made of, and Cody played his role well. He was directed to find the Sioux chief Spotted Tail, and persuade him to bring 1,000 Indians of both sexes to amuse the grand duke. The warriors staged a sham battle to amuse the grand duke, and General Custer was also there, as grand marshal of the hunt and escort for the grand duke. Custer was said to have conferred his attentions on a Sioux maiden, for perhaps the last time that would occur. There were two companies of infantry and two of cavalry, as well as the regimental band from the Second Cavalry. The army contrived to improve the grand duke's chances for a kill by tracking the southern buffalo herd, and the grand duke did succeed in killing buffalo, which was a source of pleasure both to him and also to those attending the grand affair, for a basket of champagne was distributed among the hunters whenever the prince made a kill. After the hunt, Bill Cody received some personal gifts of value from the grand duke, which in any case were not worth as much to him as the publicity he received.[5]

Cody signed on as a scout in Wyoming in the summer of 1876, but was too late for the actions that summer in northern Wyoming; instead, he was sent to the Red Cloud Agency with General Sheridan, and was there when Custer was killed on the Little Big Horn. After these events, Cody returned to North Platte, Nebraska, to try his hand at ranching, and it was apparently a Fourth of July show in North Platte in 1882 that triggered

---

[4] It appears that Cody's nickname "Buffalo Bill" was in use even before his railroad contract. Nellie Snyder Yost, *op. cit*, 16.

[5] Another famous scout, John Burwell Omohondro, better known as "Texas Jack," was also on the hunt, and it was been implied that his role was more significant than the press reports would have us believe. Herschel C. Logan, *Buckskin and Satin: The Life of Texas Jack* (Harrisburg, Pennsylvania, 1974), 52. Also, Marshall Sprague, *A Gallery of Dudes* (Lincoln, Nebraska, 1966), 95ff.

the idea for the Wild West Show that made Cody's most enduring reputation. In any case, the Wild West Show started up the following year, and from this point on, Cody's life was never far from show business.

Cody's scouting engagements for the army and for private hunters had afforded him the opportunity to see the Big Horn Basin; we know that in 1871, he was detailed by General Sheridan to bring an archaeologist from Yale to the area. Cody had two daughters, Arta and Irma, and the former married Horton S. Boal, of Chicago. It was at Arta's house in North Platte in the fall of 1888 that the Cody family entertained Mrs. George T. Beck, wife of George T. Beck, forming a connection that would be of great importance to the northern Basin.[6]

George Thornton Beck was born near Lexington, Kentucky, July 28, 1856, the fourth of five children. His father, James Beck, was law partner of James C. Breckenridge, who later became Vice President of the United States under James Buchanan; James Beck represented Kentucky in the United States House of Representatives and later in the Senate. After trying his hand at prospecting in Colorado without much success, George Beck worked for a time as a surveyor on the Northern Pacific near Mandan, but this work soon palled on him, and the summer of 1879 found him in the vicinity of Goose Creek, just east of the Big Horn Mountains, ready to take up the sheep ranching business.[7]

Young Beck bought a band of sheep from Morton Post in Cheyenne, and apparently prospered sufficiently to sell out in 1889 with a $35,000 profit. The post office of Beckton was named for him in 1884. Politics beckoned to him, and in that field he had only mixed success. In 1886 he tried unsuccessfully to secure the appointment as territorial governor from President Cleveland. He was later elected to the territorial Council, representing Johnson and Sheridan counties, and served as president of the Council in the last territorial legislature, but when he ran for the U. S. House of Representatives in the fall of 1890, he carried only Sheridan County. He also suffered defeat in his campaign against DeForest Richards in 1902.[8]

---

[6]The Yale professor, Othniel Charles Marsh, who was pursuing his studies of the aboriginal horse, was looking for fossils. Lucille Nichols Patrick, *The Best Little Town by a Dam Site* (Cody, Wyoming, 1968), 16.

[7]Senator James Beck died in office in 1890. James D. McLaird, "Ranching in the Big Horns: George T. Beck, 1856-1894," *Annals of Wyoming*, XXXIX, No. 2 (October, 1967), 157ff.

[8]The name of the Beckton post office was later changed to Milltown. On the way north with his sheep, Beck had a dispute with Moreton Frewen over the use of the range, but this did not interfere with his sheep operation.

Beck was living at Sheridan, Wyoming, when the railroad arrived there in 1892, and Bill Cody was the moving force behind a project developed to construct the Sheridan Inn, as a way station for sportsmen who came to hunt the Big Horn Mountains. The Inn opened in 1893, and although Cody did not have a financial interest in the project, he apparently did buy the furnishings. The hotel had running water and electricity for lights that was supplied by a dynamo that was turned off at midnight, forcing the nightowls among the guests to rely on candles after that hour.

Meanwhile, there was growing interest in irrigation projects for the northern Basin. Frank Mondell filed on the first project to divert water from the Stinking Water through a 48 mile canal to irrigate 155,000 acres, but this venture was never started. In the fall of 1893, Laban Hillberry and Jerry Ryan from Sheridan filed for a permit to divert water from the South Fork of the Stinking Water; the survey was performed by C. E. Wood of Otto, and the permit issued the following month, for a 28 mile canal, to be constructed at a cost of $100,000 and irrigate 246,000 acres. Hillberry did not develop this project, but instead sold his surveys to Horace C. Alger, cashier of the Bank of Commerce in Sheridan.[9]

Alger now joined with George T. Beck in a second survey of the area. Along with Beck and Alger on this survey was Horton S. Boal, who apparently told Cody of a huge reclamation project which initially contemplated the irrigation of about 400,000 acres of Carey Act land. Beck said that Cody asked to be included in the project, but it is clear that Beck considered the famous Cody, whom he called "the best advertised man in the world," a very real asset to any promotional effort. Cody became president of the Shoshone Land and Irrigation Company, while George T. Beck was the manager; the surveyor was Elwood Mead, who was also state engineer.

Mead, then 36, later became closely identified with reclamation in the West; he was working for the state engineer of Colorado before he was appointed as territorial engineer of Wyoming in 1888. After statehood, Mead became the first state engineer, and worked closely with Senators Warren and Carey to secure the passage of a law ceding arid lands to the states; the Carey Act was ultimately the result.[10]

---

[9]Permit No. 587 was issued to Hillberry and his associates on October 20, 1893, and it was to expire March 13, 1899. Jeannie Cook, *Wiley's Dream of Empire: The Wiley Irrigation Project* (Cody, Wyoming, 1990), 2.

[10]Mead was born in Patriot, Indiana, January 16, 1858 and died January 26, 1936. He was recommended for the Wyoming position by a representative of the Wyoming Development Company, which was an organization in which Senator Carey figured prominently.

In 1891, Congress began authorizing forest reserves, one of the first of which was the Shoshone National Forest, along the western fringe of the Big Horn Basin, and in 1896, the Bighorn National Forest was created on the east side of the Basin acres. Mead was opposed to the manner in which the Big Horn reservation was made. He claimed the reservation did not include the most densely timbered lands and that settlers were thereby prevented from filing on irrigable land that had not yet been surveyed. Mead left the state engineer's office to head the office of irrigation in the U. S. Department of Agriculture in 1899. He later was Commissioner of the U. S. Bureau of Reclamation. and the lake created by Boulder Dam is named for him.[11]

At the beginning, Cody and Beck were apparently equal investors in the Shoshone Land and Irrigation Company, although Cody and his close friend and partner, Nate Salsbury, soon became much larger shareholders than Beck. Bronson Rumsey of Buffalo, New York, had met Cody after a Wild West Show performance, and became interested in the Basin when Cody told him of it. He came to the Basin with George Bleistein, who owned the Iroquois Hotel in Buffalo. The group traveled through the northern Basin and when they returned east, they invested in the irrigation company; they were joined in the venture by H. Monte Gerrans, who was part owner of the company that printed Cody's promotional posters.[12]

The application of the Shoshone company was one of the first three Carey Act projects considered by the State Arid Land Board, although it was for 25,000 acres, not 400,000; Mead had cut the acreage total. The promoters hoped to earn a good profit by selling water rights at $10 per acre, for in order to buy the Carey land from the State, the settlers first had to buy the water rights from the ditch company.[13]

Cody had visited the Basin in the winter of 1895, and became impressed with the possibility of developing access to Yellowstone Park

---

[11] The Shoshone reservation of 1,566,351 acres was made March 30, 1891 and the Bighorn reservation of 1,113,516 acres was made February 22, 1897. Paul W. Gates, *op. cit.*, 674-75, Charles Arthur Guernsey, *Wyoming Cowboy Days* (New York, 1936), 46-47, and Roy M. Robbins, *op. cit.*, 316.

[12] Apparently, Cody, Beck and Salsbury originally held 400 shares each, and Alger held 200, but by 1902 Cody had 1,470, Salsbury 2,176, Beck 400 and Alger 200. Salsbury was Cody's partner in the Wild West Show. McLaird, *op. cit.*, 78.

[13] The State Board met on April 2, 1895; approval was given September 14, 1895. Carey had introduced the legislation in 1892, but it failed to pass; it finally passed Congress on August 15, 1894 and was signed by the President on August 18. McLaird, *op. cit.*, 75-77.

through Sylvan Pass, which could be served by a new town Cody proposed to call Cody or Cody City. Cody was acquainted with one Heimer, of Lincoln, Nebraska, who was with the Lincoln Land Company, and that company hoped to own the new townsite. Charles Emory Hayden was hired to survey the townsite, which was south of the river, above the DeMaris hot springs. A general store for this town was soon opened by Harrison P. Arnold, of Billings, and the commissary of the canal company was built there by George Russell.

This action by Cody apparently annoyed Beck, who expected that the townsite should be owned by the canal company. He therefore surveyed another townsite in 1896, some miles east of Cody town, and applied for the name Shoshone from the Post Office department. Since there was already a Wyoming post office under the name Shoshone Agency, the name for the new town was rejected. A second name, Richland, did not find favor with the Cody group; Cody had by now repented his earlier rashness in surveying the town of Cody, it was suggested that the name of the new town be changed to Cody. The town was laid out in 1896, and incorporated in 1901. The streets were 100 feet wide, so that freight wagons could be turned around in them. The commissary building for the canal company was moved from the old town to the new town of Cody.[14]

Bill Cody built the Irma Hotel, which was named for his second daughter; he also built a livery stable. He established a newspaper, the *Cody Enterprise*, with Colonel J. H. Peake as editor, after the demise of the *Shoshone Times*, which had published briefly beginning in 1896. Bleistein, Rumsey and Gerrans established the Cody Trading Company, and George Beck built an electric plant and became involved in other enterprises. Cody also began buying ranches, including the Carter ranch with its "Bug" brand, and the upper Belknap ranch.

In 1899, Cody was able to interest the Burlington in constructing a line from Toluca, Montana, to the new town of Cody, and in the spring of 1900 he formally offered to give the railroad a right of way across the Shoshone Irrigation Company lands, and additional lands in the townsite itself. The Cody initiative struck a responsive chord with the Burlington, because there was concern that the Northern Pacific would build south into the Basin and a Burlington extension to Cody would preempt that move. The Lincoln Land Company demanded half the townsite as the

---

[14]Patrick, *op. cit.*, 23.

price of construction to that location; it paid the Shoshone Land Company $10 per acre.[15]

The Lincoln Land Company, incorporated in 1880, was not a subsidiary of the railroad, but it was controlled by John Murray Forbes and Charles Elliott Perkins, who were chairman and president, respectively, of the Burlington. It was thus possible to ensure a high degree of cooperation between the two companies. The Lincoln company had the task of developing communities at fairly regular intervals along the route of the railroad, and it could be expected to know where the railroad was going to build. It was able to acquire land at cheaper prices than the railroad could have, and it turned over property for stations and yards at no cost to the railroad, expecting that the presence of the railroad would increase the value of the company's other lands more than enough to offset this cost. The list of Lincoln townsites in the Basin is long, and include Cody, Corbett, Cowley, Durkee, Garland, Greybull, Kane, Lovell, Lucerne, Manderson, Neiber, Otto, Rairden and Ralston.

In 1899, Edward Gillette surveyed the route for the Toluca line, toward Pryor, through Pryor Gap, and then down Sage Creek to Frannie, and on to Cody. Construction of the line began in 1900, and the first train arrived in Cody on November 11, 1901, bearing Col. Cody himself; it was followed by a special from Billlings, bearing Wyoming Senator Clarence Don Clark.

Known as the "Squaw Line," more than half of the extension was constructed through the Crow Indian Reservation, and the process of securing the right of way was laborious. Even though Congress had tried to make it easier for railroads to secure rights of way across reservations, the Interior Department insisted that under the new procedure the company must serve a copy of its route map on each of the individual Indian allottees whose land would be crossed. General Charles F. Manderson, the line's general counsel, complained bitterly that this gesture would be little understood by the Indians, saying it would make as much sense to distrib-

---

[15]The Cody offer is in a letter from William F. Cody to Charles E. Perkins, April 2, 1900. The Burlington corporate policy on the Basin line is set forth succinctly in a letter from T. E. Calvert to G. W. Holdredge, February 4, 1901. "Mr. Perkins desire was, as I understood it, to build to a point in the basin where we would be in a position to lessen the temptation of the Northern Pacific to start into the Basin with a line at some future time, and where we could establish a good trading point." Burlington railroad corporate files, Newberry Library, Chicago. By the end of April, Hill's lines had acquired the Burlington, making a competitive policy unnecessary, but this did not diminish the value of the Basin connection, which was an important element in Hill's valuation of the Burlington.

ute the Greek testament to them. Nevertheless, he admitted there was no other way to secure government approval, and directed that the person distributing the maps be accompanied by an interpreter to explain that they were not "a declaration of war or bad medicine."[16]

The Toluca line gave the railroad other experiences in dealing with the Indians. Gillette recalled that when two Indians were killed on the railroad, the situation was extremely tense, and the railroad management wisely suggested that the Indians themselves should determine what restitution should be made. After due deliberation, the Crows determined that one man who was killed was old, and "not much good," while the other, who was young, was "much good." The relatives of the first were therefore to be paid $25, and those of the latter were to be paid $100; the railroad accepted the deal with alacrity.

The Cody canal project had been approved in the fall of 1895, calling for a ditch 25 miles long and 21 feet wide at the bottom, to irrigate 25,000 acres. For a time, construction proceeded so well that the State Board opened the land for settlement in the spring of 1896, but work now became more sporadic, hampered by frozen ground that made digging impossible and also by the small saloons operating near the project. There was a break in the ditch in July and the Irma Colony was particularly hard hit; the *Red Lodge Picket* reported the population there was down to three families. Cody needled Beck about the lack of progress, and he was concerned that the state would make an unfavorable report on the canal.[17]

The investors in the canal were not faring well financially, and D. H. Elliot was appointed as land commissioner in 1897, with the task of bringing settlers to the area. The water rights were sold on easy payment terms, and the railroads gave special rates to bring settlers to Red Lodge, but the response was still not up to expectations. Elliot even hoped to obtain support for colonization from the new Social Democracy of America, which later became the Socialist Party. Eugene V. Debs and others hoped to colonize the poor in a social community in some western state, and Elliot tried to interest the socialists in the Basin. While one cannot know how such an

---

[16]The act of March 2, 1899, gave railroads the right to cross reservations by paying damages to the Indians, but did not require that they consent. The Burlington's map for the Toluca line crossing of the Crow reservation was approved March 29, 1900. Charles Crane Bradley, Jr., "After the Buffalo Days: Documents on the Crow Indians from the 1880's to the 1920's," Masters dissertation, Montana State University, August, 1970. Also, Charles F. Manderson, to W. W. Baldwin, January 31, 1900, Burlington railroad corporate files, Newberry Library, Chicago.

[17]*Red Lodge Picket*, August 1, 1896.

effort would have been received in northern Wyoming, the Socialist Party ultimately opted for political action in lieu of colonization.[18]

Finally, the State made its first inspection of the project, and in 1901, the report was issued. It was not favorable. The report noted that there had been no construction at all over nearly half the proposed length of the canal, and that 1,800 acres already patented were still without water. There was a second state inspection in 1905 and it was not until September 29, 1906 that the State approved the canal; the company turned it over to the settlers in the following year.

Another development project in the north end of the Basin was that of Solon Lysander Wiley. Born May 31, 1840 in Cambridgeport, Vermont, Wiley had later moved to Greenfield, Massachusetts. In 1884, Wiley moved to Omaha, where he was involved in numerous ventures, and in 1894 he became interested in Wyoming developments, and we find him in the Basin in that year, filing on the DeMaris hot springs on the north side of the Stinking Water.[19]

On June 1, 1895, after the Carey Act was approved, the Big Horn Basin Development Company applied for a project covering 32,000 acres, to be irrigated from the Greybull River; Wiley was an officer of the company, and Wyoming's congressman Frank Mondell was also involved in the project, as was Charles A. Guernsey; it was actually the first Wyoming project under the Carey Act. The project took over and enlarged the Bench Canal, which had been built by the Mormon colony at Burlington, which will be described more fully in the next chapter. The canal had a priority of December 19, 1896, and water rights were to be sold to settlers at $10 per acre.

In 1898, Wiley met The Rev. August C. Wunderlich, a young Lutheran minister, and urged him to bring his Lutheran community from Hemingford, Nebraska, where they had suffered crop failures. After inspecting the Wiley project in the fall of 1898, Wunderlich returned to Nebraska and organized the Evangelical Lutheran Colonization Company. Some thirty souls came from Hemingford and Rushville, Nebraska, and Ardmore, South Dakota, in the spring of 1899 and others followed that fall. The

---

[18]When the American Railway Union disbanded in June, 1897, and was reorganized into Social Democracy of America, the emphasis of the movement was on colonization, but at a second convention the following June, Debs was forced to agree that the colonization scheme was not feasible. Ray Ginger, *The Bending Cross: A Biography of Eugene Victor Debs* (New York, 1949), 195, 197.

[19]The filing on the hot springs was made with Robert Howell. Cook, *op. cit.*, 13.

colonists named their town Germania when the post office was established in 1899, but the name was changed to Emblem in 1918, because of anti-German sentiment at the time of World War I.[20]

A much larger Wiley project was involved in a conflict with another of Cody's ventures, the Cody-Salsbury Canal. The latter canal had been filed on in 1897, to irrigate 120,000 acres, using water from the Stinking Water; the total acreage would swell to 350,000 acres in 1899. For four years, Cody tried vainly to raise the $2,000,000 for the dam and canals, and the State Land Board tried to interest the U S. Bureau of Reclamation in building the project. In 1901, Wiley asked for segregation of 225,000 acres for his project, and his total would reach 245,000 by 1903; he soon saw that there was not enough water for so large a project, and the same question occurred to others, for when the Bureau began examining the Cody-Salsbury project, the Department of the Interior decided to delay the segregation of lands under the Wiley project.

Governor Fenimore Chatterton was keenly interested in land development, and he wanted development of both the Cody-Salsbury with perhaps 100,000 acres, and the Wiley project of 245,000 acres. The Bureau of Reclamation had received an allocation of $2,250,000, and it was expected that Wiley's Big Horn Basin Development Company would spend $2,000,000—the combined sum would be a significant injection in sparsely-populated Wyoming. Chatterton therefore refused to release the segregation under the Cody-Salsbury project unless the government approved the Wiley segregation, and a settlement was finally reached on this basis.[21]

The contract for the Shoshone Dam was let on September 18, 1905, at a price of $515,730. After defaults by early contractors, the dam was finally completed in January 1910, but the labor force of some 450 men had to be replenished regularly by two to four "man catchers," who were hired by the contractors to round up men for the job.[22]

In 1904, Wiley moved his base of operations to Cody, where he remained until his own town of Wiley was established in 1907, thirteen

---

[20]The Lutheran church was Zion's Evangelical Lutheran Congregation of Germania. Jeannie Cook, *op. cit., passim*. Also, Jonathan and Melba Davis, *They Called It Germania! History of Wyoming's Emblem Bench 1893-1939* (Basin, Wyoming, n.d.), 1. August C. Wunderlich was born in Missouri in August, 1872.

[21]The Wiley segregation was approved May 5, 1904. Cook, *op. cit.*, 53.

[22]Patrick, *op. cit.*, 171-72.

miles southeast of Cody. Work on the canal and associated tunnels took place between 1904 and 1908, and the project was billed as the largest irrigation project, public or private, in the United States. A town named Hamilton was laid out fifteen miles east of Wiley, and in Wiley a bank was incorporated in 1908; Wiley town lots sold for $650 to $750 each. Unfortunately, difficulties in construction at the fifth tunnel prevented completion of the ditch to deliver water in the 1908 farming season, and in October 1908, the Big Horn Basin Development Company went into receivership. Late in 1909, it was sold for $50,000 to J. W. Ramsey of Chicago, acting for the bondholders.[23]

---

[23]*Thermopolis Record*, December 11, 1909. The town of Hamilton was named for Isaac Miller Hamilton, of the Chicago banking firm of Young and Hamilton. Patrick, *op. cit.*, 131.

CHAPTER XVI

Saints in the Basin

Another early group of farmers in the Basin came at the direction of the well-organized colonization machinery of the Mormon church. The church had the experience of its own trek to Utah from the eastern states, and when colonization started from the Salt Lake City base, a comprehensive system was developed; by the end of the century more than 500 communities were formed in a distinctive way, integrating the religious, social and economic life of the people. Western Wyoming began to interest the Mormons after 1876, when a land office was opened in Evanston, near the Mormon centers in Utah, and late in 1879, the Council of the Twelve Apostles reached a decision to plant a colony in the Salt River Valley.[1]

There is a difference of opinion as to whether the first Mormon colony in the Big Horn Basin colony fits into the traditional pattern of Mormon colonization. Charles Lindsay believed that the 1893 immigration was in no sense a religious undertaking and that the colonization took place so suddenly that the church did not realize it had happened until it was too late to control.[2]

In the spring of 1892, David Patten Woodruff came to the Big Horn Basin to look over the country. Woodruff was the son of the president of Mormon Church president Wilford Woodruff, and also a distant cousin

---

[1] At least one Mormon family was already settled in the Star Valley in the middle of 1880; church officials visited the valley in August, and other settlers were soon on the way. The 1880 visit was not the first official visit, as there had apparently been a visit by Brigham Young in 1878. The colony had 60 families by 1889, and the Star Valley Stake was organized in 1892. The Star Valley Stake was organized by Joseph F. Smith, nephew of Joseph Smith, on August 13, 1892. Forrest Weber Kennington and Kathaleen Kennington Hamblin, *A History of Star Valley, Formerly Salt River Valley, 1800-1900* (Salt Lake City, 1989), 112-115, 131, 135.

[2] Leonard J. Arrington and Davis Bitton, *The Mormon Experience: A History of the Latter-Day Saints* (New York, 1979), 120, and Charles Lindsay, *The Big Horn Basin* (Lincoln, Nebraska, 1932), 164.

of John Dwight Woodruff, who had established the Embar ranch in the Basin. The Mormon president gave his consent for the exploratory trip, and the younger Woodruff took with him William Henry Packard, then 40, who would later lead the Burlington colony of Mormons; the little group was impressed with the grass in the Basin, which was then a scarce item in Ashley, Utah, where Packard lived.[3]

The favorable report on the Basin reached other ears, and in the spring of 1893, the president of the Star Valley Stake in Afton, Wyoming, visited Montpelier, Idaho, to organize a group of volunteers to come to the Basin. The Packard family came to the Basin with Woodruff, and in all, about 100 families of Mormons, from Star Valley, Bear Lake Valley and Ashley and Uinta valleys in Utah, moved to the Greybull River, about 25 miles upstream from its mouth. While most of the Mormon settlers were farmers, David Woodruff took up a ranch on the Wood River, near Meeteetse, at the 6-7,000 foot elevation.

The little Mormon colony took out a canal on the north side of the Greybull River, known as the Farmer's Canal and by the middle of August, more than five miles of the canal was complete. The Packards built a log cabin, but did not have boards for the floor. The first winter, they were visited by Indians looking for food, and when Packard returned from the mountains with a load of game he had killed, the Indians asked him to give them the legs of the deer, which they roasted for food. The settlement was named Burlington, perhaps in the hopes that the railroad of that name would be attracted to the area.[4]

---

[3]The elder Woodruff was born in Farmington, Connecticut, March, 1807, a descendant of Matthew Woodruff, an original proprietor of Connecticut, who was also the ancestor of John Dwight Woodruff. "Dr. Edward Day Woodruff," *Annals of Wyoming*, VII, No. 3 (January, 1931), 431. Wilford Woodruff converted to Mormonism in 1832. In April, 1837, he was married to Phoebe W. Carter in the house of Joseph Smith, and after two missionary journeys to England, he returned in 1846 to join the expedition to Utah. In 1848 he returned as a missionary to the eastern states and was back in Utah in 1850. Hubert Howe Bancroft, *History of Utah* (San Francisco, 1889), 435. William Henry Packard was born in Springville, Utah, August 12, 1851. Lowene Packard Saxton, *The Packard Legacy* (Sacramento, California, 1992), 135.

[4]The summary of the Burlington settlement is based in part on a typescript dated February, 1923, prepared by the Church of Jesus Christ of Latter Day Saints for the Historical Department of the University of Wyoming. The Montpelier (Idaho) *Post* carried an item regarding the journey of George Osmond, president of the Star Valley Stake, to Montpelier in May, 1893. The *Clipper* (Lander), May 19, 1893. The priority date for the Farmers Canal is November 21, 1894. *Tabulation of Adjudicated Water Rights of the State of Wyoming: Water Division Number Three* (Cheyenne, Wyoming, 1964), 60. Also, see letter from David P. Woodruff, published in the *Deseret News*, August 7, 1899 and *The Clipper* (Lander), August 18, 1893.

The Burlington settlement selected William H. Packard to be their first bishop, and although the group did not belong to any organized ward or stake, they held meetings and Sunday school sessions, and regarded Packard as their leader. It was not until 1899 that they were formally organized as a branch of the Woodruff Stake of the Church.[5]

The colonists made a false start with the idea for an all-encompassing canal to irrigate some 15,000 acres, lying between the Greybull River and Dry Creek, and when this project did not materialize there could be no crops in the year 1894; a smaller project was completed the following year, ensuring the permanence of the Mormon settlement. Soon, there were 250 families in the Burlington colony, and by 1897 they had a meeting house, also used as a public school, a grist mill powered by water, and three good sawmills, to provide building materials.[6]

In 1899, the Church authorities in Salt Lake City became concerned about the proliferation of unorganized bodies of Mormons, and appointed Apostle Abraham Owen Woodruff, another son of President Wilford Woodruff, to supervise all Mormon colonization efforts. Woodruff, who was then 27 years old, took Charles Kingston and others to visit the Burlington colony in November, to "spy out," as Kingston put it, the opportunities for colonization in the area; it was at this time that Woodruff organized the Burlington settlers into a ward of the Woodruff Stake, which was located near Evanston, Wyoming.[7]

Kingston met with William Frederick Cody, and Buffalo Bill showed

---

[5]William H. Packard died in Canada, October 29, 1917. John W. McIntosh, *History of Burlington, 1893-1963* (n.p., n.d.) Also, Andrew Jensen's field notes, Church Historical Department, Church of Jesus Christ of Latter Day Saints, Salt Lake City, Utah. A letter from James R. McNiven in the *Deseret News Weekly* of March 21, 1896 refers to Packard as bishop or presiding elder; a letter from Ambrose Hibbert, published in the *Deseret News Weekly* of March 26, 1897 refers to organized worship "since 1894." The Burlington ward was formally organized, July 30, 1899, with William H. Packard as bishop and David P. Woodruff as first counselor.

[6]*Lindsay, op. cit.*, 165.

[7]Abraham Owen Woodruff was born November 23, 1872, in Salt Lake City, in the homestead his father, Wilford Woodruff, built soon after he came to the valley in 1847. He was employed by Zion's Saving Bank and Trust Company in Salt Lake City, but did not enjoy this work. In 1893, he was called to a mission in Germany, where he became president of the Dresden branch. He returned to Salt Lake City in 1896, where he resumed work in the bank, and on June 30, 1896, he married Helen May Winters. Helen Woodruff died in Mexico City, June 7, 1904, of smallpox, and Abraham O. Woodruff died June 20, 1904, in El Paso, also of smallpox. Welch, *History of the Big Horn Basin* (Salt Lake City, 1940), 135-41. After A. O. Woodruff died in 1904, centralized control over colonization virtually ended. Leonard J. Arrington, *Great Basin Kingdom: Economic History of the Latter-Day Saints, 1830-1900* (Lincoln, Nebraska, 1958), 384. Also, Charles Kingston to Andrew Jensen, March 13, 1919, Church History Department.

him his own canal project above Cody, which was slated to be 12 miles long and cover 13,000 acres; Cody offered the project to the Mormons for $50,000, a proposal which apparently fell on deaf ears.[8]

Early in 1900, Governor DeForest Richards and Secretary of State Fenimore Chatterton visited Mormon President Lorenzo Snow in Salt Lake City, and asked that a colony of Mormons be sent into the Big Horn Basin, to assist in settling that part of Wyoming. A. O. Woodruff was placed in charge of this project and soon rumors about the planned colonies were flying: one account had 30,000 Mormons going to the Basin in the spring, to take up 180,000 acres under the Carey Act.[9]

In February, Woodruff and a party from Salt Lake City arrived in the Basin to evaluate colonization possibilities there. The group had traveled up the Oregon Short Line to Butte, and then eastward on the Northern Pacific to Red Lodge, where they were met by men from Burlington. The two wagons brought from Burlington proved insufficient to accommodate the group, but after hiring a livery rig, they proceeded to Eagle's Nest, about 18 miles east of Cody. There they were met by Buffalo Bill, who regaled the Mormons with stories of his life on the plains. They were particularly amused by his tales of the hardships the Army had endured in its ill-fated "Mormon" war of 1857.[10]

Although Cody wanted the Mormons to come to his home for further talks, the Mormons were bent on another mission; they wanted to inspect an irrigation project called the Cincinnati canal that had been surveyed by an eastern group, and was now on the point of being abandoned. A permit had been issued to the Cincinnati Canal Company on August 10, 1896, to irrigate a large tract of land on the north side of the Shoshone River. The Cincinnati company had employed Congressman Frank W. Mondell to report on the feasibility of the canal, and he had recommended against it; the permit was relinquished on December 14, 1898.[11]

---

[8]On February 24, 1900, Cody and his partner Nate Salsbury relinquished their claims to lands under the former Cincinnati Canal. Charles Welch says that Salsbury wanted $20,000 for the relinquishment, but Cody refused to support him. Welch, op. cit., 59-60.

[9]Charles A. Welch, op. cit., 53, and *Wyoming Derrick* (Casper), February 15, 1900.

[10]The story of the visit of the Woodruff party in 1900 is found in the *Deseret Evening News* of February 19, 1900.

[11]Frank Wheeler Mondell, was born in St. Louis, Missouri, November 6, 1860; he lost his parents at the age of seven, and was adopted by a Congregational minister in northern Iowa. He came west in 1887 and worked on railroad construction for the firm of Kilpatrick Brothers & Collins. He served several terms as mayor of Newcastle, and was a member of the first Wyoming state senate and president of the second state senate. He was elected to the U. S. House of Representatives in 1894, but was

The visitors from Salt Lake City were warmly received at Burlington, which then had perhaps 400 settlers, and viewed the area the Burlington colony hoped to serve from their canal, a section which they called Moroni Flat, after the angel who presented the Book of Mormon to founder Joseph Smith. Woodruff and two other men followed the survey of the proposed canal for 15 miles, half of its 30-mile length.[12]

After holding meetings in Burlington, the Utah group left to examine the Cincinnati canal survey, in a seventeen-man expedition of two four-horse outfits and one single team, generously fitted out with necessary supplies furnished by the Burlington settlers, and including a cook and assistant, wood chopper and assistants, and camp man and assistants. The expedition drove north for 30 miles, to a point near the town of Lovell, and in -10° weather crossed the Shoshone River, only to learn the ice was not strong enough to hold the rigs; they nearly drowned one horse.

The first night, they camped in an unfinished house, and the second night at a stove-less bunkhouse on Joseph Howell's ranch; the third night was spent in more comfortable, although cramped, quarters at W. A. "Jack" Morris' road ranch, where all seventeen men slept in a single room. After completing their inspection of the canal project, which they rated as excellent, the expedition proceeded to Bridger, Montana, 32 miles away, in weather that was now -20°. The following morning, the men met in a debriefing session, at which they catalogued the characteristics of the canal project, including the availability of building materials, both lumber and stone. The canal was to be 25 miles long and irrigate 18,000 acres, which could be acquired under the Carey Act.[13]

By the following April, the colonization project headed by A. O. Woodruff had received the blessing of Church president Lorenzo Snow, who had succeeded Wilford Woodruff in 1898. On January 11, 1900, Charles Kingston filed an application with the State Engineer, covering the same lands contemplated under the Cincinnati canal, and the old Cincinnati water right was transferred to him, as agent for the colony;

---

defeated in 1896; he then served in the House from March 4, 1899 to March 3, 1923. He was assistant commissioner of the General Land Office in Washington in the three years separating his House service. He died in Washington, D. C., August 6, 1939. *The Clipper* (Lander), August 19, 1898, and *Biographical Directory of the United States Congress 1774–1989* (Washington, D. C., 1989), 1518.

[12]The Burlington population estimate is contained in the *Deseret Evening News*, April 21, 1900.

[13]Charles Welch says there were 18 men in the room, but he doubtless forgot that John Croft had stayed behind in Burlington, having caught a cold. Welch, *op. cit.*, 61, and *Deseret Evening News*, February 19, 1900.

the name of the canal was changed to the Sidon Canal. It was expected that about 100 families would come to the colony, meeting at Kemmerer Bridge in Wyoming and then proceeding up the old Mormon Trail for more than 100 miles to South Pass, then to Lander, and across the Shoshoni reservation to the Embar ranch, and finally to Meeteetse and Burlington.[14]

The undertaking was highly organized, and it was expected that the 100 families would be arranged into ten companies of ten families each, and each company would have its own organization, including a chaplain to ensure religious observances. On arriving at the colony, the men were to commence work on the canal, not taking time to build houses. After the canal had been completed, so that water could be obtained for the land, houses would be constructed, and a house of worship and schoolhouse. For the time being, the colony used the post office at Lovell, although an application for its own post office was soon made.

All of these efforts were coordinated through a corporation, called the Big Horn Basin Colonization Company, a Wyoming corporation which was organized in Salt Lake City, April 9, 1900. The corporation's purpose was to build the canal and assist the settlers. A. O. Woodruff was president, and Byron Sessions of Rich County, Utah, who was then 49 years old, was vice president and general manager.[15]

Some of the settlers were delayed by bad weather, but seven companies were finally organized in late April to make the trip. To avoid slowing the entire caravan, a separate cattle company was organized to take 200 head of cattle to the Basin. There was no lack of excitement, and the symbolism of conducting devotions where the pioneers of the 1840's had camped was strongly felt.

Three of the companies were caught in a blizzard in the mountains, which lasted three days, bringing snow over two feet deep. One little girl became sick and died, and the starving horses ate the ends of fish poles and chewed on exposed portions of the wooden wagons; the settlers used their bedding to protect the horses and children, and spent the night without sleep. Some of the companies elected to enter the Basin by way of

---

[14]Arrington, op. cit., 406. Also Charles Kingston to Andrew Jensen, Church History Department.

[15]Typescript dated February, 1923, prepared at the request of the history department, University of Wyoming. Also, Welch, op. cit., 64. Byron Sessions was born November 7, 1851, in Salt Lake City, Utah; at the age of 17, he hauled stone for the Salt Lake Temple, and the next year he married Ida Twombly. They moved to Woodruff, Rich County, Utah, in 1872, and while there he accumulated considerable land, in partnership with Orlando North.

Thermopolis and to make their way down the Big Horn River to Burlington, while the rest went via Meeteetse, as originally planned.[16]

At the end of May, Woodruff gathered the people on the bank of the Shoshone River to celebrate the groundbreaking for the canal, and after conducting services, Woodruff plowed the first furrow. The colony hauled 104 scrapers from Bridger, and these, together with some brought by the settlers, were used to commence the cut of eleven and a half feet through gravel and rock. By the middle of June, the colonists had 20 acres ready for planting as gardens, and they expected to raise a small crop of potatoes that season. While still camped in a grove of trees beside the Shoshone River, a sparkling city of white tents and covered wagons, the new settlers were organized into the Shoshone branch of the Church.[17]

By the end of July, it was claimed that there were over 400 settlers in the new project, and there were two stores, as well as the Church commissary, where supplies could be purchased "as cheap, almost" as in Salt Lake City. Three miles of the Sidon Canal had been completed, and a stream six feet deep was flowing into the headgate. To save four miles of construction, a tunnel was drilled through a sandstone ridge; this proved a troublesome structure that sometimes collapsed and threatened the reliability of the system.[18]

The settlers in the Basin were soon joined by others of their religion. In September a trainload of settlers passed through Laramie, Wyoming, on their way to the Basin; there were three coaches of settlers, and thirty cars of household goods, seeds and implements. This group was led by Jesse Wentworth Crosby Jr., who was then 52 years old.[19]

By the end of October, the townsite had been laid out, and named Byron, in honor of Byron Sessions; there were 40 houses under construction. Six miles of the canal had been completed, at a cost of $30,000, and it was expected to irrigate about 3,000 acres in the spring. The land was

---

[16]*Deseret Evening News*, June 16, 1900. Also Welch, *op. cit.*, 67-68, 72.

[17]Letter of Charles A. Welch, *Deseret Evening News*, June 16, 1900.

[18]The tunnel was eventually replaced by a cut through the hill. Melvin M. Fillerup, *Sidon: The Canal That Faith Built* (Cody, 1988), 82, 83, 85.

[19]*Laramie Boomerang*, September 19, 1900, typescript dated February, 1923, prepared at the request of the history department, University of Wyoming, *Deseret Evening News*, July 31, October 31, 1900, and statistical report, December 31, 1900, Church Historical Department. Jesse Wentworth Crosby, Jr. was born in Salt Lake City, Utah, June 22, 1848, and he married Sarah Pauline Clark on October 4, 1867, also at Salt Lake City. On returning from his mission in the southern states, he moved to Panguitch, Utah, in 1873, where he engaged in stock raising and the mercantile business. He died in February, 1915. Welch, *op. cit.*, 146-48.

divided by casting lots among those who wanted a particular parcel; the cost of the 37-mile canal was $100,000, or $10 per acre, a considerable increase over the $6 per acre that had originally been estimated.[20]

As the season's work on the canal ended, Woodruff made it possible for the colonists to augment their slender resources by negotiating a grading contract for 27 miles of the new branch of the Burlington railroad from Toluca, Montana to Cody; the Mormons were given the section from Pryor Gap to Frannie. This work, which was conveniently located about 40 miles from the Byron settlement, was nominally under the supervision of Jesse W. Crosby, Jr., although the contract was apparently in the name of William H. Packard, who gave bond for its performance. Near the end of his life, A. O. Woodruff tried to interest the Utah-Idaho Sugar Company in building a sugar factory in the Mormon district, but these efforts did not bear fruit; it was not until 1916 that the Lovell factory was built by Great Western Sugar Company.[21]

Nevertheless, there were problems. Although the Church had asked that all settlers have sufficient money or supplies for at least one year, it soon became apparent that many fell short of this standard, and a report in October noted that the Burlington settlers had donated $350 of produce to the needy of the new colony. There was enough sickness among the colonists for Sessions to call for a day of fasting, that they might be healed. Unfortunately, when winter approached, the railroad now shut down the grading project.[22]

In August, Charles Kingston returned to the colony to audit its books. He found the settlers still living in tents, their money mostly gone, and nearly $3,000 in debt to Montana merchants. After consulting with Byron Sessions, Kingston contacted Wyoming Congressman Frank M. Mondell, who at the time was a director of the Burlington railroad. He urged Mondell to use his influence to get the railroad grading contract resumed; otherwise, the Mormons would be compelled to abandon the canal project and scatter to look for work.

---

[20]Welch, *op. cit.*, 91. Byron Sessions was born in Salt Lake City, Utah, November 7, 1851. In Woodruff, Utah, he went into partnership with Orlando North in the Bear River Land and Livestock Company, which purchased twelve sections of land from the Union Pacific. He came to the Big Horn Basin in 1900; he died January 6, 1928.

[21]Welch, *op. cit.*, 85, 117. Packard's wife said that Crosby wanted Packard to assign the grading contract to him, but that Packard refused because of his personal financial responsibility under the contract. Saxton, *op. cit.*, 166.

[22]*Deseret Evening News*, November 5, December 17, 1900, and Welch, *op. cit.*, 75.

Mondell took the matter up with the railroad people, and in due course, the colony sent 100 teams to resume grading. Mondell extended further help to the Mormon settlers, by securing the passage of a bill to authorize the settlers to go into Montana to take timber for their use from public lands in the Pryor mountains.[23]

---

[23]Church history records assign an $80,000 value to the contract. Charles Kingston to Andrew Jensen, March 13, 1919. The timber amendment is 31 *Statutes at Large* 1439, approved March 3, 1901. At the end of 1900, there were 325 Mormons in the Byron branch and 350 in the Shoshone branch, for a total of 675; the older Burlington ward had 343 Mormon settlers.

CHAPTER XVII

Towns and Farms in the Southern Basin

South of the Mormon colonies, near the mouth of the Nowood, were four town building efforts. In 1890, William J. Shafer had laid out Alamo on the west wide of the Big Horns opposite the mouth of the Nowood; he received his patent for the land in 1891. Alamo had a post office beginning on May 26, 1890 and there was even a newspaper, the *Alamo Argus*, owned by Will D. Edgar, which operated out of the post office until it moved to Otto in 1892, and was renamed the *Otto Mascot*; it later burned down. Shafer complained to visitors in 1893 that he had no sooner given Edgar two lots than the ungrateful editor was looking for a better deal elsewhere. Perhaps the defection arose from the fact that in the summer of 1893 Alamo consisted of one house and "some outbuildings." Still, Shafer was confident of the future, for the Burlington railroad surveyors had passed through his town, and he expected it would be on the railroad.[1]

Warren, located south of Alamo, was platted in the same year as Alamo, and perhaps the name attracted Francis E. Warren, who bought four lots, paying a total of $200, a bit more than the $30 per lot that seemed to be the going price. Berlin, which featured a circular design, with streets radiating from a central plaza, was platted on August 6, 1895. Unfortunately, this town did not attract a following, and the next year Henry Jordan platted his own town of Jordan.[2]

---

[1] *The Weekly Times* (Billings), July 29, 1893.
[2] *Basin Republican-Rustler*, December 16, 1982 and July 14, 1983. Francis E. Warren bought the lots from Joe DeBarthe on September 9, 1891. The plats of Warren, Berlin and Jordan are in the Big Horn County clerk's office; the Warren plat is dated July 3, 1890 and the Jordan plat is dated October 12, 1896.

Jordan was the site of a school and the first flour mill in the Basin. The flour mill project had been rumored as early as 1889, when the *Billings Gazette* scoffed that a ranchman at Bonanza was proposing to erect a mill and even supply part of the Billings market; in the face of such critics, Henry Jordan started building the mill in 1895 and finished it the following year. Jordan, who was born in May 1839, in Illinois, dug a short canal from the Nowood to a former channel of the river, built a dam and fed the millrace from the resulting reservoir. The mill was located on the hill, and a pipeline was planned to serve the town of Berlin.[3]

Upstream on the Big Horn was the first German colony, a small group who selected land just downstream from the area already preempted by the Colorado group. The first of this group to arrive was Charles Reinhold Pfeiffer, born in Prussia in September, 1849; he had emigrated to the United States in 1874. He was not married. We do know that in 1880, Pfeiffer and I. J. Adamson were running a bakery in Leadville, Colorado, but we do not know with certainty when Pfeiffer came to the Big Horn Basin, although it has been suggested that he came to prospect the Big Horn Mountains. He was apparently on the Big Horn in the spring of 1888, for his Pfeiffer Ditch to divert water from the Big Horn River has a priority of April 15, 1888, the first on the main stem of the Big Horn River.[4]

The main body of settlers who joined Pfeiffer was headed by the Voss family, and although Pfeiffer was apparently not related to them, all of the rest were related by blood or marriage to some other member of the group. The Voss family home was Rastow, Mecklenburg, a city in the former duchy of Mecklenburg-Schwerin, which faces on the Baltic. Johann Christoph Christian Friederich Voss was born in 1851, and it appears that when he was drafted into the Kaiser's army, he determined to leave Germany and go to the United States. They came to New York in 1888, and journeyed west to the Julesberg area, where they lived for a time on a homestead, but after a severe drought, they gave up this location, and in 1894 they moved to Wyoming. In the same year, John Voss' nephew,

---

[3]Jordan's date and place of birth are taken from the 1900 census of Wyoming. Floyd A. Bishop, State Engineer to John W. Donnell, March 3, 1966. The comment from the *Billings Gazette* was in the November 21, 1889 issue. Presumably the pipeline was to serve the town of Jordan, when it replaced Berlin, but neither municipality was destined to succeed.

[4]1880 census, Lake County, Colorado. In the 1880 census, Pfeiffer gave his age as 28, which implied a birthdate of 1852. His naturalization certificate is in his desert land entry file in the National Archives; it was issued in the district court of Fremont County, Wyoming, June 28, 1897.

Friederich (Fritz) Laudan came to the United states to join the Voss family.[5]

Matthias Bosch, who was born in Germany in February 1856, came to the United States in 1883 and settled in the Nebraska panhandle, not far from Julesberg, Colorado. The Bosch family paid the fare for Christiana's brother, John Bihr, to come from Germany in 1893, and he was thereby obligated to work for them in repayment. Two years later the Bosch family and John Bihr made the month-long trek to the Basin, where the Vosses were already settled. They traveled from Nebraska up the Platte River to Casper, and from there to Lost Cabin and over Cottonwood Pass; they spent the first winter in a cabin on the Pfeiffer place. Bosch was a charter member of the Lutheran Church at Germania, and the promotional material for Wiley's irrigation project there lists him as one of the early farmers in that area, but if he settled there, he soon left to move near the Vosses on the Big Horn.[6]

Henry W. August Wostenberg, whose wife, was the sister of Fritz Laudan, arrived in the United States from Germany in 1893 and joined the others in Wyoming. When Henry's wife died in childbirth in the summer of 1904, leaving him with five children under the age of ten, he sent for his sister Marie. John Bihr saw in Marie the qualities he wanted for the mother of his children; their first son was born the next year, and yet another family connection was forged in this tightly-knit community.[7]

In the fall of 1894, Henry Wostenburg and John Voss signified their intention to divert water from the Big Horn River through a ditch they proposed to call the Voss Ditch, at a total cost of $2,292. They expected to commence work on the ditch in September of the following year. The project did not go precisely as they had planned, but it was eventually built, after young Fritz Laudan expended a great deal of energy grubbing the sagebrush on the flats where the ditch would pass. According to one account, Fritz' hard work caused the owners to name the canal for him; in any case, the canal became the Fritz Ditch Company. The Pfeiffer Ditch

---

[5]The grand duchy was included in the German empire in 1871. Four pairs of brothers and sisters account for the family relationships. Katherina Voss, sister of John, married Frederick Wostenberg; their son and daughter Henry and Marie were married to Louise Lauden and John Bihr, Sr., respectively. Louise Lauden was the sister of Fritz Laudan, and John Bihr, Sr. was the brother of Christiana Bosch. The Vosses embarked on the ship *Sorrento* on October 17, 1888, bound for New York.

[6]*Northern Wyoming Daily News*, August 19, 1990. John Bihr, Sr. was born in 1871 in Gerstetten, near Ulm, Bavaria.

[7]Louisa Wostenberg died June 22, 1904. John Bihr, Jr. was born September 27, 1905.

was then absorbed in the Fritz Ditch, since the latter ditch had its headgate further up the river and could deliver a larger and more reliable stream of water.[8]

Across the river from the first German colony, another ditch was being developed. William Perry Townsend, who had operated the old Sullivan ferry, joined with Frank Mosegard and Louis E. Calhoun to bring water down the west side of the river to irrigate 175 acres; this Townsend ditch was enlarged to cover more land in 1902, but it suffered from the same limitation as the Pfeiffer ditch. After the turn of the century, it was absorbed by the much larger Big Horn Canal.[9]

Further south, there were a few settlers along the river. On the west side, Daniel A. "Denver Jake" Winslow was living in a cabin at the mouth of Ten Mile Creek, and south of him was the Neiber stage stop on the old Bridger Trail, operated by Bernard Neiber, an Iowan who had farmed in Nebraska before coming to Wyoming. He homesteaded on the Big Horn River in 1895 and built a dugout for the stage stop. The stage consisted of a buckboard with seats for perhaps three passengers; some had storm curtains, others left the passengers free to cope with the weather. Near the mouth of Owl Creek, the numerous Slane family, headed by Civil War veteran William T. Slane, established the Warm Springs Ditch in 1892, the third priority on the main stem of the river.[10]

The last major group to settle in the Basin arrived after the turn of the century, and they are really not a part of our story; nevertheless, they were so numerous, and their coming was so closely tied to the major agricultural developments in the Basin, that a short treatment of them is in order. They are, of course, the Volga Germans, that group of immigrants who had moved en masse from the Palatinate in the Rhineland of Germany to the Volga region of Russia in the middle of the eighteenth century, in response to a ukase issued by Catherine the Great.

Although Catherine sprang from German roots, she did not issue the

---

[8]The Voss Ditch was proposed November 10, 1894. Oral history interview of Peggy Sanders with John and Mollie Bihr, September 16, 1973, p. 4. Fritz Laudan was the only member of the first German colony who did not take up land under the Fritz Ditch.

[9]Townsend was born in Illinois, about 1836.

[10]Neiber was born in Iowa in 1859 and died in 1906. He moved to Tie Siding, Chugwater and Casper before coming to the Basin. *Daily News Sun Country Review*, November 15, 1970. See also *Northern Wyoming Daily News*, August 31, 1972. According to the census, Dan Winslow was born in Pennsylvania in May, 1867. The Warm Springs Ditch had a priority of March 31, 1892; later, it was absorbed by the Kirby Ditch, with a headgate some miles upstream. Dorothy Buchanan Milek, *op. cit.*, 84-85.

ukase in 1766 because of a desire to surround herself with Germans. She was then having trouble defending her southeastern borders from the Tatars, and she reasoned that filling the sparsely-populated borderlands with sturdy German settlers would be a cheap and effective way to reduce the Tatar depredations.[11]

So it was that the ukase was issued on July 22, 1763 and broadcast throughout the Palatinate, offering land and monetary inducements, as well as freedom of religion and exemption from military duty to those married settlers who would immigrate; the promotion proved extremely popular. To satisfy the requirement that prospective settlers be married, those who could not meet this requirement entered into mass weddings just before embarking for Russia. We do not know how durable these marriages proved to be, but when the couple had second thoughts in the fastness of the Volga region, some 900 miles from home, there may have been few alternatives that looked better.[12]

The first settlers arrived in Russia in the summer of 1764, and the migration peaked in 1767, when 68 colonies were established in that year alone. In the ensuing century and a half, the Germans toiled in Russia, and at first they suffered considerable privation; eventually, they succeeded so well that an English traveler in the region remarked on the prosperity of the German colonies. Nevertheless, the system was disturbed in a fundamental way in 1871, when the Russian government revoked many of the privileges given the German settlers, and in particular the exemption from military duty; from this point on, many settlers determined to leave.[13]

Scouts were sent out from the Volga colonies in 1874, to determine suitable destinations and between 1874 and the outbreak of World War I, 300,000 Russian Germans migrated to the United States alone; others came down from Canada in 1914, when Canada entered the first World

---

[11]Catherine, a princess of the principality of Anhalt-Zerbst, was born Sophia Augusta Fredericka, on May 2, 1769; when she converted to the Russian Orthodox Church, she took the names Catherine Alexeievna. The Empress Elizabeth died December 25, 1761, and Catherine's husband, Peter III, was assassinated, with Catherine's connivance, on July 6, 1762. Zoe Oldenbourg, *Catherine the Great* (New York, 1965), 1, 66, 202, 222.

[12]Richard D. Scheuerman and Clifford E. Trafzer, *The Volga Germans: Pioneers of the Northwest* (Moscow, Idaho, 1985), 23, 38.

[13]The ukase of June 4, 1871 revoked the privileges granted by Catherine II, in spite of the guarantee in the 1763 ukase that the military exemption to the colonists would continue "during their entire stay here." *Ibid.*, 77, 92-93, and Richard D. Scheuerman, *Pilgrims on the Earth: A German-Russian Chronicle* (Fairfield, Washington, 1974), 74.

War and many of the pacifists among the Volga Germans opted for the still-neutral United States as a place to avoid military service.[14]

When sugar beets began to be grown in northern Wyoming, the Volga Germans who had grown sugar beets in Russia in the 1850s, and later in Colorado, came to work in the fields, and eventually to settle. The Volga Germans in the Big Horn Basin eventually were far more numerous than those from the first German settlement; indeed, they tended to regard their own peculiar brand of German as the accepted language, in comparison with that brought directly from Germany by the earlier immigrants.[15]

---

[14]*Ibid.*, 96.

[15]James W. Long, *From Privileged to Dispossessed: The Volga Germans, 1860-1917* (Lincoln, Nebraska, 1988), 71. The Volga German dialect has many idioms coined during the century and a half spent in Russia.

CHAPTER XVIII

The Railroad

From its earliest beginnings, Wyoming was very much a creature of the railroad. The location of the territorial capital was decided when the crews building the Union Pacific paused for the winter on the banks of Crow Creek; the lively settlement they built survived to lead the territory when it was organized nearly two years later. As the Union Pacific passed across what is now Wyoming, it laid out the towns that gave the new territory almost all of the permanent habitations of white men in that vast region, apart from the men on the military installations and the folks in a few mining settlements at the South Pass.

The slow pace of development of the Big Horn Basin stemmed largely from its physical isolation and lack of rail transportation. The center of the territory was opened in the eighties when the Chicago & Northwestern railroad's subsidiary, the Fremont, Elkhorn and Missouri Valley Railway, came to Casper, initiating scheduled service on June 15, 1888. The Basin had no railroad at all by the turn of the century, and even after the Toluca line was completed to Cody in 1901, the rest of the Basin was without rail service.

The Burlington railroad entered Wyoming west of Alliance, Nebraska, headed for an eventual junction with the Northern Pacific in Montana Territory (this gateway was negotiated by the two railroads in 1893). This was the era of the struggle between E. H. Harriman and James Jerome Hill for control over the Burlington, and early in 1901 Hill won the competition, and the Great Northern and Northern Pacific purchased control of the line, dividing the stock between them.[1]

---

[1]The Burlington used several subsidiary companies for construction of its lines. The Grand Island & Northern Wyoming Railroad Company was incorporated on February 4, 1889, to build 236

Hill paid more than Harriman was willing to, and the line into the Basin was a part of the attraction to Hill. The Burlington's connection through Wyoming, together with the soon to be acquired Colorado & Southern, afforded the Hill lines through traffic from the Pacific Northwest to the Gulf Coast. Although the Justice Department successfully attacked Hill's holding company, Northern Securities Corporation, that case did not affect the ownership and control of the Burlington, which continued to be a Hill line.

The Burlington needed a reliable source of coal for its engines, and this requirement was met after Frank Wheeler Mondell discovered the Cambria coal field, north of Newcastle. Mondell, who would later be elected to the U. S. House of Representatives from Wyoming, was then working for the railroad construction contractor. The line for the Burlington railroad through eastern Wyoming was being located by an engineer named Edward Gillette and it is said that the town of Gillette, originally called Donkey Town, was named in his honor after he was able to shorten the route by five miles; he later remarked that he would have preferred a salary increase. The railroad was at one time planned to pass through Buffalo, but later changes sent it to Sheridan, instead, where it arrived, November 26, 1892.[2]

The completion of the Burlington railroad into Billings was at first contemplated as a step on the way to the west coast, an objective the Burlington had long considered, but when it became clear that the Burlington would build to Billings, the Northern Pacific agreed to open a gateway on

---

miles of track from the South Dakota line to the Montana line. It was opened to Newcastle on November 18, 1889, and completed to Upton August 5, 1890, after a short hiatus in the spring of 1890. The Big Horn Southern Railroad Company, incorporated December 20, 1888, built the 104 miles from the end of the Grand Island Northern at the Wyoming line to Huntley, Montana; this line was completed October 28, 1894. The Big Horn Southern was sold to the Chicago, Burlington & Quincy Railroad Company on December 1, 1897. The line from Toluca to Cody, 130.15 miles, was built by the parent company, and was opened November 11, 1901. The Big Horn Railroad Company was incorporated January 12, 1905, to build 355.13 miles of track from Fromberg, Montana to Orin Junction in Wyoming. The portion from Frannie to Worland was sold to the CB&Q on December 1, 1908. Donald B. Robertson, *Encyclopedia of Western Railroad History*, II (Dallas, Texas, 1991), 367. Also, Richard C. Overton, *Burlington Route: A History of the Burlington Lines* (New York, 1965), 258, 262-63.

[2]Edward Gillette was born on December 14, 1854, in New Haven, Connecticut. He graduated from Yale Scientific School in 1876, and worked on the U. S. Geological Survey west of the 100th meridian in 1876-81. He was a locating engineer and draftsman for the Rio Grand Western Railway in 1881-84, and locating engineer for the Burlington and Missouri River Railroad, 1884-92. Gillette was appointed superintendent of Wyoming's Water District No. 2, 1892-99, and was elected state treasurer 1907-11. He died in 1936. *Men of Wyoming* (Denver, 1915), 93.

its system for the Burlington at that location, making it unnecessary for the Burlington to build farther west. Thereafter, the Burlington concentrated on filling in its system, rather than pushing westward.[3]

The people of the Big Horn Basin were watching all of this railroad construction, and meanwhile, the surveyors were getting closer. Early in 1891, Gillette and a small party had walked up the Big Horn Canyon on the ice to examine the feasibility of constructing the line west through that defile. The party camped at the mouth of the Big Horn Canyon and began the trek upstream on March 7, 1891, when it was twenty degrees below zero. The low temperature was a welcome factor, since it eliminated the risk of flooding during the period when the party would be on the ice, hemmed in by sheer walls that sometimes soared 1,000 feet above them. Despite the difficulty of the terrain, the route was not immediately rejected, but when it was built, the Toluca line followed a different route.[4]

To the folks in the Basin, the rail connection from Toluca to Cody was good news, as the freight haul into the Basin was shortened considerably, but it did not satisfy those in the southern part of the region. The settlers along the Greybull River campaigned for a rail line extending south from Frannie. It appeared that these efforts were bearing fruit, when word reached Basin City that the Lincoln Land Company was buying land in the Burlington area. An item in the May 31, 1905 *Basin Republican* noted that Fred N. Pearson had bought a number of farms for the Lincoln company and was expected to buy more the following month.[5]

There was no shortage of land to buy, but there were too few people to use the railroad that would be built. Immigration schemes were a familiar part of the western railroad story, and early on the Union Pacific had promoted the southern part of the Wyoming country as a place to live and grow rich. In 1904, after the Burlington decided to build south into the Basin, the railroad hired D. Clem Deaver, of O'Neill, Nebraska, to head a new immigration bureau to attract settlers to the areas along the line. The following year, after a reconnaissance trip to Wyoming, Deaver was

---

[3]The Burlington had made preliminary surveys of a route to the west coast as early as 1886. The Burlington connection with the Northern Pacific at Huntley, Montana was completed on October 28, 1894; it reached Billings by using thirteen miles of Northern Pacific track to the west. The Burlington's Billings gateway was further strengthened in 1909, when the Great Northern extended its line southward from Great Falls to Billings. Richard C. Ovenon, *op. cit.*, 229.

[4]A second party visited the canyon later in 1891.

[5]The land buying in the Greybull River valley resulted in the platting of the town of Otto by the Lincoln Land Company. Lincoln Land Company townsite files, Otto, Wyoming.

quoted in a newspaper interview, "What the west needs is women. There are fully 3,000 industrious and prospering young bachelor farmers and ranchmen in the west who need wives." This remark was contained in a front page story in Omaha, with the suggestion that matrimony-minded women might write to Deaver. To Deaver's consternation, the letters began coming in some numbers, and soon he gave up trying to respond to them.[6]

If this incident proved embarrassing to Deaver, his overall effort was a success. He organized Homeseekers' Excursions to the region, and in 1913 he estimated that 8,000 families had settled there as a direct result of the railroad's promotional efforts. Deaver, Wyoming is now named for him.[7]

To the south of Basin, Charles "Dad" Worland had settled on a 160 acre land entry at the mouth of Fifteen Mile Creek, where he also built the Hole in the Wall roadhouse, in a dugout. Arthur G. Rupp, who had operated a road ranch house and post office at Welling, joined Worland in 1903, with the Hole in the Wall store. Both later moved across the river when the town moved, and Rupp established the *Worland Grit* in 1905.[8]

Early in 1903, a survey crew arrived to determine the feasibility of establishing a large irrigation project on the east side of the river. The leader of this project was Charles Fremont Robertson, then 41, an attorney from Nebraska. He came to Wyoming in April, 1903 to work on the project, and he eventually raised half a million dollars in the east to finance it. Robertson would later be the first mayor of Worland.[9]

---

[6] The former surgeon of the Union Pacific wrote a book touting the virtues of the grasslands as cattle feed, including this quote: "The cost of both summering and wintering is simply the cost of herding, as no feed nor shelter is required." Dr. H. Latham, *Trans-Missouri Stock Raising: Pasture Lands of North America* (Omaha, 1871), 15. As early as 1901, Charles E. Perkins had recommended that the Burlington build into the Basin. Deaver was 38 when he was hired in 1904; he had been register of the U. S. Land Office at O'Neill. He died in 1914. Manuscript by Robert White, American Heritage Center, University of Wyoming.

[7] Richard C. Overton, *Burlington Route: A History of the Burlington Lines* (New York, 1965), 284.

[8] Fifteen Mile Creek was named by Henry Lovell's cowhands for its distance south of Lovell's first headquarters. Rupp was born in Faribault, Minnesota, June 11, 1867. He moved to Illinois, and in 1893 to Montana, where he was in charge of the commissary for the Butte and Yellowstone Coal and Coke Company. In 1896 he moved to Wyoming, first to the mouth of Shell Creek, and then down on the Big Horn River, at Welling. Rupp sold the *Grit* in 1907; he also was the Worland postmaster until 1913, when he moved to Snohomish, Washington. He was back in Worland again in 1917, engaged in the oil business. The post office of Welling was named for Rupp's son, Wellington. Ichabod S. Bartlett, *History of Wyoming*, III (Chicago, 1918), 189, and 1910 census population schedules for Big Horn County, Wyoming.

[9] Robertson was born in Forreston, Illinois on June 23, 1862; he moved to Nebraska and was admitted to the bar there in 1889.

Robertson was joined in the Hanover project by The Rev. Dr. N. B. Rairden of Omaha, superintendent of Baptist Missions for several states. Dr. Rairden became president of the canal company and Robert E. Coburn of Carroll, Iowa, was named treasurer; Robertson was secretary and the manager of the project. The paper work for the water right on the new canal was performed by John P. Arnott, an attorney from Basin, and the canal was named the Hanover, for Arnott's home town of Hanover, Indiana; the first Hanover company, called the Hanover Canal Company, was incorporated early in 1903, with $100,000 capitalization.

It soon became apparent to the promoters of the Hanover project the land under Richard's moribund Big Horn Ditch Company was in the middle of the area they wanted to develop. Robertson therefore struck a deal with the Colorado Springs group who owned the so-called "Colorado Flats," and took over this entire tract, except for the southernmost tract near the mouth of Nowater Creek, then owned by Hiram C. Rider.[10]

The Colorado Flats thus became the core of the Lower Hanover canal, and the balance of the land surveyed was for the most part under the Upper Hanover canal. After the acquisition of the Colorado Flats, the Hanover Land and Irrigation Company was formally incorporated on July 6, 1904, with William L. Culbertson of Carroll, Iowa, as president and David T. Pulliam as vice president: Coburn and Robertson took the positions of treasurer and secretary, respectively. Culbertson was president of the First National Bank of Carroll and Coburn was cashier of that bank. Robertson and Pulliam conveyed their ditch project to the Hanover company in consideration of $25,000.[11]

It was at this point that the Rev. David Thomas Pulliam entered the scene at Worland; Robertson later commented that it was Pulliam who brought to the project the elements necessary for it to succeed, particularly the necessary financial strength. Born in 1858, Pulliam was living in Loveland, Colorado, in 1903, when he first became interested in matters in the Big Horn Basin, apparently having learned about it from Dr. Rair-

---

[10] The purchase of the Colorado Flats was financed by the Davie Realty Company of Colorado Springs. The Hanover group did not buy Richard's own land in the Colorado Flats, but later sold him the water rights for it, charging $5,000 for water rights on 400 acres. Lula Pulliam Colwell, *The Story of the Pulliam Company* (n.p., 1970-71), 4.

[11] William L. Culbertson was born December, 1844, in Perry County, Pennsylvania, according to the 1900 census, Carroll County, Iowa. He came to Iowa in 1860 and was county treasurer of Carroll County in 1875. A. T. Andreas, *Historical Atlas of the State of Iowa*, 1875 (n.p., n.d.), 536. Culbertson was the president of the First National Bank of Carroll, and Coburn, who was born in Maine in 1855, was cashier of that bank.

den and Dr. Morehouse, who were workers with the American Baptist Home Mission Society; he visited the town of Basin the following year, to commence an association that would only end with his death.[12]

Rumors about railroad building were flying in the spring of 1904. The editor of the *Billings Gazette* needled his colleagues in the Wyoming media in this fashion: "Down in Wyoming the newspapers are building roads at a rate that threatens to make them as common as cattle trails used to be before the pilgrim and his wire fence invaded the country." Nevertheless, there was soon more substantial news to report.[13]

In the middle of 1905, a group of Burlington executives stepped off what the editor called "commodious private cars" at Frannie to commence a comprehensive survey of the Basin. The Burlington group was a high level one, and included Daniel Willard, a vice president, George W. Holdredge, general manager of the Burlington lines west of the Missouri, and Thomas E. Calvert, the chief engineer. Robertson was invited to accompany this distinguished group on its tour of the Basin.[14]

The survey team traveled to Byron and Cowley before making their first camp at Lovell. Then it was on to Basin, where Mrs. Anderson at the Antlers Hotel may have tried to influence their judgment with a chicken dinner. The party went upstream to Thermopolis, stopping at Worland on the way and also at its satellite, Hanover, on the east side of the river (for Worland had not yet moved across the river). From Thermopolis, the Burlington group went to Meeteetse and Kirwin before going to Cody.

Despite the best efforts of the local leaders, the railroad men departed for the east without having made a decision favorable to the Worland area. Robertson and David T. Pulliam then took the initiative and went to Lin-

---

[12]David Thomas Pulliam was born March 22, 1858; he married Lillian Belle Rice on July 13, 1887, and died in Long Beach, California, January 26, 1939. Robertson's letter of December 10, 1940, is quoted in Lula Pulliam Colwell, *op. cit.*, 3, 4, 7, 33. Although the Pulliam family eventually received substantial returns from the investment, Pulliam wrote laconically to Robertson in 1911, "The only thing of importance that I ever went into hastily, viz., 'The Hanover,' has taught me a lesson."

[13]*Billings Gazette*, March 8, 1904.

[14]The Burlington party arrived at Frannie on July 20, 1905. The *Cody Enterprise*, July 27, 1905. Holdrege was a graduate of Harvard, and Calvert was a graduate of the Scientific School at Yale; they were both hired by the Burlington in 1870, when the railroad had barely 10 miles of track in eastern Nebraska and they became long time friends. Willard had a distinguished career, becoming a director of the Colorado & Southern after the Burlington bought that railroad; he later left the Burlington to become president of the Baltimore & Ohio. M. W. Ensign of the Lincoln office was also with the group, he handled the arrangements for the senior members. *The Big Horn County Rustler*, July 27, 1905, and Richard C. Overton, *op. cit.*, 99, 281.

coln, where they met with Charles H. Morrill, president of the Lincoln Land Company. Morrill, who was born in 1842 in New Hampshire, had come to Nebraska in 1871, and had become prominent enough in Nebraska politics to warrant the naming of a county and a town in his honor. When the First National Bank of Lincoln got into financial difficulty in 1896, Charles E. Perkins, president of the Burlington, who was a small shareholder of the bank, asked Morrill to place the bank on a sound footing so as to avoid damage to Perkins' reputation. From this early contact, Morrill moved into other businesses controlled by Perkins, and in 1896 he was named president of the Lincoln Land Company.

Morrill was familiar with the Basin, for he had been there earlier with Calvert, who was a good friend. On that trip he had met Col. William F. Cody. He gave Robertson and David Pulliam the bad news that the railroad intended to extend the line only as far south as the town of Basin, and to build a spur up the Greybull River valley. But Morrill also suggested the elements of a deal that could change this result.

The Worland party then went to Omaha, where the Hanover board met in Dr. Rairden's office to formulate a proposal to the Burlington. The price was high. The railroad wanted a 200 foot right of way and Lincoln Land Company wanted a half interest in two sections at Worland and half a section each at Rairden and Durkee, for townsite purposes. The Lincoln Land Company would be the selling agent for the lands. The board agreed to make this offer.

Morrill undertook to present the arrangement with the Hanover board to the Burlington in Chicago. Robertson was already on board the train returning west when Morrill overtook him at Alliance, Nebraska, with the glad tidings that the Burlington had accepted the Hanover proposal and would built south to Worland.

Construction of the Hanover canal began November 1, 1904, and it moved quickly, so that on June 7, 1905, Robertson could advise the *Basin Republican* that the canal was complete, extending north twenty miles from its headgate about four miles above Worland to irrigate about 17,000 acres. It was expected that the irrigated land would grow sugar beets, and Robertson emphasized that no point on the canal would be more than two and a half miles from a sugar beet dump. He also stressed that the new canal was deep enough to carry water when the river was at its lowest Since the Big Horn Canal across the river was in the process of borrowing $350,000 to carry out its construction, Robertson took care to point out that the Hanover had not issued any bonds, but instead had used the resources of its own investors.[15]

The Big Horn Canal project was incorporated in 1905 to irrigate about 30,000 acres west of the river, reaching as far north as the Greybull River. The Big Horn County Irrigation Company, had Winfield S. Collins as its first president and Charles H. Worland was one of the first directors. It was expected to build as far south as Elk Creek by the spring of 1906, but construction actually took longer, and water was turned into the canal on April 1, 1907, to irrigate 15,000 acres.[16]

The growing of sugar beets played an important part in attracting the next wave of settlers. There was a great deal of interest in the subject, and sugar plants had already been operating in Colorado at Longmont, Loveland and Fort Collins for three years or so before any were built in northern Wyoming. (Billings was assured of its sugar factory in December, 1905.) In August of 1905, there was a convention held in the new town of Worland to take commitments from farmers for the raising of sugar beets in that area. At that meeting, over 100 farmers committed 1,400 acres of Hanover lands to sugar beet culture for the Billings factory. Although the railroad had not yet arrived, the Burlington committed itself to transport laborers to the beet fields, and on September 28 the railroad publicly announced that it would be building south on the river route, ensuring that there would be a sugar factory at Lovell. The south Basin would have its railroad after all.[17]

On November 23, 1905, the Hanover Land and Irrigation Company deeded to the Lincoln Land Company the property that had been agreed upon in the earlier arrangements. Pursuant to the agreements between the companies, Lincoln held a half interest in the lands adjacent to Worland, Durkee and Rairden in trust for Hanover. Although Robertson

---

[15]Part of the Hanover canal was built by J. H. Lawson, and part by A. M. Taylor. *Big Horn County News* (Meeteetse), June 7, 1905.

[16]The canal was to begin on the west side of the river in Section 21, Township 46N, Range 93W. The capital stock was $400,000; the first directors were Otto Maier, Willis J. Booth, Charles H. Worland, Henry W.A. Wostenberg and Winfield S. Collins. *Worland Grit*, March 21, 1907 and *The Big Horn County Rustler*, May 18, 1905.

[17]*Billings Gazette*, December 13, 1905, December 3, 1906 and the *Cody Enterprise*, September 7, 1905. The first crop of beets in the Lovell area was harvested in 1907 and shipped to Billings; 680 acres were planted in 1907, and 2,500 acres were expected to be planted there the following year. *Cheyenne Daily Leader*, October 4, November 15, 1907.

implied that the Lincoln company paid nothing for the land, one of the deeds did recite a consideration of $12,550 for 600 acres.[18]

The townsite company now owned the land to lay out the two small towns of Rairden and Durkee and the larger town of Worland; on December 15, 1905, the surveyor for the Lincoln Land Company came to Worland to lay out the town on the east side of the river. When the location of the streets became known, businesses on the west side moved across and took up locations in the new townsite.

David T. Pulliam later acquired the Hanover interest in the Lincoln Land Company lands for $20,000, in partial satisfaction of a $36,000 note owed to him by Hanover. Pulliam had become discouraged by what he called the "recklessness and extravagance" of the Hanover operation, and now he wanted to end the joint ownership with the Lincoln Land Company. In the fall of 1911, he discussed splitting the property, or selling out to Lincoln Land, but finally he bought their interest, receiving the deeds in November.[19]

Construction on the line south from Frannie commenced October 3, 1905. The railroad passed the Greybull River near its mouth and proceeded up the Big Horn. A number of sources report that Basin City, the county seat, was slated to be the location of the freight terminal for the railroad. It appears that the Lincoln Land Company wanted a half section of land then owned by George N. Mecklem and Ellsworth E. Lonabaugh of Sheridan, but could not acquire it. Accordingly, the railroad moved downstream and placed its terminal there, on some 900 acres at the mouth of Dry Creek; in this manner the town of Greybull was born.

Soon the company was selling lots from a price list that ranged from $200 to $600 per 50x140 foot lot; these were handsome prices, considering the fact that only a year or so earlier, lots in Basin were selling for $60 "and up." But the future was bright: by 1916, lots in Greybull were selling for $2,000. As a nucleus for building construction, the company contracted for the construction of a large stone building in each of the towns of Greybull and Manderson, at what must have been the fairly handsome price of $13,950 for the two buildings. The company also subsidized the building of the highway bridges across the Big Horn at Greybull and Man-

---

[18]Robertson transferred about 160 acres to Lincoln Land Company, by a deed executed in Big Horn County on October 16.

[19]Lula Pulliam Colwell, op. cit., 6.

derson, presumably to enhance the salability of lots in the two towns; these bridges were completed in 1907 and 1908.[20]

Although Basin City had lost the freight terminal, it had not lost the railroad, and the tracks reached the county seat on June 21, 1906. The rails raced through Manderson, a new town laid out by the Lincoln Land Company, and graced with the name of the general counsel of the Burlington (although the company briefly used the name Zada, the name of the daughter of the Garland station agent); the townsite company thus ignored, and effectively doomed, the other town-building efforts near the mouth of the Nowood, at Jordan, Alamo and Warren.[21]

When it became apparent that the Lincoln Land Company was going to develop its own town, John Brokaw platted his own addition to the west. After some negotiations, the company was able to offer him a "business lot" in Manderson to defuse the "opposition town" movement. Prices for lots in Manderson were roughly the same as in Greybull ($200 - $600 per lot), but the future was not bright for sales; by 1919, when the town was formally incorporated, the prices were down to the range of $225-450 per lot. The population necessary for incorporation was 150, and in 1921 the state sued the town, alleging that there were fewer people in Manderson than were required, but Judge Harry P. Ilsley turned back the challenge.[22]

On July 10, 1906, the first train came to Worland, where the city fathers had taken advantage of a winter so cold the river froze solid, and had moved the entire town to the east side of the river, abandoning Charles "Dad" Worland's settlement at the mouth of Fifteen Mile creek on the west side. In 1911, the Lincoln Land Company sold its interest in

---

[20]The building contract was awarded to Elswick and Redman of Cody; it was completed by November 15, 1907. Lincoln Land Company townsite files, Greybull, Wyoming. The prices on Basin town lots are from the *Basin Republican*, August 9, 1905.

[21]The Garland station agent was Owen G. Morton and his eldest daughter was Zada L. Morton. The name of the town of Garland, which once had a bank, a newspaper and two hotels, is the subject of some dispute. In one version, it was named for Ed and Charles Garland, who had a warehouse there when the railroad arrived in 1901; Mae Urbanek relates the name to John Garland, a forest ranger. *Northern Wyoming Daily News* (Worland), June 19, 1992 and Mae Urbanek, *Wyoming Place Names* (Boulder, 1967), 82.

[22]Lincoln Land Company townsite files, Manderson, Wyoming. The population minimum had been lowered from 300 to 150 by the 1895 legislature. The Manderson incorporation petition of August 15, 1919, recited a population of 165 in 1919, and the attorney general's suit called this a "pretended census, " claiming that there were then 135, and "no more." The court refused to look behind the Big Horn County Commissioners' acceptance of the election, in which 61 voted, but 23 voted against incorporation. Case No. 2434, State of Wyoming, *ex. rel.* William L. Walls, Attorney General, *vs.* James A. Quiner, Charles H. Burritt, L. O. Gray and James Tolstrup.

the Worland, Durkee and Rairden townsites to David T. Pulliam; thereafter, Pulliam took over the role as developer of Worland, directly and later through his company, the D. T. Pulliam Company.[23]

In 1907, the Burlington railroad reached Kirby, and from there spurs were built to serve the coal mines at the new town of Gebo. S. W. Gebo had filed on the coal lands at Gebo in the summer of 1906, providing a magnet for railroad development that was not in prospect two years earlier, when the Hanover board was bargaining with Burlington for a Worland extension. At Kirby, the railroad construction paused for a time.[24]

In the spring of 1905, the Northwestern commenced construction of the extension from Casper to Lander, as part of a planned system all the way to the West Coast that was destined never to be completed, but at that time, the Northwestern seemed a good bet to build into the Basin. In May of 1905, survey crews from the Northwestern were at work between Gooseberry and Wood River, aiming at the Kirwin mines. By August, the new town of Shoshoni had been platted at the end of the proposed westward extension of the Northwestern, and a hotel and four saloons were projected; the railroad was expected at the new year, but it was actually July of the following year that passenger service from Casper commenced at Shoshoni.[25]

The folks in Thermopolis were inclined to put their money on the Northwestern, now separated from them "only" by the Wind River Canyon. Indeed, in 1905 the State Land Board granted right of way applications through the State Park to both the Northwestern and Burlington railroads.[26]

---

[23]Pulliam financed the purchase through a $20,000 note with the First National Bank of Loveland. The D. T. Pulliam Company was incorporated November 30, 1914, receiving property valued at $25,000 from David T. Pulliam. After a slow start, it eventually paid dividends to shareholders totaling $475,500, and distributed property worth $475,500 to shareholders when it was liquidated in 1969. Lula Pulliam Colwell, *op. cit.*, 6, 7, 8, 52.

[24]S. W. Gebo, who had developed coal mines just north of the Montana line near Red Lodge, filed on coal lands near what is now Gebo in the summer of 1906. The *Thermopolis Record* said that the filing, at $10 per acre, amounted to about $95,000. *Thermopolis Record*, June 30, 1906. The Burlington line reached Kirby on September 3, 1907. Richard C. Overton, *op. cit.*, 269.

[25]Shoshoni was platted by the Pioneer Townsite Company, August 8, 1905. The plat is filed in the Fremont County courthouse. See also, the *Big Horn County News* (Meeteetse), August 26, 1905.

[26]Dorothy G. Milek, *The Gift of Bah Guewana, op. cit.*, 81.

CHAPTER XIX

A Man Named Boysen

It was while the railhead for the Burlington was stopped at Kirby that Asmus Boysen advertised for bids for the first Boysen dam, and newspaper accounts painted the picture of a dam sixty feet high, to create a lake six or seven miles long and a mile or two wide; the project was expected to cost $100,000. This event was to loom large in the plans of the railroad to build through the Wind River canyon.[1]

Asmus Boysen was a Danish emigrant, born in 1868; he came to Gray, Iowa, from Illinois about 1890, and there engaged in farming; in 1900, Boysen, in partnership with his sister-in-law, purchased the bank in town, and in this period he was also buying and selling land and livestock. At one time, he owned four banks, in Gray, Templeton, Audubon and Manning, Iowa. In 1900 and 1902, he represented Audubon County in the Iowa legislature as a Republican.[2]

The curious story of Boysen's adventure in Wyoming began in the spring of 1899, when Boysen, writing on the stationery of the Iowa State legislature, requested permission to go on the Shoshoni Indian reservation to negotiate a lease to mine coal and other minerals. Boysen did not go to the Interior Department without support; early in May, the Secretary of Agriculture sent over a laudatory letter from Iowa Congressman Smith McPherson, and there were also letters from both Iowa senators

---

[1] *Cheyenne Daily Leader*, November 24, 1906, October 4, 1907.
[2] According to the 1900 census for Audubon County, Iowa, Boysen was born in July, 1868, his son Allan was born in Illinois in 1890, while his daughter Helena was born in Iowa in the following year; Boysen's wife, Anna, was also born in Illinois, in 1871. The Farmers Exchange Bank of Gray, Iowa, was established in 1893, and purchased by Asmus Boysen and Lida W. Leet in 1900; Boysen sold his interest to Leet in 1907. *Gray Community History 1881-1981*, 18. Also, *Audubon County Journal* (Exira, Iowa), November 2, 1899. The Gray and Templeton banks were private banks and the Commercial Bank in Audubon and the German Savings Bank in Manning were state banks.

and two Iowa congressmen, including the one who would be elected Speaker of the House later that year.³

It would later be claimed that Boysen was acting in concert with the Union Pacific railroad, and a fifth endorsement of Boysen's request came from John N. Baldwin, general attorney for the Union Pacific Railroad in Omaha, who was also Asmus Boysen's attorney. Baldwin was the nephew of John T. Baldwin, who had been the partner of General Grenville M. Dodge in a number of ventures; Dodge, of course, was highly influential in the building of the Union Pacific railroad. Moreover, Senator Allison of Iowa and Secretary of Agriculture Wilson had both been active in promoting the Union Pacific in Iowa and both held stock in the Credit Mobilier.⁴

It is tempting to assume that the Union Pacific was involved in some grand scheme in central Wyoming, but it is unlikely that this was so. The Union Pacific had just emerged from bankruptcy, and its new management was embarking on a reconstruction of the road, including the expensive rebuilding of the Sherman hill crossing west of Cheyenne, which commenced in the spring of 1900. In short, the Union Pacific had its plate full, without a diversion to the Yellowstone country. The more plausible explanation of so many Union Pacific figures in Boysen's camp was the fact that virtually all the politically savvy leaders in Iowa in this era had been involved in the promotion of the Union Pacific.

In due course, the Secretary of the Interior granted Boysen permission

---

³Boysen's first letter was dated February 16, 1899. There were endorsements from several in the Iowa delegation in Congress, and one from a cabinet member, who was a former Iowa congressman. The letter from James Wilson, Secretary of Agriculture was dated May 5, 1899; it enclosed a May 2 letter from Congressman Smith McPherson. The letter from Senator John Henry Gear was dated May 3, 1899, and that of Senator William Boyd Allison was dated May 4. The latter letter was also endorsed by Congressman David Bremner Henderson, who was born in Scotland on March 14, 1840, and served in the Union Army during the Civil War and wounded at Fort Donelson, causing the need for more than one amputation in future years. Henderson was elected to Congress in 1882 and was regarded as a protege of Senator Allison; he was elected Speaker of the House on December 4, 1899, and served until 1903. Donald R. Kennon, ed., *The Speakers of the U. S. House of Representatives* (Baltimore, 1986), 194.

⁴The Baldwin endorsement was dated April 19, 1899, and was directed to Congressman Henderson. Baldwin was born in Council Bluffs, July 9, 1857, the son of Caleb Baldwin. He joined the Union Pacific in Council Bluffs in 1877, and had become general attorney for the road in 1898. Alfred Sorenson, *The Story of Omaha* (Omaha, 1923), 385-86. Dodge, who had also been an Iowa congressman, had been involved in a scandal involving supplies to the Red Cloud Agency. Stanley P. Hirshson, *Grenville M. Dodge* (Bloomington, Indiana, 1967), 198. Oakes Ames sold 160 shares of the Credit Mobilier at par to eleven members of Congress, including both William B. Allison and James F. Wilson of Iowa. Maury Klein, *op. cit.*, 145.

to negotiate with the Indians, and the arena now shifted to Wyoming, where the first public indication that something was afoot on the reservation came in April, 1899, when the Lander *Clipper* reported on a flurry of speculations. It noted that there were rumors that a syndicate was "trying to get hold of the surplus land of the Wind River reservation," by long term lease. There was also an article about rumors that the agent of the Burlington railroad was on the reservation, with a view to securing a lease of coal lands; the Burlington reportedly wanted 30 years but the Indians only wanted to lease for ten. The *Cheyenne Tribune* was quoted to the effect that the Union Pacific knew of the Burlington designs on the Wind River country and had sent its surveyors out to "head off" the Burlington. In the same issue, it was reported that Senator Warren wanted the Shoshoni reservation thrown open to settlement.

A week later, the *Clipper* quoted the *Denver News* to the effect that the Burlington lease of the reservation coal lands had been signed, but needed the approval of the secretary of the interior. In May, the *Clipper* reported on a conversation with N. E. Young of Glenrock, who said he had been present when the Burlington negotiated with the tribes for a right of way across the reservation and for the coal lands. He said that Sharp Nose and Washakie were both present.[5]

In fact, something very different had happened. At the time the *Clipper* was reporting the April rumors of a Burlington lease, there was in fact a negotiation at Fort Washakie. A meeting at the fort on April 1 resulted in an agreement among seventeen men, looking toward a lease of Indian land for the mining of minerals, "principally coal." Five of the participants in that agreement were present at Fort Washakie, including Charles J. Woodhurst, a surveyor from Fort Collins, who had been working on the survey of Indian lands for the purpose of establishing allotments to tribal members.[6]

The group Boysen had assembled included a number of prominent men from Omaha. The Mayor of Omaha, William J. Broatch, was a mem-

---

[5] Young's account of the discussions with the Indians was surprisingly detailed. He said that the chiefs first held a conference among themselves, and then a mutual conference was held by the two tribes with the railroad agents, the first at the agency and a second at Fort Washakie. J. C. Burnett, the Indian trader at Fort Washakie acted as interpreter. Young declared that Thermopolis was to be a "prominent" station on the line. *Wyoming Derrick* (Casper), May 4, 1899.

[6] The seventeen participants were Adam Morrell, Josef Weis, William J. Broatch, John T. Clarke, Harry F. Clarke, Jacob Edward House, John T. Wertz, Robert C. Wertz, Reese E. Davies, Charles J. Woodhurst, Thomas Coughlan, Asmus Boysen, P. J. Barr and "four unknown." Broatch, et. al, vs. Boysen, et. al., 175 *Federal Reporter* 702.

ber; he had served as government Indian agent in Yankton and was appointed to the Missouri River Commission in St. Louis before he became mayor of Omaha. With Broatch in the group was his bookkeeper, Thomas Coughlan. Jacob Edward House was a good friend of General Grenville M. Dodge, and had served as chief engineer of the Union Pacific, before Dodge took that office. Also in the group was House's son in law, Col. John T. Wertz, as well as Wertz' brother, Robert C. Wertz. John Wertz had lived in Lander when he was allotting agent for the Wind River Reservation.[7]

The man in the group who was to cause Boysen the most difficulty in the years ahead was John Tefft Clarke, who gave his occupation as real estate and investments, and who had been involved in the first electric light company in Omaha in 1884. Clarke's father had made his fortune in freighting and wholesale jobbing in Nebraska, and became one of the largest landowners in the state.[8]

The agreement among the seventeen contemplated that the lease would issue to Boysen, and that he would assign it to another of the participants, as trustee for the benefit of the group. Ten of the men were to contribute $2,000 each over a period of two years; no explicit reasons were given for the exemption of the other six, although we can hazard some logical guesses for at least two of those. Woodhurst presumably got a free share for the knowledge of the land which he could contribute to the syndicate and Adam Morrell may have been compensated for agreeing to be the trustee for the syndicate. One of those exempted was among the "four unknown" members, which suggests that the "unknown" designation

---

[7]Jacob Edward House had been with Dodge in the Mississippi and Missouri railroad, and he superintended the building of shops for the Union Pacific and the survey of the Platte valley route. When he was the Union Pacific agent for the sale of lots in Cheyenne in 1867, Dodge named a street for him. House died in Omaha, June 22, 1908. When his will was probated, he was found to own land in at least 14 towns in Kansas and Nebraska. William J. Broatch was born in Connecticut, July 31, 1841 and died in 1922. Peggy Dickey Dircus, "Fort David A. Russell: A Study of Its History from 1867 to 1890," *Annals of Wyoming*, XL, No. 2 (October, 1968), 176-77, Stanley P. Hirshson, *op. cit.*, 153 and Alfred Sorenson, *op. cit.*, 300, 567-68. Robert C. Wertz was from Dalton, Ohio. Adam Morrell was from Omaha, and Josef Weis was from Buffalo, New York, and later New York City. Broatch, *et. al.*, vs. Boysen, *et. al.*, Case No. 288, U. S. District Court, Cheyenne. Reese Davies was from Omaha, as was Pressley J. Barr, manager of the C. F. Adams Company, whose business was installment goods. Also, *The Lander Clipper*, August 11, 1905.

[8]John T. Clarke was born December 8, 1861, in Nebraska, but later moved to Pennsylvania and then New York. His older brother, Harry Fielding Clarke, was born August 4, 1860; the two brothers were active in the Omaha real estate business with their father, Henry Tefft Clarke, who had also served in the Nebraska legislature. Also, George Austin Morrison, Jr., *The "Clark" Families of Rhode Island* (New York, 1902), 188, and *Omaha Illustrated: A History of the Pioneer Period and the Omaha of Today* (Omaha, 1888).

merely meant that the name was not disclosed in the original agreement, not that the identities were unknown to Boysen.[9]

Among those mentioned in the agreement, there is no N. E. Young, the mysterious person from Glenrock, who had told the press that he had been at the Fort when the lease was negotiated. In fact, Noah Young was none other than the Wyoming state inspector of mines. Young, who was born September, 1857, and began working in the coal mines at the age of ten; he said that he despaired of making more than a bare living at this work, and turned to bare knuckle boxing, which gave him a championship before leaving England at the age of nineteen. After working in a number of western mines in the United States, Young became superintendent of the Glenrock coal mines in 1886.[10]

Although Boysen later testified that he had employed mining experts to advise him on the lease, he did not identify the men he hired. If Young was one of those hired, the fact that he served in an official state capacity might have caused him to exercise caution on that point. But why would Young have told the newspapers that the coal lease had been negotiated with the Burlington railroad? Whether this was artful "disinformation" is impossible to tell, but it is worth noting that Young developed a reputation for overblown remarks. In any case, there is no evidence for another coal lease negotiation on the reservation in the spring of 1899.[11]

---

[9]Although Boysen may have known who the other four participants were to be, he apparently did not commit that fact to a record that has survived; later, when he was sued by some of these participants, the plaintiffs swore that the names of the "unknowns" were not known to them. Broatch, et. al. vs. Boysen, et. al., Case No. 288, U. S. District Court, Cheyenne.

[10]The Young family of Glenrock was headed by Noah Young, the state mine inspector. It seems that Noah had been the manager of Metcalf's store in Glenrock, but in the spring of 1899 was on the road selling groceries for Allen Brothers of Omaha. The Young family lived in Glenrock until May, 1899, when they moved to Cheyenne. *Natrona County Tribune* (Casper), May 18, 1899. The first state legislature had created the office of state inspector of mines, and Noah Young was appointed to that office in 1897; when the second inspector was provided for in 1903, Young was given the northern district of the slate and he served in that office until 1908. Young said he was born in Lancashire, England, and came to the United States in 1875. He worked in coal mines from the age of 10 years, and worked in Nevada, Colorado, Deadwood, and Rock Springs. He was employed at Miner's Delight in 1875 and later worked at Leadville and Coal Creek before coming to Glenrock in 1886. A somewhat different picture emerges from his entry in the 1900 census, which gives his birth date as 1857, and says he came to the United States in 1860, which would hardly give time for the sporting career in his native country. His three sons were born in Colorado in 1883, 1885 and 1887. Young died at Culver City, California, in July, 1931. *Wyoming Tribune*, July 29, 1931.

[11]At this distance in time, it is pointless to speculate whether Young might have been one of the "unknown" members of the Boysen consortium. In 1907, Young reported on a property for the Miner's Delight Mining Company, in a report which was called "flamboyant" by one writer. Robert A. Murray, "Miner's Delight, Investor's Despair: The Ups and Downs of a Sub-Marginal Mining Camp in Wyoming," *Annals of Wyoming*, XLIV, No. 1 (Spring, 1972), 53.

In due course, a lease was negotiated with the Indian agent at Fort Washakie, and confirmed by tribal councils held near the end of June. In June, Captain Herman G. Nickerson, the Indian agent at Fort Washakie, left for Washington, with five members of each of the two tribes on the reservation. On the way to Casper, one of the stages overturned, injuring an "old and lame" medicine man; this was considered a bad omen, but the Indians finally agreed to proceed with the trip, sending their injured companion back to the reservation to recover.[12]

Captain Nickerson was not without important friends in official Washington, for he had served in the same cavalry unit with William McKinley, who now was president of the United States. Near the end of June, Captain Nickerson and the Indians returned, and the *Clipper* noted that the leasing of the coal lands had been approved by the Indian Department. Although the *Clipper* story left the impression that it was the Burlington lease that had been approved, the lease actually was with Asmus Boysen, not the Burlington railroad; it was dated July 1, 1899, and was approved by the Secretary of the Interior on October 4, 1899, with minor amendments.[13]

The lease was signed for Boysen by Josef Weis, as attorney in fact; Weis, of course, was also one of the partners of Boysen. Nickerson certified to the Secretary of the Interior that the land being leased was not needed by the tribes; he further stated that he had consulted three "creditable disinterested persons" regarding the lease, and they had recommended the transaction. The three were James B. McLucas, Charles J. Woodhurst and John T. Wertz: the last two were also partners of Boysen. There is no record as to whether Nickerson knew of the connection between Boysen and his "creditable" experts, but in any case he certified that the lease was "free from fraud or deception," and that he had no personal interest in it.[14]

---

[12] *Wyoming Derrick* (Casper), June 8, 1899.

[13] *The Clipper* (Lander), April 21, 28, May 12, June 2, 23, 1899. Boysen accepted the lease amendments on October 14, 1899; in them, he was prohibited from employing people who were unacceptable to the tribes. Nickerson was said to be an old friend of President McKinley, having served with the president in the same company and regiment. *Wyoming Derrick* (Casper), December 27, 1900. Nickerson was 22 when he enlisted in Company D, of the 23rd Ohio Volunteer Infantry, and William McKinley was 18 when he enlisted in the same company; they were together in that unit until early 1863, when McKinley was moved to Company E. Marshall Everett, *Complete Life of William McKinley and the Story of his Assassination* (n.p., 1901), 134. Nickerson was named Indian Agent at Fort Washakie in 1893. The two tribal councils were held June 26, 1899.

[14] The Nickerson certification was provided to the House of Representatives in the minority report of January 26, 1905. 58th Congress, Third Session, House Report 3700, Part 2.

As originally negotiated, the lease permitted Boysen to prospect for coal in eight townships, which could have amounted to as much as 184,320 acres when the land was surveyed; ultimately it was found to cover 178,000 acres. The lease did not give Boysen the right to prospect for other minerals, but he was soon back to ask for that right, at one point agreeing to give up all except one township if he could get a lease to mine copper; the secretary blandly agreed to accept the surrender, but noted that a new lease would have to go through the entire procedure again. Boysen also told the Interior Department that he intended to construct a railroad to the reservation to remove the coal he would mine.[15]

The lease provided that Boysen would have two years in which to locate coal deposits, and to file a map defining his claim. Boysen did file a map, but the first one did not meet the requirements of the government, in part because some of the land included in the lease had not been surveyed by the government, and therefore could not be described according to legal subdivisions. Boysen went to Washington and talked to the secretary of the interior, and he would later claim that the secretary had waived the requirement to file the map. In any case, the government notified Boysen on January 22, 1901 that his lease was terminated for failure to file the necessary map.[16]

In May, 1901, Boysen nevertheless made an application for a coal vein located 15 miles from Fort Washakie and 8 miles from Lander. He also complained that he was being maligned by a group headed by Senator John Mellen Thurston of Nebraska and George de Rue Meiklejohn, the Assistant Secretary of War (also from Nebraska), who had their own designs on a mining lease.[17]

The matter then dragged on for a time, and then on March 4, 1904, the Interior Department issued a formal notice of cancellation of the lease. Why the sudden formality? The answer can be found in the *Congressional Record* for the same day, for Congressman Franklin Wheeler Mondell of Wyoming had just introduced H.R. 13481, the bill to ratify the agreement with the Indians to open the northern part of the Wind River reservation to settlement under the public land laws; Boysen's coal lease was located

---

[15] The details of Boysen's representations are contained in a letter from E. A. Hitchcock, Secretary of the Interior, dated January 26, 1905; the letter was reprinted in the *Congressional Record* for February 16, 1905.

[16] The correspondence and the lease are located in the National Archives, Record Group 75, Special Case No. 191 Shoshone.

[17] Boysen's complaint about Senator Thurston and Assistant Secretary Meiklejohn was dated January 15, 1901. Thurston was Chairman of the Senate Committee on Indian Affairs.

partly in the ceded area, and partly in the area retained by the tribes. In spite of the government action three years earlier to declare the lease forfeit, clearly somebody in the Interior Department was not so sure that the lease was really legally dead.[18]

Accordingly, in order to eliminate the supposed Boysen lease impediment, a settlement was negotiated with Boysen, and it was fortunate for him that the House Committee on Public Lands was headed by John Fletcher Lacey, congressman from Iowa. Boysen's interests may have received important help from two of the men involved in the seventeen-party agreement of 1899, for these men went to Washington to lobby for the Boysen clause that was eventually enacted. In any case, when the committee drafted the act opening the reservation, it gave Boysen the right to locate not more than 640 acres of mineral or coal lands in the form of a square; he was to pay $10 per acre for this land.[19]

The debate in the House was at times emotional, and Congressman John Joseph Fitzgerald of New York led the opposition to the Boysen settlement. He declared that the Secretary of the Interior was "violently" opposed to the provision, and he pointed out that it was inserted without the consent of congressman F. W. Mondell from Wyoming. Mondell admitted that he had not requested the provision, but refused to be drawn into the argument, noting that it was a simple way to avoid later difficulties over Boysen's rights under the lease. There was concern that Boysen could use his 640-acre option to block roads or railway routes, and to this Mondell blandly asserted that there were no "passes" where this was possible. After a somewhat heated discussion, the House deleted the provision that had been inserted by its committee and sent the bill to the Senate.[20]

When the bill came before the Senate, Wyoming's Senator Clarence Don Clark restored the Boysen provision on a voice vote. The bill then

---

[18]There is a notation that the formal notice of cancellation was "informally" sent to the Secretary of the Interior on January 25, 1905. H.R. 13481 was immediately referred to the House Committee on Indian Affairs.

[19]The two men who went to Washington were John T. Clarke and John T. Wertz. Broatch, et. al. v. Boysen, et. al., 175 *Federal Reporter* 702. The Boysen lease was dated July 1, 1899; the price he was to pay for the lands was the maximum permitted for the sale of mining lands. Boysen received his patent for 680.31 acres on May 17, 1907; he immediately conveyed the entire parcel to the Asmus Boysen Mining Company of Thermopolis. Book Q, Fremont County Deeds, 219. The acreage exceeded 640 acres, because some of the subdivisions included in the parcel were larger than 40 acres.

[20]Mondell served as congressman from Wyoming in 1895-97 and 1899-1923. He was born November 6, 1860 and died August 6, 1939. The House deleted the Boysen provision on a vote of 127-47. *Congressional Record*, February 16, 1905.

went back to the House, which insisted on its position, so that a conference committee had to be appointed. The result was practically decided when the committee included both Senator Clark and Boysen's Iowa friend, Congressman John F. Lacey; the conference version retained the Boysen amendment.[21]

Boysen's troubles were not over; he was only given thirty days after the government surveys were completed in which to locate the section of land. There was little doubt what Boysen hoped to find on the land he selected, for gold and copper fever was running high in the Copper Mountain region, just east across the reservation boundary, and a number of mining companies were incorporated to prospect the area. Boysen had a diamond drill at work on Copper Mountain, under the direction of his brother, N. P. Boysen, and late in October he moved the drill over on the reservation to help make the land selection. While there was opposition to this action, it was apparently authorized by the President himself.[22]

Prospecting with the diamond drill did not proceed very long. Early in November, two dynamite blasts damaged the engine and the drill beyond repair, and the Department of the Interior shortly ordered Boysen off the reservation. Troops were brought on the reservation, perhaps to keep the peace, or perhaps in anticipation of the "sooners" who were descending on the area which would shortly be opened under the public land laws.[23]

N. P. Boysen received an anonymous letter suggesting he leave town, but initial public reaction to this was sympathetic to the Boysens, and a public protest meeting was held in Thermopolis in their support. Despite the loss of the drill, Boysen pressed on, and in the first of a dizzying list of lawsuits, his lawyer in Cheyenne got U. S. District Judge John Alden Riner to sus-

---

[21] The Senate vote on the Clark amendment was taken February 25, 1905. The six members of the conference committee all came from west of the Mississippi; they were Clarence Don Clark of Wyoming, Chester Isaiah Long of Kansas, and William Andrews Clark of Montana from the Senate, and Thomas Frank Marshall of North Dakota, John Fletcher Lacey and John Hall Stephens, of the House. The act opening the reservation was approved March 3, 1905. 33 *Statutes at Large* 1016.

[22] Late in 1899, it was reported that there had been copper finds on the headwaters of Bridger Creek that ran twenty miles to the Wind River Canyon, where it outcropped on both sides. *Wyoming Derrick* (Casper), October 5, 1899. The Quien Sabe Mining Company, which was a fairly typical prospecting company, was formed by a Thermopolis group in October, 1905, with capital of $500,000; the Asmus Boysen Mining Company had a stated capital of $25 million. *Thermopolis Record*, October 21, 1905. N. P. Boysen came to Wyoming in March, 1905 to make his headquarters in Thermopolis. Lander *Clipper*, March 31, 1905.

[23] The diamond drill was operating in Section 9, Township 3 North, Range 7 East on November 2, 1905; the government ordered Boysen off the reservation late that day. Asmus Boysen *vs.* Harry E. Wadsworth, Case No. 286, U. S. District Court, Cheyenne, Wyoming.

pend the government's ejection order in the spring of 1906. This injunction was subsequently extended, so that Boysen's men presumably had the opportunity to obtain at least some information about the available lands.[24]

Judge Riner, who was the first United States District judge for Wyoming, was to see a good deal of Asmus Boysen and the people suing him in the years to come. Boysen's Cheyenne counsel in these actions was John W. Lacey, who has been called the most influential lawyer in the state; Lacey had been chief justice of the supreme court of Wyoming Territory and later was Riner's law partner until the latter was appointed to the federal bench.[25]

Boysen did make his selection of his preferential tract, in the northeast corner of the reservation, in an area totally outside the boundaries of his old mining lease. This section of land covered a portion of the so-called Hale lead of the Copper Mountain mineral field; the mineralization was thought to be 1,000 feet or more deep, and the *Thermopolis Record* declared, "It is a gold proposition." The selection actually made by Boysen was squarely athwart the entrance to the Wind River Canyon, across the access routes of both the railroad and the future highway, in spite of Congressman Mondell's assurances to the House that there were no passes on the reservation where such a controlling position could be achieved.[26]

Harry E. Wadsworth was the Indian agent who succeeded Nickerson, and he certainly had no love for Boysen by this time. Wadsworth now claimed that Boysen had forfeited his selection, because the provision had not been ratified by the tribes, and in any case, he claimed that Boysen could not locate his section of land outside the old lease boundaries. Boysen again went to court, and he was ultimately upheld in a case that was eventually decided by the eighth circuit court of appeals in St. Louis, and Boysen finally received the patent to his section of land.[27]

---

[24]*Thermopolis Record*, November 11, 1905.

[25]Judge Riner's initial injunction was issued April 23, 1906. Asmus Boysen vs. Harry E. Wadsworth, Case No. 286, U. S. District Court, Cheyenne. Also, *Thermopolis Record*, May 5, 19, 26, 1906. John A. Riner, born in Preble, Ohio in 1850, was appointed to the federal district court September 22, 1890; he died March 4, 1923, only two years after retiring from the bench. Rebecca W. Thomson, "The Federal District Court in Wyoming 1890-1982," *Annals of Wyoming*, LIV, No. 1 (Spring, 1982), 11-14. John W. Lacey, who was born in Indiana, October 13, 1848, served as chief justice of the Wyoming supreme court, July 5, 1884 to November 8, 1886, when he resigned to go into private practice, with the Union Pacific Railroad as a key client. Another of his partners, Willis Van Devanter, was appointed to the federal circuit court of appeals and ultimately to the Supreme Court of the United States. Lacey and Van Devanter represented the cattlemen involved in the Johnson County invasion. Lacey died in Cheyenne, February 11, 1936. [26]*Thermopolis Record*, June 30, 1906.

[27]The case of Wadsworth vs. Boysen was decided by the circuit court of appeals on November 23, 1906. 148 *Federal Reporter* 771.

CHAPTER XX

Through the Wind River Canyon at Last

After Boysen exchanged the coal lease for a section of land, the participants in the 1899 agreement suddenly appeared on the scene. Apparently nothing had been done about the partnership agreement following the issue of the lease to Boysen; indeed, the lease contained the standard provision that it was not assignable without the consent of the Secretary of the Interior, and Boysen had made no effort to obtain that consent, so that the partners could participate in the lease with him. By the same token, none of the participants had paid their contribution under the agreement, either. Nevertheless, when Boysen refused to share his section of land with the others, they sued him.[1]

Actually, not all of the participants joined in the suit, which leaves a puzzle that simply cannot be unraveled from this distance. Seven of the partners sued, and the defendants in the action included not only Boysen himself, but also Josef Weis and Adam Morrell, since these two partners had refused to join as plaintiffs. Morrell had been the trustee for the group, and Weis had signed the lease on behalf of Boysen. In an affidavit filed in support of Boysen, Morrell made the argument Boysen would also make: the lease did not result from the efforts of the group, and the agreement was never executed.[2]

---

[1] The suit against Boysen was filed July 9, 1906, even before Boysen received his patent on May 17, 1907. Broatch, et. al. vs. Boysen, et. al., 175 Federal Reporter 702.

[2] The plaintiffs were William J. Broatch, Harry F. Clarke, Robert C. Wertz, Thomas Coughlan, Charles J. Woodhurst, John T. Clarke and Mary F. House, as heir of Jacob E. House. Curiously, Josef Weis apparently never renounced the partnership agreement, and he conveyed his interest to Maurice G. Clarke on December 1, 1920; Clarke claimed it represented a one-seventh interest, because there were only seven of the original group who accepted the agreement. The action, which is Case No. 288, was filed in the U. S. District Court in Cheyenne on July 9, 1906.

Boysen also argued that the agreement was not to have been effective until signed by all, and that in any case there had been no performance under it. In the years that followed, the list of plaintiffs dwindled, as John T. Clarke and Robert C. Wertz together purchased a total of five shares in the agreement, and it was these shares that were in dispute in the subsequent litigation.[3]

When Boysen had secured title to the land, he immediately conveyed the entire tract to the Asmus Boysen Mining Company, which then conveyed an 88 acre parcel to the Big Horn Power Company, in exchange for stock of that company. For a time, Boysen's prospecting operations seemed to go well, and in the spring of 1907, his manager in Thermopolis, Niels C. Brorson, journeyed to Chicago to report to Boysen that prospects were favorable. Boysen himself visited Thermopolis in June, and reported that he had twenty men working in the mine.[4]

The mining company at first reported copper deposits running from 3% to 15%, and also four veins of "free gold;" the Williams-Luman property nearby was also thought to be rich, and it was hoped that a dredge in the river would find gold in paying quantities in the gravel in the river. Boysen had hoped that the copper outcrop that was visible in the canyon would extend onto his land, but the lode was not found when a shaft was driven into the mountain to intercept it. When none of the rosy expectations were realized, the mining operations had to be shut down. Boysen had also planned to irrigate 30,000 acres near Shoshoni by using power from the plant to pump water from the lake behind the dam, but the cost of the irrigation project was found to be greater than the developed land would have been worth.[5]

---

[3]There are allegations that all of the partners did not sign the original agreement, and perhaps that was so; in 1916, Josef Weis assigned his interest in the agreement to John T. Clarke, and appended his copy of the document, which showed the signature of twelve parties, including Boysen. Fremont County Deed Book 58, page 35.

[4]Boysen received his patent on May 17, 1907, covering a total of 680.31 acres, and the following day he conveyed the entire tract to the Asmus Boysen Mining Company; the latter company then conveyed 88.16 acres to the Big Horn Power Company of Thermopolis, in exchange for 3,500 shares of that company's stock, having a face value of $350,000. Deed records Q219, Q221 and Q223, Fremont County Clerk's office. The Big Horn Power Company was incorporated October 16, 1907, with total capital of $700,000. The original board of directors of the power company included Asmus Boysen and John N. Baldwin, the general attorney of the Union Pacific Railroad, who was also Boysen's attorney. William A. Conover, another attorney, also sat on the board; he represented the company in legal matters.

[5]Asmus Boysen testified that the lift required for the irrigation had to be 50 feet, rather the 35 feet he had contemplated when the permit was filed. Broatch, et. al. vs. Boysen, et. al., Case No. 288, U. S. District Court, Cheyenne.

If mining and irrigation projects were in trouble, so also was the dam and power plant project. The power company issued 5% gold bonds for $350,000, secured by a trust deed on the land and the water rights, as well as the dam and power plant it expected to build. The company applied for permission to build a 60 foot dam across the Wind River, at the head of the canyon, ostensibly to provide electric power for mining on Copper Mountain and the Owl Creek range. Boysen also applied for a permit to build a pipeline 6 feet in diameter and 3,930 feet long, to carry water from the river to nearby mining operations.[6]

During flood seasons, water was expected to flow ten feet deep over the dam; the 60 foot dam would permit the generation of 5,000 horsepower, enough generating capability to produce power for sale to others. The State Engineer issued the permit on May 2, 1908; the reservoir was expected to cover 1,715 acres to a mean depth of 35 feet, and the dam was expected to cost $150,000. Construction was to begin January 15, 1908, and take two years to complete.[7]

Soon, Boysen was complaining to the State Engineer that the Burlington railroad was stalling his application by its assertion that a dam of these dimensions would impair its right of way through the canyon. On his part, the state engineer was suspicious of Boysen, and he confided to Governor Brooks that he thought Boysen was working "in the interest of the Union Pacific;" the state engineer also contended that Boysen made his land selection to control access to the canyon. Governor Bryant B. Brooks called a meeting of the Union Pacific, the Burlington and the Chicago and Northwestern, to discuss the problem. Subsequently, a hearing was held by the state engineer, at the conclusion of which the height of the dam was reduced to 35 feet above the mean low water level of the stream; the spillway was to be 143 feet long.[8]

Community leaders in Thermopolis had been solidly behind Boysen

---

[6]The deed of trust from the Big Horn Power Company to Chicago Title and Trust Company was dated January 1, 1908. There were 700 bonds of $500 each, with interest payable in gold coins on the first day of January and July of each year, with the principal due in 1918. Broatch, et. al. vs. Boysen, et. al., Case No. 288, U. S. District Court, Cheyenne.

[7]The dam and reservoir are covered by the state engineer's Permit 1256.

[8]Boysen's letter of August 7, 1907 to the State Engineer was written on stationery showing his Chicago office to be in the Railway Exchange Building in that city. Governor Brooks said the meeting he called took two or three days, and was held in the courtroom of the Supreme Court. Bryant Butler Brooks, *Memoirs of Bryant B. Brooks: Cowboy, Trapper, Lumberman, Stockman, Oilman, Banker, and Governor of Wyoming* (Glendale, California, 1939), 215-16. The state engineer's determination was dated January 27, 1908. Big Horn Power Company vs. State of Wyoming, 23 Wyoming 286. The State Engineer's letter to the Governor was dated July 2, 1909.

when his diamond drill was destroyed, but when he began disputing with the railroad, there was immediate concern that his efforts might stop the hoped-for rail connection through the canyon, and the *Record* declared that the community wanted both the dam and the railroad, and was unwilling to choose between them. While the people in Thermopolis were at first fearful that the Northwestern was on Boysen's side in the dispute, they were later assured that both railroads opposed Boysen.[9]

The dimensions demanded by the state engineer created considerable difficulty for Boysen. The plan for the 60-foot dam required a cut into the walls of the canyon to create the full 143 foot width for the spillway; at the lower level contemplated for the 35 foot dam, the canyon was only 125 feet wide, and Boysen did not want to incur the expense to make the necessary larger cut for a spillway 143 feet wide. When the work was finished, the effective spillway shrank even more. Boysen built a road across the dam, carried on piers that extended nearly 15 feet above the top of the dam; the open area between the piers only amounted to a total of 89 feet.[10]

The dam was built under a contract with the Ambursen Hydraulic Company, and much of the work was performed during the winter; by heating the buttresses, it was possible to run the concrete in the cold weather without danger of freezing. Boysen said that the original estimate of the Chicago engineers was for a total cost of $160,000, only slightly more than the estimate given the state engineer; Boysen readily advanced these funds. When he came west to view the completed project, he found that the foundations had not yet risen above water level, but was assured that a further $40,000 would be adequate to complete the job. Six months later, he visited again, and found only a few feet had been added; Boysen is said to have told Johnston that the final cost was over $2 million.[11]

Actually, Boysen exaggerated the cost, although the job had overrun badly. The dam was completed in May, 1909, at a total cost of $386,000, but the power generating equipment still had to be purchased and installed. The completed dam was 50 feet high and 124 feet long, creating a lake fourteen miles long and up to two and a half miles wide, reaching to within five miles of Shoshoni. When it was nearing completion in Octo-

---

[9]*Thermopolis Record*, January 25, 1908.

[10]The roadway was 14 feet 10 ½ inches above the top of the dam and the open spillway was 89 feet 3 inches. Clarke, *et. al*, *vs.* Boysen, *et. al.*, 39 *Federal Reporter Second Series* 800, at 817.

[11]The story of the dam construction was related by Boysen to Dave Johnston in 1921.

The first Boysen dam, looking upstream, clearly showing the superstructure, a source of much litigation; it was finally removed by the Burlington railroad.

ber, the *Record* blandly noted that it had been constructed without interfering with the railroad.[12]

This was simply not so. The dimensions of the structure did not follow the terms of the permit, and the spillway was partially obstructed. Nevertheless, in Boysen's defense, it must be noted that the State Engineer admitted that he had given Boysen permission to build to the 50 foot height if the railroad did not choose to build through the canyon.[13]

Unfortunately for Boysen, the railroad did choose to build through the canyon. Writing more than thirty years after the fact, C. F. Robertson thought that the deal to bring the railroad to Worland was pivotal in the Burlington's later decision to build on to Orin junction and beyond, but this interesting speculation does not square with the facts. It was the acquisition of the Colorado and Southern Railway Company by the

---
[12]*Thermopolis Record*, October 24, 1908.
[13]Clarence T. Johnston to Justin T. Kingdon, July 2, 1909.

Burlington that gave final impetus to the completion of the line through Wind River Canyon; when the purchase of the C & S was concluded in December, 1908, it remained only to complete the line through the canyon in order to provide the Hill lines a through connection from the Pacific Northwest to the Gulf Coast.

Moreover, Asmus Boysen knew of the railroad activity in the canyon, for when he came to Wyoming to select the section of land where he built the dam, he saw two railroad survey crews at work, one for the Chicago, Burlington & Quincy on the west side of the canyon and the other, for the Chicago, Northwestern, on the east side. Although rumors continued to fly in Thermopolis that the Burlington would build south over the mountains rather than go through the canyon, the railroad had already filed its map claiming a right of way through the canyon in March of 1905.[14]

It seems clear that the reason for the Burlington route filing was to establish the right to the route before the land on the reservation became available for entry under the public land laws, pursuant to the law opening the reservation, which became effective earlier in the same month. Finally, on July 10, 1908, a fifteen month contract was let to build a line involving ten tunnels through the canyon, and construction on the north end of that project began a year later.[15]

At the beginning of 1908, the railroad sued Boysen to restrain construction of the dam and it was pressing the State to force Boysen to comply with the limitations of his permit. Bowing to these pressures, the State filed suit in the middle of 1909, to compel the Boysen company to comply with the terms of its original permit; this case did not come to trial until the end of 1913.[16]

In the summer of 1909, the Burlington let the contract for the line

---

[14]The Burlington route map was dated February 15, 1905. The Asmus Boysen testimony is in Broatch, et. al., vs. Boysen, et. al., Case No. 288, U. S. District Court, Cheyenne.

[15]David J. Wasden, op. cit., 239. The Big Horn Railway Company filed its map for the route through the canyon on March 27, 1905; the act of March 3, 1905 opened that portion of the reservation north of the Wind River to entry under the public land laws, but the act was not proclaimed until June 2, 1906, making entry available on August 15, 1906. Clarke, et. al., vs. Boysen, et. al., 39 Federal Reporter Second Series, 800, at 814.

[16]The State Engineer complained in 1909 that he had never received any assurance that the canyon route was to be followed by the railroad. Big Horn Railroad Company vs. Asmus Boysen was filed January 24, 1908, and after the line in the Basin was sold to the parent company at the end of 1908, Chicago Burlington & Quincy Railroad Company vs. Big Horn Power Company and Asmus Boysen was filed July 27, 1909. Both cases were dismissed by the plaintiffs on November 22, 1912, after the State of Wyoming commenced its action against Boysen. Case Nos. 363 and 485, U. S. District Court,

from Kirby to the connection with the Northwestern at Shoshoni to MacArthur Brothers Company of New York. While construction was still underway, high water in 1911 brought driftwood and trees against the dam, and the grade of the railroad was under water; consequently, the railroad raised the grade a further two feet so that construction trains could be run over it. When these facts were considered by the Supreme Court of Wyoming in 1915, the power company was directed to remove so much of the structure as was inconsistent with its permit.[17]

High water continued to plague the railroad and cause trouble for the Boysen interests. In 1920, the river was high enough to run through the railroad tunnels, but it did not cover the rails. The next year, the high water ran through the tunnels for six days, thirty inches over the rails, and covered 4,500 feet of track. The next year gave the parties a breathing spell, with no high water, but in July of 1923, the waters came back, four feet over the rails for five or six days; in September of the same year, there were six or seven days when the water was 52 inches over the rails, and in 1924, an ice gorge lodged against the superstructure of the dam for two or three days and flooded the tracks a foot or more. Obviously, the problem wasn't going away.[18]

Meanwhile, the Big Horn Power Company had incurred obligations in excess of its resources, and was now in financial difficulty. Asmus Boysen sold his Iowa farms in 1907 to provide money for construction. Moreover, the panic of 1907 had struck his banks, and by 1910 he would be forced to sell them to pay off depositors. According to his testimony in 1925, Boysen was totally out of funds by May of 1908. He then turned to his wife Anna, who advanced more than $200,000 to the company in 1908 and 1909, on notes which were payable at the beginning of 1918. To raise this money, Mrs. Boysen was forced to sell her 2,000 acre home ranch in Audubon and Carroll Counties, Iowa; when she died in 1910, she was left owning only the worthless Big Horn Power Company paper. These efforts proved inadequate to save the company, and by the

---

Cheyenne. Also, Clarence T. Johnston, State Engineer to Governor B. B. Brooks, July 2, 1909 and Clarence T. Johnston to Justin T. Kingdon, July 2, 1909.

[17]Traffic on the line through the canyon commenced in October, 1913. The decision against the power company was entered June 1, 1915. Big Horn Power Company vs. State of Wyoming, 23 Wyoming Reports 293. Also, Thermopolis Record, July 10, 1909.

[18]The details on flooding were provided by D. J. Nelson, assistant superintendent of the railroad at Greybull. Broatch, et. al. vs. Boysen, et. al., Case No. 288, U. S. District Court, Cheyenne.

end of 1909 it was in default on the interest payments on the gold bonds.[19]

A committee of the bondholders came to Shoshoni in the spring of 1910, but were disappointed by the lack of a viable power market and refused to advance additional funds to the company. In 1911, in order to obtain the generating equipment, the Big Horn Power Company leased its entire operation to Fremont Power Company for $10,500 per year, and the latter company completed the construction, at a cost of about $6,500. Boysen had incorporated the Fremont company in Ohio, but apparently had no significant stock ownership in it.[20]

On November 7, 1911, the Fremont Company began delivering power to customers, initially for the Boysen mining company, which was prospecting in the mountain adjacent to the dam and later to customers in Riverton and Shoshoni. Nevertheless, the operation was doomed, for once the courts determined that the superstructure had to be removed, it was no longer possible to make a profit from the shrunken level of power output. As Asmus Boysen said in 1925, "That ended the hopes of the Big Horn Power Company and Asmus Boysen...."[21]

In 1917, Asmus Boysen's only son, Allan, took over the operation, at first under the Fremont Power Company and then as Shoshoni Light and Power Company. Allan Boysen bought the stock of Fremont Power Company for $35,000, using money furnished by his aunt. He later became president of the Wyoming Power Company, which he also owned.[22]

Some of the bills for construction of the dam were not paid, and in the spring of 1910, the Shoshoni Lumber Company foreclosed a mechanics' lien of $5,206.79 on the dam and power plant; they were sold at sheriff's sale on January 31, 1916 for $7,300. The purchaser at that sale was Allan

---

[19]The notes from Anna L. Boysen to Big Horn Power Company were for $150,000 on December 3, 1908, $35,000 on July 1, 1909, $23,177.22 on July 1, 1909 and $1,629.09 on December 1, 1909. All were due January 1, 1918, with interest at 7%. The home ranch was sold to Lida L. Leet, who was married to Anna Boysen's brother, Francis M. Leet. Anna Boysen died in Aurora, Illinois. Henry B. Pogson, et. al vs. Big Horn Power Company, et. al., Case No. 1320, U. S. District Court, Cheyenne.

[20]Asmus Boysen testified that the Big Horn Power Company had between $351,000 and $352,000 to meet its obligation of $386,000. The bondholder committee consisted of J. H. Peters of the First National Bank of Alliance, Iowa, and John J. Spindler of the First National Bank of Council Bluffs. Broatch, et. al vs. Boysen, et. al., Case No. 288, U. S. District Court, Cheyenne.

[21]The Fremont company operated the facility until November, 1917. Pogson, et. al. vs. Big Horn Power Company, et. al., Case No. 1320, U. S. District Court, Cheyenne.

[22]Mrs. M. J. Stoughton was Allan Boysen's aunt. Pogson, et. al. vs. Big Horn Power Company, et. al., Case No. 1320, U. S. District Court, Cheyenne.

Boysen, who had borrowed the money to redeem it. Four years later, the property was again threatened, this time for unpaid property taxes, and Allan Boysen's aunt came forward with the money to redeem it.[23]

Finally, Allan Boysen's Wyoming Power Company took over the plant, which then was supplying power to the railroad as well as to Riverton and Shoshoni. For a time from June 1923 until October 1924, Asmus Boysen himself also worked in the plant at a salary of $125 per month. Then, a flood from Badwater Creek filled the plant with silt, and it was never restarted; Riverton and Shoshoni turned to the Bureau of Reclamation plant at Pilot Butte for their power needs.

While railroad construction work was proceeding in the canyon, Thermopolis still did not have a rail connection, and it was not until May 11, 1910, that the tracklaying crews entered that town, bringing the line from the north. Supplies for the canyon work could now be hauled from Thermopolis, rather than Kirby. It was not an easy project. In Denver, the Burlington sought 2,000 to 3,000 men for the job, which suffered from high turnover, and temporary hospitals were established at both ends of the canyon; men were buried in both places. In May of 1911, the line was completed through the canyon, and construction once again paused for a time.

For Boysen and the men who were once his partners, the endless litigation went on. The 1906 litigation under the 1899 agreement began in the U. S. District Court in Cheyenne, with the first appeal from that court to the Eighth Circuit Court of Appeals in 1910. The case went back down to Cheyenne and was appealed again to the Circuit Court in 1916, twice in 1920, again in 1921 and 1922, and was finally settled in 1930, in a case consolidating ten appeals involving four cases from the court below. The court ordered that certain of the old partners should receive a share of the property, after paying their share of Boysen's costs of development. The eleventh article of the 1930 decision repeated for the last time the require-

---

[23]The story of the dam construction is contained in a file in the Hot Springs County Museum and Cultural Center in Thermopolis. The Shoshoni Lumber Company brought suit on its mechanic's lien on March 11, 1911; the property was sold January 4, 1916, for $3,893.72, to Allan Boysen, acting on behalf of the Big Horn Power Company, who borrowed the money from Rosa L. Thompson, his sister-in-law. Clarke, et. al. vs. Boysen, et. al. and nine other cases, 39 *Federal Reporter Second Series* 800 (February 17, 1930. Ella Clarke, on behalf of herself and two other bondholders of Big Horn Power Company, brought suit to upset the judgment and sale, but her action was unsuccessful in the Wyoming Supreme Court. Clark vs. Shoshoni Lumber Company et. al., 31 *Wyoming* 205 (April 15, 1924). Asmus Boysen died in Chicago in November, 1938.

ment that the superstructure on the dam was to be removed within six months.[24]

And there was more trouble for the beleaguered company. In 1913, a Northern Arapahoe who had received an allotment on the reservation found that 42 acres of his land had been submerged by Boysen's dam, and the United States government sued the power company for the damages thus caused, obtaining a judgment for $600, one of the smaller items on a very long list. Ella R. Clarke, wife of John T. Clarke, who had acquired a majority of the gold bonds of the power company, petitioned the court to recover the interest represented by 352 of the coupons, each valued at $12.50. The coupons from the bonds still lie in the files of the court, where no one apparently cared enough to retrieve them.[25]

On June 17, 1918, John T. Clarke filed another action in the U. S. District Court in Cheyenne against Asmus Boysen and all of the other claimants in the complicated scenario. The court appointed a special master to sort out the complicated allegations and make a report, and this case was finally consolidated for decision with the appeals from the 1906 case.[26]

The trustees for the bondholders weighed in against the Boysen company in 1922, asking for compensation for the bonds that had matured in

---

[24]The court counted only sixteen participants because Adam Morrell disclaimed any interest in the agreement. The costs the participants were required to share totaled $102,678.10, consisting of $12,000 for attorneys' fees, $6,803.10 for the patent and the balance for the cost of tunnels; these costs did not include the more significant costs on the 88 acres deeded to the Big Horn Power Company. Boysen had recovered $39,125 from the sale of Boysen Mining Company stock. The cases are Broatch, et. al. vs. Boysen, et. al., 175 *Federal Reporter* 702 (January 7, 1910), Broatch, et. al vs. Boysen, et.al., 236 *Federal Reporter* 516 (October 13, 1916), Clarke vs. Boysen, et.al., 264 *Federal Reporter* 492 (April 1, 1920), Clarke vs. Asmus Boysen Mining Company, 268 *Federal Reporter* 535 (September 18, 1920), Clarke vs. Boysen, et. al., 273 *Federal Reporter* 923 (June 13, 1921), Clarke vs. Boysen, et. al., 285 *Federal Reporter* 122 (November 18, 1922) and Clarke, et. al. vs. Boysen, et. al. and nine other cases, 39 *Federal Reporter Second Series* (February 17, 1930) 800. Also, *Independent Record* (Thermopolis), August 2, 1973.

[25]Alto L. Hanaway received his allotment May 6, 1907; the value of the land submerged was judged to be $15 per acre. United States vs. Big Horn Power Company, filed October 21, 1913 and decided July 1, 1915. Case No. 765, U. S. District Court, Cheyenne. Bernard P. Wickham owned 100 shares of stock in Big Horn Power Company, which he claimed to be worth $10,000, and 20 of the $500 bonds. Bernard P. Wickham vs. Big Horn Power Company and Allan Boysen, filed July 5, 1916 and dismissed October 14, 1918 for lack of prosecution. Case No. 882, U. S. District Court, Cheyenne.

[26]John T. Clarke vs. Asmus Boysen, The Asmus Boysen Mining Company, Allan Boysen, Big Horn Power Company, Chicago Title and Trust, Chicago Burlington & Quincy Railroad, Big Horn Railroad, Shoshoni Power & Electric Company, Maurice G. Clarke, Joseph Weis, Carl H. Tiedemann, Robert C. Wertz and Midwest Power & Light Company, was filed June 17, 1918. Case No. 980, U. S. District Court, Cheyenne. Also, Ella R. Clarke vs. Big Horn Power Company, Case No. 1281, U. S. District Court, Cheyenne.

1918, but had been in default since 1910. The judgment against the poor defunct corporation was for $944,502.44, and when it was not paid, the court ordered the company's property sold at auction, with a minimum of $35,000 as an acceptable bid for the 11/16 interest, less the railroad right of way. When the sale was held, there was only one bid, that of Ella R. Clarke, who tendered $35,000. Since $215,000 of the bonds belonged to Ella R. Clarke, her bargain purchase was a hollow victory, and it soon proved to be no victory at all, as we shall see.[27]

The consolidated appeals from the 1906 case and three others resulted in an order from the Circuit Court of Appeals to remove the superstructure of the dam, and when the Boysen interests did nothing to remove it, the judge directed the Burlington railroad to deposit a bond of $15,000 with the court, and then ordered the U. S. Marshall to have the work done. The marshal let a contract for the removal at a cost of $14,136, and this amount was charged against the railroad bond. The railroad then proceeded to levy on the property of John T. Clarke to collect the balance owed. By the time it was able to realize on its executions, the bill had grown with interest to $24,797.19, and this amount was charged against Ella Clarke's recovery in the bondholder case—which she had provided from her own funds.[28]

The litigious John T. Clarke now tried still another jurisdiction, that of New York. There, he filed a number of cases against the Burlington railroad, which delayed the proceedings as well as it could, while pursuing the Wyoming cases to judgment. In the summer of 1938, Clarke's attorney complained to the federal judge in Cheyenne that he was prevailing in the New York courts, but could not stop the Wyoming cases from going against him. The judge deposited the letter with the other numerous papers in the file.[29]

---

[27]Henry B. Pogson, trustee and Augustus R. Smith, trustee, vs. Big Horn Power Company, et. al. Case No. 1320, filed December 26, 1922, U. S. District Court, Cheyenne.

[28]The U. S. Marshall hired Turpen Construction Company to remove the superstructure, in a contract approved by the court April 13, 1931; the work was completed on July 24. The cost was charged against a deposit the C. B. & Q. railroad had made with the court. The railroad recovered its payment with interest on October 25, 1938, for a total of $25,242.75, of which $24,797.19 came from the Clarke recovery in Case No. 1811, and the balance came from another small sum owed John T. Clarke by the clerk of court. Broatch, et. al. vs. Boysen, et. al., Case No. 288, U. S. District Court, Cheyenne.

[29]The letter from Albert Adams of New York City to Judge Alfred P. Murrah was dated July 25, 1938. Pogson, et. al. vs. Big Horn Power Co. et. al., Case No. 1320, U. S. District Court, Cheyenne. The New York cases were consolidated for appeal in that state, and Clarke's appeal was denied October 21, 1938. 7 New York Supplement Second Series 574. There are a number of other cases involving this situation, including Henry T. Clarke, Jr. vs. Big Horn Power Company, Case No. 1430, filed February 20, 1924 and closed for lack of prosecution, May 13, 1935, U. S. District Court, Cheyenne.

The Big Horn Basin now had a rail connection with the outside world from both north and south. Construction on the connection with the Colorado and Southern was commenced February 10, 1913, and through service between Billings and Denver was established on June 14, 1914. The railroad constructed an observation platform in the canyon, where passengers could pause for ten minutes to enjoy the spectacular view.

In the north Basin, the Toluca connection became unnecessary in 1911, when thirty miles of road were completed between Fromberg, Montana and Warren, making a direct connection between the Burlington line in the Basin and the Northern Pacific tracks from Billings. In the same year, the 75 miles of track between Warren and Toluca were taken up.[30]

It would be a while longer before the highway was built through the canyon, giving the Basin an easier road to the south. The distance from Thermopolis to Rock Springs by rail was 615 miles, and nearly 400 miles would be cut off the journey if the highway were completed. The Wyoming highway commission was organized in 1917, and highway construction was stimulated throughout the state, but funding for construction was greatly aided by the allocation of a share of oil royalties to the state.

The canyon project received impetus from the urging of Leroy E. Laird of Worland, who was a member of the highway commission in 1919 and 1920; after he was appointed highway superintendent in 1921, the canyon road project moved smartly forward. When the contract for the road was let in the summer of 1922, the highway department newsletter noted that "even the most optimistic did not expect the construction of the project to be realized at so early a date."[31]

Utah Construction Company won the contract for $294,347.80, and expected that the road could be completed "easily" by the contract deadline of April 1, 1923, but the job had been underestimated, and the company unsuccessfully tried to recover additional costs in a series of lawsuits that dragged on until 1933. The original contract deadline passed, but the road with its three tunnels did open for traffic early in 1924, although the total cost was more than double the original contracts.[32]

---

[30]Richard C. Overton, *op. cit.*, 276.

[31]*Wyoming State Highway Department Newsletter*, II, No. 3 (July 1, 1922), 18. Laird was from Emerson, Iowa, and came to the Worland area in 1904; he was the first settler under the Upper Hanover Canal. C. F. Robertson, *op. cit.*, 47.

[32]*The Billings Gazette*, July 11, 23, 1922. The contracts were let on June 1, 1922, and the road was finally cut through on January 22, 1924. The state highway commission reported the total cost at

The Boysen saga entered its final stage in 1947, when the Bureau of Reclamation commenced work on the new Boysen dam, upstream from Boysen's original structure. The new dam would be 218 feet high and 1,100 feet long at the crest, holding back a reservoir of nearly 1.5 million acre feet, and both the railroad and the highway would have to be relocated to make way for it. One of the elements of this project was the removal of the old dam, and in September, Ray R. Purdum, who had purchased the site at still another tax sale, sold the damsite and power plant to the Bureau of Reclamation for $500.[33]

Finally, in the summer of 1965, Ray Purdum's wife conveyed the remainder of the damsite to the State of Wyoming Parks Commission for the creation of the Boysen State Park, so that now the trials of Asmus Boysen are chiefly remembered in the name of the new dam and reservoir, and the state park.[34]

Long before the highway was completed through the Wind River Canyon, this region had become a part of the Wyoming society that had already grown up outside the Basin. By 1905, a state census found over 100,000 people in the state, and Big Horn County had nearly 10,000. Cody had more than 1,000 people, Lovell had over 700 and Thermopolis over 500. The frontier was gone.[35]

$581,999.46 in 1924, but a later history of the road gave the total at $700,000. Federal aid paid for 345,955.08 of the cost. *Fourth Biennial Report of the State Highway Commission of the State of Wyoming, For the Period Beginning October 1st, 1922, Ending September 30, 1924* (Cheyenne, 1924), 46, and R. L. Silver, "The Story of the Wind River Canyon Project," *Wyoming Roads*, I, No. 1 (September, 1924), 6ff. The Utah Construction litigation is in Utah Construction Company vs. State Highway Commission, decided March 13, 1933, 45 *Wyoming Reports* 403; the company had previously tried to get a hearing in the federal courts, but was turned back by the United States Supreme Court, 278 *United States Reports* 194. The road through the canyon was 13.4 miles long, with a 24 foot roadway in most places, but 20 feet in the narrower sections of the canyon.

[33]The agreement with Purdum referred to the Federal Power Commission license for the dam, which had required construction of a sluice and spillway by January 1, 1928. The damsite is in the north half of Section 4, Township 5 North, Range 6 East of the Wind River Meridian. Miscellaneous Book 30, Fremont County Clerk, at page 22.

[34]In June, 1947, the Bureau of Reclamation called for bids for the new dam and power plant. *Billings Gazette*, June 9, 1947.

[35]The census of 1905 showed a total population of 101, 817; Big Horn County had 9,842. In 1900, Big Horn County only had 4,328. Cody's population was 1,220 in 1905, Lovell 717, Thermopolis 534, Basin 370 and Meeteetse 318.

APPENDIX A

The Bridger Trail Route

While it is well known that Bridger's cutoff followed a route west of the Big Horn Mountains, there are variations in the maps and accounts of the trail. The major variety can be traced to a map drawn under the direction of Major G. L. Gillespie of the Corps of Engineers in 1876. This map shows the Bridger Cutoff following Kirby Creek to its confluence with the Big Horn, but then inexplicably veers north without crossing the river, and crosses finally at the mouth of Nowater Creek.

Both the Hedges diary and that of Major John Owen make that route extremely unlikely. Both men record distances traveled by their trains, and campsites; there is general agreement between the two, with Hedges' distance to the Big Horn (he calls it the Wind River) at 120 miles, and Owen's distance at 114 miles. From the distances given and the location of campsites, it is possible to follow approximately what the routing would have been, although Owen, in particular, has an annoying habit of giving names to watercourses that must principally reflect wildlife observed or plant growth. Thus, we have at least one willow creek, an antelope creek, a beaver creek and several dry forks and dry creeks. It does appear from both these diaries that the road came down Kirby Creek to the river and there crossed over to the west bank, where the terrain was much easier for the wagons.

Fortunately, there is a precise record for much of the route, because the trail was still visible when the government surveyors entered the Basin to perform the land office survey, and where they found the trail, the surveyors recorded it on the original survey plats.

Most of the original survey work in the trail area was undertaken in the first half of the 1880s, when the trail was only a bit more than fifteen years old, but a critical part of the trail—where it crossed the Big Horn—is not so well documented, since the original surveys of the key townships in that area were not completed until nearly ten years later.

APPENDIX B

The French Contracts

Count Robert de Mailly
à
René Vion

Contract
Billings 1er juillet 1884

Entre Monsieur le Cte Robert de Mailly-Nesle d'une part et M. René Vion d'une autre. Il est convenu.

M. le Cte de Mailly-Nesle ayant acheté du bêtail (1000) têtes environ pour la somme de (140000) cent quarante mille francs eu conféré la gérance et direction à M. René Vion.

M. René Vion l'engage.

1er A diriger et donner tous ses soins à l'exploitation.

2e A y passer au moins 7 mois sur le ranch.

3e Il payera une moitié des frais d'installation.

4e Il payera un tiers des frais du ranch jusqu'à novembre 1886 puis ensuite la moitié jusqu'au moment où il touchera pour sa part sur la vente des boeufs plus de 20000^x ou au moins 20000^x. Passé ce moment tous les frais reviendront à sa charge. Cependant si M. René Vion touchaît 20000^x une année grâce à une augmentation provenant de l'achât de nouveaux boeufs et que l'année suivante le bénéfice retouchât au dessous de 20000^x il ne payerait toujours que la moitié des frais.[1]

M. le Cte de Mailly-Nesle fera à M. R. Vion l'avance des fonds nécessaires pour le paiement des frais et M. Vion lui en fera le remboursement au pire et à mesure que les bénéfices augmenteront, M. le Cte de Mailly-Nesle aura comme garantie les parts de bénéfices de M. Vion. Comme bénéfices et au rétribution de ses soins Mr. Vion touchera.

1er La moitié de l'incris soit moitié des veaux et genesies naissant chaque année.

2e Un quart de la vente des boeufs achetés à ce jour, le prix d'achat, étant, retiré, soit un quart du bénéfice acquis depuis l'achat. M. Vion prend l'engagement de ce contrat pour la durée de six années à partir du 1er juillet 1884 jusqu'àu 1er novembre 1890.

---

[1] At an exchange rate of about 19 cents for the French franc, the count's investment of 140,000 francs would have been equivalent to about $26,600; the 20,000 franc level of activity mentioned would have been about $3,800.

A l'expiration de ce contrat, soit au bout de six années, soit dans un temps plus éloigné, si le contrat est renouvelé, la liquidation se ferait de la façon suivante, M. le Cte de Mailly retirerait sa premiere mise de fonds soit (140000ˣ) cent quarante mille francs. L'incris ou reste serait partagé égales parties, entre M. le Cte de Mailly-Nesle et M. René Vion. Autrefois si pour une cause ou pour une autre M. le Cte de Mailly-Nesle voulait ou était obligé de liquider avant l'expiration des six années, soit avant le 1er novembre 1890 la moitié du tout reviendrait de plein droit à M. Vion.

En cas de décès de M. de Mailly, la liquidation se ferait comme ci-dessus àu moins que les héritiers de M. de Mailly ne continuent dans les mêmes conditions jusqu'à l'expiration du dit contrat.

Dans le cas où M. Vion viendrait à décéder avant l'expiration du contrat, la liquidation se ferait de la façon suivante, M. de Mailly retirerait sa première mise de fonds en (betail) l'incris serait partagé en parties égales, entre lui et les héritiers de M. Vion qui doit rembourser à M. de Mailly toutes les avances faites par M. de Mailly à M. Vion.

Dans le cas où M. Vion serait obligé d'abandonner la gérance et la direction pour cause de maladies ou accidents graves, les conditions *de liquidation* restent les mêmes que ci-dessus.

Dans l'un et l'autre cas le ranch et l'installation existant au moment de la liquidation resteraient la proprieté de M. Mailly moyennant la somme de (500) dollars (cinq cents) qu'il versera à M. Vion, et à ses héritiers.

Dans le cas où M. Vion voudrait se retirer pour une autre cause dépendant de sa volonté il n'aurait droit qu'à un quart de l'incris, et aurait à payer toutes les avances à lui faite par M. de Mailly. Les conditions resteraient les mêmes si M. le Cte de Mailly-Nesle rachetait un nombre d'animaux inférieur à 500 têtes.

    Vu et approuvé
    Cte Robert de Mailly-Nesle
    R. Vion

Ont signé comme temoins
  Vu et approuvé
  Paul Fremy
  Lesley Bates

Filed for record, October 12th, A. D. 1888, 2 o'clock P.M.
  Geo. M. Hayes
  Recorder[2]

---

[2] In the margin of the document, there are three notations on the first page and one on the second, where the parties and the witnesses have signed, indicating where insertions were made in the original; it is impossible to know what these insertions were, since the clerk has copied the entire document in longhand. At the top of the second page is the notation: "Duex mots ajoutes," followed by the initials of the two parties and the two witnesses.

Entre Paul Breteché de Corbett (Wyoming)
d'une part
et Jean de Hedouville de Corbett (Wyoming)
d'autre part

Il a été convenir ce qui suit:

Jean de Hedouville ayant vendu a Paul Breteché un bande de betail marguie MO sur le flac droit pour la somme de six mille dollars monaii legale des Etats Unis payable de dix Novembre mil huit cent quartrevingt treize; Paul Breteché d'engage outre le versement de la somme ci-dessus specifice à verser a Jean de Hedouville dix pour cent sur le benefice qu'il fera lorsqu'il liquidera le betail.

Dans le cas on cette liquidation n'aurait pas lieu Paul Breteché versera dix pour cent sur tante vente partielle aperee apres recouorement de la somme de six mille dollars. Le Eatal de ces versements ne pourra exceder cinq cent dollars dans les deux cas.

Fait en double à Corbett Wyoming le 3 Juin mil huit cent quatre vingt-freize.

/s/ Jean de Hedouville   /s/ Paul Breteché

Source: de Hedouville collection.

Bibliography and Index

Selected Bibliography

Anderson, Abraham Archibald, *Experiences and Impressions : The Autobiography of Colonel A. A. Anderson* (Freeport, N. Y., 1970).
Arrington, Leonard J., *Great Basin Kingdom: Economic History of the Latter-Day Saints, 1830-1900* (Lincoln, Nebraska, 1958).
Arrington, Leonard J. and Davis Bitton, *The Mormon Experience: A History of the Latter-Day Saints* (New York, 1979).
Bartlett, Ichabod S., *History of Wyoming* (Chicago, 1918).
Brooks, Bryant Butler, *Memoirs of Bryant B. Brooks: Cowboy, Trapper, Lumberman, Stockman, Oilman, Banker, and Governor of Wyoming* (Glendale, California, 1939).
Burpee, Lawrence J., ed., *Journals and Letters of Pierre Gaultier de Varennes de la Verendrye and His Sons* (Toronto, 1927).
Burroughs, John Rolfe, *Guardian of the Grasslands: The First Hundred Years of the Wyoming Stock Growers Association* (Cheyenne, 1971).
Burton, Lloyd, *American Indian Water Rights and the Limits of Law* (Lawrence, Kansas, 1991).
Calef, Wesley, *Private Grazing and Public Lands: Studies of the Local Management of the Taylor Grazing Act* (Chicago, 1960).
Carrington, Margaret I., *Absaraka: (Ab-sa-ra-ka), Home of the Crows* (Chicago, 1950).
Chatterton, Fenimore, *Yesterday's Wyoming: The Intimate Memoirs of Fenimore Chatterton* (Denver, 1957).
Chittenden, Hiram Martin, *The American Fur Trade of the Far West* (New York, 1935).
_____. Alfred Talbot, Richardson, *Life, Letters and Travels of Father Pierre-Jean de Smet, S. J., 1801-1873* (New York, 1905).
Colwell, Lula Pulliam, *The Story of the D. T. Pulliam Company* (n.p., 1970-71).
Cook, Jeannie, *Wiley's Dream of Empire: The Wiley Irrigation Project* (Cody, Wyoming, 1990).
Coutant, C. G., *History of Wyoming and (The Fur West)* (New York, 1966).

Davis, Jonathan and Melba, *They Called It Germania! History of Wyoming's Emblem Bench 1893-1939* (Basin, Wyoming, n.d.).
DeVoto, Bernard, *Across the Wide Missouri* (Boston, 1947).
Donaldson, Thomas, *The Public Domain: Its History with Statistics* (New York, 1971).
Dresden, Donald, *The Marquis de Mores: Emperor of the Bad Lands* (Norman, Oklahoma, 1970).
Edgar, Bob and Jack, Turnell, *Brand of a Legend* (Cody, 1978).
Engebretson, Doug, *Empty Saddles, Forgotten Names: Outlaws of the Black Hills and Wyoming* (Aberdeen, S. D., n.d.)
Ewers, John C., ed., *Adventures of Zenas Leonard, Fur Trader* (Norman, Oklahoma, 1959).
Fillerup, Melvin M., *Sidon: The Canal That Faith Built* (Cody, Wyoming 1988).
Frison, George Carr, *Prehistoric Hunters of the High Plains* (New York, 1978).
Frison, Paul, *First White Woman* (Basin, Wyoming, 1969).
Frye, Elnora L., *Atlas of Wyoming Outlaws at the Territorial Penitentiary* (Laramie, Wyoming, 1990).
Fuentes, Carlos, *The Buried Mirror: Reflections on Spain and the New World* (New York, 1992).
Gates, Paul W., *History of Public Land Law Development* (Washington, D. C., 1968).
Gowans, Fred R., *Rocky Mountain Rendezvous: A History of the Fur Trade Rendezvous, 1825-1840* (Provo Utah, 1976).
Gressley, Gene M., *Bankers and Cattlemen* (Lincoln, Nebraska, 1966).
Grinnell, George Bird, *Hunting at High Altitude* (New York, 1913).
_____. *The Fighting Cheyennes* (Norman, Oklahoma, 1915).
Guernsey, Charles Arthur, *Wyoming Cowboy Days* (New York, 1936).
Hafen, Leroy R., *Broken Hand: The Life of Thomas Fitzpatrick, Mountain Man, Guide and Indian Agent* (Lincoln, Nebraska, 1981).
_____.ed., *Mountain Men and Fur Traders of the Far West* (Lincoln, Nebraska, 1982).
Hafen, Leroy R. and Francis Marion, Young, *Fort Laramie and the Pageant of the West, 1834-1890* (Glendale, California, 1938).
Haines, Aubrey L. *The Yellowstone Story: A History of Our First National Park*, 2 vol. (Boulder, Colorado, 1977).
Hamilton, James McClellan, *From Wilderness to Statehood: A History of Montana 1805-1900* (Portland, Oregon, 1957).
Hebard, Grace Raymond, *Washakie: An Account of Indian Resistance of the Covered Wagon and Union Pacific Railroad Invasions of Their Territory* (Cleveland, 1930).

Horan, James D., *Desperate Men: Revelations from the Sealed Pinkerton Files* (New York, 1949).
Hyde, George E., *Indians of the High Plains: From the Prehistoric Period to the Coming of Europeans* (Norman, Oklahoma, 1959).
_____.*Red Cloud's Folk: A History of the Oglala Sioux Indians* (Norman, Oklahoma, 1937).
_____.*Spotted Tail's Folk: A History of the Brule Sioux* (Norman, Oklahoma, 1961).
Jennings, Francis, *The Ambiguous Iroguois Empire* (New York, 1984).
Johnson, Cecil, *British West Florida, 1763-1783* (Chapel Hill, N. Ca., 1971).
Jones, Dorothy V., *License for Empire: Colonialism by Treaty in Early America* (Chicago, 1982).
Jones, William A., *Report Upon the Reconnaissance of Northwestern Wyoming, Made in the Summer of 1873 by William A. Jones, Captain of Engineers, U. S. A.* (Washington, 1874).
Journals and Debates of the Constitutional Convention of the State of Wyoming (Cheyenne, 1893).
Kappler, Charles J., ed., *Indian Treaties, 1778-1883* (New York, 1972).
Klein, Maury, *Union Pacific: The Birth of a Railroad, 1862-1893* (New York, 1987).
Kluger, James R., *Turning on Water with a Shovel: The Career of Elwood Mead* (Albuquerque, New Mexico, 1992).
Knoefel, Hugh K., *Wyoming's Bloodiest Fourth of July* (Worland, Wyoming, 1969).
Larson, Taft Alfred, *History of Wyoming* (Lincoln, Nebraska, 1978).
Latham, Dr. H., *Trans-Missouri Stock Raising: Pasture Lands of North America* (Omaha, Nebraska, 1871).
Lindsay, Charles, *The Big Horn Basin* (Lincoln, Nebraska, 1932).
Logan, Herschel C., *Buckskin and Satin: The Life of Texas Jack* (Harrisburg, Pennsylvania, 1974).
McGinnie, Anthony, *Counting Coup and Cutting Horses: Intertribal Warfare on the Northern Plains, 1738-1889* (Evergreen, Colorado, 1990).
McIntosh, John W., *History of Burlington, 1893-1963* (n.p., n.d.)
Meschter, Daniel Y., *Wyoming Territorial and Pre-Territorial Post Offices* (Cheyenne, 1971).
Milek, Dorothy G. Buchanan, *The Gift of Bah Guewana: A History of Wyoming's Hot Springs State Park* (Thermopolis, Wyoming, 1975).
_____.*Hot Springs: A Wyoming County History* (Basin, Wyoming, 1986).
Mokler, Alfred James, *History of Natrona County, 1888-1922* (New York, 1923).
Morgan, Dale L., *Jedediah Smith and the Opening of the West* (Lincoln, Nebraska, 1953).
Nadeau, Remi, *Fort Laramie and the Sioux Indians* (Englewood Cliffs, N. J., 1967).

O'Neal, Bill, *Cattlemen vs. Sheepherders: Five Decades of Violence in the West, 1880-1920* (Austin, Texas)

Overton, Richard C., *Burlington Route: A History of the Burlington Lines* (New York, 1965).

Owen, Major John, *The Journals and Letters of Major John Owen, Pioneer of the Northwest, 1850-1871* (New York, 1927).

Patrick, Lucille Nichols, *The Best Little Town by a Dam Site* (Cody, Wyoming, 1968).

Pohanka, Brian C., ed., *Nelson A. Miles: A Documenting Biography of His Military Career, 1861-1903* (Glendale, California, 1985).

Porter, Mae Reed and Odessa, Davenport, *Scotsman in Buckskin: Sir William Drummond Stewart and the Rocky Mountain Fur Trade* (New York, 1963).

Progressive Men of the State of Wyoming (Chicago, 1903).

Rollinson, John K., *Wyoming Cattle Trails* (Caldwell, Idaho, 1948).

Sandoz, Mari, *The Cattlemen* (Lincoln, Nebraska, 1958).

Smith, Helena Huntington, *The War on Powder River: The History of an Insurrection* (Lincoln, Nebraska, 1966).

Sprague, Marshall, *A Gallery of Dudes* (Lincoln, Nebraska, 1966).

Spring, Agnes Wright, *Caspar Collins: The Life and Exploits of an Indian Fighter of the Sixties* (New York, 1927).

Stanford, Dennis J. and Jane S. Day, eds., *Ice Age Hunters of the Rockies* (Niwot, Colorado, 1992).

Stanley, The Rev. Edwin J., *Life of Rev. L. B. Stateler, or Sixty-Five Years on the Frontier* (Dallas, 1907).

Stout, Tom, *Montana, Its Story and Biography* (Chicago, 1921).

Trenholm, Virginia Cole and Maurine Carley, *The Shoshonis: Sentinels of the Rockies* (Norman, Oklahoma, 1964).

Victor, Frances Fuller, *The River of the West: The Adventures of Joe Meek* (Missoula, Montana, 1983).

Walker, Tacetta B., *Stories of Early Days in Wyoming: Big Horn Basin* (Casper, 1936).

Wasden, David John, *From Beaver to Oil: A Century in the Development of Wyoming's Big Horn Basin* (Cheyenne, 1973).

Wentworth, Edward Norris, *America's Sheep Trails* (Ames, Iowa, 1948).

Williams, Robert A., Jr., *The American Indian in Western Legal Thought: The Discourses of Conquest* (New York, 1990).

Wissler, Clark, *Indians of the United States* (New York, 1966).

Woods, Lawrence Milton, *British Gentlemen in the Wild West: The Era of the Intensely English Cowboy* (New York, 1989).

_____.*Sometimes the Books Froze: Wyoming's Economy and its Banks* (Boulder, Colorado, 1985).

_____. *The Wyoming Country Before Statehood: Four Hundred Years Under Six Flags* (Worland, Wyoming, 1971).

Yost, Nellie Snyder, *Buffalo Bill, His Family, Friends, Fame, Failures and Fortunes* (Chicago, 1979).

Index

Abel, Ezekiel: 30n
Adam, Philip: 30n
Adamson, I. J: 220
Adams, Thomas B: 130
Adams, Thomas R: 134-135
Afton: 210
Ainsworth, Frank Spicer: 110
Alamo: 152, 173, 178, 190, 234; platted, 219
Alamo Argus: 178, 219
Albany County, Dakota Territory: 149
Albert, Prince of Monaco: 186
Alexander VI, pope: 25
Alexis, Grand Duke: 199
Alger, Horace C: 210
Allemand, Joseph: 144
Allen, Fred H: 92n
Allen, Mr: 134
Allison, Senator William Boyd: 238
Ambursen Hydraulic Company: 250
American Baptist Home Mission Society: 230
American Fur Company: 72n
American Railway Union: 206n
Ames, Oakes: 238n
Anable, Harry: 135
Anderson, Mrs: 230
Anderson, Abraham Archibald: 102n, 139, 185-186
Anderson, Charles W. "Badland Charley": 140
Anderson, Edward: 140
Andersonville: 140
Antlers Hotel: 230
Arapahoe Indians: 18; fight with Shoshonis, 37; water rights litigation, 160; reservation reduced, 179-180
Arikara Indians: 18
Arland: 89, 90, 102, 139
Arland, Victor: 87ff
Arnold, Harrison: 203

Arnold, John: 170
Arnott, John P: 229
Ashelby, Harry E: 92n, 96
Ashley, General William H: 28, 33
Asmus Boysen Mining Company: 244n, 245n, 248, 254, 256n
Ashworth and Johnston: 117
Ashworth, Oliver: 103
Ashworth, Richard: 96, 101, 107
Ashworth, Walter: 101n
Assiniboin Indians: 16, 159
Atlantic City: 58, 63, 170
Augur, General Christopher Colon: 52-54, 57, 59, 65

Badwater Creek: 45
Baldwin, Caleb: 238n
Baldwin, John N: 238, 248n
Baldwin, John T: 238
The Banditti of the Plains: 131
Bank of Commerce (Sheridan): 210
Bannock Indians: 39
Bar C Ranch: 106
Barrow, Merris C: 186
Barr, P. J: 239
Bar X Bar brand: 107, 141
Basin City: 156, 190-192, 230, 233; railroad arrived, 234
Basin City Herald: 163, 191-192
Bates Battle: 37-38, 80
Bates, Captain Alfred Elliott: 37-38
Bates Creek: 38
Bates, Lesley: 263
Baxter, George White: 78-79, 114, 117, 170, 192
Baxter, John A: 78n, 117
Bay State Land and Cattle Company: 83, 114-115
Bayne, Daniel V: 135-136

Bean vs. Morris: 158
Bear Creek: 171
Bear River: 159
Bear River Land and Livestock Company: 216n
Beck, George Thornton: 188, 192, 200-203, 205
Beck, Mrs. George Thornton: 200
Beck, Senator James: 200
Beckton: 200
Beckwourth, James Pierson: 32-33
Bedford, Jack: 124-125
Belknap, Captain Henry: 74-75, 101, 117, 154, 172, 185
Belknap Creek: 75
Belknap Ranch: 76
Bell, Frank: 135
Bell, Lieutenant Colonel Peter Hansborough: 183
Benbrook, B: 142n
Bench Canal: 206
Beno, Adolph: 57
Beno, Charles: 57
Bering land bridge: 13
Berlin: 220; platted, 219
Bermard, S: see Albert Nard
"Big George" gang: 135
Big Horn Basin Colonization Company: 214
Big Horn Basin Development Company: 206-208
Big Horn Canal: 231-232
Big Horn cannon: 66; photo, 67
Big Horn Canyon: 29, 47; railroad survey in, 227
Big Horn Cattle Company: 107, 110-111, 115, 134, 163n
Big Horn County: organized, 167, 188-189; photo of officials, 168; divided, 193; population (1905), 259
Big Horn County Irrigation company: 232
Big Horn County State Bank: 192-193
Big Horn Ditch Company: 162, 229
Bighorn National Forest: 202
Big Horn Oil Company: 174, 176
Big Horn Pilot: 179
Big Horn Power Company: 248, 253-54
Big Horn River: early water rights, 164
Big Horn Railroad Company: 226n
Big Horn Ranche: 101
Big Horn River: 9n
Big Horn Southern Railroad Company: 226n

Bihr, John: 221
Billings Water-Power Company: 76
Birdsley, Mr: 173
Blackfoot Indians: 16
Black's Fork of Green River: 159
Blakesley, Hal: 190
Blakesley, Lou: 190
Bleistein, George: 202-203
Bliss, Jack: 141
Bliss, James Otis: 142n
BN brand: 75
Boal, Horton S: 192, 200-201
Boise City: 148n
Bonanza: 125, 136, 151, 156, 190-192; oil boom, 174
Bonanza Herald: 175
Bonanza Rustler: 175-177, 190
Booth, Harvey: 117
Booth, Willis J: 192, 232n
Bosch, Matthias: 221
Botkin, Lieutenant Governor Alexander C: 127
Bozeman, John Merin: 42-43
Bozeman trail: 18, 46
Boughton, Edward Shuckburgh Rouse: 103n
Breckenridge, Vice President James C: 200
Boughton, Mark Vincent: 71
Boysen, Allan: 237n, 254-255
Boysen, Anna: 237n, 253
Boysen, Asmus: 237ff
Boysen dam (original): 249ff; photo, 251
Boysen dam (second): 259
Boysen, Helena: 237n
Boysen lease: 243
Boysen, N.P: 245
Boysen State Park: 259
Brave Bear, Sioux chief: 22
Breteche Creek: 99
Breteche, Florestine Daveau: 91
Breteche, Paul: 84, 91-92, 94, 96, 99, 101, 107, 138-139, 264
Bridger, James: 30n, 41; at 1851 treaty conference, 21; lays out Bridger Trail, 44-45
Bridger Creek: 45
Bridger, Montana: 213
Bridger Trail: 44, 152
Brink, Herbert: 145
Brisben, Brevet Major General James Sanks: 54
Brokaw, John: 234
Broken Back Creek: 155

Brooks, Governor Bryant B: 249
Brorson, Niels C: 248
Brown, M: 124n
Brown, Z. Thomas: 171
Buffalo: 123, 152, 197; seat of Johnson County, 151, 154
Buffalo Basin: 124
Bug Brand: 74, 203
Bull, Frank: 110
Bull, Mrs. Frank: 110
Burch, David A. "Dab": 124-125
Burdick, Henry: 178
Burlington and Missouri River Railroad: 226n
Burlington Railroad, see Chicago, Burlington & Quincy Railroad
Burnett, Fincelius G: 80
Burnett, William: 135
Burke, M. and Sons: 163
Burke, Milo: 110-111, 115
Burlington: 156
Burlington & Missouri Railroad: 173
Burlington Mormon colony: 145, 190, 206, 210ff
Burton, Frank J: 130
Bustard, Mr: 90
Byron: 215-216

Cabin Creek: 172
Calhoun, Louis E: 222
Calvert, Thomas E: 230-231
Cambria coal field: 226
Campbell, Governor John Allen: 52
Campbell, Robert: 30, 31
Camp Augur: 47
Camp Brown: 37, 54, 58, 80, 170
Camp Colter: 194
Camp Stambaugh: 58-59, 61, 83
Canton, Frank: 102n, 135
Canyon Creek: 110
Carbon County, Dakota Territory: 149; reduced by Pease County, 151
Carey Act: 166-167, 201-202, 206, 212-213
Carey, Senator Joseph Maul: 166, 186, 188, 201n
Carey, Governor Robert D: 194
Carrington, Colonel Henry Beebe: 75
Carrington, Margaret I: 18
Carter Cattle Company: 74, 203
Carter, Charles: 115

Carter County, Dakota Territory: 149; name change by Wyoming legislature, 150
Carter Creek: 74
Carter, Phoebe W: 210n
Carter, Judge William Alexander: 73-74, 149
Carter Mountain: 74
Carter, William Alexander: 74, 117, 185
Casper: 225
Catherine II, tsarina of Russia: 222-223
Champion, Nathan: 106n
Chapman, Affie: 72
Chapman, Andrew: 171
Chapman, Henry: 73, 96, 171
Chapman, John W: 72, 92n, 94n, 172
Chapmen, "Roach": 106n
Chatterton, Governor Fenimore: 189, 207, 212
Cherokee Trail: 41
Cheyenne: 197; seat of Laramie County, Dakota Territory, 149
Cheyenne Club: 108, 115
Cheyenne Indians: 18, 37, 43, 155
Cheyenne Northern Railroad: 108
Chicago, Burlington and Quincy Railroad: 128n, 203-205; Toluca line, 216, 258; purchased by the Hill lines, 225; and Boysen lease, 242; and Boysen dam, 249, 257; line through Wind River Canyon: 251ff
Chicago Northwestern Railroad: 108, 225; surveys, 235, 252; and Boysen, 249
Chioles, Count Albert: 172
Cincinnati Canal Company: 212
Cisneros, Cardinal: 25
Clark and China: 108
Clark, Senator Clarence Don: 204; and Boysen lease, 244-245
Clarke, Ella R: 255n, 256-257
Clarke, Harry Fielding: 239n, 240n, 247n
Clarke, Henry Tefft: 240n
Clarke, John Tefft: 239n, 240, 247n, 248, 256
Clark, Maurice G: 247n
Clark, Sarah Pauline: 215n
Clark, Senator William Andrews: 245n
Clark's Fork of the Yellowstone River: 36, 39, 44
Clay, John, Jr: 131
Clear Creek: 151
Clearmont: 127
Clement, Antoine: 32
Cleveland, President Grover: 79
Clifton, Cecil: 116

Cline, Joe: 98
Close, S. D: 124n
Coble, John C: 83, 105
Coburn, Robert E: 229
Cody: 190, 192, 204; seat of Park County, 194; organized, 203; railroad arrives, 225
Cody, Arta: 200
Cody Enterprise: 203
Cody, Irma: 200
Cody-Salsbury Canal: 207
Cody Trading Company: 203
Cody, Colonel William F: 192, 198-205, 211-212, 231; purchased Carter ranch, 74; photo, 196
Coffeen, H. A: 186
Cole, Senator Cornelius: 70
Collins, Lieutenant Caspar: 42
Collins, Colonel William Oliver: 42
Collins, Winfield S: 134, 174, 190-191, 232
Colorado & Southern Railroad: 226, 230n
Colorado Flats: 198, 229
Colorado Springs: 162-164, 198
Colter, John, 1807-08 journey: 10, 28
Commercial Bank (Audubon, Iowa): 237
Comstock, Henry Thomas Paige: 65
Conant, Albert A. "Pap": 174, 176
Connor, General Patrick: 47, 52
Conover, William A: 248n
Contention Ditch: 165
Cook, Josiah: 156
Copman, Jack: 76
Copper Mountain: 246, 248
Corbett: 156
Corbett, John F: 87-88, 98, 133
Corn, Judge Samuel T: 153
Corum, John J: 162n
Cottonwood Creek: 75
Cottonwood Pass: 221
Cottu, Paul A. A: 93
Coughlan, Thomas: 239n, 240, 247n
Council of the Twelve Apostles: 209
Cowley: 204
Crandall, Marvin J: 64n
Crandall's Creek: 64n
Credit Mobilier: 238
Cree Indians: 16
Croft, John: 213n
Crook County: 187
Crooked Creek: 109

Crosby, Jesse Wentworth, Jr: 215
Crow Indians: 30, 38; early sites, 14; crops and pottery, 18; 1851 treaty, 22; reservation established (1868), 23; battle with Piegans, 32-33; reservation reduced, 68; railroad construction on reservation, 204-205
Crown brand: 87, 91, 95
Culbertson, William L: 229
Cullen, Hugh: 104n
Cuming, Governor Alfred (Utah): 73
Cunningham, Neil: 179
Curran, Major Daniel: 61, 64
Cusack, Edward: 124n
Cusack, Jennie: 179
Custer, Brevet Brigadier General George Armstrong: 66, 199

Dadant, Camille P: 87
Daggett, Thomas F: 176
Dakota Territory: 148-149
Darley, Henry Algernon Cholmley: 76
Darr, David L: 192
Davies, Reese E: 239n
Dead Indian Creek: 38
Deane, John W. "Josh": 86, 155, 169-170
Deaton, William D: 126
Deaver: 228
Deaver, D. Clem: 227-228
deBarthe, Joseph: 165, 178, 219n; photo, 175
de Beyssac, R. Camille: 95
Debs, Eugene V: 205
de Bonchamps, Viscount Jules: 88
de Bonnemain, Baron: 88, 90
de Caillet, Albert: 73, 96, 99, 107
de Hedouville, Count Jean: 90, 94-95, 99, 107, 264; photo, 91
de Heursel, Count: 88
de Klopstein, Baron A: 95
de la Verendrye, Pierre Gaultier de Varrenes: 16, 27
de la Brosse, Louis: 96
de la Salle, Rene Robert Cavelier: 26
de las Casas, bishop of Chiapas: 25
de Mailly-Nesle, Count Robert-Antoine-Adrien: 92-94, 262-263
de Mandat-Grancey, Baron Edmond: 99
DeMaris Hot Springs: 203, 206
de Mores, Marquis: 78, 89, 99
de Mores, Marquise: 89

INDEX 277

de Smet, Father Pierre-Jean: 21
de Soto, Hernando: 26
de Vallambrosa, Duc: 89
Deval, Paul: 35
Dexter, Benjamin: 62-63
Dickie, David: 79
Dillard, Shelby Eli: 171
District of Louisiana: 147
Dodge, Major General Grenville Melen: 59, 238, 240
Donahue, Jack: 83, 106n, 114, 133
Donkey Town: 226
Double Mill Iron brand: 101
Double Reverse brand: 185
Dougherty, T: 64n
Douglas: 108, 191
Draper, Arthur G: 162n
Drewry, Belle: 139
Drouillard, George: 28
Dry Creek: 233
D. T. Pulliam Company: 235
du Dore, Count Jean-Yvan Barbier: 90
du Dore, Viscount Gustave-Marie Francois Barbier: 90, 95
du Fran, Philip: 106n, 133
Duncan, William P: 82
Dunivin, John S "Fat Jack": 97
Dunning, George: 131
Durkee: 204, 235; platted, 233
Dyer, John: 75, 97, 98n, 102
Dyer, Joseph: 57

Eagle's Nest: 212
East Timber Creek: 164
Ecoffey, Jules: 83
Edgell, W. S: 143
Edgar, Will D: 178, 219
EK Ranch: 79, 103, 106, 109, 114
Elk Creek: 232
Elliot, D. H: 205
El Paso County, Colorado: 162
Embar Cattle Company: 164
Embar Ranch: 66, 81, 155, 191, 210, 214
Emblem: 207
Emerson, Governor Frank C: 166n
Emge, Joseph: 144
Enderley, Dr. E. C: 142
Ensign, M. W: 230n
Enterline, Edward Elmer: 145

Evangelical Lutheran Colonization Company: 206
Evanston: 150, 197, 209, 211
Ewing, William J: 139

Fairley, David B: 162n
Farlow, Edward: 140
Farlow, Ezekiel: 140
Farmer's Canal: 210
Farmers Exchange Bank (Gray, Iowa): 237
Farris, Charles: 145-146
F brand: 75
Fencing of federal land: 79
Fenton: 156
Fergus County: 126
Fetterman, Brevet Major William Judd: 75
Fifteen Mile Creek: 124, 228
Finch, Clement: 109
Firearms: first Indian use, 15
First National Bank (Alliance, Iowa): 254n
First National Bank (Carroll, Nebraska): 229n
First National Bank (Council Bluffs, Nebraska): 254n
First National Bank (Lincoln, Nebraska): 231
First Security Bank: 92n
Fitzgerald, Congressman John Joseph: 244
Fitzpatrick, Thomas: 20, 30n, 31-32
Five Springs Creek: 77-78
Flathead Indians: 16
Fleur de Lis Ranch: 99
Flour mill: 220
Forbes, John Murray: 204
Forshee, Minnie May: 109
Fort Belknap Indian Reservation: 159-160
Fort Bridger: 58-59, 62, 65, 159; Judge Carter sutler, 73
Fort Caspar: 46
Fort Custer: 66, 128
Fort David A. Russell: 56-57
Fort Dodge, Kansas: 76
Fort Ellis, Montana: 66
Fort Fetterman: 54, 56-57, 191
Fort Fred Steele: 54
Fort Laramie: 41, 83; treaty of 1851, 20-21; treaties of 1868, 22-23; seat of Ogalala County, 148
Fort Lauderdale, Florida: 73
Fort McKinney: 151
Fort Phil Kearny: 75

Fort Raymond: 28
Fort Sanders: seat of Laramie County, Nebraska Territory, 149
Fort Washakie: 46, 78, 154-155, 169; Boysen lease, 239-240
Fraeb, Henry: 30
Franc (originally Frank): 156
Franc, Carl Augustus (von Liechtenstein): 85
Franc, Carl B. (von Liechtenstein): 85
Francis I, King of France: 26
Franc, Otto (von Liechtenstein): 85-86, 90, 107, 115-122, *passim*, 126-127, 132, 154, 170, 185, 197
Frank, Meyer: 187
Frannie: 204, 216, 233
Freeman, John: 172-173
Fremont County: 152, 188, 194
Fremont, Elkhorn and Missouri Valley Railway: 225
Fremont Power Company: 254
Fremy, Paul: 263
Frewen, Moreton: 88, 99, 101-115, *passim*, 151, 200n
Frewen, Richard: 101, 151
Fritz Ditch: 164, 221
Frontier Land and Cattle Company: 104, 106, 114-115, 133

Gallagher, William A: 138
Gallegos, Rafael: 43
Gantz, Louis: 144
Gardiner's River: 70n
Garland: 204, 234n
Garland, Charles: 234n
Garland, Ed: 234n
Garland, John: 234n
Garrison, John: 114
George, Cassel H: 137
Gebhart, Owen Thomas: 162-163, 191
Gebo: 235
Gebo, S. W: 235
Germania: 207
German colonies: 207, 220
German Savings Bank (Manning, Iowa): 237n
Gerrans, H. Monte: 202-203
Gervais, Jean Baptiste: 30
Gilchrist, Andrew: 104, 106, 108
Gillespie, Major G. L: 261
Gillette (formerly Donkey Town): 226
Gillette, Edward: 173, 204-205, 226-227

Glanagan, Edward B: 185n
Goddard, Orpheus Fletcher: 128
Gold mining: 149, 171
Gooseberry Creek: 24
Goose Creek: 200
Gordon, Captain David Stewart: 37
Gordon, George: 133
Gorman, Henry: 135-136
Government land offices: 197-198
Grand Island & Northern Wyoming Railroad Company: 225n
Grant, President Ulysses Simpson: 52
Grass Creek: 78
Great Northern Railroad: 225
Great Western Sugar Company: 167
Green River: 33
Green River County, Utah: 74, 149
Grenfell, William Henry "Willy": 111
Greybull: 234; platted, 233
Greybull (or Gray Bull) River: 36, 42, 46, 61-62, 86, 101, 124, 133, 136, 185, 206, 210
Gross, stock inspector: 135
Gros Ventre Indians: 159
Guernsey, Charles A: 206

Hamilton: 208
Hamilton, Isaac Miller: 208n
Hanaway, Alto L: 256n
Hanover: 230
Hanover Canal Company: 229
Hanover County: 194, 195n
Hanover Land and Irrigation Company: 193, 229, 231-232
Hanson, Benjamin: 124n
Hardee, Lieutenant General William Joseph: 184
Harriman, E. H: 225-226
Harrison, President Benjamin: 189
Harrison, Dr. Benjamin: 31
Harrison, William Henry: 31
Harris, John R: 178
Hart, David: 135
Hayden, Charles Emory: 203
Hayes, George M: 263
Hays, Colonel John Coffee: 183
Head, Richard G: 114
Hedges, Cornelius: 261; with Washburne-Doane expedition, 10; on Bridger Trail, 45
Heimer, Mr: 203
Henderson, George B: 177n
Henry, Andrew: 28

INDEX

Herman, Nebraska: 106
Hesse, Frederick George Samuel: 115
Hidatsa Indians: 18
Highway through Wind River Canyon: 258
Hillberry, Laban: 201
Hill, James Jerome: 225-226
Himebaugh, John A: 162n
Hitchcock, E.A: 243n
Hogan, James: 171
"Hog Ranch," on Spring Creek: 133
"Hole in the Wall": 140, 143
Holdredge, George W: 230
Holladay, Benjamin: 41
Holly Sugar Company: 167
Hollywood, John: 142-143
Hollywood, Nina: 143n
Hoodoo Ranch: 101
Hopkins, John D. "Johnny Dee": 127
Horse Creek: site of 1851 treaty conference, 22
Horses: first Indian use, 15
Hot springs: 117, 143, 179-180, 191
Hot Springs County: first proposal, 193; organized, 194
Hot Springs State Park: 235
Houghton, M. D: 112
Houlihan, William "Blind Bill": 139
House, Jacob Edward: 239n, 240, 247n
House, Mary F: 247n
Howe, Chief Justice John H: 54
Howe, Church, 55
Howell, Joseph: 213
Howell, Robert: 206
Hubbard, George: 139
Hurlbut Land and Cattle Company: 94
Hyatt and Landis: 135n
Hyatt, Elizabeth Calhoun: 174n
Hyatt, Samuel Calhoun: 174n
Hyatt, Samuel Washington: 135, 137, 151, 163, 173-174; photo, 168
Hyattville: 132, 156, 190, 192
Hyatt, William Lee: 174n

Idaho Territory: 148
Ijams, Hiram B: 132
Indian Territory: 147
In re Rights to Use Water in Big Horn River: 160
Ione Cattle Company: 103n
Irey, Joseph: 142
Irma colony: 205
Irma Hotel (Cody): 203

Iroquois League: 14
Irvine, William C: 187

Jacobs, John M. 43
Jackson, "Broken Nose": 90, 98n
Jackson "Teton": 135
Jakey's Fork: 81
Jevons, Grace McKeown: 102
Jevons, Wilfred: 102
Johnson, President Andrew: 149
Johnson County: 151, 187-188
Johnson, Edward Payson: 151
Johnson County invasion: 80, 86, 121-122, 125
Johnson, E. H. "Skew": 86
Johnston, General Albert Sidney: 73
Johnston, State Engineer Clarence T: 251
Johnston, James Charles: 101-102
Johnston, General Joseph Eggleston: 184
Joliet, Louis: 26
Jones, Capt. William Albert: 47; 1873 visit to Basin, 10, 37
Jordan: 220, 234; platted, 219
Jordan, Henry: 219

Kane: 204
Kane, Riley: 77
Kansas-Nebraska Act (1854): 147
Kansas Pacific Railroad: 199
Kansas Territory: 147
Kearny, John: 137
Kemmerer Bridge: 214
Kerr, J. S: 143
Keyes, Albert: 145-146
Kilpatrick Brothers & Collins: 212n
King, Brevet Major General John Haskell: 56, 61
Kingston, Charles: 211, 213, 216
Kirby: railroad arrived, 235
Kirby Creek: 45, 140, 144
Kirby Ditch: 222n
Kirwin: 230
Kirwin mines: 235
Knight, Jack: 135
Kutenai Indians: 16
Kuykendall, Judge William Littlebury: 49ff; photo, 48

La Bretagne: 95
Lacey, Congressman John Fletcher: 244-245
Lacey, John W: 246
La Champagne: 95

La Compagnie de comerce pour la Decouverte des nations du haut du Missouri, see Missouri Company
Laird, Leroy E: 258
Lake Mead: 202
Lamar, Lucius Quintus Cincinnatus: 79n
Lamb, Frank: 135
LaMotte, Major Robert Smith: 59, 62
Lander: seat of Fremont County, 154
Lantry, Victor G: 76
Laramie City: seat of Albany County, Dakota Territory, 149
Laramie County, Dakota Territory: 149
Laramie County Stock Association: 71
Lariour, Luke: 30n
Laudan, Friederich "Fritz": 221
Laudan, Louise: 221n
Leadville, Colorado: 220
Lea, Luke, Commissioner of Indian Affairs: 20
Leet, Francis M: 254
Leet, Lida W: 237n
Leigh Creek: 113
Leigh, Francis Dudley: 111
Leigh, Gilbert Henry Chandos: 111-113; photo, 113
Lendon, Frank: 98
Leonard, Dr. James G: 59
Leonard, Thomas: 104n
Leonard, Zenas: 30, 32
Lewiston: 148n
Ligier, Colonel: 191
Lincoln Land Company: 203-204, 227, 231-232
Lindsay, Charles: 209
Lisa, Manuel: 30
Lister-Kaye, Sir John: 114
Little Canyon Creek: 104
Little Popo Agie River: 58
Lodge Pole Creek: 43
Lloyd, Ed: 134
Lonabaugh, Ellsworth E: 233
Long, Senator Chester Isaiah: 245n
Long Hair, Crow chief: 32
Long, Major Stephen H: 10
Lost Cabin: 122, 156n
Louis and Clark expedition: 27
Louis XIV, King of France: 27
Louisiana Purchase: 27, 147
Louisiana Territory: 147
Lovell: 167, 204, 213; sugar factory, 232

Lovell, Henry Clay: 76; photo, 77-78
Lovell, Willard: 78
Lower Hanover Canal Association: 166n
Lowther, Harold Arthur: 116
Lucerne: 204
Luman, John: 82, 117, 120
LU Ranch: 78, 122, 124, 152
LU Sheep Company: 79
Lynn, Jess D: 144

Madden, Peter: 138
Madden, Thomas (perhaps John): 136-138
Magill, Joseph: 191-192
Maginnis, Chief Justice William L: 153
Mahogany Buttes: 155
Maier, Otto: 232n
Mail service: 155, 169-171
Mammoths: hunted in Big Horn Basin, 14
Man-Afraid-of-His-Horse, Sioux chief: 56
Mandan Indians: 16
Manderson: 204, 233-234
Manderson, General Charles F: 204-205
March, Albert: 86
Marney, Samuel A: 130
Marshall, Congressman Thomas Frank: 245n
Martin, Helen: 136-137
Marquette Creek: 164
Marquette, George: 155-156, 170, 172-173
Mason and Lovell Ranch: 76-77, 117, 124n, 156, 228n
Mason, Anthony L: 76, 78
Maynadier, Lieutenant Henry Eveleth: 35-36, 39
M Bar brand: 81
McCandlish, John M: 187
McClellan, George B. "Bear George": 122-123, 133, 165, 194
McCray, A. J: 98
McCulloch, J. D: 124n
McCulloch Peaks: 74
McCulloch, Peter: 74, 76
McDaniel, James: 51
McDermott, James: 136-138, 174
McDermott, Mrs. Mary: 136-138
McDermott, Philip: 136
McDermott's Butte: 138
McDermott's Gulch: 138
McDonald's Ranch: 152
McGovney, Alvan A: 162n
McHenry, Charles "Irish Charley": 62

INDEX

McKinley, President William: 242
McLaughlin, William: 172
McLeland, Charles R: 63
McLucas, James B: 242
McPherson, Congressman Smith: 237
Mead, Elwood: 159, 166, 201-202
Mecklem, George N: 233
Medicine Wheel: 19
Medora, Dakota Territory: 89
Meek, Joseph: 30
Meeteetse: 98, 156, 190, 210
Meeteetse Creek: 117
Meeteetse stage line: 154
Meiklejohn, George de Rue: 243
Meldrum, Robert: 32
Memphis and Ohio Railroad: 183, 185
Mercer, Asa Shinn: 129-132
Merrill: 150
Merritt's Crossing: 58
Merritt, General Wesley: 59
Metz, Percy W: 145-146
Meyer, Chapman and Breteche bank: 92n
Meyer, William F: 92n
Michigan Central Railroad: 76
Middle Fork of Powder River: 123
Milburn, District Judge George R: 127-128
Miles, Brevet Major General Nelson Appleton: 38, 72
Milk River: 159-160
Millais, Geoffrey: 115
Miller, Stanley: 143
Milltown: 200n
Minick, Ben: 144
Minick, William: 144
Mining law of 1866: 158
Minnesota Territory: 148
Missouri Company: 27
Missouri Territory: 147
Mitchell, David: 20-21
Mondell, Congressman Frank Wheeler: 180, 201, 206, 212, 216; discovered Cambria coal field, 226; and Boysen lease, 243-244, 246
Montana Bank of Red Lodge: 92n
MO brand: 95
Montana Supreme Court: 127
Montana Stock Growers Association: 119
Montana Territory: 148
Moonlight, Governor Thomas: 79
Moore, James Kerr: 46, 80, 170

Morehouse, Dr: 230
Morgan Franc Cattle Company: 86
Morgan, Oyer C: 125, 136
Morgareidge, Charles W: 123
Mormon colonies: Burlington, 145, 190, 206; Salt River Valley, 209
Mormon Trail: 214
Moroni Flat: 213
Morrell, Adam: 239n, 247
Morrill, Charles H: 231
Morrison, Lincoln A: 144
Morris, W. A. "Jack": 213
Morris, Frannie: 158
Morris, William Albert: 158
Morton County, Nebraska Territory: 148n
Morton, Owen G: 234n
Morton, Zada: 234n
Mosegard, Frank: 222
Mullan, Lieutenant John: 35, 36
Murrin, Colonel Luke: 52
Murrin, Thomas D: 54-55
Myer Ranch: 159

Nard, Albert "Slick": 140-142; photo, 141
Nard, Jennie Hollywood: 142
Nebraska Territory: 147
Neiber, Bernard: 222
Neiber stage stop: 204, 222
Newcastle: 212n, 226
Nez Perce Indians: 59
NH Ranch: 104, 106
Nickerson, Captain Herman G: 242, 246
Niogen Doget: 170
Noble, Worden P: 83, 105, 108, 140, 161
North Fork of Owl Creek: 152
Northern Pacific Railroad: 117-118, 200, 203; finished to Billings, 77, 154; junction with CB&Q, 225
Northern Pacific Refrigerator Car Company: 89
Northern Securities Corporation: 226
Northfield Ranch: 116
North, Orlando: 214n, 216n
Northwestern Live Stock Journal: 130
Northwestern Railroad, *see* Chicago Northwestern Railroad
Nowater Creek: 104, 108
Nowood (or No Wood) River: 36, 45, 105, 109, 111, 118, 124, 134, 136, 151; bridges across, 155; irrigation from 165

O'Brien, Nicholas J: 51
O'Day, Thomas "Peep": 123, 143
Ogalala County, Idaho Territory: 148
O'Hara, Pat: 72n
Oil exploration: 174-175
Oldis, Mr: 119
Omaha City: 148
Omohondro, John Burwell "Texas Jack": 199n
Ord, General Edward Otho Cresap: 37
Osborne, John Eugene: 126-127, 129, 166
Osmond, George: 210n
Otto: 124n, 156, 190, 192, 204; platted, 227n
Otto Courier: 190, 192
Otto Mascot (formerly *Alamo Argus*): 178, 219
Owen, Major John: 46
Owl Creek: 24, 81, 118, 124, 140, 147; early water rights
Owl Creek Livestock Company: 164
Owl Creek Mountains: 24, 41, 45, 61

Paint Creek: 171
Paintrock (or Paint Rock) Creek: 82, 109, 134-135, 151, 163
Paint Rock Record: 191
Packard, William Henry: 145, 210-211
Padlock Ranch: 143
Palette Ranchs: 139, 185
Park County: 193-194
Parmalee, Judge C. H: 145n
Pat O'Hara Creek: 72, 75
Patten, James I: 23
Payton, E. T: 179
Peake, Colonel J. H: 203
Pearson, Fred N: 227
Pease County: 151, 187
Pease, Eugene L: 151
Peay, Walter W: 124-125, 134, 164
Peters and Alston: 106
Pemberton, Chief Justice William Young: 127
Perkins, Charles Elliott: 204, 228n, 231
Peters, J.H: 254n
Peverly, H. B: 125-129
Pfeiffer, Charles Reinhold: 164, 178, 220
Pfeiffer Ditch: 164, 178, 220-221
Phelps, Louis B: 87
Pickering, Governor William: 129
Pickett, General George E: 184n
Pickett's Creek: 185, 188n
Pickett, Lieutenant Colonel William Douglas: 75, 154, 171, 183-185; photo, 168, 182

Picture Frame Ranch: 102
Piegan Indians: 32-33
Pierce, herder: 73
Pierce, John: 104-106, 110, 114
Pierre's Hole: 30
Pitchfork Ranch: 86, 119, 125-126, 197
Platte City: 148n
Platt, Senator Orville: 188
Plenty Coups, Crow chief: 95
Plunkett and Roche: 104
Plunkett, Horace Curzon: 83, 101-116, *passim*, 133n, 174
Poison Spider Creek: 45
Polygamy dispute: 150
Ponto, Glaud: 30
Popo Agie River: 30, 35, 41, 152n
Post, Morton E: 120, 200
Post offices: 156
Powder River Cattle Company, Ltd: 101
Powell: 194
Prairie Cattle Company: 102, 114
Price, Jacob: 79, 82
Provinse, H. C: 73
Pryor Creek: 95
Pryor's (or Pryor) Gap: 30, 216
Pulliam, The Rev. David Thomas: 229-231, 233
Purdum, Ray R: 259
Purdum, Mrs. Ray R: 259

Quien Sabe Mining Company: 245n

Rairden: 204; platted, 233
Rairden, The Rev. Dr. N. B: 229, 231, 235
Ralston: 204
Ramsey, J. W: 208
Ram's Horn brand: 185
Rawlins (sometimes Rawlings) Springs: 57, 151; seat of Carbon County, Dakota Territory, 149-150
Raynolds, Captain William Franklin: 35
Red Bank: 122, 152, 156, 161
Red Bank Ranch: 165
Red Bank Telephone Company: 165
Red Cloud, Sioux chief: 56-58
Red Cloud Agency: 199
Red Lodge, Montana: 73, 92, 97, 139, 156, 212
Rendezvous system: 29, 33
Reno, Major Marcus: 170
Richards, Captain Alonzo Van Ness: 161
Richards, DeForest: 161, 189-190, 200, 212

INDEX

Richards, Mrs. Harriet Alice Hunt: 156, 167
Richards, William Alford: 122, 152, 161-166, 176, 185, 188, 229; photo, 161; elected governor, 166
Riner, Judge John Allen: 245-246
Rio Grand Western Railway: 226n
Riverton: 254-255
Robertson Charles Fremont: 193, 228-229, 251
Roche, Alexis Charles Burke: 103-104, 106
Roche, Edmund Burke: 104
Roche, Lucy Maude Groschen: 103n
Rock Creek: 172
Rock Creek station: 112, 115
Rocky Mountain Fur Company: 30
Rodgers, Joseph: 125-127
Rogers, "Pistol Billy": 124
Roman Cross brand: 73
Roman Cross brand (two): 73
Rongis: 152, 163
Roosevelt, President Theodore: 186
Rose, Edward: 30
Rose, James: 134n
Rothwell, H. P: 143
Rowe, Frederick G: 162n
Rowell, Milo: 162n
Rumsey, Bronson C: 202-203
Rupp, Arthur G: 228
Rupp, Wellington: 228n
Russell, George: 203
Rustler (Otto): 190, 192
Ryan, Jerry: 201

Sabin, George: 83n
Sage Creek: 36, 95, 155; water rights litigation, 158
Salsbury, Nate: 202, 212n
Sampson, Madam: 119
San Ildefonso, 1800 treaty: 27
Saufley, Judge Mica Chrisman: 153
Sayles, Frank: 143
Schuelke, Dr. Julius: 178, 191
Seaman, John L: 124-125
Sessions, Byron: 214
7L brand: 78
76 brand: 101, 106, 151
Shafer, Jack: 179
Shafer, William J: 173, 175, 178-179; plats town of Alamo, 219
Sharp Nose, Arapahoe chief: sale of hot springs, 179; Boysen lease, 239

Sheehan, Jerry: 177
Shell Creek: 28, 37, 76, 109
Shelley, Edward: 39-41
Sherard, Henry: 140
Sheridan: 167; seat of Sheridan County, 154; railroad arrived, 226
Sheridan County: 152, 186, 188
Sheridan Inn: 201
Sheridan, Lieutenant General Philip Henry: 37, 47, 54, 199-200
Sherman, General William Tecumseh: 54, 57, 184
Shield Ranch: 87, 92, 95-96, 99; photo, 84
Shock, David: 142n
Shoshone: proposed town, 203
Shoshone Agency: 203
Shoshone Land and Irrigation Company: 192, 201-203
Shoshone National Forest: 202
Shoshone River (formerly Stinking Water): 36; dam, 207
Shoshone Times: 203
Shoshoni: platted, 235; purchased power from Boysen dam, 254-255
Shoshoni, or Snake Indians: 45, 111; origins, 16; treaty of 1863, 22; reservation established (1868), 23; hunting trip to Big Horn Basin, 24; fight with Arapahoes, 37; reservation reduced, 69, 152, 179-180; water rights litigation, 160; Boysen lease, 237-246
Sidon Canal: 214-215
Simpson, Governor Milward L: 166
Simpson, William L: 145
Sioux Indians: 37, 43; origins, 16; at 1851 treaty conference, 21-22; reservation and hunting ground (1868), 23; 1876 Custer battle, 67-68; Wyoming legislature memorial, 150-151
Slane, William T: 222
Slick Creek: 139
Sliney, George M: 124n
Smethurst, David: 97n
Smith, Jackson & Sublette: 30
Smith, Jedediah Strong: 28, 30
Smith, Joseph: 209n, 213
Smith, Joseph F: 209n
Smith, Lot: 198
Snow, Lorenzo, Mormon President: 212, 213
Snyder, Jake: 142
Social Democracy of America: 205-206
South Fork of Owl Creek: 152

South Fork of Stinking Water: 142, 201
South Pass City: 83; seat of Carter County, 149
Spindler, John J: 254n
Spoon, Peter: 30n
Spotted Tail, Sioux chief: 199
Spotted Tail Agency: 78, 88n
Spring Creek: 122-123, 133, 144
Spring Creek raid: 144-145
Stambaugh, Lieutenant Charles B: 58
Standifer, Jefferson: 49
Star Valley Stake: 209-210
Stateler, The Rev. Learned Blackman: 44
Stevens, alias "Big George" or "Red Cloud": 135
Stewart, Captain William Drummond: 31
Stewart, Robert: 109, 111, 113
Stinking Water Prospector: 171
Stinking Water River (Creek), later Shoshone: 30, 36, 46, 63, 74, 75, 76, 152, 156, 201, 206-207, 212; bridge across, 89, 117, 154
Stagner, Speed: 117
Stotts, Judge Joseph L: 145n
Stoughton, Mrs M.J: 254n
Sturgis, Thomas: 71, 105, 114
Sublette, Milton Green: 30, 31-32
Sublette, William: 30n
Sugar beets: 232
Sullivan ferry: 222
Sullivan, Patrick J: 194
Sullivan, Richard: 177
Swail, Frannie: 97n
Swan, Alexander Hamilton: 102
Swan Land and Livestock Company: 102
Sweetwater County: 70, 150; reduced by Pease County, 151
Sweetwater River: 41
Swift, Mr: 137
Swift, William L: 162n
Sykes, Eugene Frank: 109
Sykes Springs: 109
Sylvan Pass: 203

Taggart, Samuel: 171
Talbot, Major John: 55
Tatman, John J: 136-137
Tatman Mountain: 124
Taylor Grazing Act (1934): 121, 197
Taylor, General Zachary: 183
Teller, Senator Henry Moore: 180

Ten Mile Creek: 222
Ten Sleep Creek: 83, 105, 108-109, 112, 144; bridge across, 155
Thayer, Governor John M: 198
Thermopolis: 143, 180, 190; seat of Hot Springs County, 194; and Boysen dam, 250
Thermopolis, "Old Town": 140, 178
Thompson, J. W: 173
Thompson, Rosa L: 255n
Thurston, Senator John Mellen: 243
Tibbetts & Company: 115
Todd, Mrs. M. E: 134
Toluca, Montana: 203, 216
Tordesillas, treaty (1506): 26
Torrey: 179
Torrey, Jay L: 79, 82
Torrey, Captain Robert A: 37, 80, 82, 117
Townsend Ditch: 177n, 222
Townsend, William Perry: 125, 177, 222
Trail Creek: 88, 90
Trail Creek Ranch: 90
Tracy, M. C: 91
Trapper Creek: 76, 144
Trumbull, Senator Lyman: 70
Tullock, Samuel: 30
Turpen Construction Company: 257n
Twin Springs Creek: 59
Two Dot Ranch: 72
Twombly, Ida: 214n

Uinta County: 70, 194; created, 150
Union Cattle Company: 105, 114
Union Pacific Railroad: 108; builds into Wyoming, 149; involvement with Boysen: 238
Upper Sage Creek: 101
Utah Territory: 159
Utah Expedition (1857): 73, 198
U.S. Bureau of Reclamation: 207
V.U.S. vs. Douglas-Willan, Sartoris Company: 79n

Van Devanter, Justice Willis: 246n
Valentine, F. C: 73
Vetter, Philip Henry: 133-134
"Vickburg": 89
Ville de Rio Janeiro: 95
Vion, Rene: 93, 95
Volga Germans: 222ff

INDEX

von Hoffman, Louis A: 89
von Liechtenstein, see Franc
Voss Ditch: 221
Voss, Johann Christoph Christian Friederich: 220
Voss, Katherina: 221n

Wadsworth, Harry E: 246
Waln, Dow: 134
Waln, Fred: 143
Warden, S. P: 124n
Warm Springs Ditch: 222
Warren: 125, 234; platted, 219
Warren, Governor and Senator Francis Emroy: 166, 186, 219
Washakie, Chief: 58, 74, 80; photo, 12; 1874 hunting trip to Big Horn Basin, 24; Bates battle, 38; sale of hot springs, 179-180; death, 194; Boysen lease, 239
Washakie County: first proposal, 193, organized, 194
Washakie, Dick: 37
Washburn-Doane expedition: 10
Water rights: 164
Watson, Robert: 104
Watson-Smythe, W. D. "Beau": 104, 106
Weis, G: 88
Weis, Josef: 239n, 242, 247
Welch, Albert W: 134n
Welling: 228
Wertz, John T: 239n, 240, 242
Wertz, Robert C: 239n, 240, 247n, 248
Western Union Beef Company: 79
West Florida: 15
Weston County: 187n
Whaley, W. T: 83
Whetstone Indian Agency: 52
Wheaton, William: 139
Wheelan, Lieutenant James Nicholas: 59, 61-62, 65, 66
Whittington, E. Minnie: 134
Wickham, John T: 125-129
Wickwire, Byron F. "Kansas": 142n
Wiley: 207
Wiley, Solon Lysander: 206-208
Wilkins, J. Edward: 40
Willard, Daniel: 230
Willard Ditch: 78
Williams, Henry G: 94

Williams-Luman mining prospect: 248
Williams, Rose: 139
Wilson, Charles: 117
Wilson County, Nebraska Territory: 148n
Wilson, Lum: 97
Wilson Ranch: 156
Wilson, Senator William Boyd: 238
Willow Creek: 78
Wind River: 9n
Wind River Canyon: 29, 35, 38, 45; Boysen tract, 246; railroad and highway, 258
Windsor and Plunkett: 117
Windsor, Henry J: 83, 105-106, 108
Wind River Reservation: 152, 159, 179
Winn, Algernon James: 107-108, 110-115, passim
Winn, Laura Sophia Priscilla "Bea": 108n
Winslow, Daniel A. "Denver Jake": 222
Winter of 1886-87: 118-121
Winters, et. al., vs. United States: 160
Winters, Helen May: 211n
Wise: 98
Wise and Livingston: 117
Wise, George A: 96
Wise, William: 62
A Woman Taken in Adultery: 185
Wood, C. E: 201
Wood, Frank S: 190
Wood River: 86, 144, 210
Woodruff, Abraham Owen: 211, 213-214
Woodruff, David Patten: 209-210
Woodruff, John Dwight: 66, 80-82, 147, 155, 170, 210; photo, 81
Woodruff, Josephine Doty: 80n
Woodruff Stake: 211
Woodruff, Wilford, Mormon President: 209-211, 213
Worland: 144, 167, 193, 235; seat of Washakie County, 194; sugar factory, 232; platted, 233; railroad arrived, 234
Worland, Charles H "Dad": 193n, 232
Worland Grit: 228
World's Fair (Columbian Exposition): 185
Wostenberg, Frederick: 221
Wostenberg, Henry W. August: 221, 232n
Wostenberg, Marie: 221
WP brand: 83, 104, 114
Wright, Charles W: 117
Wunderlich, The Rev. August C: 206

Wyeth, Nathaniel Jarvis, 31-32
Wyndham-Quin, Charles Frederick Talbot: 115
Wynn, Isaac C: 175, 192n
Wyoming Development Company: 201n
Wyoming Parks Commission: 259
Wyoming Power Company: 254-255
Wyoming Sugar Company: 167
Wyoming State Arid Land Board: 202
Wyoming State Board of Land Commissioners: 166, 235
Wyoming statehood: 186-189
Wyoming Stock Graziers Association: 71
Wyoming Stock Growers Association: 73, 108, 130, 141; name adopted (1871), 71; reduces wages, 110; opposes leasing of federal land, 120; cattle detectives, 124-127, 177

Wyoming Territory: created, 149
Wyoming Wool Growers Association: 144

Yarnell, Charles: 64
Yarnell, Nelson: 81
Yellowstone County, Idaho Territory: 148
Yellowstone Forest Reserve: 186
Yellowstone Lake: 70n
Yellowstone Park: 38, 194, 202; established (1872), 10, 69-70
York factory: 16
Young, N.E: 239

Zada: 234
Zion's Saving Bank and Trust Company: 211n